The DELL BIG BOOK OF CROSSWORDS & PENCIL PUZZLES #7

Editor-in-Chief • Erica L. Rothstein

A Dell Trade Paperback

A DELL TRADE PAPERBACK

Published by
Dell Publishing
a division of
Bantam Doubleday Dell Publishing Group, Inc.
1540 Broadway
New York, New York 10036

Most puzzles in this book were first published in issues of the
DELL CROSSWORD ANNUAL and
DELL PENCIL PUZZLES & WORD GAMES.

ISBN: 0-440-50161-X

Printed in the United States of America

Published simultaneously in Canada

April 1989

10   9

CUK

A WORD FROM THE EDITORS

Why do people solve puzzles? Well, for one thing, with puzzles you can while away hours of leisure time pleasurably. Or, you can fill a mere minute of spare time. Some folks solve to relax and soothe a tense or troubled mind or, conversely, to sharpen one's wits and be provided with zestful mental stimulation. Puzzles give solvers the satisfaction of discovering how much they really know about a wide variety of subjects, and also an appreciation of how much more there is to learn. There's the provocative challenge of keen competition or the restful solitude of escape.

All these are answers to the question, why solve puzzles? As editors, we must give careful attention to all of them. They guide us as we select the material to be published, since there must be something for each kind of solver—and each of us is many different solvers, depending upon our level of skill, time available, and mood. Since 1932, Dell has been providing the puzzle diversity and challenges discerning solvers demand. If you're a confirmed puzzle enthusiast, you know what to expect here. But, if you're venturing into the world of puzzles for the first time, for whatever reason, you'll find a limitless new interest to explore as you turn the 320 pages of this 7th edition of *The Dell Big Book of Crosswords & Pencil Puzzles*.

For starters, there are 80 crossword puzzles, each one labeled for level of difficulty. Ranging in size from small to jumbo, in level from Easy to Challenger, you're sure to find one to suit. There are 13 diagramless crosswords, also ranging from Easy to Challenger, for those times when you want the extra dimension of not knowing where the black squares belong. Anacrostics (18 of 'em!) will fill many hours of solving for those who particularly favor these fine puzzles. Challenging, yes, but also thought-provoking, endlessly fascinating solving.

There's so much more that it's really hard to know where to begin. The contents alone take up four pages! Like decoding? Okay, 120 Cryptograms should keep you busy. Is anagramming your cup of tea? There are 5 pages of Bowl-A-Score Challenger, plus numerous other brain teasers that depend on letter-scrambling skills, such as Anagram Word Squares, Anagram Antics, and Anagram Quote. Hi-Score, Build Score, Solicross (6 of them), Spell to Score, Letter Chase, Letter Choice: All will challenge you to beat the expert's score by testing your word-forming abilities. 8 Mazes to see how well (and how quickly) you can make your way through the course.

If number puzzles are your preferred form, you won't feel neglected. There are 11 Cross Sums puzzles, plus Calculate A word, Numberama, Word Arithmetic, Number Place, Cross Numbers, and 3 Figure Logics you just won't want to miss. The Intelligence Clock is another challenge unlike any other, not to be overlooked. So, too, are the Dot Game, Word Link, Code-A-Graph, and Picture Maze. Kriss Krosses are here in multiples (15 in all), as well as those perennially popular Logic Problems. There are pages of Quotation Puzzles, Cryptoquizzes, Word Searches, Figgerits, and Laddergrams, all old favorites to millions of solvers.

It's just not possible to run down the entire list here, nor would we want to—there should be some surprises! Suffice it to say, you should find here all your old favorites, plus many, many puzzles that may well become new favorites. The only suggestion to be made at this point is: Pick up your pencil and dive right in. Start with a puzzle you've always loved or try one you've never tried before. Start with Crossword 1 on page 8 or skip to somewhere in the middle. Whichever method you choose, we wish you good solving.

The Editors

CONTENTS

• picture puzzles

• mazes

• pencil fun and word games

• brain teasers and quizzes

• number puzzles

• and don't miss...

1 EASY CROSSWORD

ACROSS

1. Steals from
5. Move slightly
9. Venice has lots of these
11. Polishes
13. "Word" from the sponsor
14. Glittery metal
16. Hack
17. Serve the purpose
18. Free (of)
20. Telegram
22. Farmer's tool
23. Ermine or seal
24. Chimney dust
26. Harbor
28. Joseph had a colorful one
29. Event at Hialeah
30. Kind (of)
32. Pizza
33. Noisy spat
34. Dress trimming
35. "The — in Spain"
37. Anxious
39. Manufacture
40. Juicy fruit
42. Observed
43. Narrow street
44. Web-spinner
46. 36 inches
47. Canoe oars
49. Stalk
51. Spring holiday
54. 60 minutes
55. Social insect
56. Go by boat
58. Close violently
59. Stingy person
61. Building top
63. Bird's limb
64. Concealed
65. Weep convulsively
67. Tattled
69. Foreman's men
70. Snug retreats
71. Implement
73. Sailors
75. Ampersand
76. Discharge
77. "From the top of your head to the tip of your —"
79. Oolong
80. That thing
81. Employ
82. Story
84. Exist
85. Latest
87. Show off
89. Fender mishap
90. Elapse

Solution is on page 288

DOWN

1. Sends by wireless
2. Forward!
3. Sack
4. Poky
5. Exhibit
6. Tilt
7. At home
8. Lose weight
9. Train parts
10. Petticoat
11. Marksman
12. Painful
15. Let fall
16. Talon
19. Entranceway
21. Great Lake
22. In want
23. Confront
25. Corner
27. Tantalized
28. Ship's company
29. Roue
31. Cravats
34. Country
36. Forty winks
38. Fertile areas
39. Spoil
41. More mature
43. Holds out
45. Water barrier
46. Favorable reply
48. Most recent
49. "Sing a — of sixpence"
50. Pull sharply
52. Corn spike
53. Noisy uprising
54. Suspend
55. Helps
57. Booty
58. Bandage (up)
59. Coal deposit
60. Plant part
62. Uninteresting
63. Desired
64. Present
66. Horseman's shoe
68. Fears
69. Profit
70. Soil
72. Spring into the air
74. Identical
76. Clenched hand
78. Insult
81. Female bird
83. Historic age
86. You and I
88. While

8

2 and 3 MEDIUM CROSSWORD

Puzzle 2

ACROSS

1. Firmament
4. Body of laws
8. Meager
12. Pizza
13. Stove section
14. Load
15. "— about time!"
16. Kitten's cry
17. Water mains
18. Lower
20. Light brown
21. While
22. Devour
23. Gamut
25. Sour
27. Nearly
28. Went first
31. Concealed
32. Chairs
33. Chestnut horse
34. Epoch
35. Gait
36. Ripped
37. Adolescence
39. Scatter seed
40. Fill the bill
42. Sauté
43. Snare
46. Aft
48. Pastoral cry
49. Fool's gold
50. Breakwater
51. Pant
52. Lubricate
53. Equal
54. Dollar bills
55. Doily

DOWN

1. Whirl
2. Small hawk
3. Recently
4. Heavenly body
5. Finished
6. Droplets on grass
7. Print measure
8. Hurl
9. Lick up
10. Notion
11. Muddle
17. Trousers
19. Sombrero
20. Savor
23. Bothersome bug
24. Space for action
25. Article
26. Publicize
27. Pithy
29. Corn spike
30. Coloring agent
32. Squirt
36. Little child
38. Proposal
39. Ginger cookies
40. Moist
41. Wood-wind instrument
43. Relieve
44. Opera melody
45. Animal skin
47. Pub drink
48. Prohibit
51. Proceed

Puzzle 3

ACROSS

1. Every one
4. Envelop
8. Owns
11. Born
12. Rabbit
13. Move on wheels
14. Find out
16. Off
17. Food fish
18. Falls short
20. Unescorted
22. Combines
23. Make (a well)
24. Spicy stew
25. Father
27. Suppositions
28. Game of cards
29. Baby bear
30. On the hour of
31. Swallows greedily
32. Cracow native
33. Slight
34. Famous reindeer
35. Bicyclist
36. Nitroglycerin: slang
37. Prompted
38. Uneducated
42. Confederate
43. Labor
44. Dove call
45. Garden plot
46. Bribes
47. A couple

DOWN

1. Hue — cry
2. Hawaiian garland
3. Bible selections
4. Intact
5. Talk deliriously
6. Exist
7. Acts on stage
8. Wolf cries
9. Sigh of misery
10. Wily
13. Wet
15. Hit on the head : slang
19. Vivacious
20. Continent
21. Hitchhiker's need
22. Nervous
24. Offenders
25. Whine
26. Encourage in crime
28. Trick
29. Solid
31. Lightheaded
32. Rain heavily
33. Use (a weapon)
34. Chills
35. Govern
36. Small piece
37. Taxi
39. Sticky stuff
40. Immediately !
41. In addition

Solutions are on page 284

9

4 HARD CROSSWORD

ACROSS

1. Attire
5. Become mellow
10. Search thoroughly through
14. Wind instrument
15. Dodge
16. Toward shelter
17. Shaded walkway
18. Talky : hyph. wd.
20. Free : 2 wds.
22. Harbor sight
23. Fate
24. Storage compartments
25. Marked with a kind of indelible "ornamentation"
28. Child's toy
31. Puddles
34. Music work
35. Caper
36. Roof overhang
37. Reproaches
38. Arabian ruler
39. Lean-to
40. Nevada city
41. Exhausted
42. Pronoun
43. Without a worry
45. Army or Navy
47. Unspecified person : 3 wds.
51. Foxy
53. Rascal
55. Dismantles : 2 wds.
57. Yugoslav river
58. Fish sauce
59. Menu
60. Portent
61. Main point
62. Lock of hair
63. Aromatic plant

DOWN

1. "Flip" : 2 wds.
2. Lessen
3. Part of a baker's dozen
4. Disparaged
5. Give in
6. Lofty retreat : 2 wds.
7. Gasp
8. Short-tempered
9. Modern
10. Church dogma
11. Exceedingly ancient : 3 wds.
12. Converge
13. Hospital accommodations
19. Footnote abbreviation : Latin
21. Prejudice
24. Mrs. Truman
26. Express a view
27. Cross : 3 wds.
29. Wednesday is named for him
30. Kind of wine
31. Mexican dollar
32. Hawaiian island
33. Catches up with
35. Is determined by : 2 wds.
37. British streetcar
41. Irish dramatist O'Casey
43. Malicious women
44. Travelers' paths
46. Upright
48. Serious play
49. Cut
50. Swedish island in the Baltic Sea
51. Party for men only
52. West African country
53. Box scientifically
54. Be concerned
56. Performance

Solution is on page 284

PICTURE THAT!

Pictured below are some well-known expressions or figures of speech. See if you can identify them all. For example, No. 1 is "Building a dream house". Answers are on page 295.

ACROSS

1. Handful
4. Document
9. Crow's cry
12. Sudsy brew
13. Wear away
14. Falsehood
15. Nothing
16. Help
17. Felony
19. Center
21. Derrick part
22. Pack away
24. Scrawl
28. Arrives
30. Healthy
31. Overhead train
32. Primate
33. Stale
35. Cushion
36. Scale note
37. Salute
38. Go by bus
40. "Rat race"
43. Consumer
44. Charity
45. Lease
47. Malice
49. Manhandle
50. Peculiar
53. Mortar trough
54. Elevate
56. Strong caustic
57. All right
58. Bit of advice: slang
59. Do needlework

DOWN

1. Cooling device
2. High priest
3. Greet warmly
4. Greenish-yellow fruit
5. Zodiac sign
6. Seed vessel
7. Mr. Sullivan
8. Fell back
9. Ascend
10. Intention
11. Very small
18. Dressing gown
20. Have debts
21. Rude child
22. Scoots off
23. Subject
25. Refrigerate
26. Sailor's holiday
27. Church officer
29. Hems and haws
34. Umbrella parts
35. Revolvers
37. Stop
39. Operate
41. Forays
42. Rub out
46. Pitcher
47. Bashful
48. Author of "The Raven"
49. Flaky dessert
51. Coloring agent
52. Nighttime moisture
55. — large, free

ACROSS

1. Liberal position
5. Opera high spot
6. Attempt
10. Flour-grinder
11. Horseman's game
12. Tease: slang
15. Quick glimpse
16. Modern: hyph. wd.
18. Human trunk
20. Verbal
21. Rudely concise
22. Jack Benny's exclamation
23. Hole of a gun
24. Exclusively
25. Lie in wait
26. On vacation
27. Man-eating monster
28. Consumed
30. Cooperate: 2 wds.
32. Pinch, as of salt
36. Lamprey
37. Continent
38. Margarine
39. — by, manages
40. Functions
41. Heavy book

DOWN

1. Lighting device
2. American Indian
3. Manicurist's tool
4. Speak candidly: 2 wds.
6. Shoot forth suddenly
7. Caps
8. Low female voice
9. Catcall
12. Uncommonly
13. Where the Renaissance began
14. Maid-summoner
17. Penniless: 3 wds.
19. Prospector's quest
21. Cowpoke's destination
23. It sounds reveille
24. Be in debt
25. Gallop easily
26. Book of charts
28. Comfort
29. Dismounted
31. Purse
33. Besides
34. Appear to be
35. Socks

Solutions are on page 284

11

7 EASY CROSSWORD

ACROSS

1. Pizza
4. Popular drinks
9. Suez —
11. Cudgels
16. Shut
17. Wash the soap from
18. Mature
19. Sponsor's message
20. Detested
22. Subdued
24. "Scram!"
25. Conducted
27. Observe
28. "I came, I —, I conquered"
29. Automobile
30. Historic periods
32. Imitate
34. Cot or crib
35. Evergreen tree
36. Plunder
38. Diet fare
40. Possessed
41. Meal "at eight"
44. Card game
45. U.M.W. members
48. Offers
49. Stories
51. Assist
52. Lacerates
54. Expert
55. Hose supporters
57. Perish
58. Expensive
60. Condensation
61. Come in
63. Camp home
64. Election selections
66. Plus
67. Streams
69. Brooch
70. Stands up
72. Chess piece
73. Weather report
75. Slippery fish
76. Period
78. Children
81. Very unusual
82. Vampire
83. Tattered cloth
85. Stool pigeon : slang
86. Exist
87. French capital
89. Storehouse
91. Dad
92. Ten-cent pieces
94. Stout cords
96. More crippled
98. Growth period
99. Choose by ballot
100. Put on clothes
101. Sturdy tree

DOWN

1. Word on a bill
2. Wayside stopover
3. Compass point
4. Weighing device
5. Staler
6. Serve the purpose
7. Timber tree
8. Sailors sail them
9. Crawls
10. Rented
11. Ship's company
12. Pot cover
13. On your feet
14. Started
15. "Saw wood"
21. Camomile —
23. Insane
26. Mends socks
29. Apple juice
31. Male child
33. Anxious
34. Prohibit
35. Skillet
37. Wager
39. Harks
40. Concealed
41. Cuts into cubes
42. Model of perfection
43. Storms
45. Penny-pincher
46. Equestrian
47. Twirls
48. Not good
50. Jurisprudence
51. Craft
53. Complete collection
56. Discontinued
59. Quick
60. Scandinavian land : abbr.
62. Outer edge
63. Choir voice
65. Foil material
66. Bother
68. Large tank
70. Withdraw
71. Most painful
73. Paths
74. Confess
75. Corn spike
77. Faucet
79. Adhesive bandages
80. Part of the Milky Way
82. Foundation
84. Precious metal
87. Wooden nail
88. Composition for one
89. Pack of cards
90. Sailor
93. Mother
95. Small vegetable
97. Myself

Solution is on page 288

12

ACROSS

1. Tropical plant
5. Heavy hammer
9. Guilt feeling
14. Woe is me!
15. Land measure
16. Stogie
17. Horse-trading
19. Old saying
20. Sault Ste. Marie Canals
21. Do an arithmetic lesson
22. Quick to learn
24. Nervous quirk
25. Persian fairy
27. Solid water
28. Religious group
29. Unnaturally pale
31. A person, at random
33. Unenthusiastic
34. Twice, in music
35. Mimic
39. Large weight
40. Talkatively
42. Big bird
43. Fashions
45. Actor, — J. Cobb
46. Whirl rapidly
47. Part of a movie cast
49. Ships' stopovers
50. Vapory clouds
53. Boat tool
54. Call heard on the city streets
55. Forty-niner's necessity
56. Hill-maker
57. Mother pig
58. Floor-duster
61. Computer
63. Incriminate
66. Unexpected pleasure
67. In the vicinity
68. Christmas weather
69. Press into ranks
70. Clan
71. 15th of March, May, etc., in old Rome

DOWN

1. Rotters
2. Hodgepodge
3. Discord
4. Set a price
5. — Gras
6. Non-alkaline
7. Decorative jar
8. Inheritance
9. Cat's dismissal
10. Concealed
11. Marble
12. Conjuration
13. Standing straight
18. Work for
23. Human beings
26. Long fish
27. Provincial
28. Indian weight
29. Emotes
30. Greasy dust
31. Trouble
32. "No" vote
34. "Home of the bean and the cod"
36. Reprove formally
37. Leave out
38. Wine casks
40. Irritate
41. Egyptian god of pleasure
44. Went first
46. White or Red —
48. Naval rank
49. Mechanical device
50. Gaiters
51. Skeleton organization
52. Beneath
54. Elaborate trips
56. Bohemian
57. Read quickly
59. Oklahoma Indian
60. Church seats
62. Otology topic
64. Born
65. Greek letter

Solution is on page 284

CHANGELINGS 1

Can you turn the first word into the second one by changing only one letter at a time? Do not change the order of the letters. Each step must be an everyday word (no proper nouns allowed.) Our answers are on page 295.

Example: TINY, tins, bins, bind, BIRD.

1. **DASH** to **SALT**   (4 steps)

2. **FEED** to **BIRD**   (4 steps)

3. **NEWS** to **ITEM**   (5 steps)

4. **PORE** to **READ**   (5 steps)

5. **STEP** to **RUNG**   (6 steps)

6. **POUR** to **RAIN**   (7 steps)

ACROSS

1. Juicy fruit
5. Plant stalks
10. Slender
14. Path
15. Candy, to a baby
16. Walk through water
17. Skip over
18. Lubricate
19. Loves greatly
21. Sopping
22. Croon
23. Thirsty
24. Consume
25. Prepare for publication
27. Redwoods
29. More peculiar
31. Enemy
32. Veteran sailors
36. Middle Atlantic State: abbr.
37. Closest
40. Harbor
41. Be wrong
43. Perish
44. Salty place
46. Bind
47. Back part
49. Discloses
52. Occur
53. Fall flower
55. Papa
56. Uncovered
58. Storehouse
60. Impolite
61. Past
64. Sofa part
65. Noah's son
66. Highest point
69. March in display
71. Label
72. Rhythm
73. Always
74. Coast
76. Neighborhood
77. Writing table
78. Dispatches
79. Sties

DOWN

1. Farmer's tool
2. Crippled
3. One
4. Was introduced to
5. Corpulent
6. Adorn
7. Electric —
8. Mother
9. Gaze open-mouthed
10. A couple
11. Bunny
12. Notion
13. Bird's home
20. Colors permanently
22. Employed
23. Clothed
26. Lair
27. Boot part
28. "Bonehead": slang
29. — glasses, binoculars
30. Takes a chance
31. Liberty
33. Fate
34. Indian family
35. Horse
38. Atmosphere
39. Social affair
42. Gnawing animal
45. Snapshot book
48. Scarlet
50. Large tank
51. Mournful
54. Peruse
57. Go to bed
59. Iron (clothes)
60. Tantrums
61. Copied
62. Donated
63. Metal sources
65. Difficult
67. Sign of the future
68. Small vegetables
70. Biblical boat
71. Large amount
72. Faucet
75. That boy

Solution is on page 284

WHAT'S WRONG?

Each sentence below contains one or more errors in spelling, grammar, or punctuation. Can you spot them all?

Answers are on page 295.

1. Did Bill ran further than Sam.
2. Mary lives in the sonny Southwest and Sue lives southwest of Salem.
3. Sum stoodents like History better than English.
4. Eather of the too boys are quiet dependible.
5. Pam, who likes swiming, preefers summer to Winter.
6. Does the loud noise effect your dispocition
7. Cathy said I believe it will reign
8. Mark was introduced to Principle Jackson when the principles had there conference.
9. The sisters were altogether in the car.
10. Is Jefferson school near Mohawk park

ACROSS

1. Coal distillate
4. Nuisance
8. Arcades have them
13. Monk's abode
17. Anger
18. "Go jump in the —!"
19. Drying cloth
20. Region
21. Stress
23. Verdi creation
24. Resound
25. Tardy
26. Melodies
28. Intones
30. Astronaut's milieu
32. Conflagrations
33. Revue sketch
34. Choose
35. Lees
36. Benediction
40. Large monkey
41. Rub out
42. Intends
43. Mongrel
44. Dweller
46. Hues
47. Bog
48. Hazard
49. Discoveries
50. Verb form
51. Apportions
54. Goods
55. Flew
56. Inclines
57. Constructs
58. Round of applause
59. Browns in the sun
60. Dwelt
61. Skid, as on skis
65. Night before a holiday
66. Quoted
67. Entices
68. Epoch
69. Defers to
71. Struggled with
72. Couple
73. Lyric poems
74. Rescued
75. Concise
76. — Island, New York City
79. Document
80. "Where have you —, charming Billy?"
81. Citrus fruit
82. Weighing device
84. Visionary
88. Portent
89. Ardent
90. Ins and —
91. Convent woman
92. Canvas shelter
93. Stalks
94. Shade of red
95. Obtain

DOWN

1. Bind
2. Sofa part
3. Supplants
4. Saucer or platter
5. Relieve
6. Slalom
7. Most irritable
8. Rocks
9. Optimists have them
10. Is in debt
11. Through
12. Relaxes
13. Pearl weights
14. "— go bragh"
15. Penitential period
16. Hangs back
22. Cut irregularly
27. Impel
29. Snake's sound
30. Mast
31. Bosun's whistle
32. Candid
33. Laths
35. Clothe
36. Submits
37. Frosting
38. Take care of
39. Avarice
41. Works on copy
42. Digs for coal
45. Finishes the laundry
46. Weary
47. Repairs
49. Counterfeited
50. Fork teeth
51. Modify
52. Furlough
53. Country roads
54. Navy women
55. Walked in water
57. Baseball gloves
58. Employed
60. Permits
61. Excellent
62. Education
63. Blue flower
64. Reduce
66. Yield
67. Great liking
70. Powerful
71. Prances
72. Fruit rind
74. City in Massachusetts
75. Harass
76. Opening for coins
77. Tempo
78. So be it!
79. Boy servant
80. Wagers
83. Spiteful gossip
85. Performing team
86. Take to court
87. High explosive: abbr.

Solution is on page 288

JOHN WHO?

Throughout history, there have been many famous men having the first name of John. Below are briefly described fifteen such famous men. Can you match each description with the full name (from the column on the right) of the man being described?

Answers are on page 295.

1. Actor brother of actors Lionel and Ethel
2. Author of "The Grapes of Wrath"
3. Loved Priscilla Mullins, who told him to "speak for yourself"
4. A signer of the Declaration of Independence
5. Prizefighter
6. "The Duke"
7. Husband of Pocahontas
8. Colonist saved from execution by Pocahontas
9. Bandmaster known as "The March King"
10. President whose election-campaign slogan was "Tippecanoe and — too"
11. Commander of the American Expeditionary Force (AEF) in World War I
12. Founder of Methodism
13. Ornithologist and naturalist, known for his paintings of birds
14. U.S. labor leader
15. First American to orbit the earth

John L. Sullivan

John Tyler

John Barrymore

John L. Lewis

John H. Glenn, Jr.

John J. Pershing

John Steinbeck

John Hancock

John Rolfe

John Wesley

John Alden

John James Audubon

John Smith

John Wayne

John Philip Sousa

MIRTHFUL MISQUOTES

Below are misquotes of familiar expressions or quotations. Can you provide the repairs necessary to return each one to its more serious, true state?

Answers are on page 295.

1. "Rome wasn't gilt in a day."
2. "People who live in grass houses shouldn't mow homes."
3. "Where there's a bill there's a pay."
4. "Wine heals all wounds."
5. "If at first you don't succeed, dye, dye again."
6. "Absence makes the heart go wander."
7. "Black is the color of my true love's stare."
8. "Too many looks spoil the troth."
9. "If the shrew hits, bear it."
10. "The sleek shall inherit the mirth."

A BEELINE FOR YOUR BUS LINE

The bus stop which you use every morning is not only on the same street on which you live, but also on the same side of the street. Nevertheless, when you leave your house in the morning, you cross the street diagonally to get to the other side. Having once crossed the street, you cross it again diagonally to reach your bus stop. In spite of crossing the same street twice, you have actually used the shortest possible way to get to the bus stop.

How can you explain such a seemingly impossible beeline to the bus line?

Answer is on page 295.

EYE SPY

The other day Mr. Carlton went shopping for new wallpaper for his apartment. From the display pictured in box 1 below, he selected a pattern and took it to a salesclerk to make his purchase. Can you tell from the jumble pictured in box 2 which pattern he picked? We'll give you a hint: Mr. Carlton picked the one wallpaper pattern shown in box 1 which is NOT repeated in box 2.

Answer is on page 295.

LADDERGRAMS 1
by IRENE R. HAYES

First, write the word that fits the first definition into space 1. Then drop one letter and rearrange the remaining letters to form the answer to definition 2. Drop one more letter, rearrange, and get the answer to definition 3. Put the first dropped letter into the box to the left of space 1 and the other dropped letter into the box next to space 3. When you have correctly solved the puzzle, the dropped letters in the boxes on the left and right, when read down, will spell out related words. Solutions are on page 295.

	1		2		3	
	4		5		6	
	7		8		9	
	10		11		12	
	13		14		15	
	16		17		18	

1. DEFINITIONS

1. Dog's restraint
2. Store's markdown event
3. Coral or Adriatic —
4. Foreigners
5. Face wrinkles
6. Optical glass
7. Vineyard fruits
8. Leaves (of a book)
9. Pod vegetables
10. Compartments, as in a diner
11. Owl cries
12. Chimney grime
13. Highway inns
14. Defrosts
15. Shade trees
16. Chicago footballers
17. Home plate, for one
18. Actor Vigoda

2. DEFINITIONS

1. Slice (the roast turkey)
2. "Indy 500," for one
3. "You — My Sunshine"
4. Idolize
5. Enjoy one of the three R's
6. Citrus drink
7. Lad
8. Biblical "you"
9. Peppery
10. Perfect examples
11. Playground fixture
12. Toboggan
13. Henry VIII, and others
14. Writing fluids
15. Relatives
16. Borsch vegetables
17. Better than better
18. Recipe abbreviation
19. Opening plays in tennis
20. Rhyme
21. Always

	1		2		3	
	4		5		6	
	7		8		9	
	10		11		12	
	13		14		15	
	16		17		18	
	19		20		21	

1	2	3	
4	5	6	
7	8	9	
10	11	12	
13	14	15	
16	17	18	
19	20	21	

3. DEFINITIONS

1. Stinging insects
2. Handles clumsily
3. Egyptian snake
4. Entertains
5. Stitched lines
6. Sen. Kennedy's State : abbr.
7. Silver, and others
8. Chaucer's output
9. Allows
10. Recluse
11. "Wagging — tails behind them"
12. Employ
13. "Do unto — . . ."
14. Electrical mishap
15. Decays
16. Songstress Bailey
17. Jump, frog style
18. Swiss peak
19. "Contrary" girl of rhyme
20. Sea extension
21. Pa's mate

4. DEFINITIONS

1. Go from first to second, in driving
2. Punches
3. "My Country, — of Thee"
4. Travel for Hiawatha
5. Story start
6. 100 years : abbr.
7. Responsibilities
8. Renditions by Donny and Marie, for example
9. Actor Knight and others
10. Barrel hoops
11. Flower holders
12. One-word advice to a spendthrift
13. Valentine symbols
14. Signs of sorrow
15. Be featured
16. "—, keepers, losers, weepers"
17. Roadside eateries
18. Homonym of "rains" or "reigns"
19. Dwelling place
20. Weeding aids
21. That woman
22. Four quarts
23. "But — came Bill . . .," from "Carousel"
24. Bank transaction

1	2	3	
4	5	6	
7	8	9	
10	11	12	
13	14	15	
16	17	18	
19	20	21	
22	23	24	

FIND THE SENTENCE

Carefully cross off words in the diagram below according to the instructions given. When you are finished, the remaining words in the diagram will be a quotation from the English philosopher Sir Francis Bacon. We have started you off by crossing off the words, if any, which contain the letter C in lines 1, 2, 3, 4, 5, 6, 7, and 8—the instruction given in number 1.

Answer is on page 295.

Do these steps in numerical order.

1. Cross out the words, if any, containing the letter C in lines 1, 2, 3, 4, 5, 6, 7, and 8.

2. Cross out the words containing the letters T O P (not necessarily together or in that order) in columns A, B, and E.

3. Cross out the words, if any, which contain any one letter at least three times in lines 8, 9, 10, 11, 12, 13, 14, and 15.

4. Cross out words beginning or ending with the letter N in column D.

5. Cross out, in lines 1, 2, 3, 4, 5, 6, 7, and 8, any of the words found in the following sentence: "The Judge took off his hat and wiped his brow".

6. Whenever the same word appears twice in columns A, B, and E, cross out the second of its appearances.

7. Cross out all words beginning with the letter L.

8. Cross out all five-letter words if any, in rows with odd numbers.

9. Cross out all words beginning with vowels in column D.

10. Cross out the words, if any, containing the three letters Y E S (not necessarily together or in that order) in rows with even numbers.

11. Cross out the words, if any, containing exactly 4 vowels in rows 8, 9, 10, 11, 12, 13, 14, and 15.

12. Cross out all words which both begin and end with the letter N.

Now, the words you have **NOT** crossed out, read in order from left to right, beginning at the top, will give you the sentence.

	A	B	C	D	E
1	WHILE	SOME	LIVE	AS	NATION
2	APPOINTMENT	SEEDY	BOOKS	ON	~~ICE~~
3	~~NICHOLAS~~	HAT	~~PLACED~~	IN	ARE
4	SYSTEM	LASTED	HIS	TO	STOP
5	~~CAN~~	THE	NOUN	BE	THESE
6	TASTED	YEARS	OTHERS	OR	~~EVACUATE~~
7	WHILE	TRIED	AND	TO	LOOK
8	NEON	EVAPORATE	YES	BE	ARE
9	MINIMUM	SWALLOWED	HELPS	AN	FORTUNATE
10	INCAPABLE	IMPORTANT	AND	AT	SIGNIFICANT
11	THERMOMETER	LASTED	SOME	NO	FEW
12	LET	NOMINATION	AUSTRIA	TO	YEAST
13	POSSESS	DESIGNATED	NEVER	BE	THESE
14	CHEWED	CHEESE	AND	IS	BURLESQUE
15	TASTED	DIGESTED	NUMERATION	US	LAST

PINWHEEL 1

The answers to the definitions below are all 6-letter words. Each answer is to be put in the diagram below so that it encircles the corresponding number. Some words will be entered clockwise, some counterclockwise; (c) after a definition means in a clockwise direction and (cc) means in a counterclockwise direction. Answers overlap in a diagram, so letters you fill in will help you with other words you might not get at first. Remember that all answers are 6-letter words. The first word, "HAWAII," has been entered into the diagram to help you get started.

Solution is on page 295.

1. James Michener novel   (c)

2. Dryer's partner   (c)

3. Freedom from disease   (cc)

4. Glass container for liquids   (cc)

5. Small piece of candy   (c)

6. Anne —, mother of Elizabeth I   (cc)

7. In abundance   (c)

8. Kind of shoe   (cc)

9. Felt afraid   (c)

10. Something bought again   (cc)

11. Area of water enclosed by a coral reef (cc)

12. Type of tea   (c)

13. One of the seasons   (cc)

14. Reserves; extras   (c)

15. Nightmares, for example   (cc)

16. Shows happiness   (cc)

17. They wear halos   (cc)

18. Snarl in a string or in the hair   (c)

19. Small, pointed beard   (c)

20. Wet through and through   (cc)

21. Ten-year period   (cc)

22. Law-enforcement personnel   (cc)

23. Untidy; messy   (cc)

24. Attractive; pleasing to the eye   (cc)

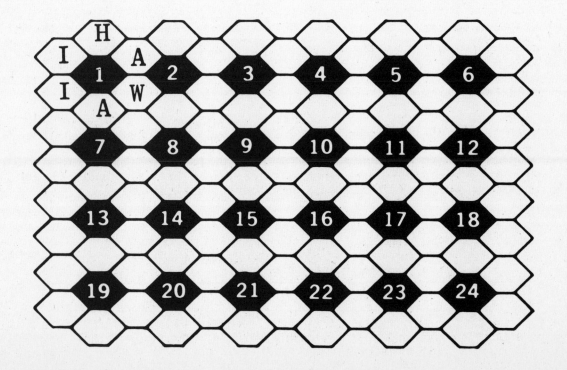

"DEAR HATTIE..."

by GERTRUDE ANDERSSON

Hattie has an "advice" column in the local Blahzette. Her advice may be somewhat sardonic, somewhat haughty—but you can always count on Hattie to be mostly humorous! Just before press time, the space bar on her "tripewriter" went on the blink and her typing was spaced incorrectly. To complicate matters, the typesetter (suffering from too-much-TV) set Hattie's reply exactly as she typed it on her faulty machine. To arrive at Hattie's advice, fill in the definitions below and then you're on your own—space-wise! Here are three of Hattie's tidbits.

Answers are on page 320.

1. "Dear Hattie: They tell me you know a lot about cars, and so I'm turning to you for help with my old clunker. It gets me where I want to go, but it shakes and rattles and makes all kinds of noises and looks terrible. What can I do to make my old car look and run better?"   RICK RACKET

Dear Rick:

Stop's opposite	Child's plaything	Belonging to us	TV show, "Let's Make a —"

Sound of hesitation	The stuff beaches are made of	While	11th letter	Letter with "bar" or "shirt"	With it: slang

Accompaniment to many Chinese dishes	Like a feather pillow	Egg layer	5th letter	Earned the blue ribbon	Plural ending

2. "Dear Hattie: Your newspaper ran a story not long ago about a man who claimed to be the happiest person on earth. The item didn't give the reason for his statement, and I'm curious to know why he felt that way. Can you tell me, Hattie, what made him so happy?"   N.V.S.

Dear N.V.S.:

Sound of a serpent	Light-switch word	Choose; pick out	Newport's State: abbr.

Average grade on a report card	—lty, not innocent	Black, sticky substance	23rd letter	Red — a beet

It follows "do" on the scale	Lincoln coin	Ancient, stringed instrument whose name sounds like "liar"	Sheriff's group in a western

Baseball position between 2nd and 3rd base: abbr.	Actor Asner

3. "Dear Hattie: My math teacher gave me a real tough homework assignment, and neither my Mom nor my Dad can figure it out. Can you give me the answer to this problem?

Wayne went to a gas station to get some gas. The Fillumup Petroleum Company was selling gas at 29.9¢ a gallon. The Squirt Station was selling gas at 32.9¢ a gallon. Wayne paid $3.85 for 11.7 gallons. The question is, where was Wayne getting his gasoline?"   STUMPED

Dear Stumped:

By — of, via	Not old	During	7th letter	— cetera, and so on

Light, ringing sound	Myself	Material for making cans	Belfast's land: abbr.	Butterfly catcher

Night, to a poet	Word with "Lauderdale" or "Knox"	25th letter	Curvy letter	Describing numbers like 2, 10, or 118

TRIANGLE TANGLE

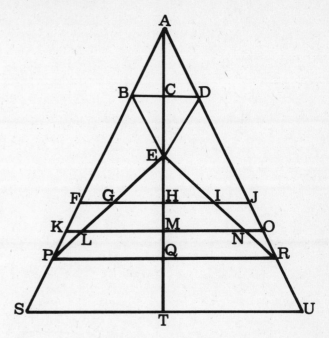

All you have to do to solve this puzzle is figure out how many triangles appear in the figure on the right. Our answer, which lists 37, is on page 295.

WORD MATCH

To solve this puzzle, add a letter to the front of each group of letters below to make it a complete word that best associates with a word or phrase from the group listed at the bottom of the page. Put the associated word onto the dotted line following the word you have made. If you have made the correct associations, the initial letters of the completed words first and associated words, next, when read from top to bottom, will result in a little truism.

Answers are on page 320.

___ime	. . . .
___ors	. . . .
___thel	. . . .
___ear	. . . .
___qual	. . . .
___avel	. . . .
___nd	. . . .
___eterans	. . . .
___arly	. . . .
___oy	. . . .
___indow	. . . .
___pple	. . . .
___team	. . . .
___cademy	. . . .
___len	. . . .
___xford	. . . .

Acuff, Administration, admiral, Award, bird, Campbell, d'oeuvres, dressing, engine, England, orange, out, polisher, rights, run, Waters

WHAT'S WRONG AT THE BEACH?   by Ralph Owen

The artist let his sense of humor have a field day in this drawing. We found 40 mistakes. How many can you find? Our list is on page 315.

WORD MINE

You are to form all the 4- and 5-letter words you can by using only the letters in the word below. We found 72 4-letter words, 38 of which are less frequently used, and 28 5-letter words, 13 of which are less frequently used. You may use a letter more than once in any word you form only if it appears more than once in the words below. Words beginning with a capital letter, plurals, contractions, foreign, obsolete, poetic, archaic, and dialect words are not allowed.

Our words are on page 320.

BALLERINA

ALPHABET TILES

Below, you are given sixteen alphabet tiles—that is, squares with letters of the alphabet in them. Insert each one of these tiles containing two letters into the diagram to get four ten-letter words—two going across and two going down. The letters in the corner squares will naturally overlap to form the across and down words. The small diagram below to the left is merely an example for you to follow. You can see that the tiles have formed the across words SAMPLE and REASON and the down words SATIRE and LESSON. The letters of one tile have been entered into the diagram to help you get started.

Solution is on page 320.

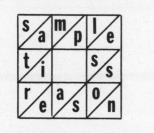

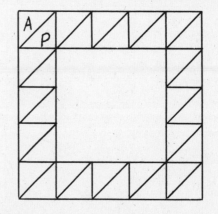

25

THE TRUTH REMAINS

Find a "mate" (that is, another picture having some logical connection) for as many pictures as you can, and cross off these combinations. Then, identify the remaining pictures and enter the first two letters of that identification in the space provided with each picture. When all the matching pictures have been crossed off and all the others correctly identified, the series of first two letters will spell out a proverbial truth.

Answer is on page 320.

CRYPTOQUIZZES 1

A Cryptoquiz is a list of related words put into a simple code. You will find that one set of letters has been substituted for the correct letters of the words in each of the following lists. The title of each Cryptoquiz, and the example, will give you a hint as to what the disguised words may be. Then look for words which might betray themselves by their "pattern" of repeated or double letters. When you've identified a word, the known letters will help you to decode other words in that list. Remember that if G stands for M in one word, it will be the same throughout that Cryptoquiz. Each Cryptoquiz has its own code.

Answers are on page 296.

1. SNOW WHITE

Example: Sleep

QNPNA SLZBYQ

DBXAMN

HFN FWAHNB

QHNDKEHFNB

DEXQEANS ZDDTN

VXQQ

DBXAMNQQ

"KXBBEB, KXBBEB

EA HFN LZTT"

YEBNQH ZAXKZTQ

2. AT THE SHOE STORE

Example: Sneakers

FTJFXQD

DNYQNPD

KFFHD

PFNJOXD

UFBBNDVYD

BPFLD

CVYL HVGD

GRUGD

COQLVOD

DPVGGOXD

3. AND A WORD FROM THE UMPIRE!

Example: Home Run!

RBZ!

FZHWXG ZYHGG!

AKSJ MSKK!

FSVG!

VSWH MSKK!

MSKX!

VRBK MSKK!

JRB'HG RBZ

RV ZYG ISTG!

ZWTG RBZ!

4. THEY LIGHT UP

Example: Flare

FKGVIN

TIKAYIBWYZ

TIKAY PRIP

GNLG ABWG

IKGZNXG

PNKFLG

IKDM

ZLXFY

FYKGVNIBNX

AMLZIBWYZ

5. ELECTED OFFICIALS

Example: Town Supervisor

YNQIEVQCJ

LWRQNCWN

FDVLQ

VEIJNEZJ

MJJWNCQT

ZWDCZEAHMC

ZWCLNQIIHMC

HMTWN

ZWHYJNWAAQN

IQCMJWN

6. ABOUT BRAZIL

Example: Amazon River

LXRRKK

DNX JK SQHKNDX

ZDQCNWNQ

SGHTWKC

CGTQD WXQR

FXGHEQNH

CQX BQGWX

BXDEGTGKCK

WQHTGQTK

DQNH RXDKCE

27

NUMBER SQUARES

Fill in the empty squares of each diagram below in such a way that the four numbers of each of the following will total 80 in diagram 1 and 1980 in diagram 2: each row, each column, each diagonal, the four center boxes, the four corner boxes, and the four boxes in each corner.   Solutions are on page 296.

1.

15	27		
33		11	
	29		
23			

2.

502	490		
494	498	500	
504	484		

ARROW MAZE 1

Copyright 1989 by
Bantam Doubleday Dell Publishing Group, Inc.

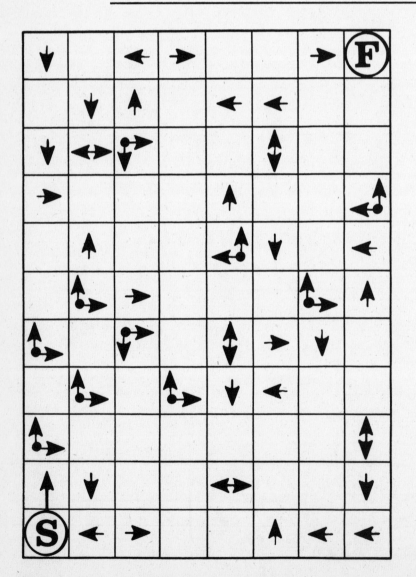

Starting at the S (start) and following the arrow leading out of that S, see if you can find your way to F (finish) in five minutes or less. When you reach a square that contains an arrow, you MUST follow the direction of that arrow. You may not simply go through a square that contains an arrow, and you may not change directions until you hit an arrow that tells you you may do so. When you reach a square that has two arrows, you may choose either direction. In this maze you MAY NOT retrace your own path.

Our solution is on page 296.

Whose Shoes?

The puzzled hotel shoemaker above had received orders to repair 12 pairs of shoes for as many guests. When the time came to deliver them, he discovered, to his dismay, that he had on hand the shoes belonging to only 11 guests. In addition, the tickets for the shoes had become all mixed up. In order to save himself the embarrassment of questioning the guests, he peeked through the keyholes of 12 different rooms and saw enough clues to determine not only whose shoes were whose, but also, by elimination, whose shoes were missing from his group. Can you do as well as the shoemaker?

Answer is on page 320.

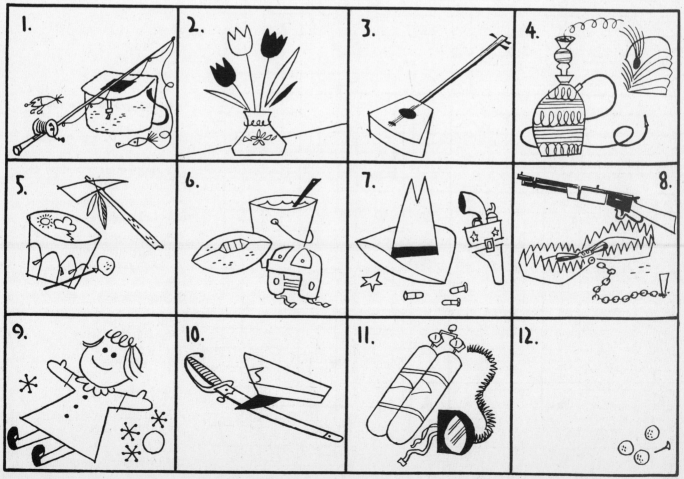

KRISS KROSS 1

Fit the words supplied with each diagram into their proper places in the puzzle squares. The words are in alphabetical order according to the number of letters. Some Kriss Krosses have a word entered in the diagram to help you get started. For example, "PURITANS" is entered into this diagram. To proceed, look for the 10-letter word whose third letter is "P." Continue in this manner until the puzzle is solved.

3 Letters

Bed *(four-poster)*
Dog *(turnspit)*
Fur *(trading)*
Gun *(flintlock)*
Hat *(cocked)*
Ink *(homemade)*
New *(land)*
Pay *(tobacco and other produce)*
Pen *(quill)*
"Sun" *(best tavern in colonies, located in Bethelhem, Pa.)*
Tea

4 Letters

Corn *(staple food)*
Door *(Dutch)*
Game *(wild)*
Lamp *(oil)*
Land *(boom, in Va.)*
Mill *(tanbark)*

Oxen
Sage *(used to preserve meats)*
Samp *(corn porridge)*
Shay *(carriage)*
Soap *(homemade)*
Well

5 Letters

Cabin *(log)*
Cargo *(from England)*
Clock *(grandfather's)*
Forts
House *(-raisin')*
Stove *(Franklin)*
Table *(puncheon)*
Walls *(whitewashed)*

6 Letters

Brooms *(birch)*
Cradle
Hearth
Lean-to

Minuet
Pewter
Piggin *(small wooden pail)*
Settle *(high-backed bench)*
Stocks

7 Letters

Doublet *(man's coat)*
Hetchel *(for combing flax)*
Indians
Periwig
Pillory
Pirates

8 Letters

Breeches *(leather)*
"Bundling"
Pilgrims
Puritans
Virginia *(richest colony)*

9 Letters

Conestoga *(wagons)*
Postrider
Tinderbox
Town crier

10 Letters

Implements *(crude)*
Ordinaries *(tourist homes)*
Trundle bed
Warming pan

11 Letters

Plantations
Springhouse *(to keep food cool)*

12 Letters

Ducking stool
Meeting house *(Quakers' place of worship)*

13 Letters

Covered bridge
Spinning wheel

Solution is on page 293

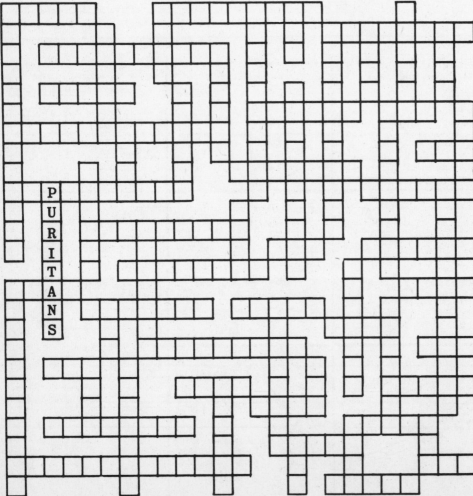

KRISS KROSS 2

3 Letters

Age

Bet

Bus

Eat

Egg

Ego

Red

Tat

Toe

4 Letters

Able

Acre

Best

Bred

Ease

Idle

Nest

Oboe

Sets

Snub

Solo

Sort

Tent

Undo

Unit

Urge

5 Letters

Above

Aster

Badge

Beret

Ebbed

Irate

Saint

Scrub

Trout

6 Letters

Absent

Battle

Beetle

Enable

Gentle

Imbibe

Little

Seemed

Settle

Studio

Tattle

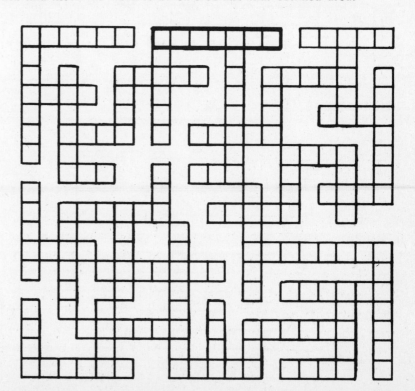

KRISS KROSS 3

SINGERS – THEN AND NOW

Puzzles which do not have a word entered in the diagram will have a heavily outlined area; if you need help
starting the puzzle, turn to page 320 and you will find listed the word to be entered into that outlined area.

3 Letters

Day (*Doris*)
Lee (*Peggy*)
Ray (*Johnny*)
Vee (*Bobby*)

4 Letters

Anka (*Paul*)
Cash (*Johnny*)
Cole (*Nat King*)
Como (*Perry*)
Dean (*Jimmy*)
Faye (*Alice*)
Ford (*Ernie*)
Gore (*Lesley*)
Gray (*Dolores*)
Keel (*Howard*)
Kirk (*Lisa*)
Lane (*Abbe*)
Lind (*Jenny*)
O'Day (*Anita*)

5 Letters

Acuff (*Roy*)
Clark (*Petula*)
Gorme (*Eydie*)
Greco (*Buddy*)
Horne (*Lena*)

Laine (*Frankie*)
Pride (*Charley*)
Reese (*Della*)
Shore (*Dinah*)
Starr (*Kay*)

6 Letters

Arnold (*Eddy*)
Bassey (*Shirley*)
Brewer (*Teresa*)
Carson (*Mindy*)
Crosby (*Bing*)
Haymes (*Dick*)
Lamour (*Dorothy*)
La Rosa (*Julius*)
Mathis (*Johnny*)
Vinton (*Bobby*)

7 Letters

Bennett (*Tony*)
Desmond (*Johnny*)
Presley (*Elvis*)
Sinatra (*Frank*)
Vaughan (*Sarah*)

8 Letters

Eckstine (*Billy*)
Stafford (*Jo*)
Williams (*Hank*)

Solutions are on page 294

KRISS KROSS 4 —"DOWN UNDER"

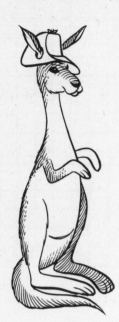

4 Letters

"Abos"
Beer (*national drink*)
Blue (*Mountains*)
Emus
Gold (*fields*)
King (*Karri, giant tree*)
Port (*Jackson*)
Pubs

5 Letters

Black (*swans*)
Coral (*Isles*)
Dutch (*traders made it known*)
Ferns (*in gorges*)
Koala (*models for our teddy bear*)
Manly (*resort*)
Pearl (*divers*)
Perth (*capital of W. Australia*)

Royal (*Theatre, at Sydney*)
Seven (*universities*)
Sheep (*stations*)
Ship's (*chandlers*)
South (*Australia*)
Sport (*cricket*)
Trees (*200 ft. high*)

6 Letters

Arnhem (*Land, reserve*)
Bottle (*trees*)
Hobart (*capital of Tasmania*)
"Little (*Miami*")
Moomba (*festival at Melbourne*)
Spring (*is our fall*)
Sydney (*capital of New South Wales*)
Winter (*is our summer*)

7 Letters

Beaches (*galore*)
Jenolan (*Caves*)
Similar (*to our climate*)
Welfare (*stations*)
Western (*Australia*)
Woolens

8 Letters

Adelaide (*capital of South Australia*)
Brisbane (*capital of Queensland*)
Canberra (*national capital*)
Kangaroo
"Stone-Age" (*aborigines*)
Victoria

9 Letters

Bandicoot (*small animal*)
Cassowary (*bird*)
James Cook (*made maps*)
Limestone (*caverns*)
Melbourne (*capital of Victoria*)
Sandstone (*cliffs*)

10 Letters

Bondi Beach
Corroboree (*ceremonial dance*)
Eucalyptus (*trees*)
"Heart-break (*Land*", *desert area*)
"Never-Never (*country*", *northern part*)
New Holland (*first name, by the Dutch*)
Queensland

13 Letters

New South Wales

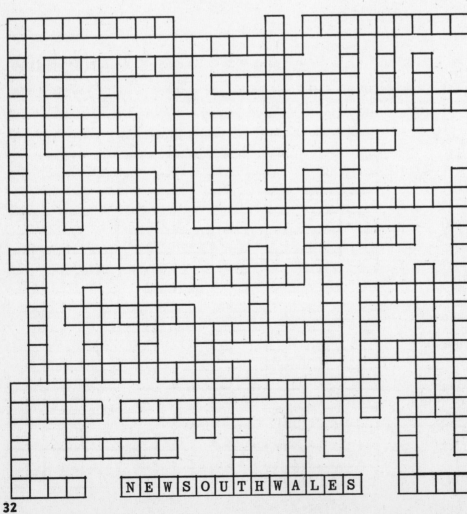

NEWSOUTHWALES

Solution is on page 293

SPORTS FAN'S VOCABULARY

If you need help starting this puzzle, turn to page 320 and you
will find listed the word to be entered into the outlined area.

3 Letters

Bag
Bat
Box
Cue
Hit
Net
Out
Pin
Run
Taw (*marble*)
Tee

4 Letters

Ball
Crew
Dash
Down
Ends
Game
Golf
Home (*plate*)
Iron
Jump
Mask
Mitt
Oars
Pass
Polo
Pool
Puck
Putt
Shot
Swim
Time
Toss

5 Letters

Agate
Canoe
Catch
Clubs
Coach
Count
Court
Derby
Field
Frame
Glove
Green
Holes
Jacks

Mound
Pitch
Plate
Races
Score
Spare
Stone (*curling*)
Track
Yards

6 Letters

Basket
Course
Dugout
Go-cart
Hazard
Hockey
Horses
Hot rod
Mallet
Mashie
Paddle

Pocket
Putter
Signal
Strike
Tennis
Umpire
Wicket

7 Letters

Brassie
Diamond
Dribble
Kickoff
Referee
Whistle

8 Letters

Halfback
Sideline

Solution is on page 293

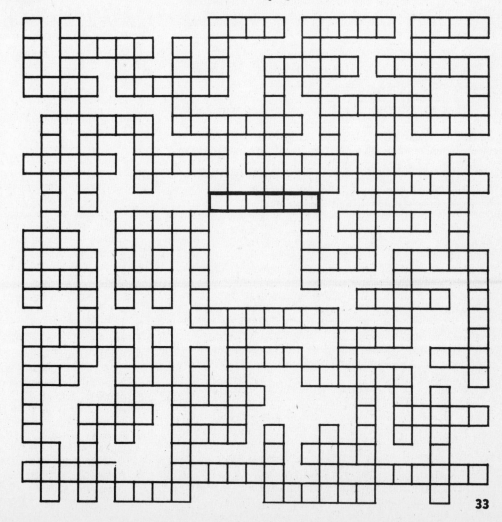

FAMOUS AMERICANS QUIZ

Each group of statements below describes a famous American of the Revolutionary period. Your task is to determine, by reading the clues, who is being described. The challenge here is to discover the answer by the earliest possible clue; do not proceed to the next clue unless you must in order to get the answer. Score yourself as follows: 1 point for each clue you need, for a maximum of 6 points per category—the idea being to get the lowest possible score.
RATING: 32 points or less is excellent; 33 to 38 points is very good.

Answers are on page 296.

A.

1. He was born in Shadwell, Virginia, in 1743.
2. He was a delegate to the Second Continental Congress and drafted the Declaration of Independence.
3. He served as the first Secretary of State.
4. While President, he made the Louisiana Purchase from Napoleon.
5. His home is called Monticello.
6. He was the third U.S. President.

B.

1. After graduating from Harvard in 1755, he practiced law in Boston.
2. Though a leading American Patriot, he defended the British soldiers accused of murder in the Boston Massacre.
3. He helped write the Declaration of Independence.
4. He was one of the negotiators of the Treaty of Paris, which officially ended the Revolutionary War.
5. He served as the new nation's first Vice-President.
6. Elected President in his own right, he served one term as the second President.

C.

1. He was born in 1756 and educated in New Jersey.
2. His service during the Revolutionary War was on Washington's staff.
3. After the War, he practiced law in New York and served a term as a U.S. Senator from the State.
4. Almost elected President, he instead served as Vice-President when the election was decided in the House of Representatives.
5. His attempt to incite rebellion in the Western territories led him to be tried for treason.
6. He killed Alexander Hamilton in a duel.

D.

1. Born in Scotland, he was probably never in America until he reached adulthood.
2. He served on English ships engaged in the slave trade.
3. After he emigrated to Virginia, in 1773, he adopted a new surname.
4. Commissioned a lieutenant by the Continental Congress, he was soon made a captain for his success in naval battles.
5. His ship, the *Bonhomme Richard,* is considered the beginning of the U.S. Navy.
6. He probably never uttered the words attributed to him, "I have not yet begun to fight!"

E.

1. He emigrated to New York in 1772.
2. During the Revolutionary War, he served as Washington's aide-de-camp.

3. A believer in a strong federal government he campaigned tirelessly for the acceptance of the Constitution.
4. Over the opposition of many, he set up a system of American currency.
5. As the first Secretary of the Treasury, he greatly influenced the course of U.S. fiscal policy.
6. He had many enemies, and was killed in a duel by the person in description C.

F.

1. Born in Virginia in 1736, he grew up in modestly prosperous circumstances.
2. Though he first worked as a farmer, he later became interested in the law and became a successful lawyer.
3. His arguments to the jury in his first case foreshadowed his talents as a persuasive speaker.
4. When, in the Virginia House of Burgesses, his speech was jeered with cries of "Treason," he supposedly said, "If this be treason, make the most of it."
5. Though he served as the first governor of Virginia after the War, he refused any federal position.
6. His most famous remark was "Give me liberty or give me death!"

G.

1. He graduated from the College of New Jersey (now Princeton) in 1771.
2. He was one of the writers of "The Federalist," which advocated ratification of the Constitution.
3. His exhaustive note-taking at the Constitutional Convention left posterity the best record of that historic debate.
4. He served as Secretary of State from 1801 to 1808.
5. Some of the policies he pursued while Secretary caused him to be the first President to serve during wartime.
6. He served as the fourth U.S. President, during the War of 1812.

H.

1. He was born in Connecticut in 1758.
2. While studying law, he worked as a schoolteacher.
3. A staunch supporter of the new Constitution, he believed in an educated citizenry as the best guarantee of democracy.
4. After the War, he wrote school textbooks stressing American values instead of British ones.
5. A man of many interests, he published works on medicine and politics as well as his well-known lexicography.
6. A revised edition of his dictionary of the English language is still used today.

"WHAT DO YOU SAY?"

Say what you see!
by A. David Kahn

Failure to identify all the pictures below doesn't mean a thing, but you can have some fun by looking over the drawings and trying to identify the well-known phrases, words, or things they suggest. For example, the words TRAFFIC CIFFART would suggest "two-way traffic." Get the idea? With each is a clue of sorts, a play on words of the answer. In some cases, it will make the answer more obvious, whereas with others, it may take a while to get the connection.

Answers are on page 296.

1

A DOG TRAIN.

2

FUELISH WASTE.

3

WAG WHEEL

IT SPOKE TO ME.

4

GOING TO THE BANK

5

LET'S GET SAUCED.

6

IF YOU DON'T GET IT,
...YOU'LL GET THIS.

FIGGERITS 1

Copyright 1989 by Bantam Doubleday Dell Publishing Group, Inc.

Your finished Figgerit will yield a little truism written onto the SOLUTION dashes. Step 1: Fill in as many words in the WORDS column as you can, using the DEFINITIONS. Step 2: Transfer these letters to the SOLUTION according to matching numbers. Step 3: If you find, for example, that the number 6 stands for "r" in one word, write "r" above 6 in all places in that Figgerit. But a letter is allowed to have more than one number, so number 9 might also stand for "r" and you'd write "r" above all the 9's too. Step 4: Work back from SOLUTION to WORDS column with any possible clues. T-E is probably THE, so try out that H in the WORDS column. Each Figgerit has a different pattern of number/letter substitutions. Word lists are on page 298.

Solutions are on page 296.

1. Definitions — Words

Housework, to some 6 12 24 9 1 32 35 20

Actors Clint or Nancy — .. 21 4 19 38 7 31

Vacation-time traveler 5 23 16 12 36 10 34

Pittsburgh football player .. 37 29 3 8 18 13 22

Mia Farrow, to Maureen O'Sullivan 9 28 14 30 26 34 13 2

Part of the weekend 15 33 27 24 35 6 17 20

Country singer, Merle — ... 26 17 25 30 11 2 9

Solution:

1 2 3 4 5   6 7 8 9 10   11 12 13

14 15 16 17 18 19 20   21 22 23 24 25 26 27

28 29   30 31 32 33 34   35 36 37 38

2. Definitions — Words

— shop, bargain spot 13 17 19 3 15 29

Dior's field 26 1 4 23 9 11 8

Use a ruler 6 5 21 10 30 19 5

Saturday-morning TV fare .. 22 7 19 16 14 27 31 10

Site of the 1980 summer Olympics 6 11 10 22 24 2

Part of a stereo speaker 16 2 20 32 13 32 28

Golfing group 25 14 12 28 4 27 6 18

Solution:

1 2 3 4 5   6 7 8   9 10

11 12 13   14 15   16 17 18   19 20 21 22 23

24 25   26 27 28 29 30 31 32

3. Definitions — Words

Rascals 24 14 9 6 3 30

In a nice, tender way 16 28 12 19 20 7 27

Mickey Rooney's real surname 8 15 26 12

Finished 4 2 18 14 25 9 21

"— Mame," famous novel, play, and movie 17 6 11 23 29 22

International agreement 1 13 31 17 20 27

Miss Garbo 9 5 10 23 17

Solution:

1 2 3   4 5 6 7 8

9 10 11 12 13 14 15 16   17 18 19   20 21 22

23 24 25 26 27   28 29 30 31

4. Definitions — Words

Low man on the military totem pole 28 14 23 10 7 36 5

Blue-ribbon holders 26 33 4 17 29 30 31

Idea 21 2 36 33 15 39

Gets in the way of; impedes 22 37 1 13 18 34 8

One easily made angry 31 38 34 29 6 11 7 19

Available fresh, as fruit: 2 wds. 20 27 8 9 35 24 3 27

Actor Tyrone and others .. 32 25 16 18 12 31

Solution:

1 2   3 4 5   6 7 8   9 10 11 12

13 14 15 16 17 18 19   20 21   22 23 24

25 26 27   28 29 30 31 32 33 34 35 36 37 38 39

5. Definitions   Words

It's said that every cloud ...
has a silver one   20   5   36   24   40   26

Verified as true   38   30   11   14   21   25

Spaghetti-sauce ingredients .   1   32   10   18   22   11   9   37

40s actress, — Goddard   28   35   17   16   4   7   13   39

Your —, royal term
of address   8   2   26   23   40   21   6   31

What a tightrope-walker ...
needs   19   27   16   18   33   34   4

Shattered completely   12   3   15   6   23   29   41

Solution:

1   2   3   4   5   6   7   8   9   10   11   12   13

14   15   16   17   18   19   20   21   22   23   24   25   26   27

28   29   30   31   32   33   34   35   36   37   38   39   40   41

---

6. Definitions   Words

It's often "stranger than ....
fiction"   4   29   18   19   26

Leisure hours: 2 wds.   10   21   3   16   34   23   6   27

"A rose is a rose . . ." ......
author   24   14   22   5   33

Coast Guard boat   12   18   4   25   32   29

Plumage   17   30   11   14   2   7   29   24

Songwriter, Cole —   28   9   21   1   13   29

Rides to hounds   15   20   33   8   31

Solution:

1   2   3   4   5   6   7   8   9   10   11   12   13

14   15   16   17   18   19   20   21   22   23   24

25   26   27   28   29   30   31   32   33   34

---

7. Definitions   Words

— Hagman, J.R. of "Dallas"   16   5   7   25   33

Very hungry   22   6   17   25   12   2   31

Moby Dick's creator   20   2   16   12   8   29   30   19

Track official   9   3   32   14   24   19   25

Soaped up for a shave   30   17   23   4   10   7   13   31

High-school subject   1   8   22   18   26   7   15

Hot-dog condiment   20   21   11   27   28   14   31

Solution:

1   2   3   4   5   6   7   8   9   10   11

12   13   14   15   16   17   18   19   20   21   22   23

24   25   26   27   28   29   30   31   32   33

---

8. Definitions   Words

Money gained after ......
expenses   3   11   2   16   21   7

Artist Moses   23   11   17   26   10   24   19

City in China   3   12   20   5   26   23

Pop singer, Johnny —   14   25   7   1   21   6

Part of the waterfront   18   8   13   11   16

Lumberjack   18   2   15   10   6   24   13   22

Wander aimlessly   24   4   17   22   10   9   11

Solution:

1   2   3   4   5   6   7   8   9

10   11   12   13   14   15   16   17

18   19   20   21   22   23   24   25   26

FIT-IN

The words to go into the diagram are listed here in alphabetical order according to the number of letters. The Across words and the Down words are mixed together. Your job is to fit them into the diagram correctly.

Solution is on page 301.

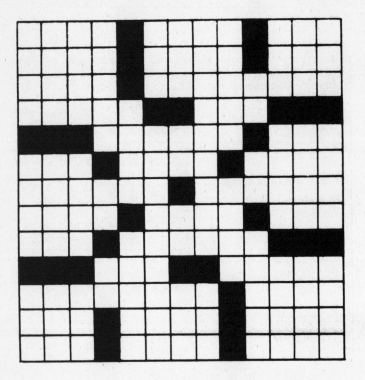

2 Letters
As
At
It
Lo
OK
Us

3 Letters
Ale
Ant
Are
Art
Ask
Coo
Has
Hay
Hid
Hod
Law
Odd
Oil
Old
One
Rip
Sot
Soy

Tow
Yes

4 Letters
Amen
Area
Dent
Dime
East
Edit
Espy
Even
Harm
Lane
Live
Lost
Neat
Need
Nero
Odor
Oleo
Open
Ores
Rest
Rods
Sell

Sent
Some
Time
Trio
Tuna
What

5 Letters
Dates
Morse
Salad
Steer
Taste
Trees

6 Letters
Enters
Refuse
Tosses
Uphill

8 Letters
Choosers
Defrosts

9 Letters
Followers
Refastens

MISSING ALPHABET

To complete the ten words below, add the 26 letters of the alphabet. Use each letter only once, and place only one letter on each dash. Foreign, slang, obsolete, or poetic words are not allowed.

Answer is on page 316.

A B C D E F G H I J K L M N O P Q R S T U V W X Y Z

1. P L A _ T I _

2. E _ _ E N S _

3. A _ A _ I N G

4. A D _ O U _ N

5. S _ U _ R E _

6. _ L I _ H T _

7. _ E A _ I G

8. _ L A N _ E T

9. _ H O _ G _ T

10. B _ _ L O _ N

WORD BASEBALL

The object of this game is to score a "home run" by forming five overlapping words (one of 3 letters and four of 4 letters) from the letters in the word below, RESPONSIBILITY. One letter goes into each dotted space in the base-ball-diamond diagram, and you may not use a letter more than it appears in RESPONSIBILITY. (It's a good idea to cross off the letters as you use them.)

To solve: Start on the pitcher's mound in the center of the diamond. Form a 3-letter word between the pitcher and the batter, placing one letter into each of the dotted areas. Next, form a 4-letter word beginning on home plate with the last letter of the word you just formed. Continue working around the bases in the same manner, following the direction of the arrows so that each word overlaps the next by one letter. If you can get back to home plate, you've scored a "home run," and you're a Word Baseball pro!

NOTE: Form only everyday English words; words beginning with a capital letter are not allowed. Our solution, which may not agree with yours, is shown on page 300.

RESPONSIBILITY

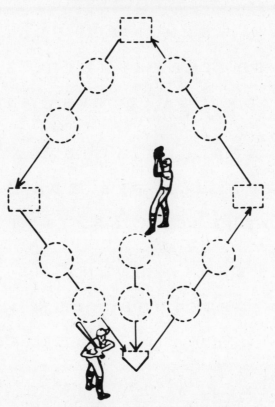

LOCKED-IN LETTERS

Using any letters you wish, fill in the diagrams below so that in each diagram you form eight different 4-letter words in crossword style. You may repeat letters, but no word should appear more than once in each finished puzzle. Plurals are allowed, but abbreviations, foreign, obsolete, slang, and poetic words, and words beginning with a capital letter are not allowed. **Our solutions are on page 311.**

1.
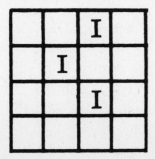

2.
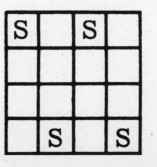

CRYPTOGRAMS

In cryptograms, you are given sentences in which one set of letters is substituted for another. The words are in their right order with a space after each. For example: A BIG CAT, M HWX UMY. Here M is substituted for A, H for B, W for I, etc. You can break each code by watching for the frequency of certain letters or the way they are grouped. You know that a single letter is usually A or I, that the word THE occurs very often in our language, as does AND. Try IS, IT, OF, and other common words when you find a group of two letters.   You'll find the solutions on page 306.

1. WNCO PJTFR FKKE JC IKTMKHMCB VQKO'AK

TMHMCB LMVQMC VQKMA WKNCR KHKC MP

VQKO CKKS VJ IJAAJL WJCKO VJ SJ MV.

2. HGTW VBJH B VWBFM B'KH UEGALGVHA DESJ

VWH ZTWSSY SD HQRHEBHFTH, ZSJH HQRHEV

TSJHZ GYSFU GFA GAAZ GFSVWHE TSLEZH.

3. ZQLE SPR'YL NULLCEV ALOFAGACPET, IL

FLYNLMAUS MLYAGCE SPR BPE'A ULGJL

ILQCEB G NPYZGYBCEV GBBYLTT.

4. CSNHN JHN ANRNHJE HTENA CL SNEV OLT

KJDU ATPPNAA FTC LUEO LUN PNHCJDU HTEN

YLH YJDETHN—CHO VENJADUK NRNHOFLQO.

5. CGJ CM WIJ MXGJZW DJVNAXGT JPJDAXZJZ XZ

OBSHXGT—JZKJAXBSSQ OIJG XW SJBVZ QCN

DXTIW CG KBZW WIJ DJMDXTJDBWCD.

6. ZP KSKLPYMW PYRK, AKMASK POF PM SKZOW

EJZP PJK LZWVYVZPKC CPZWV QMO EJYSK

AMSYPYLYZWC EZWP PM SKZOW EJZP PJK

AKMASK EYSS QZSS QMO.

7. P DATJ UOLU CTLA VOLWDV JPCC KVKLCCH

GN LWTKAE UWTKGCNE JLUNWV.

40

8. KZJHV JQP, SZE ADCSIZT LXZ DJTTZH PW

VBAAZVV PEZ HBEQ JL J LCSZ. LPTJK,

LXZK TZSJET JE ZVAJDJLPH LP IZ

WBHECVXZT IK LXZ QPMZHESZEL.

9. WSK SKJU, CBRK WSK VWDPJXS, BV PDVW

KJVBCM BQTKXWKU NBWS ZDBVDQV NSKQ

BW BV KPZWM.

10. JAPITUP DWT IHOGHZHC LHOHZGCGTA WJC

UHCLKTPHU QTAZHKCJLGTA QHKLJGAOP UTHC

ATL WJZH J LHOHVWTAH IGOO LT VJP.

11. PD HJBS LTBTLFT ZB UTHKPZEX FTLD

PWHS YZRT MST KYV XLJD PJLT—EKM

NSJM ZM WBTV MK UT.

12. BKMKXW ZYM DYMMJOPGJJM MBTJOP MV

DKOW VW MSJ SYZZMVT.

13. EGKJ, ENIJ SHJCT RMNVX, QMIJC XTNVZC

YJMWXNSWE PTJHJKJH LGW CRHJMF NX, YWX

QJHJEL FHNJC WR PTJV NX NCV'X WCJF.

14. LSAG JMLVCJTV JCV BL TGCVJBHON KCSSX

VWJV AJHN VWBHQL JCG SXVGH HSV JL

MJR JL VWGN JCG KJBHVGR.

Solutions are on page 306

CRYPTOGRAMS

15. D T P H F P D D U M F P E M P I D K J J I Z E R S J W N P I

M J K K R E P H R F R D Z I S N R U R I N I Z S T D.

16. E P B A R J A B X R J K X V M I T P Q H J T A T J G V,

I J T W - V X J A Z G D K X G V R J K X I X X E Y P G T X Z

A P Q P K X M H Y G P E A.

17. D L I I C L U B: Y V L Y U W J I C J H Q C R Q Y C Y H Y C J R

V B W T Y J U B Y V B I G C Y V Y G J A J J X Q — K J J X

L R T K V B K X.

18. V M V Y N R H Q S L F Y H Q S L Z Y K P J Y J W V K Z

L E J M V L, J Q X V M V Y N L E J M V T J L T J X R H Q S L

J P K Q S T H L J Q W V L A K Y L. (F E J A K)

19. J K H L S H L Z H Z J B W L W Z B V E Y H L H O J L F H R

G M O V L V M Z U T, "B G H B L M B G W Z E H S H L J Z

I U J Y F J Z W B W Z K J W E B H R E V L J Z C G W B H

J Z W B W Z C G W B H C J Z G H R."

20. O B H Z G O Q W Z B O D N T C P Z C M Z R G S Q R Y D T A N B

Q G X B H C X R B T B X W W Z B P G H Q G T Y F B G F A

C F Q O B P W B A W Z B A H C I B H Q B I B H S S B G H.

21. T B X Z W N K J V L B L C A Z J V E E T V A Z T V U K B

L N J K B S — J X A A V A Z L P V M N T Q P V N W N W K P V A I

B J C X A I B W B E E Q I J K B S.

22. M V H T A H J M H Y M L H J M Y J A H B K M X H A L K A R H W

Z Q Y M A H B T M V; R K Y M K L M H B M V H Q J A H

M V H A H Y E P M K L N H A Q X J M G H B M, I J A H L E P,

J B W I K B Y M J B M X H A Y N H A J B I H.

42 *Cryptograms continue on page 86.*   **Solutions are on page 306**

HEXAGON HUNT

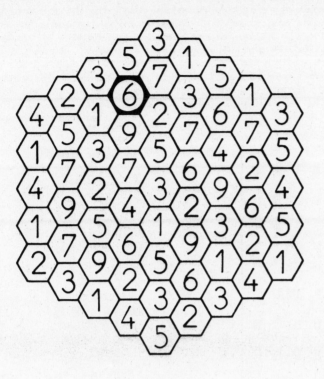

In the diagram of hexagons (six-sided figures) on the left, there are 10 "special" hexagons. These 10 are special because the six hexagons surrounding each of them contain numbers that are not only different from each other, but are also different from the number in the "special" center hexagon. We've started you off by drawing a circle in one of the 10 "special" hexagons. Can you find the other 9 in less than 3 minutes?

Solution is on page 301.

NOTE: A hexagon may belong to more than one group, and a "special" hexagon may also be one of the surrounding hexagons in another "special" hexagon group.

FUN WITH FACTS AND FIGURES

by Irene R. Hayes

NOTE: In this puzzle, no fractions are involved.

1. To begin, write down the number of days in the month of March.

2. To this figure add the number of hours in a day.

3. If thirteen couples took part in the local disco contest, how many participated? Subtract this number from your total.

4. Circle the one word in the following group *not* traditionally associated with Easter:
   BONNETS EGGS PARADE BASKETS FIREWORKS BUNNIES
   Add to your score the number of letters in the word you've circled.

5. Select (a) or (b) to correctly complete the following statement:
   In the Gilbert & Sullivan operas, (a) Gilbert wrote the text, Sullivan the music (b) Sullivan wrote the text, Gilbert the music. If you chose (a), add
   3 to your score; if you chose (b) divide your score by 3.

6. How old is John if he was born in 1954? Subtract his age from your total.

7. Next *Multiply* your score by the number of o's in the following limerick:
   There once was a lady from Hyatt
   Who tried an unusual diet,
   Cakes, cookies, and pies,
   Rolls, bagels, and ryes,
   Said her baker insisted she try it!

8. The Philadelphia Phillies won the 1980 World Series. If this statement is not false, divide your score by 2; if it is not true, add 2 to your score.

9. Next subtract from your score the numbber of misspelled words in this sentence.

10. Our answer is 17, the number of the day in March set aside for St. Patrick's Day. *Is yours?*

Solution is on page 296.

WORD SEARCH 1   FAMOUS-NAME COUNTIES OF THE USA

The Word List below contains the names of 45 counties of the USA which happen also to be the names of famous people. (In parentheses following each name is the name of just one of the States in which that particular county is located.) See if you can find them all hidden in the diagram. The names are formed in the diagram forwards, backwards, up, down, or diagonally, but they are always in a straight line and never formed by skipping over any letters. It is important to circle or cross through each word in the diagram; and it's a good idea to cross off the words in the Word List once you've circled them. Letters may be used more than once and the words often overlap. You will not, however, use all the letters in the diagram. If a word appears more than once in the diagram, but only once in the Word List, circle it only once. The words in parentheses will not be found in the diagram.

Solution is on page 300.

```
K I N G G E O R G E A N O S L I W P
D J K R A L C D C E P I K E F I H R
E G A H J E K N O T G N I H S A W I
S L M C N W O F R E M O N T L R N N
O P O L K I P S R Q X R G E F T U C
T L E V E S O O R A O S W X U H O E
O T Y V W B O O N E N Z I A L U H E
A J O H N S O N N B K K L C T R L D
B A Y E W E D O H A M I L T O N A W
E D R A W E S D A E G I I I N F C A
H A S H E R M A N I N J A H N L N R
P M K R E T R A C C L N M N A M E D
E S O F E O R N O M K R O Y F O R D
S P F Q E R T L C S R E T S U C U X
O E W A L X N B K Y Y E L P I R B Z
J E F F E R S O N D A V I S C D N D
T F H J D L E I F R A G N I D R A H
S P O C A H O N T A S Y R R E P V M
```

WORD LIST

Adams *(Colo.)*
Arthur *(Neb.)*
Boone *(Iowa)*
Calhoun *(Ala.)*
Carter *(Mo.)*
Clark *(Ida.)*
Clay *(Ala.)*
Custer *(Mont.)*
De Soto *(Miss.)*
Dewey *(Okla.)*
Ford *(Kans.)*
Franklin *(Ga.)*
Fremont *(Colo.)*
Fulton *(Pa.)*
Garfield *(Utah)*
Hale *(Ala.)*
Hamilton *(Tex.)*
Hancock *(Ohio)*
Harding *(N. Mex.)*
Jackson *(Fla.)*
Jefferson *(Iowa)*
Jefferson Davis *(Miss.)*
Johnson *(Tenn.)*
King George *(Va.)*
King William *(Va.)*
Knox *(Ohio)*
Lee *(Ala.)*
Lewis *(Wash.)*
Lincoln *(Ky.)*
Madison *(Miss.)*
Monroe *(N.Y.)*
Perry *(Ind.)*
Pike *(Pa.)*
Pocahontas *(Iowa)*
Polk *(Ore.)*
Prince Edward *(Va.)*
Ripley *(Ind.)*
Roosevelt *(Mont.)*
Seward *(Neb.)*
Sherman *(Kans.)*
St. Joseph *(Ind.)*
Van Buren *(Iowa)*
Washington *(Me.)*
Wilson *(Kans.)*
York *(Me.)*

WORD SEARCH 2

Here is a special Word Search, constructed with numbers instead of letters, but it's solved the same way as a regular Word Search. The 24 number combinations below are hidden in the diagram. The number combinations in the diagram read forwards, backwards, up, down or diagonally—always in a straight line, with no digits skipped over. To start you off, 2136 is circled.

2136	8034
2177	8070
2234	8426
2260	8476
2343	8803
2346	8830
5010	9311
5077	9367
5503	9604
5570	9676
5710	9930
5767	9963

```
0 0 7 6 9 4 9 9 3 0 8
1 3 1 0 1 6 4 3 2 4 0
7 5 5 0 3 6 7 7 2 0 7
5 4 3 1 5 1 0 6 0 6 0
9 5 2 1 7 2 2 3 4 9 2
3 7 7 8 1 6 7 4 8 2 8
6 6 0 0 3 3 4 3 6 4 8
7 3 1 0 0 7 9 0 4 7 0
4 3 6 3 4 7 7 6 6 3 3
1 0 8 9 3 0 4 7 7 6 2
1 8 3 4 9 5 5 7 7 1 2
```

WORD SEARCH 3

The idea of a Tail Tag Word Search is to form an unbroken chain of circled words in which the last letter of one word is the first letter of the next word. The number in parentheses tells you the length of each word you're looking for, and dashes are provided for writing down each word as you find it. Start with "CURIOUS," which is circled in the diagram. Continue solving by looking for a 5-letter word connected to "CURIOUS" that begins at the same "S" that "CURIOUS" ends with. That word is "STAMP," which is also circled. Your next word will be "POWER," which begins with the "P" at the end of "STAMP." Solving continues in this way throughout the diagram.

CURIOUS	(7)	_____	(5)
STAMP	(5)	_____	(4)
POWER	(5)	_____	(4)
_____	(3)	_____	(6)
_____	(4)	_____	(3)
_____	(6)	_____	(5)
_____	(4)	_____	(5)
_____	(6)	_____	(6)
_____	(6)	_____	(5)
_____	(5)	_____	(4)
_____	(7)	_____	(5)
_____	(5)	_____	(4)
_____	(3)	_____	(3)
_____	(7)	_____	(4)

```
T H R I M E H E N D F W B C
F L A T T E R B A R Y I O U
Z F N G A E I O G I R L N R
T B U I A N R U O V E D E I
E U N C D M R D I E M W D O
D E H G S S E C E R O M Y U
I W A N T Y S A P P M A T S
O L E F R G E R R O E S G T
U L O H I L V E A N E P A R
S O N I C A E S H T L M A E
S A R N K L N J S G S A I A
R E U O Y T T R A V E L L T
```

Word List is on page 303.
Solutions are on page 300.

ACROSS

1. Shuttlecock
5. Conductor's call
10. Cabbage salad
14. Fragrance
15. Large sea duck
16. Horse's gait
17. Confederate
18. Marry "on the Q.T."
19. Alleviate
20. Zest
22. Brought into harmony
24. Wind spirally
26. Urban haze
27. Merit
30. Depart: 2 wds.
34. Chopping tool
35. Spread for drying
36. Emulate
37. By way of
38. Disencumber (of)
39. Picnic intruder
40. Guido's highest note: 2 wds.
41. Possesses
44. Body of salt water
47. "— into," attacked
48. Scandinavian land
50. Legation
52. Military unit
53. Slant
54. Short-bladed weapon
57. Required
61. Reddish-brown horse
62. Select group
66. Invisible emanation
67. Opening bet
68. Glossy fabric
69. Go by boat
70. Come together
71. Sound from the nest
72. Otherwise

DOWN

1. Wild hog
2. Inactive
3. Bun
4. Refrigerant: 2 wds.
5. Place of activity
6. Lubricate
7. "Fuss and feathers"
8. Corded fabric
9. Imagine: 2 wds.
10. Santa's vehicle
11. Temporary grant
12. Church recess
13. Garden menace
21. Classify
23. Misplace
25. Headed
26. Mineral spring
27. Challenged
28. Banish
29. Closed car
31. Some faces
32. Conclusion
33. Greasy
41. Timid rodent
42. Sofa part: 2 wds.
43. The heavens
44. Obstinate
45. Distinguished
46. Capable
49. Loadstone
51. Relaxed: 2 wds.
54. Small amount
55. First-rate: 2 wds.
56. Fence opening
58. Twofold
59. Goddess of discord
60. River valley
63. Regulation
64. Follower of: suffix
65. Even score

Solution is on page 284

WHAT'S THEIR LINE?

From each group of four possibilities, can you pick the one word that is most closely associated with the given profession? Answers are on page 296.

1. CARTOGRAPHER: a. skits b. maps c. carts d. cartridges
2. CHOREOGRAPHER: a. cording b. coring c. ribbing d. dancing
3. ETHNOGRAPHER: a. anthropology b. paces c. cookery d. fashion
4. ORTHOGRAPHER: a. drawing b. spelling c. coloring d. pasting
5. PHONOGRAPHER: a. lights b. seeds c. disks d. sounds
6. PHYSIOGRAPHER: a. nature b. leisure c. denture d. posture
7. RADIOGRAPHER: a. helms b. X-rays c. qualms d. radio
8. STENOGRAPHER: a. cymbals b. idols c. medals d. symbols
9. TOPOGRAPHER: a. tops b. rhymes c. rivers d. tapers
10. TYPOGRAPHER: a. painting b. printing c. weaving d. branding

ACROSS

1. "Shoot the breeze"
5. Standard
9. Certain leather
13. Squalid place
14. Diva's forte
15. Carp
16. Slacken
17. Confined
18. Humiliate
19. Place to find a "scoop": 2 wds.
21. Sheer linen
22. Cowed
23. Noisemakers of a sort
25. Arctic weather word
28. Doorway part
29. Burdened
30. Chess situation
35. Affirm
36. Covered with stratified rock
37. Quite old
38. Luncheon necessities
40. Fetch
41. Feudal gentleman
42. Lower in rank
43. Ladies' man
47. Singer Horne
48. On the move
49. Lazy
54. Tiny insect
55. Make docile
56. — horn, althorn
57. Cajoled
58. Olive genus
59. Smear
60. Golf gadgets
61. Garrison
62. Goals

DOWN

1. Henri Soulé's title
2. Rime
3. Likewise
4. Junior prom set
5. Took forty winks
6. Mountain nymph
7. Phone call
8. Fabrics
9. Famous Boston name
10. Benefit
11. Extra-strong thread
12. Escapes
15. Rustler's concern
20. What Castor is to Pollux
24. Confederate
25. "Pad"
26. Speak incoherently
27. Thought
28. Point of view
30. Baseball position
31. A preserve
32. Exchange premium
33. Encamp
34. Move cautiously
36. Shortly
39. Coated with metal
40. Inclination
42. Make null and void
43. Entire extent
44. Burning
45. Famous Boston name
46. Theater boxes
47. Sources of vitamin C
50. Symbol of virtue
51. Spirit
52. Shirt ornament
53. Weeps

Solution is on page 284

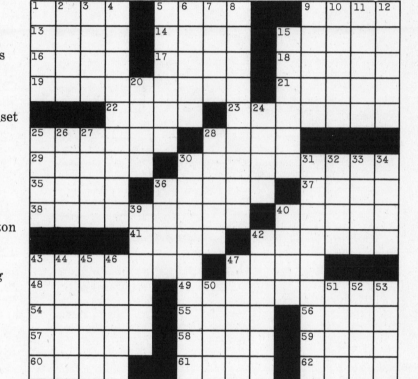

CHANGELINGS 2

Can you turn the first word into the second one by changing only one letter at a time? Do not change the order of the letters. Each step must be an everyday word (no proper nouns allowed). Our answers are on page 296.

1. **TALL to LILY**   (4 steps)

2. **PULL to WEED**   (5 steps)

3. **CALL to OUTS**   (5 steps)

4. **SHORT to STOPS**   (6 steps)

5. **HEAT to WAVE**   (6 steps)

6. **BRAVE to RAIDS**   (8 steps)

13 and 14 EASY CROSSWORD

Puzzle 13

ACROSS

1. Raise
5. One of the "Little Women"
8. Desire
12. Scent
13. Hatchet
14. Neighborhood
15. Extremely
16. Edge
17. Appear (to)
18. Consume
19. Museum exhibit
20. Attending
21. Unsightly
23. Tiny insects
26. Last
28. Pastry
29. — and downs
31. By mouth
32. Fiery
33. Huge continent
34. Decay
35. Cereal grain
36. Small
37. Requires
39. Cat's "sigh"
40. Myself
41. Young fellow
42. Likely
45. Desk light
48. Winter ailment
49. Adhesive
50. Aid and —, help
51. Wheel track
52. Is ill
53. Refuse to admit
54. I do!
55. Seasoning

DOWN

1. Like greatly
2. Notion
3. Lucky
4. Attempt
5. Wed
6. Way out
7. Jewel
8. Squander
9. Anger
10. Understand
11. Hog meat
19. Everything
20. Beerlike drink
22. Sal, for one
23. Conniption
24. Continent "down under"
25. Rotisserie rod
26. In favor of
27. Press
28. Kettle
30. Speak
32. Possesses
33. Atmosphere
35. Lyric poem
36. Purchase
38. Vacant
39. Sulks
41. Ocean's color
43. Tug
44. Try out
45. Stripling
46. — Lincoln
47. Squad members
48. Sauté
49. Helium

Puzzle 14

ACROSS

1. Forty winks
4. Shut violently
8. Catch sight of
12. Lubricant
13. Apple center
14. Mass of money: slang
15. Education problem
17. Cutting edge
18. Advised
19. Sharp ache
20. Deserved
22. Comic strip
25. Bit of news
26. Remedies
27. Suffice
28. Zeus was one
29. Strongholds
30. Also
31. At home
32. Ridiculous
33. Eskimo gear
34. Demolish
36. Thick-headed
37. Cake layer
38. Witnessed
39. Blueprints
41. Sports event
44. Symbol of marriage
45. Pepper's mate
46. Recline
47. Betting advantages
48. Individuals
49. Health resort

DOWN

1. Sign of assent
2. Melody
3. Conspired
4. Nagging shrew
5. Like a showy tie
6. Mr. Linkletter
7. Pine Tree State: abbr.
8. Divides
9. Cliburn's instrument
10. — Town, city in 7-Down
11. Golf mound
16. Ode, for one
17. Exposes
19. Social event
20. Inflexible
21. Make amends
22. Type of hair
23. Aromas
24. Lasso
26. Red or blue
29. Discharges
30. Deep passages
32. Insect bites
33. Three equal one yard
35. Music rack
36. Fender mishaps
38. One and only
39. Paid athlete
40. Pot cover
41. Preserve
42. Tiny taste
43. Beverage
45. Thus

Solutions are on page 284

ACROSS

1. Back talk
5. Desist
9. Cavalry sword
14. Lively dance
19. Dismounted
20. Volcanic overflow
21. Occupation
22. Cognizant
23. Mexican coin
24. Help in wrongdoing
25. Deride
27. At home
28. Touch gently
30. Stiff
32. Entertain lavishly
33. Cozy room
34. Walk pompously
37. "Deep and dreamless — "
38. Conceal
39. Bank (on)
40. Stumble
41. Make amends
42. Duel measurement
43. Chapeau
44. Disencumbered (of)
45. Baa
46. Remedy
47. Explosion sound
50. Ran
52. Barrel
53. Business associate
54. Read
55. Punctuation mark
56. Hostile incursion
57. Latin salutation
58. According to
59. Droop
60. Overstuffed
61. Stupefy
62. Fixed charges
65. Preserve
67. Swiftness
68. Cleveland's lake
69. Search
70. A few
71. Definite article
72. Immense
73. Use a ledger
74. Weary
75. Introduce into a discussion: 2 wds.
79. Ineffectual
81. Wait
82. In the interim
83. Peaceful
84. Tree trunk
85. Mutual concord
86. By way of
87. Tavern
88. Horse's gait
89. Make happy
90. Bird's bill
91. Elapse
93. Severe discomfort
94. Misfortunes
95. Dips into coffee
96. Hardwood
97. Russian news agency
98. Occurrence
99. Kitty
100. Skyward
101. Kerosene burner: 2 wds.

103. New Zealand bird
105. Sharp taste
109. Fishing net
111. Senior
112. Send forth
113. Bright thought
114. Penetrate
115. Suspicious
116. Contradict
117. Requirement

DOWN

1. Enervate
2. Beerlike beverage
3. Family member, for short
4. Clog: 2 wds.
5. Louver board
6. Cafe bill
7. Burden too heavily
8. Long-suffering
9. Dismantle
10. Barren
11. Ill-behaved
12. Building
13. Move back
14. Strong wind
15. Reverent fear
16. Musical note
17. Bay window
18. Coin
26. American Indian

29. On the hour of
31. Gosh!
33. Explode
34. Razor hone
35. Bosh!: slang
36. Passenger
37. Spirited horse
38. Listen!
39. Enthralled
41. Change
42. Shove
43. Crowd of animals
45. Military installations
46. Discard: 2 wds.
47. Track part
48. Musical show
49. General course
51. Indian coin
52. Composed
53. Ashen
55. Soil
56. Impolite
59. Desire
60. Renown
61. Exhausted
62. Picture puzzle
63. Get up
64. Ferocious
65. Disarrange
66. Learning
67. Gleam
69. Flexible tube
71. Smidgen
73. Famous Quaker

74. Incline
75. Thrashes
76. Specified
77. Eskimo boat
78. Pinnacles
80. Camera eye
81. Blessing
82. When the dinner bell rings
84. Take offense
85. Made a sharp little sound
88. Drape ornament
89. Preceding night
90. Interrupt: 2 wds.
91. Hesitate
92. Colorado city
93. Chum
94. Each without exception
95. Perform
97. Layer
98. Always
99. Compassion
101. Individual
102. Lyric poem
104. Triumph
106. Fruit drink
107. Born
108. Roam about
110. Tag player

Solution is on page 288

ACROSS

1. "Ernani" composer
6. "I —, I melt, I burn"
10. Inclination
14. Regional dialect
15. Beyond
16. Platonic model
17. Vehicle for winter
19. Adroit
20. Corrode
21. Bore, as ill will
22. Ladder rung
23. Joel Chandler Harris' — Rabbit
24. Pittsburgh pro
26. Fruit for jelly
29. Approach
30. Bay window
31. Floating ice sheet
33. Lingerie item
37. Taj Mahal site
38. Fry lightly
39. Elephant's-ear, e.g.
40. Garden herb
41. Airplane maneuver
42. Urchin
43. Hyson and gunpowder
45. To no avail
47. Least prudent
50. Canadian Indian
51. Spirit in "The Tempest"
52. Unfounded
53. Famous featherweight
56. Hindu lady of high standing
57. Winter-driving aid
60. — the Red
61. Type of mortgage
62. Cognizant
63. Regatta
64. "Wozzeck" composer
65. Licit

DOWN

1. Holding device
2. Poetress Millay
3. Something very funny
4. Indian Ocean boat
5. Lacking virtue
6. American poet: 2 wds.
7. Eager
8. Colloidal substance
9. Before
10. Shakespearean work, "The — : 2 wds.
11. Perfect
12. Set sail
13. More recent
18. Actor, Reginald —
22. Overwhelming amount
23. Make a beginning: 3 wds.
24. Rich dessert: 2 wds.
25. Of a certain age group
26. Anthracite, e.g.
27. Advocate earnestly
28. To laugh: French
32. Old-time card game
34. Metallic fabric
35. Rainbow
36. Famous operatic soprano
38. Le Sage's novel "Gil —"
42. Widespread
44. Lamprey
46. One's identity
47. Less common
48. Australian cockatoo
49. Chinese
52. Highway of Caesar's day
53. Wampum
54. Book of the Bible
55. Rind
57. Ecclesiastical vestment
58. Never: German
59. Lambkin's ma

Solution is on page 284

BIBLE QUIZ

Each drawing below suggests the name of a character in the Bible. Can you name all eight? Answers are on page 296.

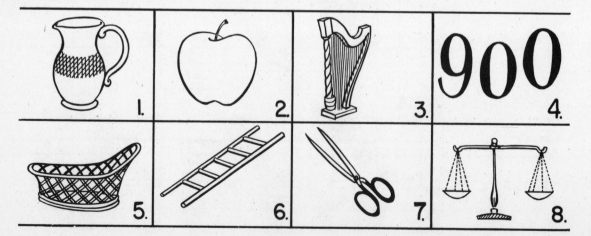

BIBLE CROSSWORD by RUSS CARLEY

ACROSS

1. Man that is born of a — is of few days, and full of trouble
6. They make haste to — innocent blood
10. Yea, I judge not mine own —
14. Man shall not live by bread —
15. Thou shalt not — the name of the Lord thy God in vain
16. So the Edomites r—ted from under the hand of Judah
17. Who hath gathered the wind in his —?
18. — rebuke is better than secret love
19. Thou shalt not suffer a witch to —
20. Adam called his wife's name —
21. The words of the covenant, the — commandments
23. The young lions roared upon him, and —
25. On the seventh day thou shalt —
27. These are his sides east and —
30. And forgive us our debts, as — forgive our debtors
31. — is me for my hurt!
33. Thou art lukewarm, and neither cold nor —
35. When they make a long blast with the — horn . . . the wall of the city shall fall down
39. They brought their offering before the Lord, six covered —s, and twelve oxen
42. Jesus was born in Bethlehem of Judea in the days of — the king
44. I will stand on the — of the hill
45. Take bow and —ows
46. They were sore amazed in themselves b—nd measure
48. And he showed me a pure river of water of life, —ar as crystal
49. Th— was no room for them in the inn
50. Now Eli the p—st sat upon a seat by a post of the temple of the Lord
51. In four quarters were the porters, toward the east, west, north, and —
53. Teach me, and I will hold my tongue: and cause me to understand wherein I have —
55. Was not — Jacob's brother?
57. We know that the law is good, if a man — it lawfully
58. Many shall run to and —
59. Greater love hath — man than this
61. The fathers have —n sour grapes
63. But if ye do not forgive, neither will your Father which is in heaven forgive your —passes
67. When ye see a cloud rise out of the west, straightway ye say, There cometh a —
71. Stand in —, and sin not
73. Be in rest and at e—
74. The Lord separated the tribe of —
75. For — was first formed, then Eve
78. Make a joyful — unto the Lord, all ye lands
80. O f—t, and every tree therein
81. Lord, dost thou not — that my sister hath left me to serve alone?
82. The ox knoweth his —, and the ass his master's crib
83. The words of his mouth — smoother than butter
84. And Saul — David from that day and forward
85. And when he sowed, some — fell by the wayside

DOWN

1. One cake of oiled bread, and one — out of the basket of the unleavened bread
2. I am like a green — tree in the house of God
3. Pharaoh called for — and Aaron
4. The Lord is my shepherd, I shall not w—
5. As a bird that wandereth from her —
6. He that is without sin among you, let him first cast a — at her
7. —py is the man that findeth wisdom
8. He that se—th findeth
9. Then came to him certain of the Sadducees, which — that there is any resurrection
10. As with the buyer, so with the —
11. Hate the —, and love the good
12. — of money is the root of all evil
13. They . . . left their tents, and their horses, . . . and — for their life
22. The poor man had nothing save one little — lamb
24. A time to rend, and a time to s—
26. No man can serve — masters
28. But his wife looked back from behind him, and — became a pillar of salt
29. The chariots shall be with flaming —es
32. These are the two anointed —, that stand by the Lord of the whole earth
34. Moses went out, and —d the people the words of the Lord
36. If thine enemy be . . . thirsty, give him w— to drink
37. It is — blessed to give than to receive
38. Have they not —? have they not divided the prey
39. Be— of false prophets
40. The sun also —eth
41. Behold, I bring you good tidings of —t joy
42. He that troubleth his own — shall inherit the wind
43. The roebuck, and the fallow —
47. It is vain for — to rise up early, to sit up late
52. They that sow in —rs shall reap in joy
54. I w—e them with ink in the book
56. Wherefore be ye not —, but understanding what the will of the Lord is
58. For many are called, but — are chosen
60. Be ye d—rs of the word, and not hearers only
62. For every kind of beasts, and of birds, and serpents, and of things in the sea, is —
64. The Lord —d hail upon the land of Egypt
65. Bl— are the meek: for they shall inherit the earth
66. Over— to set the people awork
67. He that is — to anger appeaseth strife
68. — is the patience of the saints
69. Thou anointest my head with oil; my cup runneth —
70. The — is not to the swift
72. All the days of — were nine hundred and five years
76. And God called the light —, and the darkness he called Night
77. Stolen waters — sweet
79. Pay me that thou —st

Solution is on page 285

ACROSS

1. Unexpected joys
7. Desert "ship"
12. Empty or worthless
13. Amphitheater
14. Stop
15. Captures
17. Uncommon
18. Factual
19. Solidify
20. That thing's
21. Residence
22. History topics
23. Myself
24. Helpful pointers
25. Sack
26. Mistakes
28. Loving embrace
31. Poetic "before"
32. Damage
33. At home
34. Heap (up)
36. June flower
37. Dollar bill
38. Lyric poem
39. Fishing cord
40. Shade of red
41. Ocean frontage
43. Less colorful
44. Alleviates
45. Razor
47. Frozen rain
48. Lofty buildings

DOWN

1. Movie house
2. Laughs loudly
3. Otherwise
4. Sudsy brew
5. Toward
6. Teems
7. Watchfulness
8. "Roses — red"
9. Get the —, understand
10. Penetrate
11. Endures
14. Legal wrong
16. Regret
18. Surpasses
21. Put on the payroll
22. Friendly
24. Ripped
25. Uncovered
27. Set free
28. Lawsuit
29. Evildoers
30. Scoff
32. Trustworthy
34. Asks (a question)
35. Visionary
36. Free (of)
37. Tanker
39. Itemize
40. Greeting from afar
42. Visualize
43. Rabbit's foot
46. Westward —!

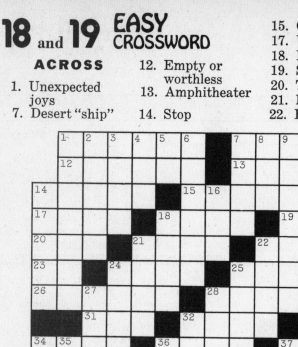

ACROSS

1. Split — soup
4. Location
8. Newcastle has these
10. Arrived
11. Vials
13. Opera selection
14. Crusades
15. Pocketbooks
17. Be "off the beam"
18. Boiled slowly
20. Drone or queen
21. Possessed
22. Was in session
24. Junk
26. Fashions
28. Tilt
29. Is able to
30. Negative vote
32. Postpones
34. Expert
35. Happier
38. Printers' purchases
39. Fence segment
40. Forsakes
43. Land measure
44. Is venturesome
45. Mrs. Truman
46. An illuminant

DOWN

1. Kitchenware
2. Consume
3. Everyone
4. Burned with hot liquid
5. Peel
6. Fail to include
7. Dolls' parties
8. Right
9. Stitched
11. Exposes
12. Proverb
14. Flytrap
16. Sour fruits
18. Formed
19. Faucet
23. Lease-holders
25. Puzzles
26. Spring month
27. Discharges: slang
29. Minded
31. I do!
33. Conducted
35. Be greedy
36. Shoestring
37. Melodies
38. Makes angry
41. Droop
42. Epoch

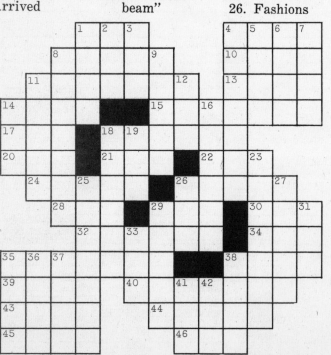

Solutions are on page 285

ACROSS

1. Farm storage places
5. Extremely pale
10. Egyptian lizard
14. Friend: French
15. Rope with a running knot
16. Dramatist O'Casey
17. Achieve control: 4 wds.
20. Puts in
21. Relieve
22. Is situated
23. Assistant
25. Soothsayers
27. Lamb, for one
31. He opened Japan to U.S. commerce
32. Tropical beast
33. God: Latin
34. Goddess of discord
35. Surfer's delight
36. Equal
37. Subject of many fibs
38. Italian movie star, Sophia —
39. Electric catfish
40. Council meetings
42. Evangelist Graham
43. Is over
44. Ramble
45. Unsophisticated
48. Italian nobleman
52. Not well: 3 wds.
55. Fen
56. Down from a duck
57. The Pentateuch
58. Compressed bundle
59. English city
60. October birthstone

DOWN

1. Figures in a crèche
2. Sign
3. Humorists
4. First colonists
5. Anoints
6. Spiritual parts of people
7. School dances
8. Dr. Rhine's interest: abbr.
9. Born
10. Elizabeth —, actress
11. Business transaction
12. "Two Years Before The Mast" author
13. Singer Williams
18. Hirsute
19. Detection device
23. Colorado culture center
24. Egyptian goddess
25. Once-popular suiting
26. American Indians
27. Roof edges
28. Standard of perfection
29. Down at the heels
30. High peaks
31. Vegetable
32. Mountain lakes
35. He painted "American Gothic"
36. Cabbage palm
38. Ship
39. Lasso
41. Harsh
42. Mistakes: slang
44. Propelled a boat
45. Without feeling
46. Wild ox of Celebes
47. Mickey Mantle, to some
48. Grant
49. Boutique
50. Whey
51. Russian sea
53. Wire: abbr.
54. Hasten

Solution is on page 285

VOCABULARY QUIZ 1

This Vocabulary Quiz will test your word knowledge. 8 right answers puts you in the big league, vocabulary-wise. 6 right is average and 4 right means more work is needed in the vocabulary department. Answers are on page 296.

1. If SALVAGE is to rescue, what is SELVAGE?
2. If DISCUSS is to talk over, what is a DISCUS?
3. If SILLY is foolish, what is STILLY?
4. If FAIL is to be unsuccessful, what is a FLAIL?
5. If BURNT is scorched, what is BRUNT?
6. If WHILE is although, what is WILE?
7. If DÉCOLLETÉ is low-necked, as a gown, what is DECOLLETE?
8. If TARDY is late, what is TAWDRY?
9. If WON'T is will not, what is WONT?
10. If SHOTGUN is a weapon, what is a SHOGUN?

MAZE 1

Starting at the arrow at the top of the circle, see if you can find your way to the inner circle without crossing any lines and without retracing your steps. Our best mazer did it in just two minutes. Can you do it even faster than that?

Solution is on page 315.

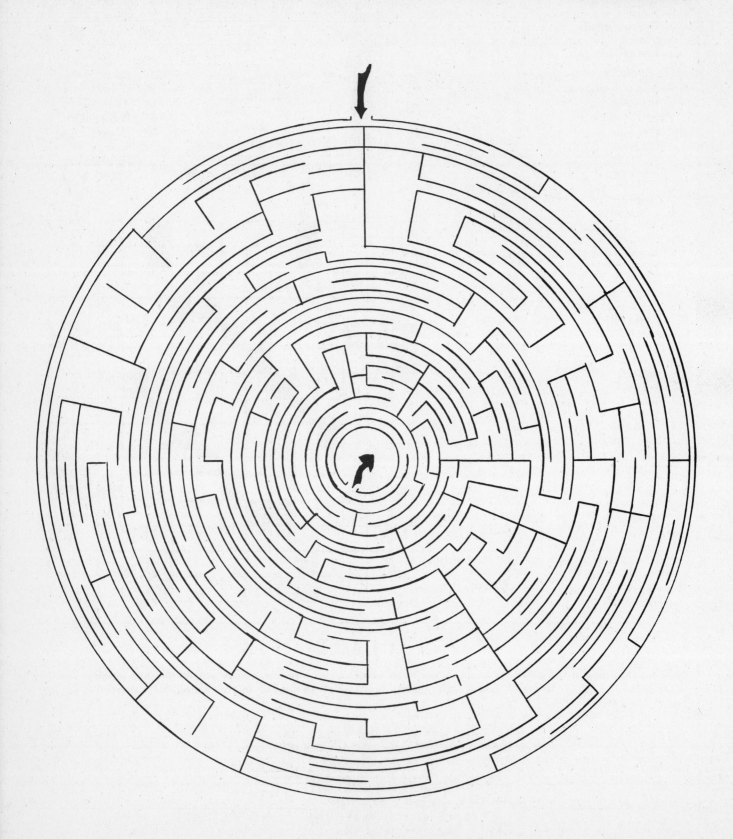

ALPHAGRAM

In the diagram below, there are 26 rows across, each with one empty box. Insert different letters of the alphabet into the empty boxes in the diagram (one letter per box) to form words reading across. We have listed the letters of the alphabet above the diagram and, since each letter may be used only once, it's a good idea to cross off a letter as you use it. Each word you form must be of five or more letters, but not every letter in each row will necessarily be used in forming a word. Words beginning with a capital letter are not allowed. Do not rearrange any of the letters already in the diagram.

Example: In the first row across, you should insert an "N" into the empty box to form the word ALIEN. As you can see, you have used only four letters in the row in addition to the letter you have inserted. The letter you insert may be the first letter of the word you are forming, the last letter of the word (as in alien), or somewhere in between. Remember, each word you form must have FIVE OR MORE letters.

Solution is on page 301.

A B C D E F G H I J K L M N O P Q R S T U V W X Y Z

S	H	A	L	I	E		C	Y	C	L	O	N
P	O	R	P	O	N		I	G	I	D	I	C
H	I	R	E	S	H		A	G	U	E	L	L
P	A	L	M	E	T		A	N	D	I	D	E
S	A	P	R	E	S		C	I	R	C	L	E
J	A	P	A	I	S		M	E	B	O	D	Y
L	Y	R	I	C	S		S	T	A	T	E	R
S	A	L	V	O	T		O	R	N	A	S	K
A	T	T	I	R	A		U	N	I	O	R	Y
O	R	E	P	R	I		A	N	D	R	E	W
K	O	B	E	S	H		M	P	O	O	L	S
C	O	L	O	N	I		E	A	V	O	I	D
S	P	R	O	V	O		E	X	C	L	U	D
T	U	R	B	I	O		T	W	I	T	H	Y
I	N	B	O	R	A		C	E	B	R	A	N
P	A	S	A	N	K		E	R	R	U	N	K
T	A	P	O	L	O		Y	E	L	L	O	W
E	Y	E	B	R	O		T	H	E	S	I	S
C	A	P	T	I	N		L	A	T	T	E	N
W	H	O	N	B	O		C	A	T	I	N	E
O	P	I	L	A	S		U	E	L	C	H	E
D	I	O	D	E	X		R	O	G	E	N	Y
C	O	P	P	A	D		S	T	R	E	S	S
A	T	O	R	E	A		Y	I	E	L	D	S
S	C	A	N	A	R		P	A	G	O	D	A
A	R	E	C	E	N		T	R	A	N	K	Y

WORD ARITHMETIC 1

These are long division problems in which letters are substituted for numbers. Solve the problem, determine the number value of each letter, and when the letters in each one have been arranged in order from 0 to 9 they will spell out a word or words.   Solutions are on page 296.

1. 0 1 2 3 4 5 6 7 8 9
```
              B I T
      _____
O A T | C A L I C O
        I B C O
        T T B C
        T L A P
          S I C O
          S A X C
            A B A
```

2. 0 1 2 3 4 5 6 7 8 9
```
                L I E
        _____
F I R E | D E A L E R
          C F A I
          L P D I E
          L A D P E
            F H L H R
            L D L I P
              D P A
```

3. 0 1 2 3 4 5 6 7 8 9
```
               N U T
      _____
H O G S | T O G G L E
          S E U N
          L E E L
          H O G S
            N O T R E
            N H E O N
              R L S
```

4. 0 1 2 3 4 5 6 7 8 9
```
            G O B
      _____
R O B | N I B B L E
        I O N W
        E G W L
        E F G N
          G R O E
          G E R B
            I I W
```

5. 0 1 2 3 4 5 6 7 8 9
```
            A L E
      _____
L A W | B E L I E F
        B B B M
        M U W E
        U F H L
          M W U F
          M B I H
            M B F
```

6. 0 1 2 3 4 5 6 7 8 9
```
              I N N
        _____
L A I N | H A T I N G
          G N T B
          G B I N
          I C A N
            G K B G
            I C A N
              L B H A
```

7. 0 1 2 3 4 5 6 7 8 9
```
                A I M
        _____
S O M E | M A R I N E R
          M M F O I
          I N A O E
          S O M E
            M F R L R
            N M A A R
              M L E L
```

8. 0 1 2 3 4 5 6 7 8 9
```
              P O T
      _____
E K E | E C H O E S
        K P B S
        K H C E
        K E H C
          C T C S
          C U H B
            K T S
```

9. 0 1 2 3 4 5 6 7 8 9
```
              A L L
      _____
P I E | H E A L T H
        H L H H
        H T H T
        H I I T
          H G R H
          H I I T
            C E
```

LOGIC PROBLEM 1.

THE BOYS FROM CENTRAL AMERICA   by Evelyn B. Rosenthal

NOTE TO SOLVERS: This Logic Problem is not a difficult one. It has been chosen especially for those of you who are new to Logic Problem solving.

Five boys whose families come from Central America are upset that their North American friends can't keep their countries straight. Felipe commented to the Guatemalan boy, "It's reasonable that they don't know the smaller cities of Danli, Flores, and La Palma, but two of us are from capitals; everybody should know Managua, Nicaragua and San Jose, Costa Rica." From the following clues, can you find each boy's full name and city and country of origin?

1. The Lopez boy does not come from Danli or Nicaragua.

2. The Sanchez boy, who is not Carlos, is from Honduras.

3. The Lopez and Rodriguez boys both have first names beginning with P.

4. Pedro's family is not from Flores.

5. Neither Pablo nor the Rodriguez boy is from La Palma.

6. The Lopez boy is not from El Salvador, and Juan is not from Honduras.

7. Neither Carlos, whose last name is not Diaz, nor Pedro is from Danli.

8. The Hernandez and Rodriguez boys are not from Nicaragua.

Solution is on page 296.

If you care to use the chart below in solving this problem, you do so by entering all information obtained from the clues using, perhaps, an X to indicate a definite "no" and a dot to show a definite "yes." Remember: Once you enter a definite "yes" (dot), place a "no" (X) in all the rest of the boxes in each row and column that contains the dot.

	Diaz	Hernandez	Lopez	Rodriguez	Sanchez	Danli	Flores	La Palma	Man.	San Jose	Costa Rica	El Sal.	Guat.	Hond.	Nic.
Carlos															
Felipe															
Juan															
Pablo															
Pedro															
Costa Rica															
El Sal.															
Guat.															
Hond.															
Nic.															
Danli															
Flores															
La Palma															
Man.															
San Jose															

QUOTATION PUZZLES 1

Copyright 1989 by Bantam Doubleday Dell Publishing Group, Inc.

In each puzzle below, you are to fit the letters in each column into the boxes directly above them. The letters may or may not go into the boxes in the same order in which they are given. It is up to you to decide which letter goes into which box above it. Once a letter is used, cross it off the bottom half of the diagram and do not use it again. A black square indicates the end of a word. When the diagrams have been filled in, you will be able to find the completed quotations by reading across the boxes.

Answers are on page 296.

1.

A	A	O	A	M	O	N	T	I	H	O	R	O	M	Y	I	A	E	S
E	T	L	D	K	W	K	A	S	O	E	F	A	T	E	S	N	R	R
L	L	N		S	A	R	E	T	U	P	T		G	H	T	T	G	B
T		N			E	E		N	N					U	E	H		

2.

E	C	E	R	P	V	A	T	S	N	L	H	A	S	K	N	U	G	R
I	N	W	S	I	E	A	I	E	I	I	E	C	N	D	I	T	O	L
		P	H	D	T	T	K	H		T		S	N	U	P	M	B	Y
			E	A	S	S	T	I		S		I	O			N	R	

3.

P	H	R	N	E	T	M	L	N	P	O	A	W	A	R	H	C	G	T
M	E	E	E	T	O	I	E	E	O	A	R	S	O	H	M	N	U	S
T	A	I	L	L	T	H	S	C	F	R		N	T	T	O	E	I	
		R	F	O	I	T	A	N	E	E		F	I	R	I	O	R	

4.

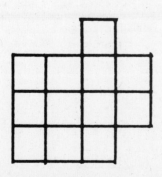

R	A	T	H	E	O	M	B	B	X	S	W	R	H	T	E	O	D	N	N	O	E
N	M	C	T	A	S	F	Y	E	Y	A	A	A	E	E	I	G	G	I	O	G	U
	O	R	D	T	R			E	I	H	P	U	R	T		N	F	Y		L	
		O			O							T	S	E		N	E	T		T	

5.

S	T	G	F	O	E	E	C	O	E	N	N	M	S	M	T	M	S	G	I	G	I
S	A	H	E	O	M	S	B	R	A	T	D	T	I	S	A	E	A	F	A	R	E
A		L	I	S	D		N	U	P	I	I	E	A	S	P	N	A	S	O	M	
R			O	R	R				S	D	I					S		N	E	R	

6.

C	B	P	O	O	O	K	G	U	E	W	E	U	D	S	N	I	N	W	P	Y	H
A	E	E	Y	F	I	N	N	U	T	P	O	C	G	I	T	G	I	G	A	O	E
H	T		E	L	U	S	S	O	S	T	I	D	T	H	W	A	L		N	I	T
	O								N	N	E	N				R	Y	A		T	

LETTER LINK 1

Copyright 1981 by Dell Publishing Co., Inc.

B E F G I K L N O R T V

See if you can place the letters above into the diagram in such a way that by moving horizontally, vertically, and/or diagonally from square to square (without skipping over any squares) the following sentence can be spelled out:

BE NOT LOOKING FOR EVIL.

NOTE: Put each letter into the diagram only once, even though you will use some letters more than once in spelling out the sentence. You may stand on a letter and use it twice in direct succession.

Our solution, which may not agree with yours, is on page 299.

HEXAD PUZZLE

All you have to do to solve this Hexad is fit the ten pieces on the right below into the grid so that each line across and each line down contains the six different symbols pictured above the grid. The squares and black diamonds already in the grid are there to help you figure out how the pieces fit together and should not be moved or changed in any way. Likewise, each of the ten pieces must be kept as a unit as it is pictured. The pieces can be turned in any direction to fit into the grid. Remember, when you're finished, no symbol will be repeated with a line either across or down. As a starting help, we'll tell you that the piece indicated by the arrow goes into the upper left-hand corner of the grid. **WARNING: This is a toughie!**   Solution is on page 291.

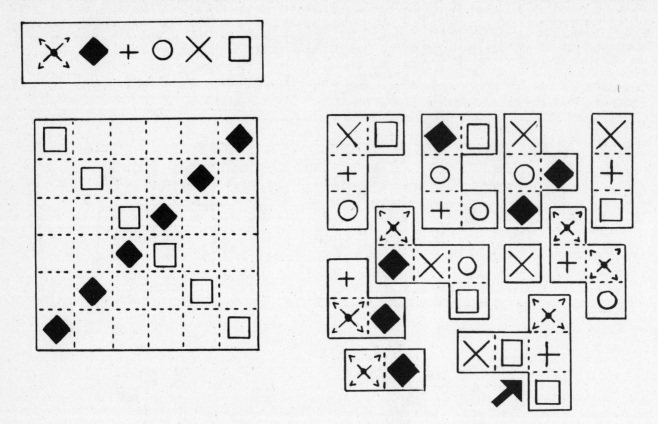

THREE LITTLE WORDS

The challenge here is to make three 3-letter words from each 9-letter word below, using the letters (each one one time only) from left to right in the order in which they appear in the given word. Your first 3-letter word must begin with the first letter of the 9-letter word. You may skip over letters to select your other two letters, but do NOT rearrange the order of the letters. Your next 3-letter word must begin with the first UNUSED letter of the six remaining letters. The third word should then be spelled out by the remaining three letters. If the given word contains repeated letters, you must use the first letter as you come to it before using the repeated letter. For example, if the given word were AMUSEMENT, your first little word (which must begin with A) could be "ant." Returning to the left so your second little word can begin with the next unused letter (M, in this case), you could make "mum." The three remaining letters as they appear must spell out your third little word—"see." Remember, you will use each letter only once, so cross each one off as you use it. Form only real, everyday English words; obsolete, archaic, and poetic words are not allowed, nor are slang words or words beginning with a capital letter. **HANDICAP:** When you are finished, all fifteen little words should be different.   Answer is on page 296.

1. G A T H E R I N G

2. D O M I N A N C E

3. M O N A S T E R Y

4. R E A R R A N G E

5. S T A G E H A N D

WORD STEPS

The idea of Word Steps is to make a progression of words in the fewest possible steps in the following manner:

Beginning with a given word (STRONGHOLD, for example), which can be split to make two smaller words (STRONG, HOLD), use the second part (HOLD) to form a new word (HOLDOVER, HOLDOUT, etc.).Continue forming words in this manner until you can arrive back to the first part of the given word.

Example: *STRONGHOLD* (1) HOLDOVER (2) OVERHEAD (3) HEADSTRONG. Try to form as few words as you can for the best score. Each word must be a real word; no proper names, foreign words, slang, obsolete, or dialect words are allowed, nor are hyphenated words or two-word phrases. Two games are given below; in the first one, the given word is PERSON and we used four steps to solve it. In the second game, we needed 4 steps with the given word PITFALL. See how well you can do. Our answers, which may differ from yours, are on page 297.

1. PERSON (4 steps)

2. PITFALL (4 steps)

CATEGORIES 1

The idea of this word game is to think of words that belong to a given category and which also begin with the letters used to spell out the category. For example: If the category were GEMS, you would name a gem beginning with "g," then one beginning with "e," etc. Your answers might be garnet, emerald, moonstone, and sapphire. Here the name of the category is LET'S TRAVEL and you are to name a foreign country to which you might travel. There are many choices, of course, so your answers will probably not agree with ours, given on page 297.

L _____

E _____

T _____

S _____

T _____

R _____

A _____

V _____

E _____

L _____

THE NAME GAME

Using each of the letters below once and only once, add any vowels (a, e, i, o, or u) as many times as necessary to form the names of five 5-letter birds. Our answer is on page 297.

B

G G

L L

N N

Q

R R

S

V

1. _ _ _ _ _

2. _ _ _ _ _

3. _ _ _ _ _

4. _ _ _ _ _

5. _ _ _ _ _

AROUND THE BLOCK

In this puzzle, the correct answer for each definition below is a 4-letter word. Start the word in one of the four squares encircling the corresponding number. The words may go in either a clockwise or counterclockwise direction; it is up to you to determine which. Letters in adjacent words will help you figure out which squares the letters go in. The first word, DRUM, has been entered to help you get started.   Solution is on page 315.

1. Tom-tom, for example
2. Flower having a thorny stem
3. Make airtight
4. Open-handed blow
5. Like "the driven snow"
6. Look quickly and furtively
7. Trim for lingerie
8. — year, year having 366 days
9. Had on, as clothing
10. Close one eye and open it quickly
11. Part of the face below the mouth
12. Assist; aid
13. Nothing
14. Short test
15. Matching coat and
    pants or skirt
16. Golf stroke on the green

PYRAMID

Using only the letters given below, build a pyramid of words on the dashes provided in the following manner: first, find a 1-letter word from among the given letters, write it on the uppermost dash, and cross if off the list of letters. Then, by adding another letter either BEFORE or AFTER your 1-letter word, form a 2-letter word, write it on the next set of dashes, and cross off those two letters. Continue in this manner with each step down the pyramid, adding a letter to either the beginning or end of the word above it. Do not rearrange the order of the letters as you form each new word; and don't forget to cross off the letters as you use them, as each letter is used one time only.   Our answer is on page 297.

A A A A A   ——

M M M M P   —— —— ——

P R R R T   —— —— —— ——

                        —— —— —— —— ——

                      —— —— —— —— —— ——

SILLY DILLIES 1

by L. G. Sims

Failure to identify the six Dillies below doesn't mean a thing, but you can have fun trying. Each drawing is the artist's literal interpretation of a common word or phrase. For example, a drawing of a cat sitting atop a telephone pole would suggest "POLECAT." Get the idea? Answers are on page 297.

CRYPTOQUIZZES 2

A Cryptoquiz is a list of related words put into a simple code. You will find that one set of letters has been substituted for the correct letters of the words in each of the groups below. The title of the group, and the example, will give you a hint as to what the disguised words may be. Then look for words which might betray themselves by their distinctive spellings. When you've identified a word, the known letters will help you to decode other words in the group. Remember that if G stands for M in one word, it will be the same throughout that Cryptoquiz. Each group has its own code.

Answers are on page 297.

1. "S" CREATURES
Example: snail

C Y X H

C L Y Y Z

C N B T N

C T X N Y

C Z X O O G J

C D B F O O Y H

C U G O N

C J X H H G J

C J X T

C Y X   H F G T

2. WATERCRAFT
Example: rowboat

K A C D Q Z K

L Z G N K

H Z B T D Q Z K

C T Z H H - D Q K K Q F J P

D Q Z K

M J E E L

M E J B C N K J E

F Q K Q E D Q Z K

G Z R Q J

H K J Z F D Q Z K

N Q A H J D Q Z K

3. DESCRIPTIVE COLORS
Example: wine-red

S B X - P D A K S

F S A K - K R M X H

Z U N N V H - W D U Q

D B P Q - D H Z

P A X X V H - W D H H S

D A P M S ' F - H W W

P V B H

P U P Q - P V B H

E M Z S M W R X - P V B H

N H U - W D H H S

V H E A S - Q H V V A K

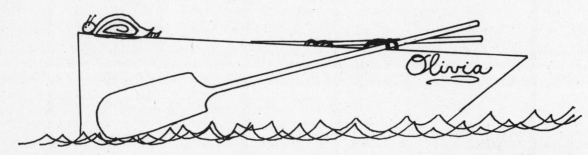

4. EDGED IMPLEMENTS
Example: axe

N W X N N I E N

W K X N Y T

K R Z W K Y Z

W R E O X U S   L U X A Y

W T Y R O Y E

N W E R D Y E

D E Q U X U S   N K Y R E N

U R X T   W T X D D Y E

D I W L Y Z L U X A Y

N X W L T Y

5. CITIES THAT END IN "O"
Example: Chicago

X N   M Z E G

E Z A   D Y Z A L V E L G

G Y N Z A R G

M C X F N G

E Z A   R V X J G

F C D D Z N G

K G N X R G

E Z L Y Z B X A K G

Y X A G

Z B Z Y V N N G

6. SHAKESPEAREAN LADIES
Example: Olivia (*Twelfth Night*)

C J A H   Z J T P Q E F

R M C W Q E

P W J K T J

T D V A Q C W J

T J C N M V K W J

D N F Q C W J

A Q G A Q Z D K J

T C Q D N J E V J

F Q V Z W J

N D V E W J

PRESTO-CHANGO!

By changing ONE letter of each word in each group below, you can form three new words that are related to each other in some way. Do not change the order of the letters. For example, TRUCE—FAR—BUT could be changed to TRUCK—CAR—BUS (all modes of transportation). Answers are on page 297.

1.	MELLOW	GREED	GLUE
2.	LAME	BULL	SHAME
3.	POST	THYME	TERSE
4.	LOON	DEW	ROAD
5.	PRONE	RIND	BELT
6.	PINCH	BAIL	CUT
7.	KNOW	DILL	RATIO
8.	DRUG	BENT	BEND
9.	STARE	PLAN	ARTS
10.	CHEST	MORE	HOARD

RED-WHITE-AND-BLUE QUIZ

Can you find the word or phrase containing "red," "white," or "blue" that answers each of the definitions below? Answers are on page 297.

1. Waters Moses crossed
2. U.S. President's home
3. Architect's plans
4. Inexpensive, fixed-price restaurant meal
5. Tactful fib
6. British soldiers of 1776
7. World charity organization
8. First-place award
9. Irving Berlin holiday song
10. Foaming ocean wave
11. Very seldom
12. Grand, impressive welcome
13. Kentucky's nickname
14. Descendant of aristocrats
15. Moscow plaza
16. Banner of truce
17. Giant Pacific Coast tree
18. Nickname for the robin
19. Useless possession that is costly to maintain
20. Completely unforeseen
21. Something that distracts attention from the main issue
22. Like a high-priced, secure stock
23. Type of automobile tire
24. January event in the Linen Department

CATEGORIES 2

The idea of this puzzle is to think of words that belong to a given category and which also begin with the letter used to spell out the name of that category. For example: If the category given were GEMS, you would name a gem beginning with the letter "g," then one beginning with "e," then one with "m," and one with "s." Your answers might be garnet, emerald, moonstone, and sapphire. Below are 3 Categories for you to try. Our answers, which may differ from yours, are on page 297.

1. LANGUAGES

L_____
A_____
N_____
G_____
U_____
A_____
G_____
E_____
S_____

2. BLOSSOMS
plants or flowers

B_____
L_____
O_____
S_____
S_____
O_____
M_____
S_____

3. SALT WATER
creatures of the sea

S_____
A_____
L_____
T_____
W_____
A_____
T_____
E_____
R_____

HIDDEN VEGETABLES

In each sentence below the name of a vegetable appears, but it is hidden within the words of the sentence. For example, in sentence 1, the vegetable is RADISH (hidden in extra dishes). Can you find all the others?

Answers are on page 297.

1. We're going to need extra dishes for our reunion dinner.

2. Edgar Allan Poe could spin a chilling tale as well as write haunting poems.

3. If lemonade is too tart I choke and sputter while I'm drinking it.

4. I think I shall be eternally amazed by people who can do math problems in their heads.

5. Whether it was politic or not, the senator decided to vote for the wage bill.

6. The one time I visited Boston I only had a few hours between planes.

7. Cheerleading candidates are judged by their pep, personality, and ability.

8. Questions about operating a new camera can be answered by reading the instruction manual.

9. In some models of a foreign-made car, rotary engines are being used.

10. If your breakfast includes an egg, plan to watch your intake of other foods having high cholesterol levels.

11. We were able to spot a total of twenty Canadian geese at the bird sanctuary.

12. Sometimes a person who appears quiet has a delightful sense of humor.

13. Harry sprinted for a cab, bagel in one hand and briefcase in the other.

14. At the last turn I passed a sign advertising a flea market.

15. Eula found writing a term paper on the atom a tough assignment.

PICTURE PERFECT?

Picture B is a mirror image of picture A . . . or is it? If you're really eagle-eyed, you'll be able to spot the ten things in picture B that are not exact mirror images of their counterparts in picture A. Consider yourself very perceptive if you can do it in less than three minutes.

Answers are on page 297.

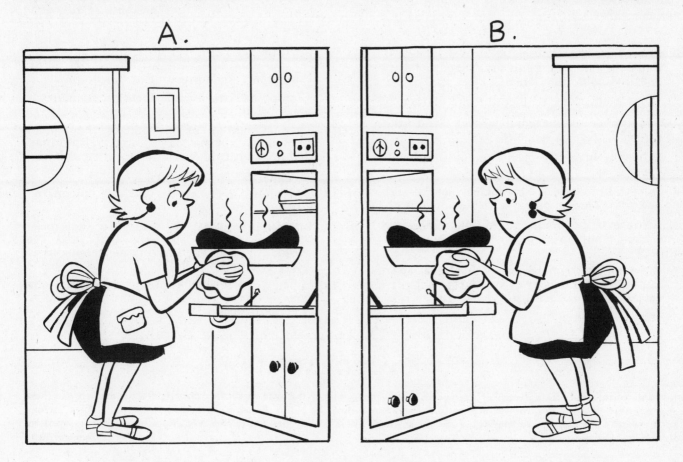

STARGRAM 1

For some pure anagram fun, find a Mystery Name which lies jumbled in the words below. First, rearrange all the letters of each line to form common English words which are made up of two shorter words (for example, "insure" or "manage"). Then, rearrange the letters marked with a star to spell out the Mystery Name.

Solution is on page 297.

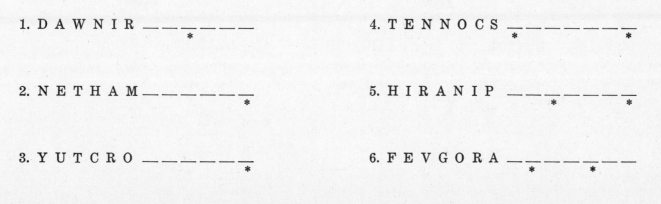

1. D A W N I R _ _ _ _ _ _
                    *

2. N E T H A M _ _ _ _ _ _
                       *

3. Y U T C R O _ _ _ _ _ _
                       *

4. T E N N O C S _ _ _ _ _ _ _
                       *   *

5. H I R A N I P _ _ _ _ _ _ _
                        *   *

6. F E V G O R A _ _ _ _ _ _ _
                      *   *

Mystery Name (T.V. comedian) _ _ _   _ _ _ _ _ _

SOME PUMPKINS

by Irene R. Hayes

In the statements below, the word "pumpkin" has been substituted for a common word. It stands for the same word in all the sentences. Try to discover what the "pumpkin" is. If you discover the word by No. 9, you are an expert "pumpkin-picker"!

Answer is on page 297.

1. How versatile "pumpkins" are! Indeed, it would be mind-boggling to try and list their multitudinous functions.

2. Most occupations require the use of them.

3. "Pumpkins" can be small, large, strong, weak, hot, cold, open, closed, etc.

4. Many products are marketed for the care of "pumpkins."

5. In certain instances "pumpkins" can be high, low, first, second, old, new, heavy, or light.

6. Because of the importance of "pumpkins," the word, "pumpkin" has taken on many meanings.

7. A "pumpkin" can be one of two sides in an argument; influence; active part; control; a certain unit of measure; signature; worker; etc.

8. One can "pumpkin" down, up, over, out, or in. It is permissible to be at "pumpkin" or on "pumpkin," but never out of "pumpkin."

9. "Pumpkins" are a basic form of communication.

10. The articulation or jointing of the human "pumpkin" is more complex and delicate than that of comparable parts in any other animals.

11. The human "pumpkin" has 27 bones.

12. CALLIGRAPHY is the art of "pumpkin" writing.

13. Do you agree that "the 'pumpkin' that rocks the cradle is the 'pumpkin' that rules the world," or that "a bird in the 'pumpkin' is worth two in the bush"?

14. If you've guessed what pumpkin stands for by this sentence, you deserve a congratulatory "pumpkin" shake!

QUOTEGRAM

Solve this puzzle by placing each of the words below onto one of the sets of dashes directly below the words. Then put the letters into the diagram according to the number below the letter. Work back and forth between the diagram and the words until you have completed the puzzle and will discover the quotation. We have entered one word to help you get started.

Answer is on page 320.

1	2 T		3	4 S		5	6	7		8	9 H	10	
11	12	13	14	15 L	16	17	18	19	20		21	22	23
24 T		25	26 E	27	28	29	30	31	32		33	34	35
	36	37 A	38	39	40	41	42	43	44		45	46	47
	48	49	50		51	52	53	54	55	56	57	58	

BUTTON   CHERISH   DETROIT
FACTORY   INTONE   SHIVER
STEALTH   THYME   TUITION

S T E A L T H
4 2 26 37 15 24 9

___ ___ ___ ___ ___ ___ ___
51 23 38 8 14 43 31

___ ___ ___ ___ ___ ___ ___
54 34 12 52 1 27 39

___ ___ ___ ___ ___ ___ ___
47 46 53 33 18 30 58

___ ___ ___ ___ ___ ___ ___
25 50 21 29 6 3 55

___ ___ ___ ___ ___ ___
45 16 48 28 57 5

___ ___ ___ ___ ___
7 49 44 36 35

___ ___ ___ ___ ___ ___
32 22 56 13 10 11

___ ___ ___ ___ ___ ___
40 41 17 19 20 42

SKILL-O-GRAM 1

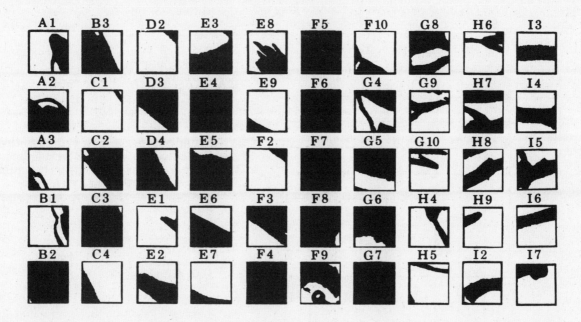

Each square above contains one part of a complete picture. Using a pencil or pen, you are to copy exactly what you see into the diagram below. Use the letter-number combinations as a guide, and draw exactly what is in each box above into the correspondingly numbered box below. Start with A-1, drawing in the box where Row A and Column 1 intersect. Then, draw in A-2, A-3, etc. and continue right through to the end. The result will be a finished picture, as skillfully drawn as if by an artist. The artist's picture is shown on page 291.

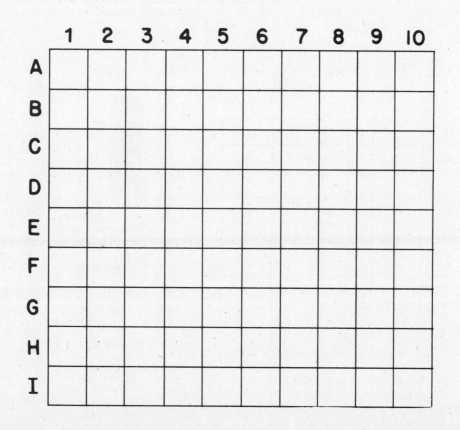

1 and 2 EASY DIAGRAMLESS

Puzzle 1

ACROSS

1. "—, Kindly Light"
5. Dining tool
9. Not on
12. Unemployed
13. Prophetic sign
14. Female deer
15. Grows old
16. Go by auto
17. Stale
18. Esteem
20. Nobleman
22. Undivided
23. Cunning
24. Either/—, contract phrase
26. Arise
29. Owns
30. A duo
31. Narrated
32. Carpet
33. Podiatrist's concern
34. Building wing
35. — in hand, humbly
36. Close ties
37. Myself
38. Saucerless cup
39. Distant
40. Bellow
42. Borders
46. Statute
47. Burden
49. Blue-pencil
50. Had dinner
51. Great Lake
52. Musical sound
53. I agree!
54. Cozy rooms
55. Assassinated

DOWN

1. Falsifier
2. Rim
3. Dark beers
4. Lose hope
5. Power
6. Leave out
7. Scarlet
8. Bends in prayer
9. Smell
10. Came after
11. Nourished
19. Cease
21. "Yes" vote
23. Droop
25. Decomposes
26. Stalk
27. Put up with
28. Everybody
29. Hermit's home
30. Two fives
32. Tattered cloth
33. Fails to recall
35. Threw hard
36. Saloon
38. Mother
39. Loses color
41. Has debts
42. Principal
43. Pagan god
44. Almost 30-Down
45. Simmer
46. Deposit
48. Unrefined metal

Puzzle 2

ACROSS

1. Tarries
6. Ruin
8. Take a chance on losing
9. Was in debt
11. Rhymester
12. Santa's cry
13. Witnessed
15. Bird's home
16. Young pooch
17. "Welcome" rug
19. Before
20. Martini liquor
21. Bridal "path"
23. Morning: abbr.
24. Roams
26. A — carte, menu term
27. Takes the bus
29. Male sheep
30. Garment's edge
31. Pigpen
32. Moist
33. Tabbies
34. Stitch
36. Commercial
37. Fourth planet from the sun
38. Immerses in water
40. Neither cold nor hot
41. Collects
43. In want

DOWN

1. Toward L.A., from N.Y.
2. Inquire
3. That thing
4. Infantry company
5. Plant seeds
6. Limited table fare
7. Okay!
8. Garden flower
10. Water barriers
11. Allows
12. Ten tens
14. Billfolds
15. Approaches
16. Brooch
18. Baseball nines
20. Fuel for 33-Down
21. Branch
22. Exists
24. You and I
25. Dine
28. Imparted color to
30. Injure
32. What "haste makes"
33. Automobiles
35. Toupee
37. —, Queen of Scots
39. Skillet
40. Marry
42. That man

Solutions are on page 292

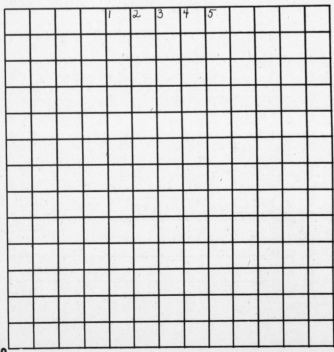

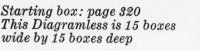

ACROSS

1. Scorch
5. Cavity
6. Flash of lightning
10. Songstress Fitzgerald
11. Cupid
12. White lies
16. Escaped
17. House: Spanish
18. False god
19. Oriental sauce for meat, fish, etc.
20. Was aware of
21. Entertainer Autry
22. "Spider-work"
24. Experienced person: 2 wds.
26. Fly high
29. Tidy
30. Liked better
33. Neckwear
34. Clip neatly
36. Peers narrowly
39. Horse-drawn, two-wheeled carriage
41. Yours and mine
42. African country
45. Knock loudly
47. Latvian capital
48. Employ
49. Facts and figures
50. Gulf of —, between Arabia and Africa
51. Ireland: poetic
52. Dull pain
53. Remain
54. Pest on Rover
55. Small sea bird

DOWN

1. Head cooks
2. "The Legend of Sleepy —"
3. Looking intently: 2 wds.
4. Do one of the "3 R's"
6. Rear part
7. Arabian country
8. Go broke: 3 wds. (slang)
9. Fishing boat
12. Boxer
13. Brain storm
14. West Germany's capital
15. Snow vehicle
23. Punch; strike: slang
25. Short seam
27. Skilled workman
28. Harness part
31. Brings
32. Excavate
35. Marvel
36. Wading bird
37. British pound sterling: slang
38. Egg on
40. Accumulate
43. Opera melody
44. Contradict
46. Song of joy
49. "Goofy"

Starting box: page 320
This Diagramless is 15 boxes wide by 15 boxes deep

Solution is on page 292

VOCABULARY QUIZ 2

1. "Mom, when you say your laundry is piled up a mile high, you are uttering an overstatement not meant to be taken literally, or, as we learned in English class today, a (hypogenous; hyperbole)."

2. "I dearly love you, Martha, but after that dinner of rawhide roast beef, petrified parsley, and rigid coffee, I don't think it's unloving of me to (prescribe; proscribe) a few professional cooking lessons."

3. "Ted, turn down that amplifier; Sue, lower your voice a little. With you two musical geniuses, the howling dog, the TV, and your mother's eggbeater, my ears are beginning to ache and I can't afford a trip to the (orologist's; otologist's) just now."

4. "Sir, I need some help. I want to buy a chatelaine for my niece and would appreciate it if you would direct me to the (lingerie; jewelry) department."

5. "Do I get seasick? I get queasy just watching the (vitriolic; vortical) motion of the clothes in the machines down at the laundromat!"

6. "Got to get together and talk about that new ad, George. Call my secretary and arrange for a (colliery; colloquy)."

7. "I'm not Queen Elizabeth, Ralph, I'm your wife. Stop being (ignominious; obsequious) and, instead of all that bowing and scraping, just tell which it is —the Mets game tonight or the Mets game tomorrow night."

Answers are on page 297

4 MEDIUM
DIAGRAMLESS

Starting box: page 320
This Diagramless is 15 boxes wide by 15 boxes deep

ACROSS

1. Immense
5. Give the villain his due
9. Detest
11. Hiding place
12. Small ornamental tower
14. Illinois city
15. Rate of speed in music
16. Misbehaved: 2 wds.
18. Low river dam
19. South African of Dutch descent
20. Porker
22. Hostelries
23. Melancholy
24. Pursuit
26. Ravine
27. Subdue
28. That man
31. — food
33. Sharp bark
35. Hereditary character determinant
36. Russian sea
37. Blab: 2 wds.
39. Relative of the canary
41. Firmly established
42. Port
44. Game fish
45. Dig (into)
46. Rope fiber
47. Jump, kangaroo style

DOWN

1. Large cask
2. Border upon
3. Like Shakespeare's "Kate"
4. Harass
5. Stopped
6. More frigid
7. Lean-to
8. Arrangement
10. Fasten again
11. Chocolate drink
13. High craggy hills
14. Punches, ring style
17. Resentment
21. Small narrow ravine
25. Brilliancy
26. Easily duped
27. Altercation
28. Warm, as food: 2 wds.
29. Cove
30. Canasta play
31. Obi
32. Mountain nymph
34. Capital of Western Australia
35. What a pessimist spreads
38. Knowledge based on tradition
40. Variable star
43. Twilled fabric

Solution is on page 292

TRAVEL FRACTIONS

To solve: Follow the arithmetic signs below and if you are correct in your "travel math," each row will yield the name of a vacation place. For example: The fraction: one-third FIREPLACE (the first three of the word's nine letters) plus one-half STAR (the first two of the word's four letters) would equal FIRST. **Solutions are on page 297.**

ACROSS

1. Peach stone
4. Dalmatian marking
8. Volcanic peak
9. Checkerwork
11. Refuse to listen (to) : 4 wds.
14. C, for one
15. Suit part
16. Uprising
18. "Actions are — epochs": Byron
19. At this place
20. Fish delicacy
21. Sketch
23. Church song
24. Lukewarm
28. Fixed charge
30. Draw forth
31. Dodge; shun
34. Inexperienced
35. Make late
36. On vacation
39. Shout
42. Dust cloth
43. Receipts
47. Speak
48. Jaunt
50. Skip over
51. Cast a ballot
52. Do something risky: 3 wds.
55. Circumstance
56. Otherwise
57. Not burdensome
58. Type of bread

DOWN

1. — over, study minutely
2. Hostelry
3. Instruct
4. Blade of grass
5. Dish
6. Simpleton
7. Cake layer
8. Marked down: hyph. wd.
10. Creamery
11. — de force, ingenious feat
12. Female antelope
13. Space
14. Be drowsy
17. "Sawbuck"
22. Take a spouse
23. Cure
25. Weak
26. Winter hazard for motorists
27. Homonym of "do"
28. Nourished
29. Miss Arden
32. Period of time
33. Ugly sight
36. Museum display
37. Twist out of shape
38. Nimble-footed
40. Overdue
41. Caustic
43. "Whistle stops"
44. Friendship
45. Caboodle's "partner"
46. Anesthetic
49. Smooth (a road)
51. Clamping device
53. Affirmative
54. Summer pest

MEDIUM 5
DIAGRAMLESS

Starting box: page 320
This Diagramless is 15 boxes wide by 15 boxes deep

Solution is on page 292

BODY ENGLISH QUIZ

The unique feature of this quiz is that the answer to each definition below is a part of the body. See if you can get a perfect score without consulting an anatomy chart.

Answers are on page 298.

1. Young cow
2. Potato buds
3. ⅓ of a yard
4. Weapons
5. Servings of corn
6. Core

7. Makes fun of: slang
8. Make one's way by shoving or jostling
9. Journey segments
10. Be chief of; command
11. Farm laborers
12. "In the know"

Starting box: page 320
This Diagramless is 15 boxes wide by 15 boxes deep

ACROSS

1. Homonym of "all"
4. Spoil
7. "Aloha" gift
8. Nuance
10. Lawyer's degree: abbr.
11. Righteous
12. The "less deadly" of the species
13. Cowboy actor, Gene —
14. "Faint heart ne'er — fair lady"
15. Actor Tamblyn
17. Really communicate: slang
18. Sudsy
21. U.S. Treasury agent: hyph. wd.
23. Appointment
24. Farming tool
25. Angry reaction
26. Conceit
27. Disposition
28. Friend: French
29. Imitator
30. City and county in Nevada
31. Hawker
33. Bankroll: slang
34. Hibernia
35. Supervised
36. Dark, durable wood
39. Impala, e.g.
41. Skip the light fantastic
42. Guido's highest note: 2 wds.
43. Change
44. Bird's nest: French
45. "O Sole —"
46. Perth's river

DOWN

1. Part of Poe's full name
2. How about it?
3. One who ends a tyranny
4. Trade center
5. Jewish month
6. Depend
8. Big success
9. Common or usual
12. Swab
14. Approach an end
16. Colorado Indian
17. Home
18. Pilsner
19. Important chess piece
20. Tokyo, formerly
21. Mouth: slang
22. Marcel Marceau, for one
23. Tax deduction
27. Squalid
29. Cassius Clay
32. Laundry machine
33. "Guerra," to Virna Lisi
35. Warmed up, as a pitcher
36. Dutch cheese
37. Island east of Java
38. Aware of: slang
40. Charles Lamb's pseudonym

Solution is on page 292

WORD S-T-R-E-T-C-H

Copyright 1989 by Bantam Doubleday Dell Publishing Group, Inc.

Make the longest word possible from each word listed below by putting letters in the spaces which appear before and after each letter. Your new word may start and finish at any point, but you may not skip over any letters or spaces. Foreign words, or words beginning with a capital letter, are not allowed. Score yourself one point for each letter of the new word you make. For example:

_A_I_M_

_A C I D M_   R A P I D M_   _A X I O M S_

You might form ACID for a score of only 4 points; RAPID for only 5 points; or AXIOMS, the longest word, for 6 points. In the game below, a score of 36 is very good; 40 is excellent; anything over 45 puts you in the "experts' corner." Our expert's score of 50 points is on page 298.

1. _S_U_B_
2. _R_E_T_R_Y_
3. _D_O_M_E_S_
4. _T_R_I_P_L_E_
5. _M_U_L_A_T_T_O_
6. _R_E_S_T_R_I_C_T_

ACROSS

1. Tiny amount
4. Lacking color
5. Evil one
6. Character in "The Tempest"
7. Courtroom testifier
10. London theater district
14. Part of a Scotch costume
16. He's a menace in the cornfield
17. Frightening
19. Wind instrument
20. Give up: 3 wds.
22. Ellipsoidal
23. Injures
24. Microscopic opening
25. Droop
26. Ogled
27. Sure, lady!: 2 wds.
33. Latin dance
34. Implored
35. "Cabbie's" concern
36. Kitchen pest

DOWN

1. Ship's crane
2. Foreign
3. Certain girl at a ball
4. Persian fairy
5. Black bird
8. Delayed by evasion
9. Hindu garment
10. Punish severely
11. Sphere
12. Owl's cries
13. Has debts
15. Legends
17. Famous European family name
18. — Boothe Luce

20. Contend (with)
21. Landing place
28. House slipper
29. Ethical

30. Filled with wrath
31. Mets' center fielder

32. Insane

Starting box: page 320
This Diagramless is 15 boxes wide by 15 boxes deep

Solution is on page 292

CROSS SUMS 1

In Cross Sums puzzles, the numbers in the black squares refer to the **TOTAL** of the numbers which you are to fill into the empty squares. The number written **ABOVE** a slashed line refers to the empty squares directly to the **RIGHT** of that number. A number written **BELOW** a slashed line refers to the empty squares directly **BELOW** that number.

No zeroes are used here and no number higher than nine. An important point: A number cannot appear more than once in any particular number combination. We have filled in one number combination to start you off.

Solution is on page 301.

by MILDRED PEKELSMA

Using the definitions at the left, fill the words into the WORDS column. Then transfer the letters from the WORDS column into their corresponding places in the diagram. It is not necessary to know more than a few words to begin solving. Work back and forth from diagram to WORDS column until both are filled in. A black square denotes the end of a word. Your completed diagram will yield a quotation; and the first letter of each word in the WORDS column, reading down, will spell out the author and the work quoted.

Word lists are on page 312.   **Quotations are on page 308.**

DEFINITIONS   WORDS

A. Polite; courteous — 77 12 29 140 170 178 41 59

B. Scene of Cornwallis' surrender — 44 191 54 138 11 150 82 113

C. Turns down — 71 14 195 151 201 91 181

D. Not intentional — 27 117 149 70 111 55 137 163 78 5

E. Navigable streams, canals, etc. — 63 53 146 125 15 45 186 98 160

F. Uses handbills or air media — 88 196 179 30 171 116 8 68 100 37

G. Try to influence legislation — 124 194 3 155 42

H. Mocking; ridiculing — 67 32 187 79 72 157 13 161

I. From all appearances — 112 36 182 114 9 104 80 164 120

J. Advisory panel composed of experts: 2 wds. — 43 89 177 145 10 57 108 204 103 73

K. One who "hears a different drummer" — 143 34 86 165 16 153 200 83 106

L. Free from bondage — 110 193 147 94 141 24 52 136 84 172

M. Most foolhardy — 142 173 127 85 62 17 162

N. Wing added to a building — 167 101 158 21 33

O. Word for Mr. Magoo — 56 199 2 192 81 28 90 61 169 105 134

P. Weight-lifting equipment — 31 129 99 1 123 180 58 203 92

Q. Republicans, collectively: 3 wds. — 128 65 122 25 166 46 118 109 51 183 76 60 4

R. Lawful title — 64 18 184 48 135 154 87 38 96

S. Alert and efficient: 3 wds. (slang) — 6 152 26 175 130 74 119 35 66

T. Propriety; morality — 144 115 148 156 7 174 189

U. Signaler — 190 188 50 159 22 75 198

V. A weather report — 139 39 185 20 202 93 131 121

W. Going in the wrong direction: 3 wds. — 107 69 168 132 176 19 205 40 97 47

X. Far apart or far away — 95 197 133 102 23 49 126

1 P	2 O	3 G	4 Q	5 D	6 S	7 T	8 F	9 I	10 J		11 B	12 A	13 H	14 C	15 E	16 K	17 M		18 R	19 W	20 V	21 N
	22 U	23 X	24 L	25 Q	26 S	27 D	28 O	29 A	30 F	31 P		32 H	33 N	34 K	35 S	36 I	37 F	38 R	39 V	40 W	41 A	42 G
	43 J	44 B		45 E	46 Q	47 W	48 R	49 X		50 U	51 Q	52 L	53 E	54 B	55 D	56 O	57 J	58 P	59 A		60 Q	61 O
62 M		63 E	64 R	65 Q	66 S	67 H	68 F		69 W	70 D	71 C	72 H	73 J		74 S	75 U	76 Q	77 A	78 D	79 H	80 I	81 O
	82 B	83 K	84 L	85 M		86 K	87 R	88 F	89 J	90 O	91 C	92 P		93 V	94 L	95 X		96 R	97 W	98 E	99 P	100 F
101 N	102 X	103 J		104 I	105 O	106 K	107 W	108 J	109 Q	110 L	111 D		112 I	113 B		114 I	115 T	116 F	117 D	118 Q	119 S
120 I		121 V	122 Q	123 P	124 G	125 E	126 X	127 M		128 Q	129 P	130 S	131 V	132 W	133 X		134 O	135 R	136 L	137 D	138 B
139 V	140 A		141 L	142 M	143 K	144 T	145 J	146 E		147 L	148 T	149 D	150 B	151 C	152 S	153 K	154 R		155 G	156 T	157 H	158 N
159 U		160 E	161 H	162 M	163 D	164 I	165 K	166 Q		167 N	168 W	169 O	170 A	171 F		172 L	173 M	174 T	175 S		176 W	177 J
178 A	179 F	180 P	181 C	182 I		183 Q	184 R		185 V	186 E	187 H	188 U	189 T		190 U	191 B	192 O	193 L		194 G	195 C
					196 F	197 X	198 U	199 O	200 K	201 C		202 V	203 P	204 J	205 W						

DEFINITIONS   **WORDS**

A. Sharp in practical affairs
139 6 122 200 149 74

B. Famous Lon Chaney role "of the Opera"
136 131 169 201 5 53 94

C. Scope; reach
35 198 132 121 187 80

D. Rainy-day funds: 2 wds.
196 30 147 177 97 103 39

E. Haggish old women
62 33 128 179 206 52

F. Became level: 2 wds.
104 158 165 141 197 115 59 9 68

G. America's Cup race, for one
170 61 130 8 105 210 153

H. Perceptible to the ear
41 190 155 3 15 110 171

I. It's composed of rachis, vane and quill
133 157 113 69 92 192 10

J. Dangerous denizen of Southwest deserts
191 84 36 64 119 152 164

K. Intuitive knowledge
11 114 106 182 32 70 176

L. Transformed
151 20 195 194 186 111 156

M. Long and difficult, as a journey
188 42 202 16 140 81 116

N. One gear position on a car
145 48 175 172 22 203 120

O. Something "there is always time for"
40 95 129 112 189 23 162 58

P. Roly-poly
209 193 148 63 60 86

Q. Funeral oration
83 134 205 46 180 102

R. Decorate with raised designs
161 107 47 28 88 183

S. Fluffy little pets
146 178 99 123 89 29 184

T. In apple-pie order
17 124 76 199 44 143 108 207 137

U. Weighty; influential
37 117 174 72 98 167 50 154 160

V. Turn a cold shoulder to: hyph. wd. (slang)
100 150 163 18 49 208 142

W. "The — Dodger," Dickens character
118 25 19 67 87 135

X. African —, delicate plant
55 185 173 73 125 45

Y. Acid-on-metal art
101 126 168 181 144 14 77

Z. Unattached man
204 166 12 127 56 109 159 138

AA. — money, bargain-binder
21 24 57 38 71 75 91

BB. Made more comfortable
7 13 90 54 51

CC. Under no conditions
4 26 96 34 82

DD. Ruined; unfinished
1 78 43 66 85 93

EE. Puts "in hock"
2 79 31 27 65

1DD	2EE		3H	4CC		5B	6A	7BB		8G	9F	10I	11K
12Z	13BB	14Y		15H	16M	17T	18V		19W	20L	21AA	22N	23O		24AA	25W	26CC		27EE	28R	29S
30D	31EE		32K	33E	34CC	35C	36J	37U	38AA	39D		40O	41H	42M	43DD	44T		45X	46Q		47R	48N
	49V	50U	51BB		52E	53B		54BB	55X	56Z	57AA	58O		59F	60P	61G		62E	63P	64J	65EE
66DD	67W	68F		69I	70K	71AA		72U	73X	74A		75AA	76T	77Y	78DD	79EE	80C	81M	82CC	83Q		84J
85DD	86P		87W	88R	89S	90BB	91AA	92I	93DD	94B		95O	96CC	97D	98U		99S	100V	101Y	102Q
103D	104F	105G		106K	107R	108T	109Z	110H	111L	112O		113I	114K	115F		116M	117U	118W	119J	120N	121C	122A
	123S	124T	125X		126Y	127Z	128E	129O	130G	131B	132C	133I	134Q	135W		136B	137T	138Z	139A	140M	141F
142V	143T	144Y	145N	146S		147D		148P	149A	150V	151L		153G	154U	155H		156L	157I	158F	159Z	160U	161R
162O		163V	164J	165F	166Z	167U		168Y	169B	170G	171H		172N	173X		174U	175N	176K	177D	178S	179E	180Q
	181Y	182K	183R		184S	185X	186L	187C	188M	189O	190H	191J	192I		193P	194L		195L	196D		197F	198C
199T	200A	201B	202M	203N	204Z	205Q	206E		207T	208V	209P	210G

3 ANACROSTIC

by MARIE WEST

DEFINITIONS   WORDS

A. Cheese named for the English town where it originated — 66 174 195 165 153 43 112

B. Merely theoretical — 161 91 123 49 19 99 28 186

C. Dan Rather or Howard K. Smith, e.g. — 159 5 212 128 84 144 223

D. End of the day — 196 219 154 35 173 143 17 182 96

E. Musical interval — 199 6 124 51 209 104

F. Fondness for "the good old days" — 106 130 215 160 95 197 189 102 181

G. Ahead of time — 138 54 218 185 24 100 77 175 122 113

H. Negligent; lax — 57 94 82 162 2 145

I. Catch up with — 111 176 36 10 224 85 120 63

J. Prayer — 198 26 133 214 119 64

K. Cherished remembrance — 142 11 222 59 72 115 183 87

L. Was greatly agitated — 46 167 75 101 4 206 86

M. Village settled by Mayflower passengers — 118 137 56 207 172 31 18 166

N. Merchandise at a charity sale — 190 216 14 156 67 203 177

O. Easy on the budget — 121 69 208 188 179 103 169 134 47 62

P. Arrow parts — 147 21 213 132 108 60

Q. Situation where a solution can't be found — 152 194 52 141 105 13 210

R. Charles G. —, Vice President under Coolidge — 168 40 110 127 97

S. Deliriously happy — 155 32 192 20 136 146 201 220

T. Not forced or phony — 163 109 184 73 139 1 151

U. Closemouthed — 125 157 42 221 180 27 211 202

V. Decisive encounter — 193 80 149 34 170 107 114 16

W. They provide traction on sports shoes — 148 68 164 37 204 116

X. Surpasses in excellence — 187 58 178 117 88 158 171 129 79

Y. — printing, lithographic process — 150 131 217 55 140 38

Z. Pretty small: hyph. wd. — 200 71 92 191 205 135 9 126

AA. Fund-raising event — 30 83 41 15 25 78 90

BB. Spectator — 70 48 53 7 81 44 22 93

CC. Pollyanna outlook — 89 39 3 61 74 23 12 50

DD. United closely — 33 8 98 29 65 45 76

[Grid of numbered/lettered cells]

78

DEFINITIONS   WORDS

A. Overly sentimental   100 186 14 197 124 51 139

B. Fresh and vigorous   206 8 56 123 158 23 94 167

C. Type of early sports car   152 36 143 193 78 91 12 196

D. Fixed costs of operating a business   192 85 52 5 163 101 198 147

E. Familiar appellation   9 170 60 126 45 212 116 112

F. Extracts water (from)   130 29 203 156 190 122

G. Posing a threat   106 180 127 50 159 71 13

H. Witness; note   99 103 65 177 16 150 184

I. Adds a little liquid to   157 86 76 194 151 21 185

J. Pleasant; amiable   47 108 207 113 95 144 77

K. — Rhodesia, former name of Zambia   42 33 59 132 210 17 92 199

L. "— is to do and say the nastiest thing in the nicest way": I. Goldberg   46 67 182 211 22 169 117 1 154

M. Little bouquet   34 53 81 146 160 131 172

N. Unyielding; unrelenting   75 175 155 11 166 118 31

O. Very close, as a contest: 3 wds.   90 39 148 6 205 121 68 136 72 64

P. A wedding vow   165 55 179 134 88 209 73

Q. New Englanders   115 83 188 213 133 140 27

R. Of or like the fairer sex   178 41 183 173 128 96 107

S. Outmoded; obsolete   89 26 153 111 191 61 174

T. Voices disapproval   189 18 161 63 142 28 176

U. Stalling for time   200 97 3 168 43 208 125 135

V. Summon by sorcery   138 162 120 105 181 25 214

W. One who rows a boat   149 10 84 187 57 119 204

X. Unruly; disorderly   110 195 66 145 49 141 201

Y. Violent act   102 109 171 20 79 129 38

Z. Causes anger; festers   114 30 164 202 137 104 70

AA. What one good turn deserves   44 74 4 82 69 62 40

BB. Get rid (of)   7 32 48 37 58 98 15

CC. Side branch   2 24 54 80 35 19 93 87

1L	2CC	3U	4AA	5D	6O	7BB	8B		9E	10W	11N	12C	13G		14A	15BB	16H	17K		18T	19CC
20Y	21I		22L	23B		24CC	25V	26S	27Q	28T	29F	30Z	31N	32BB	33K	34M		35CC	36C	37BB	38Y
	39O	40AA	41R	42K	43U		44AA	45E	46L		47J		48BB	49X	50G	51A	52D		53M	54CC	
55P	56B	57W	58BB	59K		60E	61S	62AA	63T	64O	65H		66X	67L	68O	69AA		70Z	71G	72O	73P
	74AA	75N	76I	77J	78C		79Y	80CC		81M	82AA	83Q	84W	85D	86I	87CC	88P	89S	90O		91C
92K	93CC	94B	95J	96R	97U	98BB	99H	100A	101D		102Y		103H	104Z		105V	106G	107R	108J	109Y	110X
	111S	112E	113J	114Z	115Q		116E	117L	118N		119W	120V	121O		122F	123B	124A	125U	126E	127G	128R
129Y		130F	131M	132K	133Q	134P		135U	136O	137Z	138V	139A	140Q	141X		142T	143C	144J	145X	146M	147D
	148O	149W	150H	151I	152C	153S	154L		155N	156F	157I		158B	159G	160M		161T	162V	163D	164Z	
165P	166N	167B	168U	169L	170E	171Y	172M		173R	174S	175N		176T	177H	178R	179P	180G	181V	182L		183R
	184H	185I	186A	187W		188Q	189T		190F	191S	192D	193C		194I	195X	196C	197A		198D	199K
	200U		201X	202Z	203F	204W	205O	206B		207J	208U	209P	210K		211L	212E	213Q	214V

by LOISANNE VAN SCIVER

Quotation is on page 308.
Word list is on page 312.

DEFINITIONS   WORDS

A. Code of morals
68 4 154 120 48

B. Exposed to view
7 52 172 32 119 74 105

C. Everlasting
65 10 130 39 88 176 109

D. Beverage with ambrosia
54 108 18 80 140 183

E. Subdued in tone and color
124 40 118 164 100

F. Well known by reputation
161 2 33 25 145

G. Handworked blanket
90 3 45 169 117 135

H. "Skoal!," e.g.
153 46 69 177 127

I. Howl; wail
96 5 126 42 158 70 143

J. Contest of cowboy skills
87 53 13 132 101

K. Lack (of)
56 91 12 139 186 77 111

L. Item used in several Word J events
116 81 159 8 182 61

M. Shockingly ugly
51 14 187 112 166 171 38

N. Formed by volcanic action
84 168 44 144 113 19 134

O. A symbol of authority
123 178 106 15 31

P. — Zone, area between the Tropics of Cancer and Capricorn
22 95 131 151 6 58

Q. Children's card game: 2 wds.
184 92 83 34 73 62 107

R. A 33 rpm, e.g.
150 122 170 136 110 24

S. Wet behind the ears
93 147 185 128 173 16 167 41

T. "Prexy" or "veep," e.g.
179 76 114 17 104 157 67

U. "For purple mountain majesties; Above the — plain"
26 82 49 174 146 155 102

V. Neonatal
142 29 148 125 181 138 63

W. Sail closer to the wind than another
149 78 21 99 162 27 121 141

X. Miser
165 30 180 137 60 156 98

Y. Archie Bunker's pet word
50 163 133 115 20 72

Z. Pleasant sound
160 103 86 129 175 37 152

AA. Members of the peerage
9 75 89 97 59 55

BB. Farewell appearance: 2 wds.
1 94 36 57 79 23 47 66

CC. Blue-penciling
35 71 43 85 11 28 64

1 BB	2 F	3 G	4 A		5 I	6 P	7 B	8 L	9 AA	10 C		11CC	12 K		13 J	
14 M	15 O	16 S	17 T	18 D	19 N	20 Y	21 W		22 P	23BB		24 R	25 F	26 U	27 W	28CC	29 V		30 X	31 O
32 B	33 F		34 Q	35CC	36BB	37 Z	38 M		39 C	40 E	41 S	42 I	43CC	44 N	45 G		46 H	47BB		48 A	49 U
50 Y	51 M	52 B	53 J	54 D	55AA		56 K	57BB	58 P		59AA	60 X	61 L	62 Q	63 V	64CC		65 C		66BB	67 T
68 A	69 H	70 I		71CC	72 Y	73 Q	74 B		75AA	76 T		77 K	78 W	79BB	80 D	81 L	82 U	83 Q		84 N	85CC
	86 Z	87 J	88 C	89AA	90 G	91 K	92 Q	93 S		94BB	95 P	96 I	97AA	98 X		99 W	100 E	101J	102U	103Z	104T
105B		106O		107Q	108D	109C	110R	111K	112M		113N	114T		115Y	116L	117G	118E	119B	120A	121W	122R
123O	124E		125V	126I	127H		128S	129Z	130C	131P	132J		133Y	134N		135G	136R		137X	138V	139K
140D	141W		142V	143I	144N	145F		146U	147S		148V	149W	150R	151P	152Z		153H	154A	155U	156X	157T
	158I	159L	160Z		161F	162W	163Y		164E	165X	166M	167S	168N	169G		170R	171M	172B	173S	174U	175Z
		176C	177H		178O	179T		180X	181V		182L	183D	184Q	185S	186K	187M				

DEFINITIONS   WORDS

A. Favorite phrases
144 187 117 95 26 3 41

B. Close tightly, as fists
74 20 42 165 195 121

C. Free-throw lanes, in basketball
78 208 189 55 123 36 104 8

D. Unfriendly; passionless: hyph. wd.
164 100 22 120 73 162 44

E. Chaplin movie of 1952
84 91 188 39 50 18 160 103 64

F. Flighty; explosive
57 108 135 10 72 130 207 145

G. Biblical wife of King Ahasuerus
126 179 166 31 4 49

H. Quick review or summary
11 83 173 107 60 90 184

I. Restlessness; anxiety: 2 wds.
5 101 70 185 33 202 193 149

J. Fine —, subtlety in intrigue: 2 wds.
133 9 48 65 159 56 109 129 76
112 24

K. Meriting attention
69 210 96 6 28 116 201 128 136 154

L. Grasp the opportunity or abandon it: 4 wds.
35 106 198 82 186 156 77 119 174 206
147 176 47

M. Keeping one's eyes peeled: 3 wds.
200 52 97 152 167 114 67 110 146 80

N. Rehashes (another's mistakes): 2 wds.
75 148 175 16 203 181

O. Felix —, German composer (1809-1847)
105 150 59 204 25 169 32 46
113 161 94

P. Extreme; total: hyph. wd. (slang)
87 168 134 209 13 190 58 71

Q. Person's characteristic manner of existence: 2 wds.
85 170 17 157 45 102 163 93 66

R. Private school attended by F.D.R.
53 177 37 140 98 14

S. Gives or confers upon, as pleasure
155 199 21 2 68 139 54

T. Creator of trivial verse
40 158 62 118 211 27 1 153 127

U. Heavy or oppressive burden: 2 wds.
89 23 197 178 38 183 51 171 115 79

V. Avoids adroitly
63 19 142 182 81 192

W. NBC, CBS and ABC
124 191 151 132 137 141 111 212

X. Contrary to statutes
29 92 122 43 15 205 138

Y. Pioneer ranchers' word for farmers
34 143 131 61 194 7 86

Z. Medieval symbol of a challenge
125 180 99 88 30 12 172 196

1 T	2 S		3 A	4 G	5 I	6 K	7 Y		8 C	9 J	10 F	11 H	12 Z	13 P	14 R	15 X	16 N		17 Q	18 E	19 V	20 B
	21 S	22 D	23 U	24 J	25 O	26 A	27 T		28 K	29 X	30 Z	31 G		32 O	33 I	34 Y	35 L	36 C	37 R	38 U	39 E	40 T
41 A	42 B	43 X	44 D	45 Q		46 O	47 L	48 J	49 G	50 E	51 U	52 M	53 R	54 S		55 C	56 J	57 F	58 P		59 O
60 H	61 Y		62 T	63 V	64 E		65 J	66 Q	67 M	68 S	69 K	70 I	71 P		72 F	73 D		74 B	75 N	76 J	77 L	78 C
	79 U	80 M	81 V		82 L	83 H	84 E	85 Q	86 Y		87 P	88 Z	89 U		90 H	91 E	92 X	93 Q		94 O	95 A	96 K
97 M	98 R	99 Z	100 D	101 I		102 Q	103 E	104 C	105 O		106 L	107 H	108 F	109 J	110 M		111 W	112 J	113 O	114 M
115 U	116 K	117 A		118 T	119 L	120 D	121 B		122 X	123 C	124 W	125 Z	126 G	127 T		128 K	129 J	130 F	131 Y		132 W
133 J	134 P	135 F		136 K	137 W	138 X	139 S		140 R	141 W	142 V	143 Y		144 A	145 F	146 M	147 L	148 N	149 I	150 O		151 W
152 M	153 T	154 K		155 S	156 L	157 Q		158 T	159 J	160 E	161 O	162 D	163 Q		164 D	165 B	166 G	167 M	168 P	169 O	170 Q	171 U
172 Z	173 H	174 L		175 N	176 L	177 R	178 U	179 G		180 Z	181 N	182 V		183 U	184 H	185 I	186 L	187 A		188 E	189 C
190 P	191 W	192 V	193 I	194 Y	195 B	196 Z		197 U	198 L		199 S	200 M	201 K	202 I	203 N	204 O	205 X	206 L	207 F	208 C	209 P
210 K	211 T	212 W																			

PATCH PUZZLE

If you put the correct vowel (a, e, i, o, or u,) into each blank square in the diagram below, you will have a finished crossword, with real, everyday words reading across and down. When you are finished, no word should appear more than once in the diagram. Our solution, which may differ from yours, is on page 301.

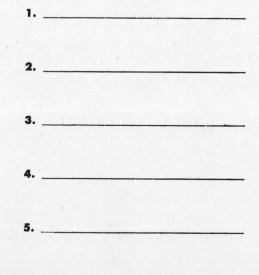

STAR SCRAMBLE

In each section of the star below there are five scrambled letters. Add the "O" from the center circle to each group of five letters and form five common 6-letter words; however, your words may NOT start with "O." When you have formed your words, take the first letter of each word, add the "O," and form one final 6-letter word, but this word MUST begin with "O."

Answer is on page 298.

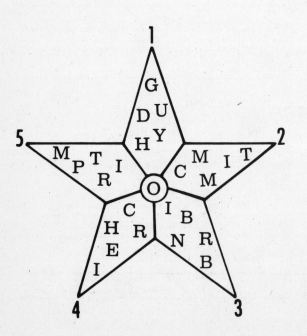

1. _____

2. _____

3. _____

4. _____

5. _____

Bonus word: _____

PICTURE REBUS

by Ann Wolf

Below is a little truism told in pictures. To read it, express in words what is represented by the illustrations. If a picture is followed by a plus or minus sign, you are to add or subtract those letters from the preceding word. If no plus or minus sign is present, it signifies the end of one word and the beginning of the next one. Answer is on page 298.

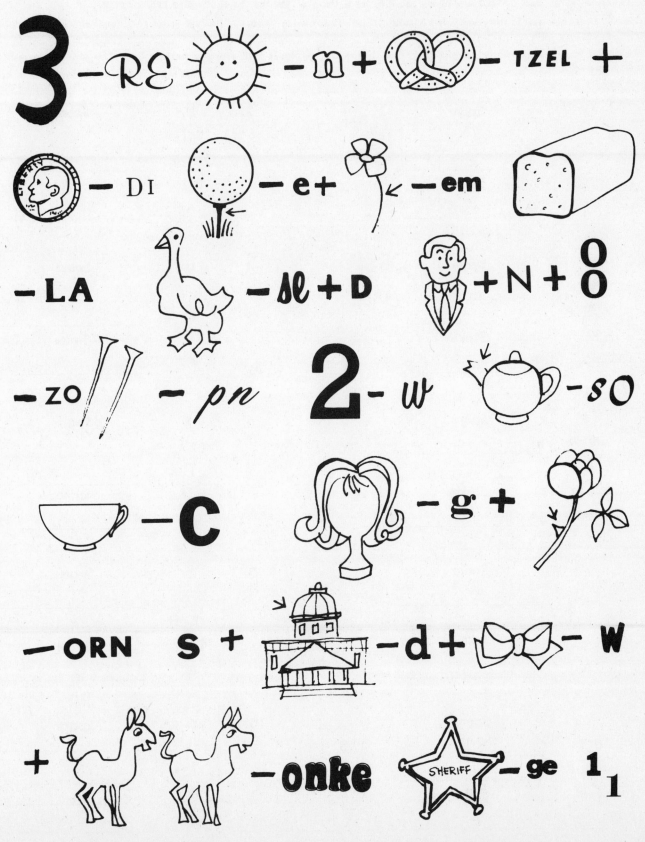

BOWL-A-SCORE CHALLENGER 1

Copyright 1989 by Bantam Doubleday Dell Publishing Group, Inc.

In this bowling game your "pins" are the groups of letters below. In order to score a "strike," you must unscramble (anagram) the "pin" letters of each group and form one 9-letter word. The starting letter for each "strike" word is given. To score a "spare," rearrange the scrambled letters of each group into two words, with no letters left over. Words beginning with a capital letter are not allowed for either "strikes" or "spares." In forming your "spare" words, you may not simply split the "strike" word in two parts and use both exactly as they appear in the "strike" word. For example, FORE and CASTER would not qualify as a "spare" for the "strike" word FORECASTER.

SCORING: Score 20 points for each "strike" and 10 points for each "spare." Perfect score (10 "strikes" and 10 two-word "spares") is 300.

Warning: This game is really tough! Only word bowling geniuses will score a perfect 300. The words we made are on page 298.

1.   V   **Spare**
       S S
       N O R   _____
       E G   **Strike**
       E   **G** _____

2.   U   **Spare**
       T T
       O P S   _____
       E L   **Strike**
       A   **P** _____

3.   Y   **Spare**
       S U
       L O P   _____
       E H   **Strike**
       A   **P** _____

4.   U   **Spare**
       T U
       P R S   _____
       E L   **Strike**
       C   **S** _____

5.   P   **Spare**
       N P
       E E G   _____
       A D   **Strike**
       A   **A** _____

6.   T   **Spare**
       M S
       H I K   _____
       E F   **Strike**
       A   **M** _____

7.   Y   **Spare**
       R U
       S T T   _____
       E I   **Strike**
       A   **A** _____

8.   Y   **Spare**
       K N
       E E H   _____
       C D   **Strike**
       A   **H** _____

9.   Y   **Spare**
       S U
       N O P   _____
       E M   **Strike**
       D   **P** _____

10.   Y   **Spare**
       P R
       G I N   _____
       C E   **Strike**
       A   **P** _____

DOVETAILED WORDS

Two 6-letter words, with their letters in the correct order, are combined in each row of letters. To solve the puzzle, find both words. There are no extra letters, nor is any letter used more than once. In a line like CHROENESASTE, or cHrOeNESasTe, you have the two words CREASE and HONEST.   Answer is on page 298.

Words

1. T R U R E N I T A P I N_____   _____

2. C E H O V O R L U S V E_____   _____

3. A D N E Y S I W G A N Y_____   _____

4. B E C L I K A B O L E N_____   _____

5. P A F R O F I P R E L M_____   _____

6. S U S M A L M A R I T Y_____   _____

7. W I N I D T I H I G O N_____   _____

8. G R E N A R A D G E R E_____   _____

9. M U T H E I C T I N C Y_____   _____

10. O V E R N E N E A R T E_____   _____

SPELLATHON

Copyright 1989 by Bantam Doubleday Dell Publishing Group, Inc.

The idea of Spellathon is to spell as many 5-letter words as you can by moving along the connecting lines from one letter to another in the diagram below. Do not skip letters. You may come back to a letter and use it twice in the same word (as in "ceded"); but do not stand on a letter using it twice in direct succession (as in "added"). Words beginning with a capital letter, foreign words, slang, contractions, obsolete, dialect, archaic, or poetic words are not allowed. Our list of 47 words, 11 of which are less frequently used, is on page 298.

NOTE: In this Spellathon, plurals ending in "s" and present-tense verbs ending in "s," such as "sings," are not allowed. Your list of words:

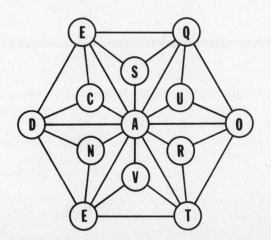

Cryptograms begin on page 40.

23. MN'P S AKTR XMPK LKTPVW XIV QWVXP XISN

WVN NV PSR—LTVAMJKJ IK JVKPW'N PSR MN.

24. DCJXJYZBIJDYD BXL ZDZBIIP HLJYVLX

CLDDJQJDYD HSX SCYJQJDYD—TZDY VBCCP

QLAJZQD.

25. ITMMHII BI MHVALBEGD VHGLABOH. AZH QKVH

KN BA L QLE QLD ZLOH, AZH QKVH KN AZHQ

ZH'GG NBEX ZH ZLI.

26. J LGJE HW GHPC J THRJM. HI HX HW J

IJHGDMC, UB JKBDUX BI LDIIHUR OHGG CNCM

KJPC HX SMJO—HI J AHR WDTTCWW,

CNCMEABSE OJUXW J ABZ.

27. KQ JNN VSW IRNNRKHL KQ LHKMQNJPWL VSJV

QJNN WJXS MRHVWG, RV'L SJGZ VK IWNRWFW

VSJV VSWGW JGWH'V JV NWJLV VMK JNRPW.

28. KEXMX SMX KEMXX HSVL VPJ HDAA FXK

LPZXKEDYF WPYX: WP DK VPJMLXAT, EDMX

LPZXPYX, PM TPMRDW VPJM BDWL KP WP DK.

29. AQUDRKUDA K PDJKDZD RYD SQOJM SQHJM PD

UHBY PDRRDO QLL KL SD YCM YCM LDSDO

AQ-BCJJDM KUEOQZDUDIRA.   **Solutions are on page 306**

30. A K X ' Y   B I B J   P B Y   Y U B   L B N Y   R K Q   U C I B   A K X B

N K   Z C J   L B   Y U B   N Y C X A C J A   Z K J   Y U B   J B N Y

K Z   R K Q J   P D Z B .

31. W R D   L M K   J V   B C Q Q D L   H C Z ' V   U D V W   S N J D Z L

U D B C X V D   R D   M S S D N V   Z M   C L E J B D ,   Z D E D N

W N J D V   W M   U M N N M O   H M Z D P ,   C Z L   R C V Z ' W   C Z P

J Z - Q C O V .

32. P R T   P Q   H J T   G T W H   H J D R A W   X G P M H   J X C D R A

X R   X H H D Y   D W   H J X H   B P M   E P R ' H   J X C T   H P

Y Z T X R   D H   X Z Z   P M H   H P   U X S T   V P P U   Q P V

B P M V   Y X V .

33. G Q   Z B C   F Z S W C I O W I L   B T W U   V   H G L L H W   O Z C W

D C B I G I F   V I U   V   H G L L H W   H W T T   F C V Q L G I F ,   J W

O G F X L   X V S W   V   H G L L H W   O Z C W   D C Z T D W C G L R .

34. L W   B J H T E   G P   Q Y P F W   L O   P R P Y S J U P   N J H T E

Z F R P   F   A P N J U E   N Z F U N P ,   G H W   T L O P   E J P A U ' W

D Y J K L A P   K F U   F U S   A H N Z   W Z L U Q .

35. Q N C C X J Y   J Q   V S C   A N C I I   K I   I J Y C V S K G R   V S B V

K I   N C B U U L   R D B N B G V C C X   J G U L   V J   V S J I C

A C N I J G I   H S J   J H G   J G C .

36. L W K Z N   V C W V Z C   L H Z Z   M S C   Z W X A - G R X N C N

H B M C O - N R X X C O   P V C H Q C O   " A K P M   W B   S W X W O " ?

Solutions are on page 306

CRYPTOGRAMS

37. NXGZ WKRG PZTPCPTMJE HGIKRGW IKZWIPKMW

BXJB XG PW PFZKLJZB, XG XJW RJTG J

WBJLB BKNJLT KHBJPZPZF YZKNEGTFG.

38. XZQVAGQVX OTJA ATV MVJXZEGH QGEI OZYFI

XTYA ZYA, ATV FZBV-MYFVI TVJMA JFFZOX

AZ VEAVM.

39. IH UHGPX BF NCEHIK GULN QO PBNVQL GES

VUGSCVCQE VQ PXQJH VQSGK GES CLFHSH

VQLQUUQI.

40. WJSB JQ JGH FPWZCLYUJL CLUBHIHBUBHW JQ

DPFW OPL PDFPTW AB UHGWUBX UJ UPRB

SPLT IBHQBOUDT YJJX JLBW PLX CLUBHIHBU

UZB OJSSJL WBLWB JGU JQ UZBS.

41. QDPA JPY SGHBDGL LXRRSTRL JHR JKDGV

JL WBV WDH YBLXJVST JL J HRAJQ HDKR

NBVT J QDPA VHJBP BL WDH J HJSR.—

WHJPSBL KJSDP

42. HCIHVBP VR VIIVPCHCVK VRHBK HMEK CKHV

F PVMKL VR PHFDIBLB.

43. RKEB-ILRPLAELGK PDG HK DR RDNLRBFLGT

NM FMC DR LGICETKGPK.

44. UKRQHJHN QK GWJQ GB JEE KRUB JUUBIQBA

KR LJCQW, KCE XBBOX QK WJMB TBUKOB J

IHCRUCIJE UJDXB KL QHKDTEBA GJQBHX.

Cryptograms continue on page 141.

Solutions are on page 306

LETTER SWITCH

Each of the nonsensical sentences below can be changed into a quotation by replacing one letter in each word with one of the letters listed in the parentheses following the sentence. Every word in each sentence must have one letter changed (including the 1-letter words "a" and "I"), but do not change the order of either the letters in the words or the words in the sentence. For example: I SWITCH ON TIRE (A I M T) becomes A STITCH IN TIME—the four letters in parentheses having replaced the I, W, O, and R in the words of the nonsensical phrase. The letters in parentheses are in alphabetical order, which is not necessarily the order in which you will use them. Each letter in parentheses will be used only once.   **Answers are on page 298.**

1. KEEN TREE NO THY DREADS ON THE MOUTH.   (E F M P T U Y Y)

2. AT AS OILY WREN HEN BEGAN DO WARSHIP CHAT THEN BEGUN GO CROW.   (G H I I I I M N O T T T Y)

3. THROB I DUCKY FAN ONTO TOE SET, ANY WE WILT COMB US WITS I FIST ON HIM SOUTH.   (A A A D E H H H H I I L L M M P S W)

4. THEN HE GAVE GOT THAT BE LONE, YE DUST DOVE WHAM ME RAVE.   (H H L M N T V W W W W W W)

5. THY PACE IF DOT SO TIE SHIFT, NOT TEE BOTTLE DO SHE STRUNG.   (A E H H N O R R S T T T W)

6. OF YON WORLD BY HEALTHY, THANK ON HAVING AT WILL IS IF BETTING.   (A E E F G I I O S S U U W)

SHARED LETTER QUIZ

The names of the four American colleges in each numbered group below have only one shared letter; that is, there is only one letter which appears in every name in that group. Write that shared letter on the dash to the right of each group. When you have found the 8 shared letters, unscramble them and you will find the name of another college. Can you do it in 5 minutes or less?   **Answer is on page 298.**

1. Emmanuel, Fairmont, Hampshire, Oakwood   _____

2. Anderson, Edgewood, Harvey Mudd, Huntingdon   _____

3. California, George Fox, Lafayette, Pacific Union   _____

4. Brigham Young, Duquesne, Florence, Kirkland   _____

5. Houghton, Minnesota, Rockefeller, Wilberforce   _____

6. Fitchburg, Manchester, Northwestern, Waynesburg   _____

7. Amherst, Buena Vista, Marshall, Rockhurst   _____

8. Centenary, Hamilton, Livingstone, Marquette   _____

WORD SEARCH 4

Hidden in the diagram below are the names of 51 things that can be found in the produce department of a super-market: fruits, vegetables, and a few of those "extras" which are often located in that department. Some of the words are plural and some singular, but they are all four or more letters in length. See how many you can find without the help of a Word List. PEARS is circled to get you started. Space has been provided for you to write down the words as you find and circle (or cross through) them. If you keep your list in approximate alphabetical order, you can avoid repeated searching for a word you've already found. REMEMBER: Don't circle words within words, and if a word appears more than once in the diagram, circle it and count it only once.

Word List is on page 298.   Solution is on page 300.

YOUR WORD LIST

```
O P I N S R A P M X Q S T O R R A C
K F I G S A M C G R E E N B E A N S
R S K N N Y E P U M P K I N B P D E
A B E A E L B O T A M O T M M O S N
G G N P E A P P L E S H H T U T M U
A A R R A S P E A S B C K Y C A O R
B E Y B N R G P T W P I N R U T O P
A G T A E G G P L A N T O B C O R N
T A E L M A W E N E N R M G A O H O
U B X F R S B R E H R A E W N R S L
R B H L R E Q S S T N A L P T A U E
F A I M E H U A P A P A Y A A N M M
S C D T D W U L V E P E M S L G E R
E T S I D Q U B A O L G R N O E D E
M Q S A S M Q C A S C A G O U S L T
I G T L T H H V R R E A X I P Y M A
L E T T U C E A K P B F D N E A V W
S H C A N I P S C A L L I O N S Z A
```

The terms in this puzzle are part of the truck driver's colorful vocabulary. You'll find their definitions on page 298. Solution is on page 300.

```
P I G G Y B A C K C A T S T R I P
U E R D D N A P D O O D L E B U G
T D A A V I A T O R S K I N S O W
O A X N N I C H Y B W G E R D O O
N E A A U R O H C N A W S S S S O
T H M E M T R G H H M R H R R D D
H D I K L Y W E S Z P B E E B O C
E A T O F F L A T B E D E B N O H
A E A M D N A R G A R R T U A K U
I D H S T C A B Y O O R T M J C C
R A G E K I P O G T N L U B O A K
Y G I L B I L N O R I G F L C B Y
X O B I G R I G G E R K O E K Y P
O O B T L Y R E L U M W A B E D I
B L A W L R P R O O B O G E Y R N
E I E F O Z O S P O T S E E R I U
L T A C K C A B Y H S I F R O B P
```

WORD LIST

1. Anchor	12. Cab	22. Gear bonger	32. Mule	42. Rig
2. Aviator	13. Cowboy	23. Grandma	33. P and D	43. ~~Shag~~
3. Bareback	14. Deadhead	24. Gypsy	34. Peanut wagon	44. Skins
4. Bible	15. Dog	25. Horse	35. Piggyback	45. Smoke
5. Big hat	16. Donut	26. Hot load	36. Pigtail	46. Spot
6. Big rigger	17. Doodlebug	27. Iron	37. Pike	47. Stack
7. Birdyback	18. Fishyback	28. Jockey	38. Pin up	48. Strip
8. Bogey	19. Flatbed	29. Lie sheet	39. Pots	49. Swamper
9. Box	20. Floater	30. Lowboy	40. Put on the air	50. Tack
10. Break it	21. Flying orders	31. Maniac	41. Rag	51. Woodchuck
11. Bumblebee				

FIGGERITS 2

Copyright 1989 by Bantam Doubleday Dell Publishing Group, Inc.

Your finished Figgerit will yield a little truism written onto the SOLUTION dashes. Step 1: Fill in as many words in the WORDS column as you can, using the DEFINITIONS. Step 2: Transfer these letters to the SOLUTION according to matching numbers. Step 3: If you find, for example, that the number 6 stands for "r" in one word, write "r" above 6 in all places in that Figgerit. But a letter is allowed to have more than one number, so number 9 might also stand for "r" and you'd write "r" above all the 9's too. Step 4: Work back from SOLUTION to WORDS column with any possible clues. T-E is probably THE, so try out that H in the WORDS column. Each Figgerit has a different pattern of number/letter substitutions. Word lists are on page 302. Solutions are on page 298.

1.

Definitions	Words
Unknown person	36 30 18 23 10 5 34 35
Migraine, for example	2 19 9 33 38 27 22 26
Balderdash!	29 7 6 36 3 32 20 19
Athlete's coach	37 8 15 4 14 19 35
Alp	12 17 31 6 11 28 4 39
Was ready for; expected	13 21 38 4 1 26 40
Searched (for)	25 31 10 24 3 16

Solution:

1 2 3　4 5 6 7 8 9 10 11　12 13 14

15 16 17 18 19 20　21 22 23 24　25 26

27 28 29 30　31 32 33 34 35 36 37 38 39 40

2.

Definitions	Words
Walks in a parade	25 7 16 20 26 29 4
Actor Holden	2 27 12 13 33 1 18
Ways of social behavior; deportment	6 1 17 30 5 23 28
Rose of —, biblical plant	35 21 15 16 24 8
Mitch — of sing-along fame	32 3 11 13 14 23
Spouse	9 27 22 31
Scientists, Marie and Pierre —	20 19 16 10 34

Solution:

1　2 3 4 5　6 7 8　9 10 11 12

13 14 15 16 17　18 19 20 21　22 23 24 25

26 27 28　29 30 31 32 33 34 35

3.

Definitions	Words
Tom —, Twain character	35 25 14 12 20 5
Cardigans, for example	7 29 4 8 36 20 16 21
Sleepy —, Ichabod Crane's territory	24 15 19 32 34 10
East coast Ocean	1 17 31 11 26 28 6 33
Apparitions	3 18 38 13 23 22
Very small	17 27 2 37
Court plea	3 39 30 9 23 37

Solution:

1 2 3 4 5　6 7　8 9 10 11 12 13

14 15 16 17 18　19 20 21 22　23 24 25 26

27 28　29 30 31 32　33 34 35 36　37 38 39

4.

Definitions	Words
Broadcast on "the tube"	34 11 14 22 17 3 30 25
Was very unsteady	20 7 10 12 29 33 19
Bank employee	9 13 2 14 27 35
Purplish flower of the British Isles	21 16 1 26 38 33 5
Big "goof"	10 29 36 8 19 16 5
Sound physical condition	24 18 4 28 37 32
Jonathan or Shelley —	6 15 23 31 18 35 30

Solution:

1　2 3 4 5　6 7 8 9　10 11

12 13 14 15 16 17 18 19　20 21 22 23　24 25

26 27 28 29 30　31 32 33　34 35 36 37 38

5. Definitions — Words

Atlanta's baseball team 25 5 33 21 14 31

Entire; whole 27 20 15 9 13 4 32 30

Male geese 34 2 35 8 10 24 17

Choke 31 18 24 36 7 34 13 26

Common salad ingredients ... 3 11 19 6 38 28 30 17

Actor, Tyrone — 12 23 1 22 24

— Olympus, home of the Greek gods ... 29 11 16 37 3

Solution:

1 2 3 4 5 6 7 8 9 10 11 12 13 14

15 16 17 18 19 20 21 22 23 24

25 26 27 28 29 30 31 32 33 34 35 36 37 38

6. Definitions — Words

Little fingers 9 3 19 29 16 22 37

"Capistrano" bird 25 15 1 6 11 20 33

Matted; snarled 21 24 28 13 18 7 36

This gets done on washday .. 17 8 27 19 32 23 14

"Blue" part of the week ... 4 10 31 32 24 14

Graduating student 2 26 31 30 12 35

Curly-haired dog 5 10 34 36 17 26

Solution:

1 2 3 4 5 6 7 8 9 10 11 12 13 14

15 16 17 18 19 20 21 22 23 24 25 26

27 28 29 30 31 32 33 34 35 36 37

7. Definitions — Words

Makes sooty 19 35 30 4 25 11 7 27

The "Windy City" 4 14 36 16 23 32 8

Seed used in rye bread 13 5 29 15 22 18 1

Princess Grace's daughter ... 13 30 17 2 24 31 6 38

Beethoven's "Moonlight —" . 27 21 37 12 28 26

It's often "stranger than fiction" 10 17 3 20 33

Bread spread 19 3 9 34 11 29

Solution:

1 2 3 4 5 6 7 8 9 10 11 12 13 14

15 16 17 18 19 20 21 22 23 24 25

26 27 28 29 30 31 32 33 34 35 36 37 38

8. Definitions — Words

Lone Star State 31 12 7 20 19

Chocolate, vanilla, etc. 16 21 8 35 26 30 19

Fib: 2 wds. 28 2 34 27 6 14 22 12

Comic strips 23 4 11 37 15 3 19

Rub this on a sore muscle ... 33 18 11 10 9 24 25 1

Source of great wealth: 2 wds. 38 29 21 13 9 22 25 17

"The —," 1980 horror film .. 19 32 10 25 36 5 38

Solution:

1 2 3 4 5 6 7 8 9 10 11 12 13

14 15 16 17 18 19 20 21 22 23 24

25 26 27 28 29 30 31 32 33 34 35 36 37 38

LADDERGRAMS 2

by IRENE R. HAYES

First, write the word that fits the first definition into space 1. Then drop one letter and rearrange the remaining letters to form the answer to definition 2. Drop one more letter, rearrange, and get the answer to definition 3. Put the first dropped letter into the box to the left of space 1 and the other dropped letter into the box next to space 3. When you have correctly solved the puzzle, the dropped letters in the boxes on the left and right, when read down, will spell out related words. Solutions are on page 299.

	1	2	3	
	4	5	6	
	7	8	9	
	10	11	12	
	13	14	15	
	16	17	18	

1. DEFINITIONS

1. Overseas telegrams
2. Bundles (of hay)
3. Tight closure
4. "Throbbers"
5. Prolonged look
6. Direction of a sunrise
7. Augusta is its capital
8. Prayer ending
9. "Ol' — River"
10. Small
11. Name
12. Cause to slant
13. Singlebreasted sports jacket, often a solid color
14. Striped animal
15. Uncovered
16. Tom —, Huck Finn's friend
17. Take an oath
18. Armed battles

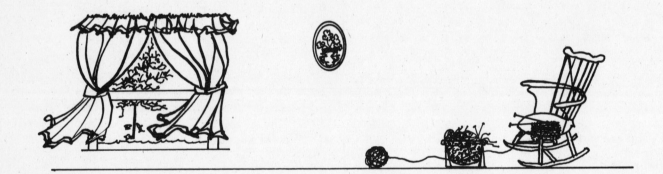

2. DEFINITIONS

1. Flying toys
2. Locale
3. Fasten
4. Snowy season
5. Act the author
6. Grow weary (of)
7. TV collie
8. Store's markdown events
9. Young girl
10. Our planet
11. Jack rabbit
12. "Rings on — fingers . . ."
13. Baby —, person hired to take care of one's children
14. Makes an effort
15. Ascend
16. Borscht vegetables
17. Optimum
18. Abbreviation in recipe
19. Long window curtains
20. Fifth tire
21. Pod vegetables

	1	2	3	
	4	5	6	
	7	8	9	
	10	11	12	
	13	14	15	
	16	17	18	
	19	20	21	

1	2	3	
4	5	6	
7	8	9	
10	11	12	
13	14	15	
16	17	18	
19	20	21	

3. DEFINITIONS

1. Quicker!
2. Song oldie, "— You've Gone"
3. Be afraid
4. Bread spread
5. Very cruel person
6. Mr. Parks, popular emcee
7. Quarrel
8. One's equipment
9. Grow old
10. Particles, as of snow or soap
11. Faucet problems
12. Beerlike beverages
13. Banquetlike meal
14. Has dinner
15. Occupied a chair
16. Simple (to do)
17. One's chance to speak
18. While
19. Rosary segments
20. Home plate is one
21. Actor Vigoda

4. DEFINITIONS

1. Disgraced
2. Titles for knighted ladies
3. Summertime drinks
4. Leaves out
5. Fine rain
6. Rockies or Appalachians: abbr.
7. Sinai and Vernon
8. Animal nose
9. Eject
10. Kept a tally of
11. Wrapping strings
12. Curtain supports
13. Shriek
14. Measures of land
15. Autos
16. Blossom segments
17. Slumbered
18. Allows
19. Tuning knobs
20. Travel via ship
21. Namesakes of actor Pacino
22. Rented
23. Distributes the cards
24. Boys

1	2	3	
4	5	6	
7	8	9	
10	11	12	
13	14	15	
16	17	18	
19	20	21	
22	23	24	

21 MEDIUM CROSSWORD

ACROSS

1. Supermarkets
7. Soaks (up)
11. Use a "Louisville Slugger"
14. Come to a place
15. Inactive
16. Speak dishonestly
17. *Nein*
18. Vitality
19. Jump
20. Fruit drink
21. Probed (into)
23. Violent anger
25. Female members of the family
27. Imitated
29. Farmer's possession
31. Inquire
32. Fruit rich in vitamin C
34. Read quickly
36. One-dish meal
39. Distress signal
41. Optician's study
43. Be in debt
44. Advancements
48. Made impassable
50. Tiny vegetable
51. Apiece
53. Johnny Cash hit, "A Boy Named —"
54. "Lights out" song
56. Wander
58. Do a mending job
62. Snakelike fish
64. Enclose (a package) in paper
66. Knowledge
67. More swift
70. Hat part
72. Chinese export
73. Annoy
74. Of the air: prefix
76. This very minute!
78. Toward
79. Hawaiian garland
80. Scorch
81. Game bird
83. Husband or father
84. Trees
85. Perceived

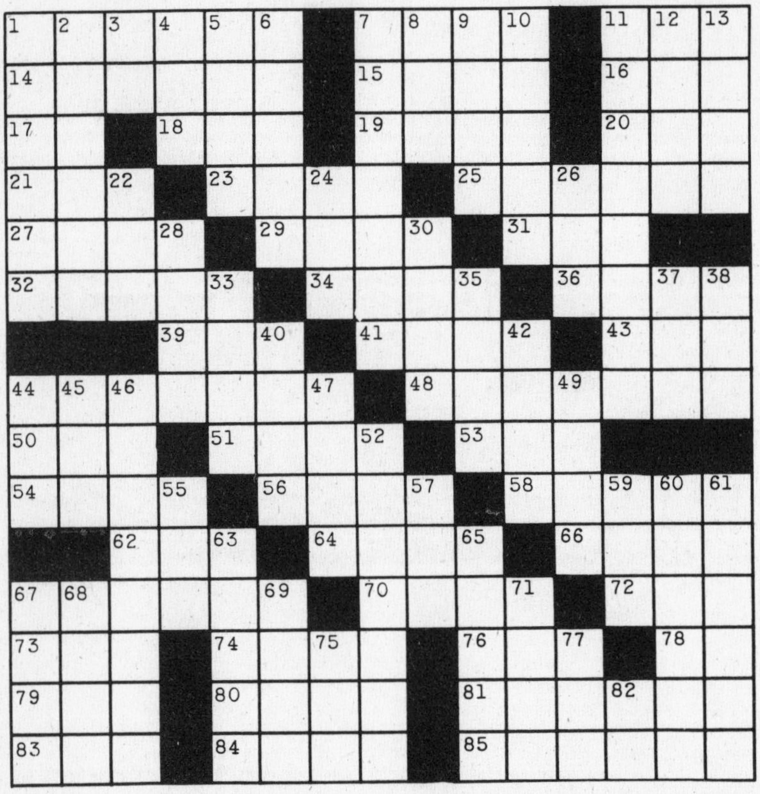

1 2 3 4 5 6 7 8 9 10 11 12 13
14 15 16
17 18 19 20
21 22 23 24 25 26
27 28 29 30 31
32 33 34 35 36 37 38
39 40 41 42 43
44 45 46 47 48 49
50 51 52 53
54 55 56 57 58 59 60 61
62 63 64 65 66
67 68 69 70 71 72
73 74 75 76 77 78
79 80 81 82
83 84 85

DOWN

1. Summertime shoe
2. Group of performers
3. Either
4. Tear (apart)
5. Always
6. Calyx leaf
7. Library sign
8. Lyric poem
9. Plot
10. Reddish-brown
11. Asphalt road surfacing
12. Assistant
13. Golf pegs
22. Jewel
24. Car fuel
26. Curvy letter
28. Quantity of medicine
30. Time divisions
33. "Nary a bit"
35. Certain snares
37. Lamb's mother
38. Marry
40. Be featured
42. Dinner course
44. Likely (to)
45. Ocean
46. Leather for gloves
47. Flat-bottomed boat
49. Sound (a bell)
52. Ports
55. Gel
57. Disfigure
59. Kindergartener
60. Wrinkle
61. Made warmer
63. Rental contract
65. Ignition knocks
67. Photographer's purchase
68. Scope; range
69. Film-holder
71. Oliver Twist's request
75. Lamb's father
77. Came in first
82. You and me

Solution is on page 285

NOTED WOMEN MATCH

The names of noted women are scrambled in Columns A, B, and C—their first names are in Column A, middle names are in Column B, and last names are in Column C. Can you match each woman's complete names with the occupation in Column 1, which made her famous?

Answer is on page 298.

Column 1	A	B	C
1. Authoress	Margaret	Rose	Anthony
2. Poetess	Marie	Jane	Alcott
3. Mystery writer	Mary	Boothe	Grimaldi
4. Reformer	Edna	Roberts	Luce
5. Princess	Gypsy	Sklodowska	Canary
6. Frontier woman	Clare	Brownell	Smith
7. Performer	Grace	May	Skinner
8. Physicist	Martha	Otis	Rinehart
9. Playwright	Cornelia	Chase	Curie
10. Monologuist	Louisa	Kelly	Millay
11. U.S. Senator	Susan	St. Vincent	Lee

ACROSS

1. Sailor's swab
4. Ruin
9. Postage sticker
14. Sick
15. Rental agreement
16. Sum
17. Ocean
18. Dine
19. At that time
21. Toward
22. Walk with shaky steps
24. Halt!
25. Grass moisture
26. Spinny toy
27. Killed
28. Complimentary ticket
29. Plant stalk
31. Expensive
32. Plot to build on
33. Paving material
34. Suds producer
35. Fondle
38. Mr. Jolson
39. Coin opening
40. Clock dial
41. That boy
42. More suitable
44. Challenge
45. Go to —, deteriorate
46. Crimson
47. Triumphs
48. Cat's feet
49. Cabbage salad
51. Swine
52. Evergreen tree
53. Chart
54. Four-posters
55. Gives medical care to
58. That thing
59. Painful spot
60. Perish
61. "A Boy Named —," Johnny Cash song
62. Ice-tea garnish
64. Stock portion
66. United
67. Rub out
68. Domesticated
69. Guided

DOWN

1. Fog
2. Margarine
3. Serving dish
4. Slumber
5. Fruit
6. Grain
7. Exists
8. Envelope's content
9. Stair
10. Heavy weight
11. Attending
12. Spouses
13. Farm implements
20. In what way?
23. — Thumb
24. Strike with open hand
25. Palm fruit
27. Chair or pew
28. Skin opening
29. Pierce with a dagger
30. Story
31. Room entrance
32. Shoestring
34. Arctic vehicle
35. Detroit products
36. Exhibit
37. Collections
39. Simmer
40. Cooling devices
43. Snare
44. Excavates
45. Lady's umbrella
47. Broadest
48. Crusty dessert
49. Mona Lisa's mystery
50. Afterward
51. For each
52. Liberated
54. Skeleton part
55. Children often use this as a swing
56. Melody
57. Plant beginning
59. Distress signal
60. Water barrier
63. Mother
65. Laughter sound

Solution is on page 285

SILLY DILLIES 2

For some fun, look over the drawings and damaged words below and try to identify the familiar expressions, phrases, or words they suggest. The number below each little picture is for identification only and is not part of the picture itself. As a start, the answer to No. 1 is "Cross over the bridge." Answers are on page 299.

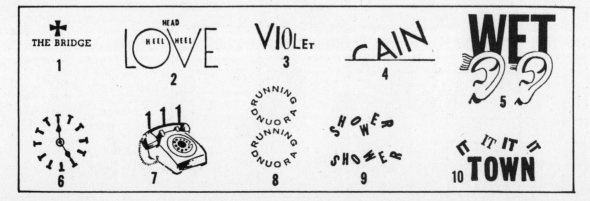

ACROSS

1. Like most schools
5. Loud sound
10. Thick slices
15. Raid
17. — *corpus*, legal writ
19. Dangers
21. Instantly: 4 wds.
23. Visualize
25. Hikes
26. Card game for two
27. Be chummy (with)
29. Supreme Being
30. Lily genus
32. Brobdingnagian
33. English architect
34. Hoodlum
35. Leanings
37. Large mackerel
39. Bowl for gravy
40. Humorous
41. Anticipatory
43. Artisan
46. Racing official
49. Headware
50. Metal bar
53. Yellow jacket
54. Cut of beef
55. Well-chosen
58. Opera melodies
59. Silky fabric
60. Toggles
61. Monk's title
62. Genuine
63. Facilitates a course: 3 wds.
65. Saucy
66. Bean holder
67. Stupefied
68. Violinist's need
69. Recipient
70. Dawns
72. Gaynor or Leigh
73. Arm parts
74. Instruct
75. Gem surface
76. With the most promptness
77. Complete standstills
80. Go swiftly
81. Mythical strong man
84. Kennedy Cabinet member
85. Sprinter's goal
87. Persian fairies
91. Scorch
92. Beer ingredient
93. Optical glass
95. Talk wildly
96. Foil alloy
97. Muddied
99. Threshes
101. Power agency: abbr.
102. Zoo attraction: 2 wds.
104. Amusement park attraction: 2 wds.
107. French hackney coach
108. Flunky
109. Gratify
110. Rapidity
111. Spirited horse
112. British county

DOWN

1. Pair
2. Prayer
3. Convenient abbr.
4. Water barrier
5. Cavalry-officer's mount
6. Ceiling beam
7. Competent
8. Vast expanse
9. Diced meat dish
10. Pianos
11. Flat failure: slang
12. Desert dweller
13. Sizable
14. Neglect
15. Young pigeon
16. To — his own
18. Braggadocio
20. Hog's nose
22. Cup holder
24. Short-tempered
28. Spoiled child
31. Everlasting
34. Slight color
36. Cloys
38. Takes place
39. Tree covering
40. Desires
42. Acquire
44. Hialeah or Churchill Downs: 2 wds.
45. Foggy
46. Musical symbols
47. Ripped away: 2 wds.
48. Minos' daughter
49. Recoiled in fear
51. Crime
52. Armored towers
54. Sheltered inlets
55. Namely: 2 wds.
56. Man's name
57. Newest
59. Labyrinth
60. Attacked
63. Turkish title
64. Trustworthy
65. Hunting dog
67. Chops fine
69. Sag
71. Detecting device
72. Lord or Lemmon
73. Court
75. Stimulates
76. Picturesque
78. Emptied
79. Quiet period
80. Pierced with a sharp object
81. Book of the Bible
82. Robber
83. Hawaiian porches
86. Affirm
88. Wickerwork palm
89. Play the market
90. Look fixedly
92. Roger or Melba
94. Spill, as water
97. Houston university
98. Specks
99. Ice mass
100. Dr. Jonas —
103. Fold
105. Fate
106. Lay eyes on

Solution is on page 288

Crossword 24

ACROSS

1. Moist or damp
4. Coin deposits
9. See 25-Across
12. Anger
13. Portable boat
14. Commit perjury
15. Aerialist's swing
17. Take for one's own
19. Some
20. Ah me!
21. Tower's top
24. TV commercial
25. Shed tears
28. Reservoir
29. Matured
31. Roman "eleven"
32. Depart quickly
33. Inquiry
34. Nothing
35. Exists
36. Salary boost
37. Marco —
38. Mexican coin
40. Myself
41. Military man to-be
42. Nudge
44. Coop occupant
45. Lamp covering
47. Full length movie
51. Assist
52. Frost products
54. Give utterance to
55. Tiny
56. The ones here
57. Lamb's mother

DOWN

1. Humorist
2. Be mistaken
3. "4 o'clock cup"
4. Play locale
5. Indolent
6. *Un* or *uno*
7. Headed for
8. Zoo favorite
9. Shut
10. Mr. van Winkle
11. Still
16. Public grounds
18. Daybreak
20. Sun-dried brick
21. Airport runway
22. Short rest
23. Country hotel
24. "The people — as one man"
26. Banish
27. Steersman
29. Sooty dirt
30. Plural of "I"
33. Family member
34. Silent greeting
36. Crucifix
37. Breathe hard
39. Kind of shovel
41. Stop
43. Complied with
44. Skirts' edges
45. Logger's tool
46. Hasten
47. Service charge
48. Application
49. Uncooked
50. Look at
53. My goodness!

Crossword 25

ACROSS

1. In a —, bewildered
4. Holler
9. "Wild blue yonder"
12. Nocturnal bird
13. Rough
14. Meat or apple dish
15. Understand clearly
17. — the icebox, has a snack
19. Square of three
20. Young horse
21. Dental problem
23. Competition
26. All —, finished
27. Carved gem
28. That man
29. Bow the head
30. Appointments
31. Heavy weight
32. Approve
33. Metal bolt
34. Arguments
35. Get better
37. More awful
38. Eager
39. Hen's quarters
40. Fatigued
42. Make remarks
45. Wrath
46. Escape from
48. Payable
49. Mike's friend
50. Temptress
51. First number

DOWN

1. In favor of
2. Have debts
3. Looked quickly
4. Like patent leather
5. Misty air condition
6. Crude metal
7. You and me
8. Royal seats
9. Malice
10. Young goat
11. Word of approval
16. Untruthful person
18. Low female voice
20. Heavenly body
21. Giver
22. Call forth
23. Purvey food
24. Exhibits
25. On edge
27. — in, collapsed
30. Separates
31. Submarine missile
33. Wander
34. Den or study
36. Editor's mark
37. Certain chairpersons
39. System of laws
40. Tilt
41. Lyricist Gershwin
42. Pinto or Mustang
43. Convent dweller
44. Golf mound
47. Roman six

Solutions are on page 285

99

26 HARD CROSSWORD

ACROSS

1. Wood for furniture and flooring
6. "Pineapple"
10. Lose color
14. Poe's middle name
15. Iridescent gem
16. Certain change
17. Shore
18. Not in accord: 3 wds.
20. Even one?
21. Decays
23. Weak; diluted
24. Kin of martens
26. Treasury of information
27. "Wind In the Willows" character
28. Coffee, tea, or milk
32. Nursery-rhyme Jack
34. One allergic reaction
35. Look at
36. Bear's retreat
37. More elegant
38. Polaris or Phad
39. Curved path
40. Burn slightly
41. — on, behave childishly
42. Treat gently: 3 wds.
44. Pudding starch
45. Henpecks
46. A famous Jimmy
49. Sanctuary
52. Mailed
53. Object in mind
54. Exaggerate
56. Small egg
58. Snack
59. Dutch cheese
60. Saltpeter
61. "Call of the Wild" vehicle
62. Feet: slang
63. Impertinent

DOWN

1. Large parrot
2. On one's own responsibility
3. What pranksters do: 3 wds.
4. Spanish "the"
5. Beg earnestly
6. They often go with saddles
7. Musical composition
8. Wrestling surface
9. Be dissipated, as a storm: 2 wds.
10. He wrote "Camptown Races"
11. Pot "sweetener"
12. Sambar or axis
13. Catch sight of
19. Bus riders
22. "Long in the tooth"
25. Fly high
26. Landing place on a river
28. Game of chance
29. M. Scott Carpenter, et al.
30. Trappings
31. Weird
32. Pitcher's plate: slang
33. Trim away
34. Intimations
37. Moved nervously
38. Adventure tale
40. Hidden difficulties
41. Boxes
43. Hardened
44. "Centre and sire of of light"
46. Judges
47. Holders for hot plates
48. Corundum
49. Deprives of
50. — eye, spell
51. Celebration
52. Male animal
55. Commotion
57. Passing through

Solution is on page 285

THINKING THINGS THROUGH

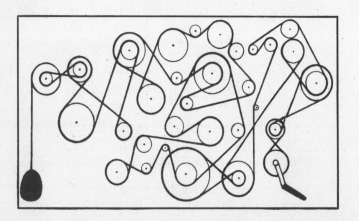

It will take a logical mind to figure this one out. You really do think things through if you can decide whether you must turn the crank at the right (in the picture on the right) in a clockwise or counterclockwise direction in order to raise the weight at the left.

The answer is on page 299.

ACROSS

1. Pack tightly
5. Muffin ingredient
9. Do the marketing
13. Mouth parts
17. Wolf's gait
18. Country road
19. Own
20. Inactive
21. Kiln
22. Created, as a military unit
24. Intend
25. Fate
27. Gratuity
28. Word for a bride
30. Pen and —
31. Bed-linen item
33. Fortune
34. Evil spirit
37. Boot part
38. 1,440 minutes
40. Halfhearted
44. Steady
45. Chairman of the —
47. Golfer's accessory
49. Challenge
50. Gave a meal to
51. Low shoe
52. Decayed
55. 2,000 pounds
56. Testimonial
58. To a businessman, it's money
59. Gains knowledge
61. Spigot
62. Splinters
65. Athlete ineligible for the Olympics
66. Radio interference
69. Paradise
70. Inventor's protections
74. Small bed
75. More recent
77. Trail
78. Cry of discovery
79. Singles
81. Little child
82. Portion
84. Eagerly anticipating
85. Tries
87. Moisten
89. Generation
90. Duke, earl and baron
91. TV writer Serling
93. Floating platforms
95. On a — with, equal to
96. Liberty
100. Behold
101. Flee: 2 wds.
105. Ore deposit
106. Expert; skillful
109. Ripped
110. Dismounted
111. A Great Lake
112. The "A" in B.A. or M.A.
113. Wicked
114. Obtains
115. Becomes firm
116. Mislay
117. Circus "performer"

DOWN

1. Dolt
2. Wander about
3. Zoo attractions
4. Refer to casually
5. Not written on
6. Risqué
7. Aesop fable, "The Grasshopper and the —"
8. Nor
9. Molded
10. Chapeau
11. Above
12. Foot lever
13. Restricted
14. Notion
15. Scheme
16. Dispatched
23. Contend
26. Hotel
29. Speck
31. Soft —; flattery
32. Rag
34. Skillful
35. Always
36. Ponders
37. Large books
39. Up to now
41. Clientele
42. Common metal
43. Lairs
45. Except
46. Chauffeurs
48. Snakelike fish
51. Student
53. Foretoken
54. Intensity, as of color
57. Stout stick
58. Ebb and flow
60. Exist
63. X, Q, J, or Z
64. The "new frontier"
66. Gael
67. Actor, Franchot —
68. Hipster's word for "man"
71. Devoured
72. God of thunder
73. Droops
76. Pull on a rope
77. Porkers
80. Thoroughfares
83. Sideways
84. Ventilates
86. Turf
88. Savors
90. Prospector's item
92. Heads : slang
94. Specialist's charge
95. Throb
96. Old Glory
97. Actor's part
98. Revise a manuscript
99. Female horse
101. Furrows
102. Worked at a loom
103. Opera melody
104. Shout
107. Take a chair
108. To and —

Solution is on page 288

ACROSS

1. Ham's son
5. Food fish
9. Male deer
13. Winter vehicle
17. Kitchen item
19. Advance: 2 wds.
21. Awaken: 2 wds.
23. Propped (up)
25. Unnamed person
26. Material for combs: 2 wds.
28. Stored away
30. Informal dance
31. Trap
33. Escape: slang
34. Stop gradually: 2 wds.
36. Actress Claire
37. Aroma
39. Make amends
40. Political radical
44. Evade
45. Highlander
46. Wearies
48. Unusual
49. Industrial fuel
50. Thick slice
52. Decimal point
53. Commonwealth
54. React to a severe blow on the head: 2 wds.
56. Cringe
57. Actress Miles
59. Hit with little balls of paper
61. Go to bed
62. Disabled
63. Skin blemishes
65. Staggered
66. Kind; sort
67. Got along
68. Nursery visitors
71. Insults
73. Become semisolid
74. Be mad about
76. Marshy inlet
77. Hurls
79. Noisy quarrel
81. Subdue
84. Glacial snow
85. Phrase for a lack of similarity: 3 wds.
89. Sloping passage
91. Chemical suffix
92. Sophia —
93. Schedule
94. Actress Powers
95. "N" in U.S.N.A.
97. Golf gadget
98. Atmosphere
99. Help in crime
100. Infect
101. Wharves
103. Tempo
104. A Gershwin
105. Passed on
107. Wire barrier
108. Nonprofessionals
110. Advanced study group
112. Whine tearfully
113. Hash
114. Comrade
117. Massage
119. Urgently
120. Pull apart
121. Thick soup
122. By word of mouth
124. Strong winds
126. Requirement
127. Storage room
129. Subcontract: 2 wds.
131. Protect
133. Business matters
136. Miss Lollobrigida
137. Cold-shoulder
139. End of the train: 2 wds.
143. Quick peek: hyph. wd. (slang)
144. Disconcerted
145. White-plumed heron
147. Drug container
148. Object of attack
149. Light rain
151. Stupidity
153. Charms
155. 1952 nickname
156. A person
157. Actress Lupino
158. Make lace
159. Supple
163. Skip along quickly
167. Roadway machinery
171. Equality
174. Closest
176. Fur garment
177. Entices
178. Summary
180. River in New York
181. Singer Logan
182. Unchanged: 2 wds.
183. Contributed
184. World War II rifle
187. Longed for
189. Unnerved
191. Vagrant
194. Kinship
196. Short letters
197. Malice
198. Twelve months
202. Support
204. Substantial
206. Man's nickname
207. Racing position
208. Props up
210. Decanters
212. Moved forward
214. Sluggish
215. Fierce fighter
216. Crude material
217. Demons
219. In a dressing gown
221. Cloth pattern
222. Unruly child
223. Freudian term
224. America: abbr.
225. Sources
227. Cause of harm
228. Sea eagle
229. Pen: French
230. Certain moisture
231. Fixed ratio
233. 1861 alliance: 2 wds.
237. Swamps
238. Short, sharp cry
240. Weak—, timid
241. Fabric amounts
242. Salary hike
243. Autumn shade
244. Bother
246. Distinguishing quality
248. Sun to sun
249. Metal bolt
250. Weight of India
251. Cayenne
254. Turn inside out
256. Pry bar
257. Dreaded
260. Rejected: 2 wds. (slang)
262. Habituate
264. Rescues
265. Refuses politely
267. Behaved
268. Geological layer
270. Number suffix
271. Sightseeing trip
272. China —
273. Chemical element
274. Slide sideways
275. One who believes all motives are selfish
277. Die
279. Sudden activity
281. Tease
282. Punctuation mark: abbr.
283. Solid foundation
285. Poisonous snake
286. Real-estate broker
288. Corded fabric
289. Error correction
291. Properly situated: 3 wds.
296. Easy to see
298. Pelted with pebbles
299. All gone!: 2 wds.
300. Feminine name
301. Transfer designs
302. Breakfast order
303. Recent events
304. Hamlet, for one
305. Contradict

DOWN

1. Boy Scout assembly
2. Put into action
3. Cobbler's "job"
4. Hair dye
5. Hoard
6. In this place
7. Likely
8. Singing twosome
9. The man's
10. Fire residue
11. Coarse grass
12. Spring flower
13. Flashy
14. Bank transaction
15. Do wrong
16. Open formally
17. Gloomier
18. Bring back, as to health
19. Tolerate
20. Filch
21. Careless
22. Supplicate
23. Smaller
24. Designated
25. Inoculations
27. Was in session
29. Old-fashioned
32. Becomes drowsy
35. Lozenge
38. Hard to control
40. Mooed
41. — out, supplemented
42. Bridge term
43. Tropical plants
45. Leading; chief
47. Fence steps
49. Retribution: slang
51. Machine part: 2 wds.
53. Freezing rain
55. Noah's refuge
56. Billiard shot
58. Core
60. Journey segment
62. "—, MacDuff": 2 wds.
64. Milt
67. Gem face
68. Cosmetics
69. Fool
70. Jazz dance
72. Work hard
74. Merciful
75. Smother
76. Filled with ennui
77. Leggy bird
78. Sluggard
80. City near Quebec
82. Afternoon performance
83. Green stone
84. Approaches
85. Dynamite inventor
86. Wonderland girl
87. Cheerless
88. Titles
90. Arctic explorer
92. Dessert offering: 2 wds.
96. Hard candy: 2 wds.
100. Doctrine
102. Place
106. Miss Gardner
107. "Sack"
109. New Haven school
111. Wrath
113. Disarranged
114. Review of troops
115. Garment sleeve
116. Released
118. Pay (the cost)
121. Ponder (over)
122. Instrument board
123. Fencer's move
125. Appear to be
128. Catalogue
129. Effervesce
130. Hand (in)
132. Dozes
133. Chicken —, lunch dish: 3 wds.
134. Know beforehand
135. Mist
136. Newspaper
138. Furthermore
140. Actor's aid
141. The best in sports history: hyph. wd.
142. Akin
144. Conclusion
146. Sea movements
148. Sesame
150. Korean soldier
152. Sailor
154. Pen for pigs
160. River in Poland
161. Tall tree: 2 wds.
162. Flat tableland
163. "Lifts"
164. Revealed
165. Actress, Vera-—
166. Motive
167. Stared fiercely
168. Stratagems
169. Parched
170. Ladylike
171. Yearn
172. Whatever happens: 3 wds.
173. Decay
175. Balkan native
179. Nudge
185. Midday
186. Poetic "grief"
188. Citizen of: suffix
189. New frontier
190. Rustic
191. Gossip
192. Wearing boots
193. Python
195. Insubordinate
197. Hard taskmaster: 2 wds.
199. Spike of corn
200. Agrees (to)
201. Chemical substance
202. Scrub clean
203. The masses
205. Prohibit
207. Carpenter's tool
208. Massive
209. Packs away
211. Specter
213. Actor, Reginald —
214. Slaves
215. Actor Cabot
218. Daring feat
220. Group of ten
221. Barrie character
222. Strong rush of air
226. Cubic meter
229. Nosy one
232. Slipped by
234. Breathe hard
235. — pro nobis
236. Roof edges
237. Dealer in mink and skunk
239. Spoke shrilly
243. Kingdom
245. Went first
247. Placed accurately
249. Musical show
250. Dry, as wine
251. Green Bay —, football team
252. Gauge
253. Wine: 2 wds.
255. Corner
256. Vietnamese neighbor
257. Ate heartily
258. Completely
259. Muffles
260. Out-of-date
261. Hang fire
263. Cover completely
264. Rice or wheat
265. Business transaction
266. Slumbered
269. Read superficially: 2 wds.
272. Flash flood
275. Shows concern
276. Church law
278. Compass point
279. Perceive
280. Budged
283. Lingered (over)
284. Alaska mining town
286. Restraint
287. Oriental food
290. Saturate
292. Immediately
293. Bitter vetch
294. Days of yore
295. Extinct bird
297. — Cupid

Solution is on page 291

ACROSS

1. "Staff of life"
6. Petticoat
10. Tablecloth substitutes
14. Wash lightly
15. Saga
16. Pagan god
17. Unusual
18. Tailor's tool
20. Soft drink
21. "Go —, young man"
23. Actor Milland
24. Mike's friend
26. Toward
27. Cure
29. Conducted
30. Vat's contents
31. Inns
34. Part of a cowboy's gear
36. New Year's —
37. Dissolves
39. Parts of chairs
42. Landlord's income
44. Counts calories
46. Clutch
47. Command
49. Birds' homes
51. Sooner than
52. Glossy paint
54. Bellowed
56. In a fury
58. Hydrogen is one
59. Coal containers
60. TV commercial
61. That woman
62. Possessed
63. Stockings
67. Alone
69. Wakens
72. Spring month
73. Maple or oak
74. Margin
75. Alert
77. Stage décor
78. Exploit
79. Entranceways

DOWN

1. Forehead
2. Go by car
3. Terminates
4. Since
5. Lair
6. Pilfer
7. Woman
8. Indisposed
9. Stole a look
10. Fine rain
11. Fuss
12. The present time
13. Roofing material
19. Obliterated
22. Definite article
25. Appends
28. Another 73-Across
29. Endures
30. More expensive
31. Brave man
32. Finished
33. Took care of
34. Hard metal
35. Lower limb
38. Queues
40. Grow weary
41. Hotfooted it
43. "Five and —" store
45. Walk purposefully
48. Violent anger
50. Male heir
53. Damaged
55. Cigarette residue
56. Spars
57. Worship
59. Founded
61. Garden tools
62. Gargantuan
64. Fail to include
65. Hoard
66. Observes
68. Permit
70. Poem of praise
71. Droop
76. Scale note

Solution is on page 285

STARGRAM 2

To solve Stargram, rearrange all the letters of each line below to form common English words which are made up of two shorter words (for example, "daybreak" or "cutaway"). Next, rearrange the letters marked with a star to spell out the Mystery Name. **The answer is on page 299.**

1. T U G H O N S   _ _ _ _ _ _ _
                       *

2. E E V I H E B   _ _ _ _ _ _ _
                         *

3. H O R G N O F   _ _ _ _ _ _ _
                         *

4. F A W L Y A H   _ _ _ _ _ _ _
                                 *

5. K I P S I N G   _ _ _ _ _ _ _
                       *

6. F O N D F E S   _ _ _ _ _ /_ _ _ _
                         *

7. O L L P H E B   _ _ _ _ _ _ _
                       *   *

Mystery Name   _ _ _ _   _ _ _ __
(Recording Artist)

ACROSS

1. Close-fitting
6. Trade
10. Arizona city near Phoenix
14. Brass is one
15. Type size 1/6" high
16. Wicked
17. Builder's needs
19. Semester
20. Employ
21. Literary drudge
22. Views
24. Random amount
25. Diversion
26. First-rate
29. Chinese-restaurant dish: 2 wds.
32. Deadly pale
33. "Land of hope and —"
34. Parseghian, of football
35. Not active, as business
36. Gibe
37. Be radiant
38. Understanding
39. Salt solution
40. Throb
41. Shoplifter's act
43. Laughed like a donkey
44. Low spirits
45. Swarm
46. On a ship
48. Stitched line
49. Wrath
52. Weaver's frame
53. Receptive to new ideas: hyph. wd.
56. Female voice
57. Impulse
58. Dinner course
59. Ordinal number suffixes
60. Spree: slang
61. Abrasive substance

DOWN

1. Forbidden: var. sp.
2. Woes
3. Mucilage
4. Garden tool
5. Tropical storm
6. One "ingredient" of little girls
7. Flirt with the eye
8. Perform
9. Traveler's document
10. Measuring instruments
11. Sooner or later
12. Paddock papa
13. Charity
18. Certain passageway
23. Facsimile
24. Hearty dish
25. Glistened
26. Chores
27. Small island
28. Certain small structure: 2 wds.
29. Adhered (to)
30. Worn away
31. Steered wildly
33. Advances
36. Tested: 2 wds.
37. WW II battle-field in the Pacific
39. Grow hazy
40. Basis for an argument
42. Los —, where the atom bomb was developed
43. Shine
45. Belief
46. Wings
47. Lock part
48. Utah state flower
49. Unemployed
50. Raise, as children
51. Whirlpool
54. Golf teacher
55. Viet —

Solution is on page 285

WORD HUNT

Using the letters in the diagram at the right, see how many kitchen items or the names of kitchen equipment you can find. Start anywhere and move in any direction, but do not skip over a letter. You may go back to a letter and use it more than once in the same word. Can you top our culinary expert's list of 42 items, which is on page 299?

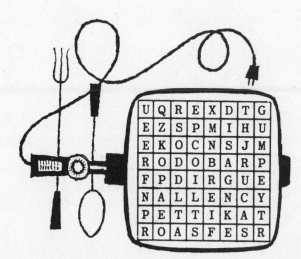

HIDDEN FABRICS

In each sentence below the name of a type of fabric appears, but it is hidden within the words of the sentence. For example, in sentence number 1, the name is SATIN (hidden in "sat in"). Can you find the other twelve fabrics?

Answers are on page 299.

1. Elyse could hardly see the performance on stage because she sat in the third balcony.

2. When you're hungry, the lunch line never seems to move.

3. Edging ham with pineapple and cherries enhances its appetite appeal.

4. If the checkout lines at my supermarket were any longer, I could cook a week's dinners in the time it would take to buy them.

5. Customs procedure presents no problems to a travel veteran.

6. Even though we have a small garden I manage to grow plenty of salad vegetables.

7. Herman usually eats too much if fondue is on the menu.

8. Our baseball coach used to slam us line drives to sharpen our reflexes.

9. Kathy always asks for two olives in her martini.

10. According to Erica, licorice is less fattening than chocolate.

11. Mothers tend to nag about leaving crayons on the floor.

12. An infected tonsil kept Mindy out of school for a week.

13. If I sleep on that old cot tonight I'll have a back ache tomorrow.

CAN YOU SPOT THE ODD ONES?

Only 2 of the keys pictured below do NOT have exact twins. All but 2 of the ballet dancers have a mate who is wearing the same dress. Can you spot the odd ones in each picture?

Answers are on page 299.

1.

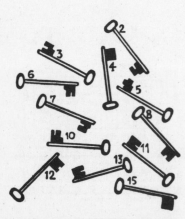

2.

CROSS PATHS

Copyright 1989 by Bantam Doubleday Dell Publishing Group, Inc.

Start at the box indicated by the arrow. There are four circles in that box; that tells you that you must move through four boxes; you may move through those four boxes either across or up, but not diagonally. Any move may be in the same direction as your previous move, or you may change direction when you start a move, but you may move in *only one direction per move*. Each time you land in a box, your next move must be through however many boxes are indicated by the number of circles shown in the box you land in. You always have the choice of moving up or down, or left or right, as long as there are enough boxes in the diagram to move the indicated number of boxes. You may cross your own path, but do not retrace it. Start at the arrow and see if you can get to the box marked F for Finish in less than 4 minutes.

Solution is on page 311.

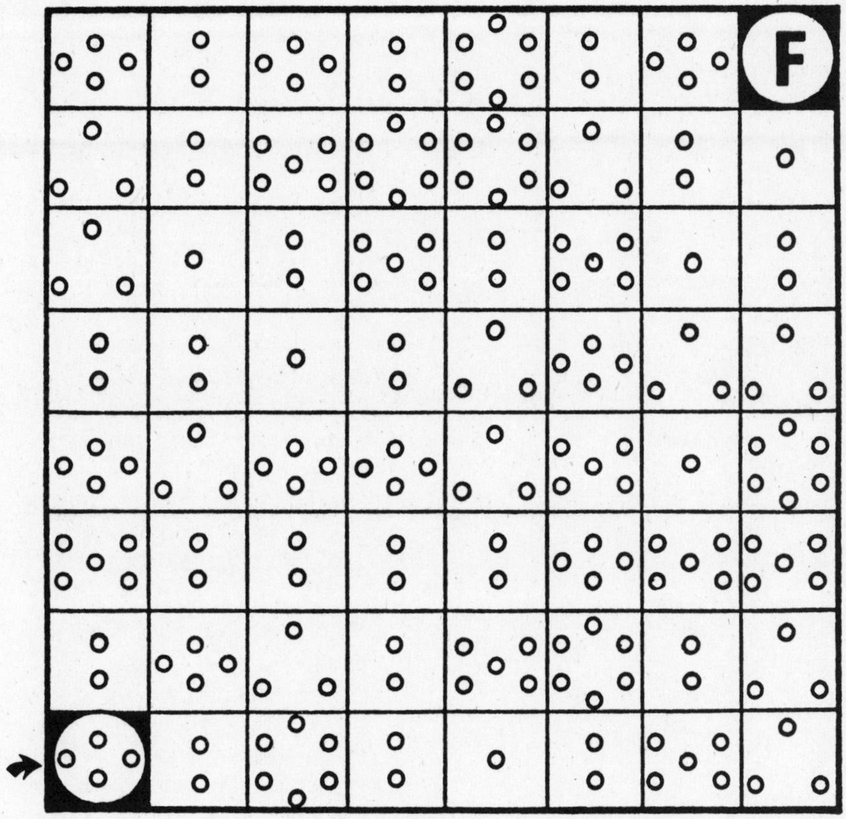

SWITCH FIVE

Without rearranging the order of the letters, you are to change every letter, one step at a time, so that your five steps will have changed every letter in the word. Each change you make must result in a real word, and once you have changed a letter YOU MAY NOT CHANGE THAT LETTER AGAIN. Your words should be everyday words; use no proper names, foreign or poetic words, contractions, or archaic words. You may change the letters in any order, and you may change to a letter which appears in the original word.

Your solutions may differ from ours shown on page 299.

1. THROW

2. CHORD

FIGURE LOGIC 1

by L.G. Horsefield

Solve Figure Logic by completing some simple arithmetic problems, which will enable you to move from clue to clue through the puzzle.

TO PROCEED: Look at the diagram at the bottom of the page and note that the number "19," answering clue 17-Across has been entered as a starting point. Your next step might be to 2-Down, which reads "Twice 17-Across," or to another clue that mentions 17-Across. Continue solving by going from clue to clue as needed.

You might discover that, at times, you will not be able to complete an entire number at first; but you may be able, by logic, to determine what one or more of the digits must be. If you enter those digits into the diagram, they may help you solve other clues, and you can eventually return to the unfinished numbers and finally complete them.

CLUES ACROSS

1. 7-Down minus 17-Across
4. Consecutive digits in order
7. 5-Down multiplied by 17-Across
8. Seven times 11-Across
10. Last two digits of 4-Across
11. Three times 1-Across
13. 10-Across plus 17-Across
14. Digits of 4-Down in a different order
16. Its digits total twenty-five
17. One-third of 5-Down
18. One hundred less than 1-Across
19. 10-Across plus 13-Across
22. One hundred more than 17-Across
25. One-quarter of 21-Down
26. Four times 10-Across
28. One-third of 13-Across
29. Five times 33-Across
31. 16-Across plus 23-Down
33. Four times 7-Down
34. Three more than twice 4-Across

CLUES DOWN

1. Seven times 7-Down
2. Twice 17-Across
3. Same digit three times
4. Thirteen times 18-Across
5. One-eighth of 4-Across
6. Seven times 16-Across
7. One-third of 4-Across
9. Three times 22-Across
12. 13-Across plus 17-Across
15. Digits of 22-Across reversed
16. One-third of 8-Across
19. 5-Down plus 10-Across
20. 1-Down plus 31-Across
21. Four less than 10-Across
23. Five times 14-Across
24. Eight times 22-Across
26. 7-Down plus 10-Across
27. 18-Across multiplied by 25-Across
30. 17-Across plus 32-Down
32. 8-Across divided by 1-Across

Solution is on page 294.

CROSS SUMS

NUMBER 2

In each of these Cross Sums, we have not filled in a digit combination. Instead, we have shaded one area in the diagram. If you need help starting the puzzle, the digit combination to go into that area is listed on page 320.

Copyright 1989 by Bantam Doubleday Dell Publishing Group, Inc.

NUMBER 3

Solutions are on page 301

KEY POINTS 1

There are 7 key letters listed below. Add one of these key letters to each word below (using a *different* key letter for each word) and then rearrange (anagram) the letters to form a new word. HANDICAP: TRY TO REARRANGE THE LETTERS IN SUCH A WAY THAT THE KEY LETTER YOU HAVE ADDED APPEARS AS THE FOURTH LETTER IN EACH OF THE NEW WORDS. Plurals, words beginning with a capital letter, and foreign words are not allowed. Place the new words on the dashes provided (one letter per dash). When all the new words are in place, count 1 point for each letter in the new words and 5 points for each key letter that appears as the fourth letter in the new words.

Our perfect score of 77 points is on page 309.

Average score: 55 points   **Superior score: 66 points**

```
┌─────────────────┐
│  KEY LETTERS    │
│  A E H K N O T  │
└─────────────────┘
         ↓
```

FROST   1. _ _ _ _ _ _

LAST   2. _ _ _ _ _

UNREAL   3. _ _ _ _ _ _ _

MEANT   4. _ _ _ _ _ _

PLENTY   5. _ _ _ _ _ _ _

WALL   6. _ _ _ _ _

TRACE   7. _ _ _ _ _ _

SEQUENTIAL MAZE

finish

The key to solving this maze is finding the sequence, that is, the numerical progression, which will enable you to go from the 0 at START to the 50 at FINISH following only the numbers in the sequence. You may not cross or retrace your path, and you may not skip over any number.

Solution is on page 311.

start

PATCH QUOTE

Enter the 22 words from the list below **HORIZONTALLY** into the diagram so that every box is filled. The letters already in the diagram are letters in most of the words to be entered. (Two of the shorter words in the list have no letters already entered, but you will be able to enter them as you solve.) Some words will continue from one line to the next, and since no divisions between words have been given, it's a good idea to place a heavy dot before and after a word as you enter it into the diagram (· WORD ·), and cross it off the list. You will use all of the words listed. When you have completed the diagram, you will find a quotation by Voltaire reading from left to right beginning at the top. Solution is on page 299.

AND	OF
ARE	PHILOSOPHY
DISCOVERY	PRACTICE
GOOD	THAT
IMPORTANT	THE
IS	THE
IS	THE
MOST	TRUE
OBJECTS	TWO
OF	WHAT
OF	WHICH

T			I		O			Y
	F			T	I			U
		D		E	P		C	
			F	T		T	W	
			G	O		A	R	
		W		O	S		M	
	T			O	B			T
O			I		S			Y

QUOTATION PUZZLES 2

Copyright 1989 by Bantam Doubleday Dell Publishing Group, Inc.

In each puzzle below, you are to fit the letters in each column into the boxes directly above them. The letters may or may not go into the boxes in the same order in which they are given. It is up to you to decide which letter goes into which box above it. Once a letter is used, cross it off the bottom half of the diagram and do not use it again. A black square indicates the end of a word. When the diagrams have been filled in, you will be able to find the completed quotations by reading across the boxes. Solutions are on page 299.

1.

O	O	B	O	H	U	R	A	I	A	H	D	N	C	V	I	R	O	I
O	I	U	W	R	S	L	E	C	N	E	E	N	E	A	N	S	T	F
L	N	P	R	P	E	Y		R	T	N	A	U	Y		E	I		N
L			E	I	T	H				A		R			T	A		N

2.

H	H	Y	R	T	L	M	S	L	I	V	W	N	Y	E	D	I	O	H	K	A
H	S	E	I	E	E	E	I	O	L	E	E	E	T	E	W	W	W	E	I	T
T	E	W	S	E	C	W	D	S	N	T	Y	A	V	O	R		T	R		C
		N		L				I		A	N		T				B	H		

3.

C	V	T	R	S	R	F	M	E	M	T	G	E	D	S	T	N	S	A
U	I	E	Y	F	C	G	E	I	A	A	I	W	A	A	I	C	N
E	E	N		Y	O	O	R	N	A	E	A	A	V	A	U	D	E
I	D					I			C		H	N				O	

4.

S	V	T	S	W	S	T	E	E	R	D	M	M	C	N	R	S	O	V	H	N	N
I	O	I	H	O	E	E	D	N	T	O	R	S	I	H	O	O	E	U	U	E	T
H	V	W	E	A	F	D	E	F		O	B		C	U	E	E		W	R	P	L
		E			T			M			O		T	L		E			E		

5.

N	E	E	A	E	E	I	T	O	N	N	L	L	O	O	H	O	R	O	S	S
O	H	U	T	G	R	F	T	N	M	A	L	C	A	T	N	E	S	N	M	A
B	G	T	N	O	R		R	I	A	N	A	N	N	M	E	S	N	S	L	E
T	M	I		G			G	H	A	A	S		O	T	P		E			E

6.

R	C	L	M	O	S	A	A	P	E	I	I	I	D	H	E	B	T	O	B
E	D	E	B	A	W	R	A	N	I	X	D	D	A	N	A	I	C	T	A
N	O	O	L	Y	G		T	H	T	M	T		O	L	A	I	I		U
F	S		Y	E			I		A	N	E			G			N		
							E												

LETTER LINK 2

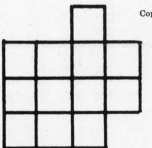

A E F H I L N O R S T W

See if you can place the letters above into the diagram in such a way that by moving horizontally, vertically, and/or diagonally from square to square (without skipping over any squares) the following sentence can be spelled out:

THE REASON OF THE LAW IS THE LAW.

NOTE: Put each letter into the diagram only once, even though you will use some letters more than once in spelling out the sentence.

Our solution, which may not agree with yours, is on page 319.

LOGIC PROBLEM 2

JUNIOR BASEBALL TRYOUTS

by Randall L. Whipkey

At the Junior Baseball League's tryouts, Nabors and four friends tried out for selection by the league's five teams, one of which is the Lions. Each boy tried out for a different position, and each was selected to play for a different team. From the clues below, can you determine each boy's full name and position and the team for which he now plays?

> NOTE: The battery consists of the pitcher and catcher; the infielders are the first baseman and the shortstop.

1. Andy and the Mason boy tried out as infielders; neither was chosen by the Leopards.
2. Andy wasn't picked by the Jaguars, and Chad wasn't picked by the Leopards.
3. The Parks boy, who wasn't picked by the Leopards, tried out for neither first base nor the outfield.
4. The two who tried out for the battery are Bobby and the one selected by the Cougars, who isn't the Parks boy.
5. The Ogden boy wasn't taken by the Panthers.
6. Donny, whose last name isn't Land, wasn't picked by the Cougars.
7. Neither the pitcher nor the shortstop is Chad, nor is the last name of either boy Parks.
8. The Ogden boy, whose first name isn't Eddie, did not try out for outfielder.
9. The catcher wasn't chosen by the Panthers.

Solution is on page 302.

If you care to use the chart below in solving this problem, you do so by entering all information obtained from the clues using, perhaps, an X to indicate a definite "no" and a dot to show a definite "yes." Remember: Once you enter a definite "yes" (dot), place a "no" (X) in all the rest of the boxes in each row and column that contains the dot.

	Land	Mason	Nabors	Ogden	Parks	1st base	short-stop	pitcher	catcher	out-fielder	Coug.	Jag.	Leop.	Lio.	Pan.
Andy															
Bobby															
Chad															
Donny															
Eddie															
Cougars										
Jaguars										
Leopards										
Lions										
Panthers										
1st base					
shortstop					
pitcher					
catcher					
outfielder					

LOGIC PROBLEM 3

SUPER SEVEN

by Randall L. Whipkey

One of the features on WCOZ radio is the "Super Seven Show," when the top seven hit records in the Cozy Valley listening area are played in order from seven up to one. This week seven different rock groups, each recording for a different label, are in the Super Seven. From the following clues, can you determine which group has which number record and the record company for which the group records?

1. The Countto Five's record is one position below the one on Nadir Records but one position above the one by the Gotta Good Beats.

2. The record by the Sparkle Band is below the one on the Sol label on the charts but above the Smyth Brothers' hit.

3. The record on the Trolley label ranks one position above the recording on Jemm Records, which is above the Diamond Needles' hit.

4. These three records occupy consecutive positions, from top to bottom, on the Super Seven: the FooManChoose recording, the record produced by Avocado Records, and the hit by the Group of Wrath.

5. The Smythe Brothers' hit, which is not on the Speck label and is not number four on the list, is charted above the record on the Heart label.

Solution is on page 303.

	Avocado	Heart	Jemm	Nadir	Sol	Speck	Trolley	1	2	3	4	5	6	7
Countto Five														
Diamond Needles														
FooMan Choose														
Gotta Good Beats														
Group of Wrath														
Smythe Bros.														
Sparkle Band														
1							
2							
3							
4							
5							
6							
7							

CIRCLE BACK PUZZLE

Copyright 1989 by Bantam Doubleday Dell Publishing Group, Inc.

Starting with the given letter "H," and following the numbers in order, fill into the wheel diagram the words defined below. Each word overlaps the next one by one or more letters, and the last word will end with the same "H" you started with. Solution is on page 294.

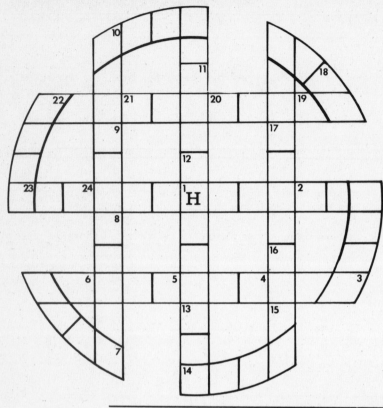

1. "Home" for an airplane
2. Act of reaching a destination
3. Small passage between buildings
4. Watched sharply
5. Bongo, for one
6. Person who has not attained majority
7. Like a circle
8. Entranceway
9. Reddish-brown coating on iron
10. Shake; shiver
11. Subtraction word
12. Having an attractive figure
13. Caustic soap ingredient
14. Bird of prey
15. One of Santa's helpers
16. Hazy; misty
17. Every twelve months
18. Affirmative answer
19. Ooze
20. Remove the skin from
21. Force that brings good fortune
22. Child's toy flown in the air
23. Terminate
24. What bakers knead

WORD INSERT

Copyright 1989 by Bantam Doubleday Dell Publishing Group, Inc.

For each word in Column A, select from Column B the word which, when inserted intact between two of the letters of the Column A word, will form a new, longer word. The words in Column B are in no particular order. Use each word one time only. For example, if you saw the word BEING in Column A and the word AM in Column B, you could insert AM into BEING to form the new, longer word BEAMING (BE-AM-ING). Solve in this manner until you have all ten longer words.

Answers are on page 299.

COLUMN A	COLUMN B
1. SING	ALL
2. TUNE	US
3. POLE	TRAIN
4. BET	ARK
5. MEN	IT
6. HEED	WIN
7. DOES	EIGHT
8. GROG	RIB
9. MET	AT
10. HEN	AID

_____

_____

_____

_____

_____

_____

_____

_____

_____

_____

SHAKESPEARE OR THE BIBLE?

Though you might think that you could tell very easily whether a quote came from the Bible or from one of Shakespeare's plays, it's often not so simple. Remember that the King James Version of the Bible, which we have used for this quiz, was translated in 1611, about the time that Shakespeare was writing his plays. The 10 quotes below are either from the Bible or Shakespeare; your task is to try to figure out which is from where.

Answers are on page 299.

1. The words of his mouth were smoother than butter, but war was in his heart.

2. Sweets to the sweet.

3. The time is out of joint.

4. If a house be divided against itself, that house cannot stand.

5. Your sin will find you out.

6. Take thine ease, eat, drink and be merry.

7. He hath eaten me out of house and home.

8. Men's evil manners live in brass; their virtues we write in water.

9. We see through a glass darkly.

10. Many waters cannot quench love, neither can the floods drown it.

HOURGLASS WORD PUZZLE

The lower half of this hourglass is waiting for the letters from the upper half to drop down and form new words. Find these words by reading the definitions below and taking the needed letters from the top of the hourglass. However, each time you remove a letter or letters from words in the top section, complete words must be left behind. For example, if you need an "S" and there are two choices, such as the "S" in SONG and the "S" in SCARED, you must take it from SCARED so that the full word CARED is left (if you took the "S" from Song you would then have ONG, and that is not a complete word). You must work the definitions in order, otherwise you will not be able to follow this rule. You may have to rearrange the order of some letters as you take them from a word.   Solution is on page 302.

Definitions

1. Finale

2. Strong wind

3. — down, reduces speed

4. Shipping container

5. — aid, sound amplifier

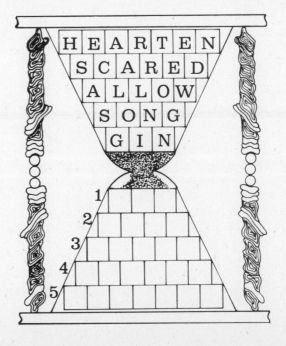

FIGGERITS 3

Your finished Figgerit will yield a little truism written onto the SOLUTION dashes. Step 1: Fill in as many words in the WORDS column as you can, using the DEFINITIONS. Step 2: Transfer these letters to the SOLUTION according to matching numbers. Step 3: If you find, for example, that the number 6 stands for "r" in one word, write "r" above 6 in all places in that Figgerit. But a letter is allowed to have more than one number, so number 9 might also stand for "r" and you'd write "r" above all the 9's too. Step 4: Work back from SOLUTION to WORDS column with any possible clues. T-E is probably THE, so try out that H in the WORDS column. Each Figgerit has a different pattern of number/letter substitutions. Word lists are on page 304.   Solutions are on page 302.

---

1.   Definitions   Words

Vow; give one's word ...... ___ ___ ___ ___ ___ ___ ___
                          18 26 9 35 31 14 27

Having short hours, as a .... ___ ___ ___ ___ ___ ___ ___ ___
 job: hyph. wd.   18 1 10 17 29 13 35 27

Flowering tree .... ___ ___ ___ ___ ___ ___ ___
                          11 6 25 5 16 20 33

Symptom of a head cold .... ___ ___ ___ ___ ___ ___ ___ ___
                          12 15 31 22 24 3 27 32

Frosty of song, for one .... ___ ___ ___ ___ ___ ___ ___
                          14 15 21 8 35 28 15

—, march!, military .... ___ ___ ___ ___ ___ ___ ___
 command   2 23 10 30 1 19 33

Walking: 2 wds. .... ___ ___ ___ ___ ___ ___
                          4 15 7 20 34 17

Solution:

1		2	3	4	5		6	7		8	9	10	11	12

13	14		15	16	17		18	19	20	21	22

23	24		25	26	27	28	29		30	31	32	33	34	35

---

2.   Definitions   Words

Los —, California .... ___ ___ ___ ___ ___ ___ ___
                          8 29 1 17 23 32 34

Royal color .... ___ ___ ___ ___ ___ ___
                          14 35 3 30 24 13

Mommas and poppas .... ___ ___ ___ ___ ___ ___ ___
                          30 28 16 37 6 11 38

"Dial M for —," .... ___ ___ ___ ___ ___ ___
 Hitchcock thriller   27 15 9 4 37 36

Blinks, as lights .... ___ ___ ___ ___ ___ ___ ___
                          21 31 33 7 25 13 18

Washington city .... ___ ___ ___ ___ ___ ___ ___
                          34 5 22 11 19 31 10

Leave hurriedly: 2 wds. .... ___ ___ ___ ___ ___ ___ ___
                          4 2 38 12 20 26 19

Solution:

1	2	3	4	5	6	7		8	9	10		11	12	13

14	15	16	17	18	19		20	21		22	23	24

25	26	27	28	29		30	31	32	33	34	35	36	37	38

---

3.   Definitions   Words

They masquerade in .... ___ ___ ___ ___ ___ ___
 "sheeps' clothing"   17 28 34 4 11 27

Children's game .... ___ ___ ___ ___ ___ ___ ___
                          30 33 18 7 24 22 8

"Horse opera" .... ___ ___ ___ ___ ___ ___ ___
                          26 14 8 20 22 32 16

Painting of a person ...... ___ ___ ___ ___ ___ ___ ___ ___
                          1 3 2 12 10 25 35 21

Military garb .... ___ ___ ___ ___ ___ ___ ___ ___
                          15 16 19 29 31 6 30 8

He owns the presses, ... ___ ___ ___ ___ ___ ___ ___
 in publishing   1 2 19 23 36 5 32

In a sharp, grating manner . ___ ___ ___ ___ ___ ___ ___
                          13 9 18 27 13 34 37

Solution:

1	2	3	4	5	6	7	8		9	10	11		12	13	14

15	16	17	18	19	20	21	22	23		24	25	26	27

28	29		30	31	32	33	34	35	36	37

---

4.   Definitions   Words

Baby minder .... ___ ___ ___ ___ ___ ___
                          28 7 1 37 17 34

Presidential surname ...... ___ ___ ___ ___ ___ ___ ___
                          5 2 32 13 19 30 25

Bye-bye, in Britain .... ___ ___ ___ ___ ___ ___ ___
                          8 16 26 17 34 10 21

Songwriter, Stephen .... ___ ___ ___ ___ ___ ___
 Collins —   20 6 19 15 35 22

Prepares, as an athlete ..... ___ ___ ___ ___ ___ ___
                          23 3 12 27 11 31

Oven pan .... ___ ___ ___ ___ ___ ___ ___
                          18 21 33 28 29 4 22

Grave; not kidding .... ___ ___ ___ ___ ___ ___ ___
                          19 9 3 36 14 24 31

Solution:

1	2		3	4	5	6	7	8	9		10	11

12	13	14	15	16	17	18	19		20	21	22	23	24	25	26

27	28		29	30		31	32	33	34	35		36	37

5. Definitions — Words

Eternally .... —24 —5 —8 —9 —39 —20 —15

Artist who painted his mother ...... —34 —30 —35 —13 —14 —19 —40 —27

Lacking .... —3 —35 —14 —1 —7 —17 —29

Drops (the ball), in football .... —6 —23 —32 —18 —19 —37 —10

Plant (an area) again with trees ..... —8 —11 —25 —16 —41 —31 —10 —33

Makes safe .... —21 —12 —36 —17 —15 —26 —28

". . . to the — of Tripoli" ... —22 —4 —38 —8 —2 —28

Solution:

—1 —2   —3 —4 —5   —6 —7 —8 —9 —10 —11 —12 —13

—14 —15 —16 —17 —18 —19 —20 —21   —22 —23 —24 —25 —26 —27 —28

—29 —30 —31 —32   —33 —34 —35 —36 —37   —38 —39 —40 —41

6. Definitions — Words

Dressy clothes: 2 wds. (slang) .... —8 —28 —5 —13 —25 —18 —33 —30

Anteroom of a theater or hotel .... —28 —29 —17 —26 —1

Very small person .... —22 —34 —19 —33 —9 —7

Gene —, one of the singing cowboys ..... —16 —3 —20 —11 —27

What "truth is stranger than" .... —15 —12 —4 —35 —31 —2 —32

Job opportunity .... —14 —23 —24 —6 —34 —32 —8

Poke fun at .... —10 —21 —5 —30 —24

Solution:

—1 —2 —3   —4 —5 —6 —7   —8 —9 —10   —11 —12 —13

—14 —15   —16   —17 —18 —19   —20 —21 —22 —23 —24 —25

—26 —27   —28 —29 —30 —31 —32 —33   —34 —35

7. Definitions — Words

Irritable .... —23 —28 —15 —34 —2 —22

U.S. money unit .... —31 —24 —17 —21 —11 —13

— Pitcher, Revolutionary War heroine .. —30 —32 —4 —21 —18

El —, place of great riches .. —8 —19 —13 —11 —31 —24

Make wet, as a postage stamp .... —25 —29 —33 —1 —6 —14 —12

Miss Kennedy .... —10 —15 —28 —9 —16 —3 —20 —26

Links game .... —35 —7 —5 —27

Solution:

—1 —2 —3 —4 —5   —6 —7   —8 —9   —10 —11 —12

—13 —14 —15 —16 —17 —18   —19 —20 —21 —22   —23 —24 —25 —26

—27 —28 —29 —30   —31 —32 —33 —34 —35

8. Definitions — Words

New York baseball player .. —3 —14 —18 —29 —33 —20

Hand digits .... —34 —1 —21 —19 —27 —31 —11

Counted (on) .... —30 —28 —21 —15 —33 —10

Like ground talcum .... —12 —4 —6 —10 —20 —31 —24

In a courteous manner ..... —26 —7 —9 —32 —22 —13 —23 —36

Verb tense for tomorrow ... —2 —8 —22 —17 —31 —13

Pass one's lips inadvertently: 2 wds. —25 —35 —32 —16 —7 —5 —22

Solution:

—1 —2   —3 —4 —5   —6 —7 —8 —9 —10

—11 —12 —13 —14 —15   —16 —17 —18 —19 —20 —21 —22 —23 —24

—25 —26 —27 —28 —29   —30 —31 —32 —33 —34 —35 —36

WHAT'S ZAT?

Don't know what a ZAT is? You can still come up with the right answers here because your job is to find out what a ZAT is. Of course, a ZAT is something different in each case below. First study the boxes marked ZAT and NON-ZAT—each of the figures in the ZAT box IS a ZAT; each of the figures in the NONZAT box is NOT a ZAT. (Assume that all figures are correctly and proportionally drawn. It is the elements involved that count, not how they are drawn.) Then look at the five choices beneath those boxes and see if you can tell which one is a ZAT (only ONE will be a true ZAT). Now comes the hard part—can you put into words WHY the one you have chosen is a ZAT? Most people can understand an abstract concept (which each of these is an example of), but have great difficulty putting that concept into words. Score 10 points for each ZAT correctly identified, and 10 points for each correct explanation (your explanations don't have to be in the exact words we use). Any score above 80 is excellent.

Answers and explanations are on page 302.

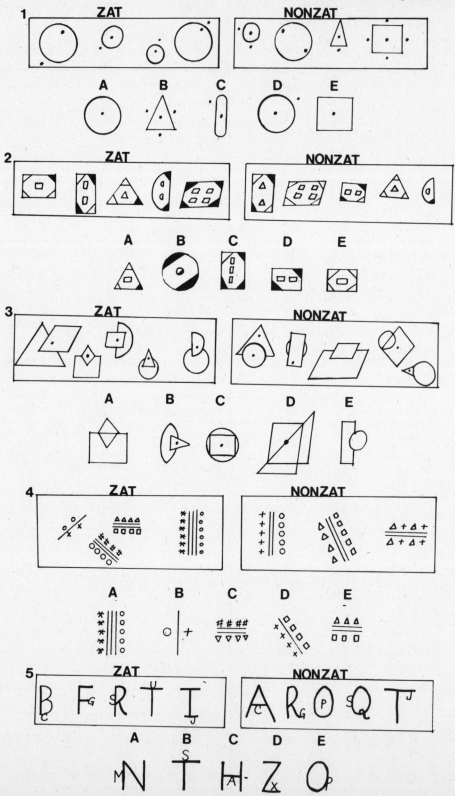

BOWL-A-SCORE CHALLENGER 2

Copyright 1989 by Bantam Doubleday Dell Publishing Group, Inc.

Solve this Bowl-A-Score Challenger as you did the one on page 84. This time, though, your "strike" words will be 10-letter words instead of 9-letter words. The same rules apply, however: The starting letter for each "strike" word is given; you form your two-word "spares" the same way, by rearranging the scrambled letters into two words, with no letters left over. You may not simply split the "strike" word into two parts and use both exactly as they appear in the "strike" word for your "spare"; for example, FORE and CASTER would not qualify for the "strike" word FORECASTER.

Scoring: Score 20 points for each "strike" and 10 points for each two-word "spare." Perfect score is 300.

WARNING: This game is really for experts! Only the most expert word bowlers will score a perfect 300. HINT: If the "strike" word stumps you, work on the spare words; sometimes this helps with the "strike" word. Our words are on page 302.

1. N S U C   **Spare**
   I E I   _____
   R Y   _____
   T
   Strike I _____

2. S C D S   **Spare**
   A N L   _____
   I E   _____
   P
   Strike P _____

3. N R I A   **Spare**
   I Y O   _____
   L L   _____
   G
   Strike O _____

4. N T V W   **Spare**
   G H L   _____
   E E   _____
   A
   Strike W _____

5. R R T U   **Spare**
   L M N   _____
   A I   _____
   A
   Strike I _____

6. N O S U   **Spare**
   E I M   _____
   C D   _____
   A
   Strike M _____

7. N O R R   **Spare**
   H I L   _____
   C E   _____
   C
   Strike C _____

8. O P R T   **Spare**
   H I M   _____
   C E   _____
   A
   Strike M _____

9. M N S T   **Spare**
   H H I   _____
   E E   _____
   A
   Strike H _____

10. R T T T   **Spare**
   I P R   _____
   E I   _____
   A
   Strike T _____

If you need help starting this puzzle, turn to page 320 and you will find listed the word to be entered into the outlined area.

3 Letters
Koa (*trees*)
Poi
USA

4 Letters
Hilo (*city*)
Hula
Leis
Luau (*feast*)
Oahu
Shop
Tapa (*cloth*)

5 Letters
Akaka (*Falls*)
Aloha
Fleet

Kauai*
Mango
Palms
Sugar
Vines
Waves

6 Letters
Banana
Divers
Ginger (*blossoms*)
Hawaii
Native
Niihau
Papaya

7 Letters
Banyans

Craters
Islands
Kilauea
Molokai
Pacific

8 Letters
Hibiscus
Honolulu
Mauna Kea
Mauna Loa
Ti leaves
Ukuleles

9 Letters
Lava rocks
Taro patch
Volcanoes

10 Letters
Breadfruit (*tree*)
Coral reefs
Outriggers
Pineapples
Surfboards

11 Letters
Archipelago
Diamond Head (*volcanic crater*)
Fern forests
Flower carts
Grass shacks
Pearl Harbor
Sightseeing

12 Letters
Barking Sands (*beach*)
Coffee bushes
Fishing coves
Waikiki Beach

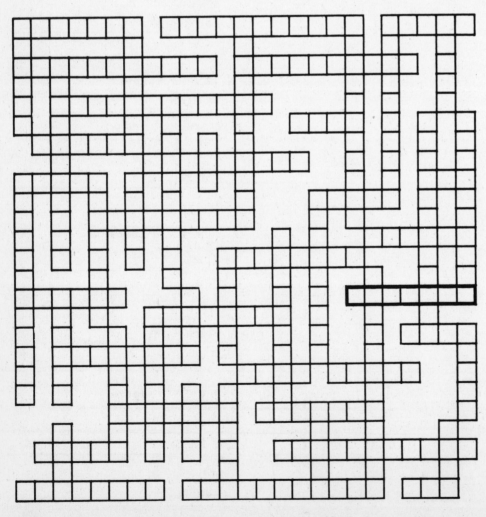

Solution is on page 293

KROSS NUMBER

Solve this like a regular Kriss Kross, putting numbers instead of words into the diagram. If you want help getting started, the number that goes into the heavily outlined area is listed on page 320.

3 Digits

018
078
237
384
385
576
607
705
891
908
999

4 Digits

0378
1861
2341
2486

3652
3747
4071
4361
4796
5676
6290
7177
7554
7987
8178
8325
8796
9034
9174
9777
9869

5 Digits

05597

09728
24786
27343
32567
37801
47682
48375
74368
79706
89136
90907
91036
93250
97836

6 Digits

098634
346986
687416

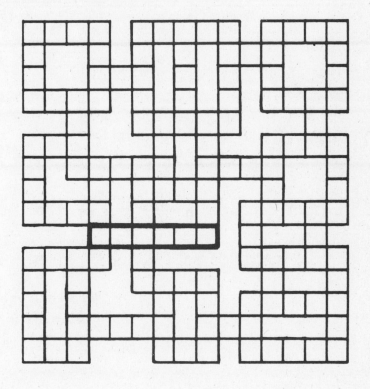

EASY DOES IT

If you need help starting this puzzle, turn to page 320 and you will find listed the word to be entered into the outlined area.

4 Letters

Abet
Aide
Aver
Bone
Bore
Comb
Come
Ease
Else
Name
Noon
Note
Numb

Rent
Roan
Sent

5 Letters

Alone
Amber
Baron
Canon
Least
Needs
Robot
Scene
Shrub

Strum
Strut
Tabor
Tenon

6 Letters

Absorb
Banner
Barren
Cannon
Cannot
Carrot
Ermine
Runner
Treats

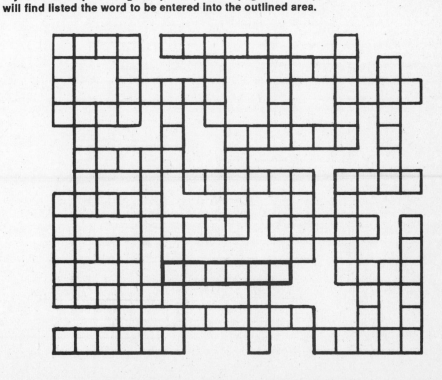

Solutions are on page 294

KRISS KROSS 9

The words for this Kriss Kross can all be found in the rows of letters below. They always overlap each other by one or more letters, and they will be found by reading from left to right without skipping over or rearranging any of the letters. Some of the overlapping letters appear in several words. For example, the "N" in SHIN appears in 1 additional word. Only everyday words are used, and no abbreviations, proper names, slang, or foreign words are allowed. However, present-tense verbs may end in "s." When you have written all the words on the dashes below, solve the Kriss Kross as usual putting those words in their proper places in the diagram. NOTE: The words WILL NOT appear in alphabetical order, as in a usual Kriss Kross listing.

4-letter words:

S H I N D I A L T O I L Y O U R G E A R L I F E Y E D (12 words)

5-letter words:

F R O S T A K E N T E R S E R V E R S E V E R Y O D E L (10 words)

6-letter words:

S A C R E D I T O R R I D D L E A V E N G E (7 words)

7-letter words:

E N T R U S T E E P L E A S E S S I O N E S E L F I S H I N G L E (9 words)

Word List is on page 302

Solution is on page 294

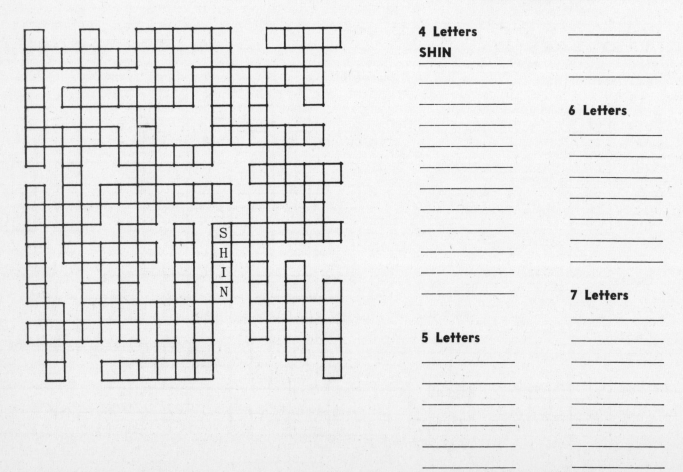

YOUR WORD LIST

4 Letters
SHIN
_____   _____
_____   _____
_____
_____   **6 Letters**
_____   _____
_____   _____
_____   _____
_____   _____
_____   _____
_____   _____
_____   **7 Letters**
5 Letters   _____
_____   _____
_____   _____
_____   _____
_____   _____
_____   _____
_____   _____
_____   _____
_____

Solve this Kriss Kross in the usual way, but instead of words, letter-number combinations are to be entered into the diagram. All the combinations which begin with numbers are listed first, followed by those combinations beginning with letters. Be careful, though, this one is tricky!

5 Units

3VM5F

5M64M

75C3M

A3L6M

C3M3X

C3V7H

C4H6C

C5V6F

C6AVX

C8H7F

H5V36

J3FM7

J8M3C

L56C7

M3FA6

V65FX

V67JH

V8C7H

XM6M4

6 Units

3VXA6A

5JXC4M

5L3F56

7H6A3M

7H6AV4

A3H6M7

A5JH67

C5H6M3

C7M8AJ

F5MC3V

H6F5M3

L3VX6M

L5M3H7

L6AV4J

L8M6CH

LH4M68

M5J37L

M6AC3L

V7M6HX

XLM4L8

7 Units

4C7M8L6

4L8A3CA

4M6C5ML

4VM6J3H

6ML8V35

7F4M36A

A5XM67V

FV73H4V

FX4CA6V

H3J6A7J

H5M3C4X

J4H6M8A

L5M6VH8

L8M6X3A

M6LA3VX

MA63CL8

V3A4MC8

8 Units

5AX43M7F

5L7M64AV

8A4J6M3F

8CA8M3L7

8F3CH6M5

A5M6J5H3

C7HA3LC6

CA4V76M3

H3AV86MV

H3CM6JV7

H86J3V43

M3A6AX3V

M8V3CA6F

X4C76V8M

Solution is on
page 293

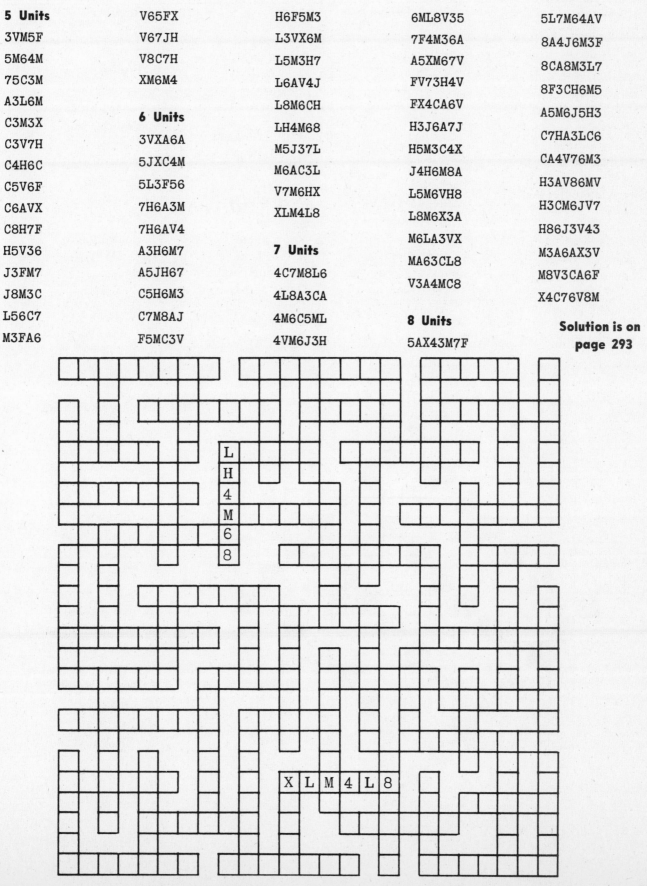

ACROSS

1. Lowly dwelling
4. Flower-holders
6. Take the prize
7. Help
9. Cords
13. Harbors
17. Exchange
18. Father
20. Maiden
21. Intense anger
22. Swimming place
24. Pastry dessert
25. Fashion topic
26. Smite
27. Attached to
29. Wooden nail
31. Laundry material
32. Sack
33. Ink stain
35. Chum
37. Plant stalk
38. Baseball club

39. Petroleum
40. Morning: abbr.
42. "—, my darling daughter"
44. That man
45. Remain
47. Metal container
48. Malt drinks
50. Mother
51. Have lunch
53. Either
54. Tubby
55. Perish
56. Black bird
58. Pitcher part
60. Violent rebuke
62. That lady
63. Acute distress
64. Stenographer's notebook
66. While
67. Prohibit
68. Hairless

69. Knock
71. Shoe tips
73. Noisy
74. Corner
76. You and I
77. Tantalize
78. "Old-hat"
80. Doctored
82. Encountered
84. Aged
85. Within the law
87. Agree silently

DOWN

1. Suspend
2. You and me
3. Asian shrub
4. Creeping plant
5. Drink slowly
6. Broad
8. Lassie, for one
9. Rivers
10. Hobo
11. Tatters
12. Speck
14. Lacerate
15. Stumble
16. Slumber
19. One
22. Swine
23. Puppet
25. Garden tool
26. Sombrero
28. Flat refusal
30. Merry
31. Take illegally
32. Laurel
33. Coal container
34. Story
36. Sour fruit
37. Novel by Haggard
38. Saloons
39. Cereal grain
41. Myself
43. Carpenter's tool
46. Toward
47. Bottle top
48. Ventilate
49. Burned with hot liquid
52. Gift to a waiter
54. Speedy
55. Lair
57. Free (of)
59. Separates
61. Musical note
62. Owns
63. Hesitate
65. Scoot
67. Red vegetable
68. Steamer or liner
70. Small vegetable
72. Cry of pain
73. Heavy metal
75. Shade tree
77. Narrate
79. Elongated fish
81. Highway
83. Twice five
86. Ready, set,—!

Solution is on page 288

ACROSS

1. Commend
7. Sinews
12. Soft, floppy toy: 2 wds.
14. Chuckled
16. European country
17. Egg-shaped
19. A Gershwin
20. Nothing more than
21. Be vainglorious
22. Rouse
23. Perch
25. Far East
27. Space vehicle
30. Hardy
31. Everything
32. In the — of, defying
34. Phantom
37. Party for men only
39. Pig's nose
41. Indian of Brazil
42. Sheer linen
44. Star in Cygnus
46. Take to court
47. Church parts
49. Go off the —, be rash: 2 wds.
51. Was lenient with
53. Dark red dye
54. Facility
55. Magnificence
57. Wind instrument
61. Also
62. Type of electronic tube
63. Mister in Mayagüez
64. Twitting
66. Decrease
68. Being untruthful
69. Praises highly

DOWN

1. Decorous
2. Deserve
3. Culture medium
4. Inactive ones
5. Oriental sauce
6. — Paso
7. Drum signal
8. — and cry
9. For example: abbr.
10. D.C. landmark: 2 wds.
11. Canarylike bird
13. Unfinished business: 2 wds.
14. — Vegas
15. Move quickly
18. Large tub
21. Tree trunks
22. Vision
24. Not at home
26. Carpet
27. Throw
28. Female voice
29. Perfectly obvious: 3 wds.
30. Rumbled loudly
33. Shoe tip
35. Made, as yarn

36. Fit to be —, very angry
38. Stare angrily
40. Very small
43. Miss Arden
45. Big —
48. Ornamental trim
50. Evident
51. Install
52. Entire jury
53. Coal scuttle
56. Day by day record
58. Open
59. Cotton plant pod
60. Greek war god
62. Sustained noise
63. Number
65. Spanish "yes"
67. All of us

Solution is on page 285

KEY-LETTER SCORE 1

Copyright 1989 by Bantam Doubleday Dell Publishing Group, Inc.

Add any letter to each word below and then rearrange (anagram) all the letters to form a new word. HANDICAP: TRY TO REARRANGE THE LETTERS IN SUCH A WAY THAT THE SAME LETTER APPEARS AS THE THIRD LETTER IN EACH OF THE 10 NEW WORDS. Plurals, proper nouns, and foreign words are not allowed. Place the new word onto the dashes. When all the new words are in place, circle the one letter that appears the most times in the third column. This is your key letter and you get 10 extra points every time it appears as the third letter in one of the new words. Score 5 points for each anagram you make. Our perfect solution of 150 points is on page 309.

Average score: 100 points

Superior score: 120 points

TRACE 1. _ _ _ _ _ _

CABLE 2. _ _ _ _ _ _

MOTEL 3. _ _ _ _ _ _

SLEEP 4. _ _ _ _ _ _

TOPIC 5. _ _ _ _ _ _

RODEO 6. _ _ _ _ _ _

GREEN 7. _ _ _ _ _ _

SCARE 8. _ _ _ _ _ _

WATER 9. _ _ _ _ _ _

PRICE 10. _ _ _ _ _ _

ACROSS

1. Chirp
5. Sooty dirt
10. That woman
13. Preclude
14. Shoestrings
15. Pot cover
16. Idolize
17. Native metal
18. Slip on ice
20. Sun-bather's goal
21. Do a full gainer
23. Sailors
24. Raised railroad
25. Metal thread
26. Breathe quickly
27. Step
28. Short-handled axes
32. Gush forth
34. Thick soup
35. Fish eggs
36. Pork fat
37. Tilts
38. Decrease
39. Possessive pronoun
40. Harbors
41. Mislays
42. Speculations
44. In this place
45. Ball-points
46. Bird's bill
47. Musical tone
49. Accent
52. Tie
53. Mother's Day month
54. Dried plum
55. Stroke, as a dog
56. Make joyful
58. Help
59. Racket
61. Moves upward
62. Shoe tip
63. Oaks and maples
64. Adjusts, as a clock

DOWN

1. Foot throttle
2. Black
3. Hearing organ
4. Prophesy
5. Hand covering
6. Underdone, as roast beef
7. Drink-cooler
8. Myself
9. Perfume
10. Slender
11. Conceal
12. Paradise
13. Engagement
19. Narrow slat
22. Anger
23. Gluts
25. Fend (off)
26. Portions
27. Pocketbook
28. Seeks
29. Rub out
30. Sound quality
31. Beholds
32. Narrow cut
33. Footway
34. Peels
37. Nickels, for example
38. Labor
40. Gift
41. Maestros
43. —up, unfold
44. Egg-layer
46. Snacks
47. Prices
48. Potato buds
49. Small quarrel
50. Singing group
51. Impolite
52. Foundation
53. Spar
55. "Deep-dish" dessert
57. Falsehood
60. Either

Solution is on page 286

BUILD-A-WORD

Copyright 1989 by Bantam Doubleday Dell Publishing Group, Inc.

To build-a-word, begin with the first word in Column A, then select a word from Columns B and C so that the three small words form one large word; for example, AN NOT ATE. Do this for each line from one to ten so that ten large words will result.   Answer is on page 302.

	A	B	C
1	PATH	ON	WAY
2	LIT	IS	MOTH
3	HA	TEN	LOGICAL
4	ART	A	GRAPH
5	PA	OR	LOAD
6	WAG	HO	TED
7	TOM	HE	ABLE
8	BE	O	DIES
9	FAR	LA	TRIES
10	MA	BIT	ROW

1. _____
2. _____
3. _____
4. _____
5. _____
6. _____
7. _____
8. _____
9. _____
10. _____

Bible Crossword by RUSS CARLEY

ACROSS

1. Take heed — no man deceive you. *Matt. 24:4*
5. They had on their — crowns of gold. *Rev. 4:4*
10. We . . . will do all that thou shalt — us. *II Ki. 10:5*
13. A time to love, and a time to —. *Eccl. 3:8*
14. There appeared unto him an — of the Lord. *Luke 1:11*
15. The crooked shall be — straight. *Luke 3:5*
16. The Garden of —
17. Let him first cast a — at her. *St. John 8:7*
18. No man was — to answer him. *Matt. 22:46*
19. It came — pass. *Luke 20:1*
21. There came wise m— from the east. *Matt. 2:1*
22. I — all thy precepts . . . to be right. *Ps. 119:128*
24. The kingdom of heaven is — hand. *Matt. 3:2*
26. Blessed are the —e in heart. *Matt. 5:8*
28. Absalom sent — throughout all . . . of Israel. *II Sam. 15:10*
29. His sons . . . turned aside after lucre, and took —. *I Sam. 8:3*
31. The angel — unto him, Fear not. *Luke 1:13*
32. We cannot speak unto thee b— or good. *Gen. 24:50*
33. Brother of Moses
34. — is the kingdom, and the power. *Matt. 6:13*
35. I am — old man. *Luke 1:18*
36. Nothing bettered, but rather — worse. *Mark 5:26*
37. She shall — forth a son. *Matt. 1:21*
38. Give me children, or — I die. *Gen. 30:1*
40. They shall be — white as snow. *Isa. 1:18*
41. It shall be a reproach and a —. *Ezek. 5:15*
42. He set the royal — upon her head. *Esth. 2:17*
43. To him that knocketh — shall be opened. *Matt. 7:8*
44. My lips shall —r praise. *Ps. 119:171*
45. Who hath — you to flee from the wrath to come? *Matt. 3:7*
46. God created the heaven and the —. *Gen. 1:1*
48. Make bare the —, uncover the thigh. *Isa. 47:2*
49. Firstborn of Judah
50. Ye shall see no more vanity, nor — divinations. *Ezek. 13:23*
52. — good to them that hate you. *Matt. 5:44*
53. —ther was taken unto king Ahasuerus. *Esth. 2:16*
55. Thou art a priest for — after. *Heb. 5:6*
56. Cleanse the lepers, — the dead. *Matt. 10:8*
59. Consider the lilies of the field . . . they — not, neither do they spin. *Matt. 6:28*
63. Num—, Old Testament Book
64. Cause me to understand wherein I have —. *Job. 6:24*
65. John was cast — prison. *Matt. 4:12*
66. I . . . will — them as gold is tried. *Zech. 13:9*
67. Moses . . . was mighty in words and in —. *Acts 7:22*
68. Sleep on now, and take your —. *Mark 14:41*

DOWN

1. — Lord is my shepherd; I shall not want. *Ps. 23:1*
2. When he — opened the book, he found the place. *Luke 4:17*
3. I — no pleasant bread. *Dan. 10:3*
4. Lot . . . pitched his — toward Sodom. *Gen. 13:12*
5. Make —te, and get thee quickly out of Jerusalem. *Acts 22:18*
6. — ye in at the strait gate. *Matt. 7:13*
7. Being in . . . —y he prayed more earnestly. *Luke 22:44*
8. He lieth in wait secretly as a lion in his —. *Ps. 10:9*
9. The same night Peter was — between two soldiers. *Acts. 12:6*
10. As newborn — . . . ye may grow. *I Pet. 2:2*
11. Their words seemed to them as — tales, and they believed them not. *Luke 24:11*
12. The shipmen — that they drew nigh to some country. *Acts 27:27*
15. None shall want her —. *Isa. 34:16*
20. Their throat is an — sepulchre. *Rom. 3:13*
23. Let us pass over unto the other —. *Mark 4:35*
24. The ark rested in the seventh month . . . upon the mountains of —. *Gen. 8:4*
25. Your — shall be upon your heads. *Ezek. 24:23*
27. Give — this day our daily bread. *Matt. 6:11*
28. The Gospel according to — Luke
29. He hath taken a — of money with him. *Prov. 7:20*
30. I — my knees unto the Father. *Eph. 3:14*
31. His face did — as the sun. *Matt. 17:2*
32. I will ask of you one question, and — me. *Mark 11:29*
34. God also gave them up . . . who changed the — of God into a lie. *Rom. 1:24, 25*
35. Man shall not live by bread —. *Luke 4:4*
37. The people . . . — the wall, to throw it down. *II Sam. 20:15*
38. Ye do —, not knowing the scriptures. *Matt. 22:29*
39. I am . . . the beginning and the —. *Rev. 21:6*
41. We — away from him that speaketh from heaven. *Heb. 12:25*
42. As a — is full of birds, so are their houses full of deceit. *Jer. 5:27*
43. We . . . forgive every one that is —ed to us. *Luke 11:4*
45. — give thee thanks. *Rev. 11:17*
46. Hearken unto me — one of you. *Mark 7:14*
47. The very h— of your head are all numbered *Matt. 10:30*
48. Their eyes have they c—; lest they should see. *Acts 28:27*
51. Give . . . for God loveth a cheerful g—. *II Cor. 9:7*
52. In the morning will I —ct my prayer unto thee. *Ps. 5:3*
54. Grievous words — up anger. *Prov. 15:1*
57. Blessed — the meek. *Matt 5:5*
58. I must ne— go and see it. *Luke 14:18*
60. They twain shall be of — flesh. *Mark 10:8*
61. That which groweth of — own accord . . . thou shalt not reap. *Lev. 25:5*
62. Remember —'s wife. *Luke 17:32*

Solution is on page 286

35 and 36 HARD CROSSWORD

ACROSS

1. Small branch
6. Plait
11. Water holder
12. Came down
14. Enthusiasm: French
15. From one place to another: 3 wds.
17. Total
18. Flycatcher bird
19. Face feature
20. By
21. Place of refuge
22. "Stone of the side"
23. Disproves
25. Noblewomen
26. Verily!
27. A "fickle food upon a shifting plate"
28. Thing often "brought home"
30. Says "uncle": 2 wds.
33. Assert
34. Cars for hire
35. Yes, in Ponce
36. Mr. Gehrig
37. Destined
38. Husbands
39. Imagined
41. — goods, clothing
42. Depict: 2 wds.
43. A planet
45. *Chaudement*
46. Blossom part

DOWN

1. Greeting
2. Baby carriage, in London
3. Sprinted
4. Supposition in a Kipling poem
5. Retaliate: 2 wds.
6. "Gray matter"
7. Talk wildly
8. Be a help to
9. Afire: 2 wds.
10. Scoff at
11. Actor Romero
13. Figures (out): slang
16. Has creditors
18. Eucharistic plate
21. Ready wit
22. Jesse —
24. Confront realistically: 3 wds.
25. King of Judah
27. Repaired: 2 wds.
28. Wood lighter than cork
29. Affirm
30. Attendance
31. Of good effect
32. Liquid measures
34. Flavorful
37. Baseball term
38. "— Lisa"
40. Money at stake
41. Held a session
44. Concerning

ACROSS

1. Smooth-spoken
5. "Holed up"
8. Mountaineer's hound
12. Miss Horne
13. Gormandized
14. Wicked
15. Feed-bag fare
16. Florida Indian
18. Get by effort
20. — idol, male actor
21. Highway
23. Jewel
24. Word with "interior"
27. Joke: slang
30. Golf club
31. Bukhara product
32. Verb form
33. Hungry Horse or Flaming Gorge
34. Society "bud"
36. Offer a price
37. Roof edge
38. Certain; secure
42. Hazard
45. Legal action to recover goods
47. Tatted edge
48. Jutting rock
49. Glacier material
50. Nicholas Udall's school
51. In this place
52. Give leave to
53. Look after

DOWN

1. Incandescence
2. Shakespeare king
3. Interoffice "telephone"
4. Oboe's kin
5. Is carrying
6. Particular
7. Rabble rouser
8. Fabric for jeans
9. English river
10. Sly artifice
11. — club, singing group
17. Via Appia, for one
19. — and feathers
22. Reckless chap
24. Filled the bill
25. Pitcher's statistics: abbr.
26. Clumsy boat
27. Produce
28. School subject
29. Mild expletive
32. Tiny ripple
34. Dreadful
35. Spigot
36. Be filled to capacity
38. Roguish
39. Withered
40. Box, in a way
41. "Devil's bones"
43. Sacred image
44. Impart
46. Clear gain

Solutions are on page 286

ACROSS

1. "Stardust" is one
2. New Mexico, the — of Enchantment
9. Sudden attack
13. Drying cloth
14. Minnesota, the — State
16. California, the — State
18. Michigan, the — State
20. A nickname of Arkansas: 2 wds.
22. At home
23. Field of glacial snow
24. Wings
25. Sun god
26. Want
29. Mr. Arnaz
31. June 6, 1944: hyph. wd.
32. Halt!
34. Defeat completely
36. Site of Busch Stadium: 2 wds.
38. Baseball great, Roger —
39. Omit
41. City in the Buckeye State
42. Diamond facet
43. Show Me State: abbr.
45. Blunder
47. New Jersey, the — State
49. The Cotton State: abbr.
51. Musical perception
52. Old Dominion State: abbr.
53. Mix, as cake batter
56. Title of respect
57. Bob and dip, as bait
58. Play division
60. Beaver State: abbr.
61. Insignificant person
63. Little Rhody: abbr.
64. DDE's nickname
65. Not: prefix
66. Highest point
69. West Point freshman
71. Sioux State: abbr.
72. Goddesses of the seasons and hours
73. African antelope
77. "Biggest Little City in the West"
79. Feminine accessory
80. Treasure State
82. Narrated
84. Not present
85. Magnolia State: abbr.
86. Cornhusker State: abbr.
88. Seven —, world's navigable waters
90. Great Britain and Northern Ireland: abbr.
91. Indonesian island
92. This and —
94. Pelican State: abbr.
95. One of the 13 original States: 2 wds.
99. Philadelphia, the "City of — Love"

102. Mr. Power of film fame
103. Akron, the "— City"
105. Assumed name
106. Looked at
107. Dainty trimming
108. Pinches

DOWN

1. Oklahoma, the — State
2. Night bird
3. Silver State: abbr.
4. Secluded valley
5. Texas, the — State: 2 wds.
6. Tailless monkey
7. Granite State: abbr.
8. New entrant into society, for short
9. State flower of 5 states
10. Height: abbr.
11. Gem State: abbr.
12. U.S. "Motor City"
13. Minneapolis and St. Paul, the "— Cities"
14. Donates
15. Keystone State city
16. Neutral color
17. Certain tides

19. River separating Oklahoma and Texas
21. Its capital is Juneau: abbr.
27. Dawn goddess
28. — University, Durham, N.C.
30. Class; kind
31. Musical pair
32. Store events
33. Capital of 95-Across
35. Weary
37. Rain — shine
38. Wet, sticky earth
40. Illinois, the — State
42. Treat for Polly
43. The Bay State: abbr.
44. Man's name
46. Planet's curved path
48. Be of use to
50. Grand Canyon State
54. — ore, Minnesota mine output
55. Pull apart forcefully
59. 4th Jewish month
62. Jaunty
67. Negative vote
68. Indiana, the — State

69. Maine, the — State: 2 wds.
70. Seth's son
72. Iowa, the — State
74. MDs' assistants
75. That thing
76. Prohibit
78. Bullfight shout
79. Visit frequently
80. Wire-diameter measures
81. Detest
83. "Big D", Texas city
85. Female horse
87. Rodent
89. Utters
91. Tennessee, the Big — State
93. Comparative word
96. Ironic, as humor
97. Namath of football
98. Actor Brynner
99. English radio-TV network: inits.
100. Inventor Whitney
101. Torn place
104. College degree: abbr.

Solution is on page 288

ACROSS

1. Goulashes
6. Give cues to
12. Sprite
13. Given freely
15. Make amends
16. Former: hyph. wd.
17. Common experiment subject
18. Boisterous
20. One Caesar's name
21. Cut quickly
23. Aye, aye
24. Berlin product
25. Got away
27. Fencing move
28. A Taylor
29. Family
30. Playing card
33. Subtracts
37. *Uber*
38. Separate
39. Actor's quest
40. Prohibit
41. Nautical crane
43. Golf-ball position
44. Skyscraper, for one
46. — with, abounding in
48. Recuperate
49. Strode back and forth
50. Go away
51. Soils

DOWN

1. Few and far between
2. Giants
3. Strangely enticing
4. Come in first
5. Prophet
6. Tilled the soil
7. Outer parts
8. "Reason should direct and appetite —"
9. Converged
10. "Clink"
11. "The — Of The Shrew"
14. Shelf
19. Hear !, in court
22. Whiter
24. Dawn
26. Sewer's aid
27. Teapot part
29. Type of military cap
30. Like "a judge"
31. Side-stepped
32. Italian seaport
33. Amuse
34. Cotton fabric
35. Hot-dish stand
36. Bayard and Rosinante
38. Speeder
41. Opera singer
42. Draws upon
45. Dandy
47. Track circuit

ACROSS

1. Crops acreage
5. Assail
11. Forbidden
12. — *bleus*, master chefs
14. Thing of value
15. Cut glass
16. Article
17. Follow orders
19. A Gabor
20. Coat with solder
21. Sprint or mile
22. Harassed
24. Crazy: slang
26. Animal with a "rudder"
28. Vim
30. Decrees
34. Washbowl
36. Poet Sandburg
37. Brag
40. Romaine
42. Pod vegetable
43. Soufflé item
44. Steadfast
45. Utter
46. Resilient
49. Get up
51. Renewal, as of interest
52. Barber's tool
53. Decorous
54. At that time

DOWN

1. Mode
2. It makes the heart "grow fonder"
3. Caviar
4. Engine
5. Stress
6. Rightist
7. Attempt
8. Newspaper items
9. Doves' homes
10. Jack
11. Tell secrets
13. Thin board
18. Channel markers
22. Flower plot
23. Newsman Sevareid
25. Spheres
27. Male voice
29. Gun: slang
31. Overturn
32. "If this be — make the most of it"
33. Murderer
35. Wintry "stalactite"
37. Malt brew
38. Eyes leeringly
39. Century plant
41. Sting
44. King's decree
47. Comedian Caesar
48. Power project: abbr.
50. Stadium sound

Solutions are on page 286

ACROSS

1. Clothes-tree hooks
5. Festival
9. Auction
13. Cudgel
17. Land measure
18. Copy
20. Employ
21. Munch on
22. Help
23. Harbor
24. Roam about
25. Shoe tip
26. Conclusion
27. Cautious
28. Coldest season
29. Tidy
31. Figure
32. Snake's tooth
33. Upper air
35. Ilk
36. Hung around
40. Stringed instrument
41. Defraud
42. Moves upward
43. Poem of praise
44. Go wrong
45. Dip doughnuts in coffee
46. Lacks
47. Confine
48. Leasing
50. Rows
51. Famous Greek
52. Bonnet
53. Jokes
54. Distress call
55. Inn
58. Army vehicles
59. Misrepresent
63. Approve
64. Droops
65. Large bundle
66. Also
67. Samovar
68. Niagara sight
69. Listen!
70. Burn
71. Unevenly
73. Register
74. Glove fabric
75. Count (on)
76. Fewer
77. Equal
78. Ten years
81. Some horses
82. Illuminated
83. Biting humor
86. Smooths (out)
87. Soft drink
88. Doze
89. "Stash away"
90. — julep
91. Moon
93. Capri, for one
94. Visits

95. Unfold
96. Mimics
97. Appear

DOWN

1. Treaty
2. Reverberate
3. Novice
4. Make samplers
5. Cyclops was one
6. Among
7. Cover
8. Attending
9. Hurricane
10. Breezy
11. Fate
12. Print measure
13. Alter
14. Bits of thread
15. Impel
16. Malt liquor
19. Separately
24. Resounds
26. Listener's "loan"
27. Labor
28. Decreases

30. Snakelike fish
31. People
32. Clenched hands
33. At any time
34. Weary
35. Warble
36. Golf course
37. Rove
38. Brink
39. Stag or doe
41. Tap (a baseball) lightly
42. Talks wildly
45. Clock face
46. Hornets
47. Price
49. Those people
50. Whirls
51. Stockings
53. Bread spread
54. Lustrous fabric
55. 60 minutes
56. Gumbo
57. Strong taste
58. Joyful
59. Scoot
60. Else

61. Highway
62. Ripped
64. Big spoon
65. Quartet member
68. Nurtures
69. Snake's sound
70. Hint
72. Gives
73. Licit
74. Obstinate
76. Burdened
77. Hookahs
78. Parking lights
79. Great Lake
80. Ice-cream holder
81. Short letter
82. Tardy
84. Inactive
85. Abound
87. Weaken
88. Pinch
89. The boy's
91. As a result
92. Musical tone

Solution is on page 288

CRYPTOQUIZZES 3

A Cryptoquiz is a list of related words put into a simple code. You can spot familiar words by their "pattern" of repeated or double letters, and you can solve the rest if you remember that if G stands for M in one word, it will be the same throughout the list. A new code is used for each Cryptoquiz. Answers are on page 303.

1. "FOR RENT"

Example: Cabin

Q J Q N W T X V W

Z C D F X

F W D O P C

J X V W Z C D F X

S C M W

I X Q Y Z   Z C D F X

Y C W W Q R X

M D N V P F Z X O   N C C T

I D V R Q S C U

Y Z Q S X W

2. CAMPER'S GEAR

Example: Cooking stove

A P X A

K H P P I Y X U   S T U

M Y C K A – T Y N   R Y A

R X T I K T O R

M Y P H N   U H T K K P K

M H T K L H Y U L A

C B I P

O B V I T K K

I B O R P A   R X Y M P

O T X A P P X

3. ON A WESTERN SET

Example: Jail

A Y U K B

V Y W T T U

K T A A Y W

K T T Z B T X V L

R X U Z B T X V L

Y M T R L

V O Y R W L

V C T Z L B T X V L

B T O L W

K B X A K B

4. ASTRONAUT'S WORLD

Example: Mission control

A B R P C R R

A K Q Y L X

U V K L J H K A Z

L C G G K Y S   G C S Q A J

I C L Z J P   U P K N J U

A Q Y K I   C I E B P

U V A K U X S C H Y

S J E I B J R B Y N U

U V K L J U Q B P U

H J B N X P A J U U Y J U U

5. PUTTING OFF THE ISSUE

Example: Sorry, return Tuesday

T G E ' X   H N B B   W K ,

   S P ' B B   H N B B   L G W

C N L J P   X G C G Y Y G S

N E G X M P Y   X V C P

H G C P   J N H D

I P Y M N I K   B N X P Y

X Y L   E P Q X   S P P D

E G X   Y V R M X   E G S

K G C P   G X M P Y   T N L

K X G I   V E   N R N V E

6. REVOLUTIONARY BATTLES AND SIEGES

Example: Lexington

A M L W G C   Z K E E

A P I H P L

F P L F P C N

H K F P L N G C P R B

S P C W H P D L

Y C K L F G H P L

E P L R   K I E B L N

A C B L N S D K L G

I B C B H P R B

D Z K H G   Y E B K L I

SKILL-O-GRAM 2

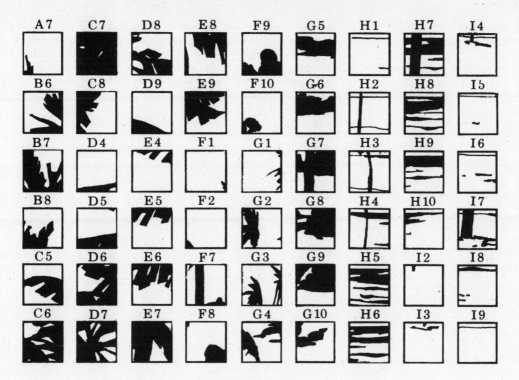

Each square above contains one part of a complete picture. Using a pencil or pen, you are to copy exactly what you see into the diagram below. Use the letter-number combinations as a guide, and draw exactly what is in each box above into the correspondingly numbered box below. Start with A-7, drawing in the box where Row A and Column 7 intersect. Then, draw in B-6, B-7, etc. and continue right through to the end. The result will be a finished picture, as skillfully drawn as if by an artist. The artist's picture is shown on page 294.

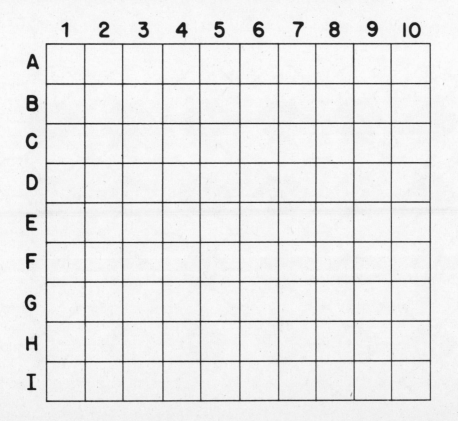

PINWHEEL 2

The answers to the definitions below are all 6-letter words. Each answer is to be put in the diagram below so that it encircles the corresponding number. Some words will be entered clockwise, some counterclockwise; (c) after a definition means in a clockwise direction and (cc) means in a counterclockwise direction. Answers overlap in a diagram, so letters you fill in will help you with other words you might not get at first. Remember that all answers are 6-letter words. The first word, "SNEEZE," has been entered into the diagram to help you get started.

Solution is on page 311.

1. "Product" of a nose tickle   (cc)

2. Highest point; summit   (c)

3. Long, vehement speech; harangue   (c)

4. Adjusts (to)   (c)

5. Towards the rear, on a ship   (c)

6. Person who scolds and faultfinds continually   (cc)

7. Not tough, as meat   (cc)

8. Fireplace floor   (c)

9. Taunt (a public speaker)   (cc)

10. Plant stems   (cc)

11. Help; aid   (c)

12. New Orleans pro football team   (c)

13. Cut molars, as a baby   (c)

14. Rebuke severely   (cc)

15. Opposite of debit   (cc)

16. Sew   (cc)

17. Sharp-edged sculptor's tool   (c)

18. Hidden   (cc)

19. Shakespeare's "Prince of Denmark"   (c)

20. Clever; smart   (c)

21. Chauffeur, for one   (cc)

22. Put (something) into something else   (c)

23. Delay; stay behind   (cc)

24. Crisp fold in trousers   (cc)

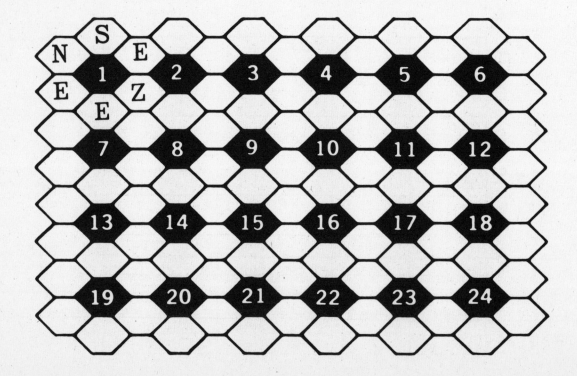

TWO FOR EACH

Each word in the CLUES column has some application to a listing in Columns A and B. Can you find the two correct lines to go with each of the ten clues? Nine right is very good, seven right is passing.   Answer is on page 302.

CLUES	A	B
1. mysteries	a. entrance	a. foam
2. hats	b. Little Boy Blue	b. Old King Cole
3. gold	c. Miss Marple	c. Colonial bed
4. Abraham	d. gorgonzola	d. Easter Parade
5. canopy	e. Sutter's Mill	e. Gabriel
6. salt	f. square dance	f. Christie
7. fiddlers	g. Mary Todd	g. Midas
8. horn	h. milliner	h. Wisconsin
9. bubbles	i. pipes	i. Atlantic Ocean
10. cheese	j. potato chips	j. Sarah

ANAGRAM ANTICS

Job Hunting

The odd-looking words below are men and women's occupations, in anagram form. Unscramble each word and place the name of each occupation into its corresponding squares in the diagram. When you are finished, and if you have solved all seven correctly, the letters in the heavily outlined boxes (reading down) will spell out the occupation of "one who likes to wrap a lot."   Solution is on page 302.

1. S T R I F L O

2. C H R T B U E

3. G N O R S E U

4. D R O O N A M

5. S T E D N I T

6. R E H S C A I

7. I O R N T A J

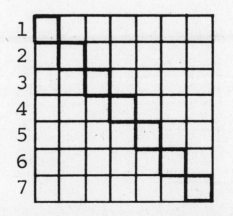

WORD ARITHMETIC 2

These problems and the ones on the opposite page are long-division problems. To solve a problem, determine the number value of each letter. When the letters in each one have been arranged in order from 0 to 9 (using the line over the 0 to 9 for your letters), they will spell out a word or words.

Solution is on page 303.

1. 0 1 2 3 4 5 6 7 8 9

```
              PAT
TOLL | PECTATE
       TOLL
       IASYT
       CYCCS
        ATLTE
        AASLE
         ELPS
```

2. 0 1 2 3 4 5 6 7 8 9

```
             ANTS
HAT | NOMISMS
      OTOI
      OTMS
       ONIS
       HAMM
        CICO
        CRTS
         COON
         ASH
```

3. 0 1 2 3 4 5 6 7 8 9

```
             RIG
HAW | WIGGLY
      WLAP
      RRGL
      WTWW
       IAGY
       RGIH
        RPR
```

4. 0 1 2 3 4 5 6 7 8 9

```
              HAIR
BLOB | TUBULAR
       BLOB
       RRTIL
       RIRUW
        HALLA
        HITAI
         ILTRR
         HTLIU
          AAWA
```

5. 0 1 2 3 4 5 6 7 8 9

```
              NUT
LASS | ENTENTE
       ETAST
       LGLLT
       ESESL
        EGALE
        SISN
         OLI
```

6. 0 1 2 3 4 5 6 7 8 9

```
             NED
ANT | TWEED
      UWT
      AWLE
      KUT
       SLD
       SAW
        AD
```

7. 0 1 2 3 4 5 6 7 8 9

```
              TOE
BIRD | DOUBLED
       DIRDU
       RDODE
       TOBIK
        ULIED
        URDBL
         TEIR
```

8. 0 1 2 3 4 5 6 7 8 9

```
              SEE
BEET | BEACHES
       BTSCE
       BASOE
       HXMBO
        HSATS
        HXMBO
         TMXC
```

9. 0 1 2 3 4 5 6 7 8 9

```
             BYE
ITCH | BRUNCH
       BCTH
       YRRC
       YIYH
        EYBH
        ENRT
         INH
```

10. 0 1 2 3 4 5 6 7 8 9

```
              E O N
ICES | HOSTESS
      H C O I C
       O T E E S
      L S L L O
       P H H H S
      P O E C H
       L N H O
```

11. 0 1 2 3 4 5 6 7 8 9

```
              S H E
NODE | HOSANNA
      H B N O D
       B N X N
      N O D E
       H B S S A
      H H B E A
       N D H T
```

12. 0 1 2 3 4 5 6 7 8 9

```
              G E T
AGED | TRACING
      T I N G E
       G A A Y N
      G Y E N R
       I R G Y G
      I C N D G
       A G R C
```

13. 0 1 2 3 4 5 6 7 8 9

```
              N O
ILLS | GIVEN
      K I I E
       I P O P N
      S K L G
       I N G E
```

14. 0 1 2 3 4 5 6 7 8 9

```
              P I
PEP | PRICE
      M C E A
       I G E E
      H H E G
       I L A
```

15. 0 1 2 3 4 5 6 7 8 9

```
              L E E
CUBS | GUESSES
      I S G G H
       N C H G E
      N I G H G
       N U N C S
      N I G H G
       L G S H
```

ANTONYMS QUIZ

An antonym is a word opposite in meaning to a given word. For example, HOT is an antonym for COLD. In each case below, there will be one word of the four choices that is *most nearly opposite* in meaning to the word in capital letters. This quiz is not easy, so if you can pick out 7 of the antonyms you will have done a good job.

Answer is on page 303.

1. COURTEOUS: (a) scrupulous   (b) insolent   (c) cheerful   (d) aesthetic

2. PREPOSTEROUS: (a) apologetic   (b) outrageous   (c) reasonable   (d) unique

3. TURBULENT: (a) placid   (b) jet-propelled   (c) redundant   (d) incongruous

4. PREMEDITATED: (a) ardent   (b) loquacious   (c) beneficial   (d) impromptu

5. IMPETUOUS: (a) confused   (b) controlled   (c) incidental   (d) ashamed

6. INCREMENT: (a) reduction   (b) rainy   (c) effect   (d) rationalization

7. INAUGURATE: (a) argue   (b) unsettled   (c) terminate   (d) open

8. CERTAIN: (a) dubious   (b) particular   (c) positive   (d) debenture

9. EMANCIPATION: (a) liberation   (b) integration   (c) capitulation   (d) imprisonment

10. DOGMATIC: (a) stubborn   (b) credible   (c) compliant   (d) lissome

CRYPTIC PLACES

The illustration below is a State of the United States, with the location of a city indicated by an asterisk (*). Both the city and State, and a message about that city, have been coded with another set of letters just like a Cryptogram or Cryptoquiz. Your job is to "crack" the code and learn what the message is. See the instructions for solving Cryptograms, page 40, for solving hints. If you can't get started, the name of the city and state is given on page 320.

Answer is on page 303.

OQLSGDP   JNQLH
(*city*)

IQUBNLUQL
(*state*)

HXS   PSDZ-OQLQLY

QLZRUHGK   IXQBX

BGSDHSZ   HXQU   HNIL   QU

QLDBHQAS   LNI.   XNISASG,   D

CSI   BSLHRGK-NPZ   UHNLS

XNRUSU   NL   UXDMSGDY

UHGSSH,   ERQPH   EK   BNGLQUX

OQLSGU,   DGS   G·SUHNGSZ   DLZ

MSJH   NJSL   HN   AQUQHNGU.

LETTER INSERT

All you have to do to solve Letter Insert is to place the letters of the word ELECTION (using each letter one time only) into the empty squares of diagram 1, and the letters of the word RETURNS (again using each letter only once) into the empty squares of diagram 2 in such a way that 4 everyday words are formed reading across and 3 everyday words are formed reading down in each diagram. The letters which have been inserted into each diagram should not be rearranged in any way.

Our solutions are on page 303.

ELECTION

RETURNS

1.

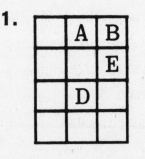

2.

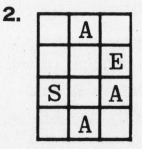

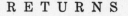

45. ZIJ AJHHCN NIC BHNBQD UJTHBSJD ZIBZ IJ'D

GCLCUQ'D ACCH KSCLBLHQ IBD IXD

DMDKXTXCGD.

46. JYMBSU'L QYM FVQRL'F VWWVHGUL LXVL

LYSVQ'F LVPVLRYU JRLX HGWHGFGULVLRYU

RFU'L FY XYL, GRLXGH?

47. IVMTM HR SLI UNEV ANS HS UMCHEHSM;

RIHDD IVMTM HR TMJDDX J QLLC CMJD LA

UMCHEHSM HS ANS.

48. YC JTBHM KN L RTTM YMNL CT JLHH SYELCN

DXYSD CXN "CXBRKTLCD."

49. BWTYKOBHD ZBET WJYT LJJA PJ TBP PZBH

MTJMIT KH BHX JPZTY OJRHPYX KH PZKD

QJYIA—BHA WJYT PXMTD JL DPYKOP AKTPD

PJ AKDOJRYBST PZTW LYJW TBPKHS KP.

50. P JNPXQ JNCJ C SCX'W KTCPX BTPYPXCGGE

PW BXGE C WSCGG, KCTTDX CJJPU, CXV OD

WJBUQ PJ OPJN ONCJ OD UNBBWD.

51. NCVZXUC KBX TZEC DTC MBPCO BW UMCCVT,

JD QBCUH'D HCVCUUZOJIK WBIIBP DTZD KBX

TZEC Z DZICHD WBO VBHECOUZDJBH.

Solutions are on page 306

52. PS PA GMSKJDKYPUJKV SD BFJS JU GMHGUAG

DX SPOG JUY ODUGV HGDHEG BPEE QD PU

DKYGK SD QGS ADOGSFPUQ XDK UDSFPUQ.

53. IYXOX COX IUM XHJOXVVDMGV KMO UYDLY

SMB GXXW GM IOCGVQCIDMG. MGX DV IYX

VRDQX MK C LYDQW; IYX MIYXO DV IYX UCP

MK C VRCQQ JBJJS'V ICDQ.

54. GCBE J VHQ CJUE'X J VPPK NBV XP UXJEK

PE, CB GMNN OPUX NMWBNQ APEAPAX J NJOB

BZAHUB.

55. JP JC DQJPW Y IXP NWPPWO PX LWNYPW Y

DQWCPJXH RJPVXQP CWPPIJHZ JP PVYH PX

CWPPIW Y DQWCPJXH RJPVXQP LWNYPJHZ JP.

56. X PLL KJOU NLJGWLOP SN KHPU KOXNGXTM

KSDT GS GWL LJOGW GSTXMWG.

57. QGHM RJM QGH JPHKJXH QJBTJMHK CDKNR

WYPH ODZQGR DLQ DW HJUG MHJK WDK QGH

XDPHKZOHZQ. CH SDLIQ QGH TJYS WHSHKJA

CDKNHKR SD OLUG IHQQHK.

58. RHBF EC'CH B WCBH LBF XDL WYC CFC

WYBW WDLC BEX RBWDCEQC QBEEMW XHF.

Solutions are on page 306

59. YX GVUVJE TLABJ LW LHH XVA EVC
LGJ GVUVJE TLABJ LUVCW QB, LGJ YX DB
LHH NWVVJ LHVGB YG WIB ULWWHB VX
HYXB, DILW L TVHJ, JABLAE VHJ DVAHJ
WIYN DVCHJ UB.

60. YVWG HJN EUJYR FRR LFH, GFANUFRRH HJN
DWWR LJE-AQUWL FA GQEVA.

61. OLVVQ RN JK LPI ASPPLO ORWE TSKISI ESJI,
UJVVQRKH J PLJI LA ASJWESVN OERUE ES
TSPRSCSN RN PSJI.

62. ZGCGZYLU'E KGQTM SOLHYUS—YZ LPDYLBETM
URDRO HGURE; ZL IYUQ KLOR URH HGME LI
ZGCYUS, LBO TRGQROE ZGC ZXRYO POGYUE.

63. WZH LKT UZM UQRR SMW HOMSMCQDH CGT
HEHSWKGRRT ZGEH WM GLMSQDH.

64. XIYVBGN LVODKB NJ NJYIDANA: HTBG DG
YGVBIVBOBZJXBV KJYGNIDBA, VJG'N VIDGE
NTB HLNBI; DG VBOBZJXBV KJYGNIDBA,
VJG'N WIBLNTB NTB LDI.

65. OKN DJYT JP R MJTTGNW DRJGJYQ XAOPJTN
XAW BJOSKNY TXXW JY OKN JYBZ UGRSBYNPP
XM OKJP YJQKO.

66. HR CVOLQLUGO LIKGO LW G IKHVUAGUR.
KZKARVEK WNVBOI TK AKWCKUQKI GW GE
LEILZLIBGO, TBQ EV VEK LIVOLFKI.—GOTKAQ
KLEWQKLE.

Cryptograms continue on page 185.

Solutions are on page 306

WORD SEARCH 6

HIDDEN NUMBERS

Here is a special Word Search, constructed with numbers instead of letters, but it's solved the same way as a regular Word Search. The 24 number combinations below are hidden in the diagram. The number combinations in the diagram read forwards, backwards, up, down or diagonally—always in a straight line, with no digits skipped over. To start you off, 6729 is circled.

```
2 0 1 3 8 8 9 4 8 1 2
0 1 9 6 8 7 1 9 5 1 2
9 6 5 5 6 7 2 9 0 1 0
0 9 9 7 8 7 0 5 9 1 8
5 1 6 4 5 8 7 3 3 9 0
0 3 6 6 1 1 7 8 3 5
8 9 0 9 0 6 2 6 9 1 8
2 8 9 7 7 0 5 2 7 9 5
9 0 1 8 7 1 3 5 8 0 8
0 1 3 9 8 1 8 9 4 0 1
2 6 4 4 7 1 0 4 5 9 3
```

2034	5217
2090	5278
2184	5307
2193	5387
3876	6649
3897	6695
3960	6701
3980	~~6729~~
4405	7132
4462	7135
4518	7560
4593	7563

WORD SEARCH 7

"I" RHYMERS

Hidden in the diagram below are 36 words, each of which rhymes with the letter "I." No word has the letter "I" in it, and no word is less than three letters long. See how many you can find without a Word List. Space is provided for you to write down the words as you find and circle (or cross through) them—and don't forget to include "REPLY," which has been circled to get you started. No word ends in "S," is a proper noun, or is a foreign word. If you find 30 on your own, consider it a good search.

YOUR WORD LIST

```
Q Y R Y Y T Z Y O B H S
L U L L A B Y C R U U K
S G P L Y Y C Z Q T S Y
S P X A Y U L Y J T N O
A P R O P H Q S Y E M Z
O D Y Y R X S O D R Q E
U R L S Z T Q Z Y F E D
T F E U U E Y R H L R Y
C O M P L Y R W W Y L E
R C E P L F Z Q T E Y L
Y F R L R Y H E R E B Y
Y Y G Y P U C C O E R P
```

Word List is on page 303.
Solutions are on page 300.

```
P O H S S E N I S U B A C C O U N T
E N T Y E N O M M C D O V R E Y U B
L O A N U I T U O N R A P R O F I T
F I R M E B I S E P L E A S E L A S
I L I V E M T V O U C H E R L D T S
N L F D E O E R E Q N E T A B E R T
A U F R S C A S H K F E B O O X U O
N B P X A T G A I N L D V I N N S C
C R E D I T E D E A L E R E D J T K
E N I O C C N S S B R O K E R A G E
D S N P N S T E S H Y P R I C E C X
L E Z A S T L M E A S W P U Y A O C
O G L O T O M A R T R T R A R Y L H
G A L I H C D R T I I R O T T R L A
B W D W V K H K T I E B E R N A E N
F U N D S E V E G N P L E A E L C G
A L I A T E R T C T F A R D R A T E
T R E A S U R Y X K L I C E N S E S
```

WORD LIST

Account	Buyer	Debt	Mart	Shop
Agent	Capital	Delivery	Money	Stock
Appraisement	Cartel	Draft	Net	Stock exchange
Arrears	Cash	Entry	Order	Store
Assets	Check	Fees	Overhead	Sum
Audit	Coin	Finance	Par	Tariff
Balance	Collect	Firm	Premium	Tax
Bank	Combine	Funds	Price	Trade
Bid	Corporation	Gain	Profit	Treasury
Bill	Cost	Gold	Rate	Trust
Bond	Credit	Lease	Rebate	Underwriter
Brokerage	Currency	Licenses	Retail	Value
Bullion	Deal	Loan	Revenue	Vend
Business	Dealer	Loss	Salary	Voucher
Buy	Debit	Market	Sales	Wages
				Wholesale

Solution is on page 300

BOWL-A-SCORE CHALLENGER 3

Copyright 1989 by Bantam Doubleday Dell Publishing Group, Inc.

Solve this Bowl-A-Score Challenger as you did the one on page 84. This time, though, your "strike" words will be 10-letter words instead of 9-letter words. The same rules apply, however: The starting letter for each "strike" word is given; you form your two-word "spares" the same way, by rearranging the scrambled letters into two words, with no letters left over. You may not simply split the "strike" word into two parts and use both exactly as they appear in the "strike" word for your "spare"; for example, FORE and CASTER would not qualify for the "strike" word FORECASTER.

Scoring: Score 20 points for each "strike" and 10 points for each two-word "spare." Perfect score is 300.

WARNING: This game is really for experts! Only the most expert word bowlers will score a perfect 300. HINT: If the "strike" word stumps you, work on the spare words; sometimes this helps with the "strike" word. Our words are on page 303.

1. N A D R   **Spare**
    T O C   _____
    E T   _____
    C
    Strike C _____

2. P P T Z   **Spare**
    I I N   _____
    E G   _____
    A
    Strike A _____

3. E A E I   **Spare**
    C R T   _____
    A V   _____
    T
    Strike R _____

4. N O R T   **Spare**
    I I N   _____
    C F   _____
    A
    Strike I _____

5. R S T U   **Spare**
    K N O   _____
    C D   _____
    A
    Strike S _____

6. R S T Y   **Spare**
    N O O   _____
    E F   _____
    E
    Strike F _____

7. N N N S   **Spare**
    G H I   _____
    A E   _____
    A
    Strike S _____

8. I M R U   **Spare**
    O E L   _____
    T N   _____
    A
    Strike T _____

9. I L L S   **Spare**
    E H I   _____
    B D   _____
    A
    Strike D _____

10. M O R T   **Spare**
    C H I   _____
    A C   _____
    A
    Strike A _____

CROSS SUMS

NUMBER 4

In each of these Cross Sums, we have not filled in a digit combination. Instead, we have shaded one area in the diagram. If you need help starting the puzzle, the digit combination to go into that area is listed on page 320.

Copyright 1989 by Bantam Doubleday Dell Publishing Group, Inc.

NUMBER 5

Solutions are on page 301

PICTURE MAZE

by JESSICA CLERK

To solve, simply shade in with a pencil or pen all of the shapes below that contain dots. We think you'll like what you see when you've finished.

Solution is on page 319.

HOW WELL DO YOU FOLLOW DIRECTIONS?

by ELEANOR FARINA

This is a puzzle designed to test how well you can follow directions. If you follow all of the directions given below exactly, you will change DIAMONDS into a phrase sometimes associated with them. Be sure to work carefully, in order, step by step, for this puzzle is tricky. We have provided space for solving and have started you off by printing DIAMONDS, the direction given in step Number 1. Only super directions-followers will solve this puzzle correctly on the first try!   Solution is on page 304.

1. Print the word DIAMONDS.

1. DIAMONDS _____

2. Remove the 1st consonant from the left and replace it with a G.

2. _____

3. Remove the 2nd vowel from the left and the 2nd consonant from the left; replace them with L and S respectively.

3. _____

4. Insert an R to the left and right of the 2nd vowel from the left.

4. _____

5. Insert an O in the 1st position at the left and after each 3rd letter thereafter.

5. _____

6. Place an I in the 6th position from the right.

6. _____

7. Insert a B between the 2 identical vowels which appear side by side.

7. _____

8. Move the 1st consonant from the right so that it becomes the 6th letter from the right.

8. _____

9. Insert a T after the 2nd S from the left.

9. _____

10. Insert an F in the 4th position from the right.

10. _____

11. Move the 4th consonant from the left so it becomes the 4th letter from the left.

11. _____

12. Remove the 5th vowel from the left and re-place it with E; then place another E in the 4th position from the right.

12. _____

13. Locate the 5th, 6th, and 7th letters from the right; reverse their order.

13. _____

14. Insert an A in 1st position at the left.

14. _____

15. Remove all O's.

15. _____

WHAT'S THE ANSWER?

ANIMAL KINGDOM

by Eugene T. Maleska

ACROSS

1. Rough sound
5. Moses' scout
10. Jockey's crop
14. Killer whale
15. Of the birds
16. Use a whetstone
17. Lookouts' platforms: hyph. wd.
19. Capri, for one
20. Intimidate
21. Role
22. Rag
24. Trolleys running late at night: 2 wds.
26. Summaries
27. Dobbin's fare
28. Carried along
29. Stir up
32. Puppy's "hello"
33. George or T.S.
37. Persian elf
38. Levelheadedness: 2 wds.
40. Angers
41. Brown pigment, in oil painting
42. Layout
43. Ursa Minor: 2 wds.
45. Harridans
46. Resin
47. Timetable abbreviation
48. Recipient of a check
49. Helps in crime
51. Bit of wit
52. Mooring ropes
55. Marine reptiles
59. Isolate
60. June bugs
61. Compass point
62. Rub the wrong way
63. Famous suffragist: 2 wds.
66. Spanish pot
67. Contort
68. Eye layer
69. Something for an "operator"
70. Indian in the British army
71. Comedian Lahr

DOWN

1. Italian boy's name
2. Sioux missile
3. Frown angrily
4. Fido's offering
5. — Islands, off NW Africa
6. States firmly
7. Inventory
8. Adjectival suffix
9. Rouse to action
10. Burdensome possession: 2 wds.
11. Throws (a party)
12. Arm of the sea
13. Titled Britons
18. Former Belgian prime minister
23. Choreographer DeMille
25. Decorative stamp: 2 wds.
26. Turned-down corner of a page
28. Tonsorial artists
29. Plug of wood
30. Jeopardy
31. Mountain crest
32. Australian badgers
34. Dental filling
35. Missouri river
36. High-strung
38. Color
39. "Goof"
44. Defamation
48. Race-track word
50. Builds
51. Innocence
52. King of Judea
53. Old-womanish
54. Author Cather
55. Trunk
56. "Split"
57. Set foot in
58. Attack: 2 wds.
60. Coffee-making method
64. Veneration
65. New reporter

Solution is on page 286

CROSS NUMBERS

The idea of Cross Numbers is to arrive at the figures given at the bottom and right-hand column of each diagram by following the arithmetic signs in the order they are given in the diagram (that is, from left to right and top to bottom) using only the numbers above each diagram. Solutions are on page 304.

A

1 2 3 4 6 7 8 9

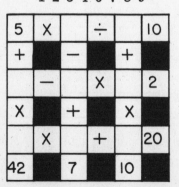

B

1 2 3 4 5 7 8 9

C

1 2 3 4 5 6 8 9

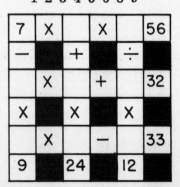

ACROSS

1. Started
6. Scatter
11. Hole-making tool
14. Perfume
15. Abode
16. Sheep's bleat
17. Golf-ball position
18. Pledge
20. Invite
21. Muddle
23. Kiln
24. Fake jewelry
26. Behindhand
28. Wealth
29. Revolve
32. Gleam
34. Similar
35. Fetch
36. Merry
39. Agree (with)
40. Magnificent
41. Companion of faith and charity
42. Weeding implement
43. Commerce
44. Bather's need
45. Lofty self-respect
46. Tyrolean peasant skirt
47. Saw eye to eye (with)
50. Part of the china set
51. Bank transactions
52. When it's "soft" it's flattery
54. Work at the city desk
58. Pull hard
59. Walk unsteadily
62. Expert
63. Lifetime
64. Bird of prey
65. Frequently
67. Cherry-colored
68. Velocity
69. "Beauty and the —"

DOWN

1. Soothing oil
2. Lake —, where Perry defeated the British
3. Leaves
4. Exist
5. "Grab forty winks"
6. Push rudely
7. Large book
8. Destruction
9. Curvy letter
10. "Crying buckets"
11. Make ashamed
12. Squander
13. Minnesota sights
19. By —, by memory alone
22. Quench
25. Deed
27. Devoured
28. Watermelon remnant
29. Reckless
30. Mixture
31. Current
32. Class
33. Queue
35. Small nail
36. Graduate's robe
37. Mimicked
38. Shout
40. Grating
41. Mount
43. Locks of hair
44. "Thanks," to a waiter
45. It's "mightier than the sword"
46. Fool
47. Sacred table
48. Kind of chisel
49. Had a tantrum
50. Confined
52. Wise
53. Eye amorously
55. Group of facts
56. Sherbets
57. Canvas shelter
60. Spigot
61. Actor Reiner
66. Santa —, New Mexico

Solution is on page 286

VACATION FROM VEXATION?

This little quiz is designed to amuse, not confuse you. All of the fictional characters below speak up about vacations. From the clues given (written in the modern vein) see how many you can identify. Answers are on page 303.

1. "Get away for a weekend? Now, really! What am I going to do with all those kids? Besides the repairmen are coming in . . . yep, the old shoe leaks!"

2. "Reservations? What are the jet rates for one adult and seven dwarfs?"

3. "A vacation? You kidding? I'd jump at the chance. I'm so sick of this boring existence. Spin, spin, spin. Gold, gold, gold. And no union covers this trade, either!"

4. "OK, OK, OK. So he might turn into a handsome, rich prince. Meanwhile, I would like a change from this *beastly* place!"

5. "Nah, no vacations for me. See, I got it too easy. I can wish myself off to any planet, anywhere, any-time. Right now all I wish is that I had some silver polish. My hand's getting all green from rubbing this lamp. Whoops, wow, that was fast! See what I mean?"

6. "You know how I'd get a rest, don't you? No trips, no cruises, just bring that rhyme about me up to date! Do me a favor, how about some plain, ordinary cornflakes! Forget those curds and whey, curds and whey, curds and whey. . . ."

7. "Crazy, man! I dig you and your noise about time off, but well, like I dig what I'm doing the most! Course, if you could come up with a 'Rhythmic Rats' Convention,' then I'd communicate! C'mon over to my pad, man, I blow a mean pipe. Those 'cheese-grabbers' dig me the most. Man, when I blow, they go!"

43 EASY CROSSWORD

ACROSS

1. Book parts
6. Small ponds
11. Small bed
14. Oak-tree nut
15. One-way sign
16. Stir
17. Pronoun
18. Steals from
20. Before
21. Object used for catching butterflies
22. Neither
24. Moistens
26. Lifeless
28. Stumble
30. Well-behaved, as a child
32. Attempts
35. Ocean
37. Regrets
39. Canvas shelter
40. Pilfers
43. Trail
45. Pigpen
46. Exclamation of surprise
47. Genuine
49. Falsehoods
51. Overhead railroad
52. Exist
54. Place for inserting coins
56. Withdraw from public life
58. Harbor
60. Ripped
62. Boy
63. Perspire
65. Acid in taste
67. Tiers
70. Harvest
72. Bucket
74. Pouring part of a pitcher
75. Lowly dwelling
77. Ventilate
79. Break off suddenly
81. Perform
82. Employ
83. Roofing material
85. Drain
87. Furious
88. Singing voice
89. Paid out money

DOWN

1. Use oil colors
2. Marlon Brando, for one
3. Depart
4. Blunder
5. Feature of Sun Valley
6. Clergyman
7. Either
8. Unrefined metal
9. Nobleman
10. Sugary
11. Gum drops, for example
12. Lyric poem
13. Small child
19. Ask for a handout
23. Ascend
25. Chowder, for one
27. Skill
29. Table fruit
31. Distribute cards
33. Come in
34. Fashion
36. Malt beers
38. Agitate
40. Washing bars
41. Hurl
42. Taste of the ocean
44. Back of the foot
48. Plunder
50. Asterisk
53. Built
55. Pitfall
57. Pagan god
59. Roofing material
61. Pencil rubber
64. "Skoal!", for example
66. Soft metal
68. Broaden
69. Volleyball, for one
71. Heap
73. Young girl
75. Sound from a beehive
76. Washington is its capital: abbr.
78. Sped
80. Energy
84. As far as
86. You and I

Solution is on page 286

WHAT'S THE NAME?

Allow yourself 10 seconds per question to decide what first name each of the groups of three below has in common. 9 right is excellent, 7 right is good, 5 right is just passing. Answer is on page 304.

1. Taft, Burns, Browning
2. Johnson, Houston, Goldwyn
3. Whitman, Shirra, Raleigh
4. Clay, Longfellow, Lodge
5. Jefferson, Edison, Dewey
6. Madison, Cooper, Buchanan
7. Mead, Truman, Smith
8. Burton, Nixon, Byrd
9. Key, Drake, Bacon
10. Truman, Lauder, James

There are zany definitions in this Crazy Crossword, so please look out for traps. For example, 34-Across is "Cow catcher", and the answer is LASSO. The clues are sly, so be careful.

Solution is on page 286.

ACROSS

1. Good Scotch device for raising hair
6. Cat's bark
10. What *your* face looks like in a photo; not *my* handsome puss!
13. Unlike Gaul, this was divided into two parts
14. Soviet song like "Sioux City Sue"; "Volga City —"
15. Prominent Alto, well known in California
16. Fetter-weight bracelets
17. Now, here's a gal who's really on her toes
19. What dieting Fatso did between between-meal snacks
21. "Sonny: Come home. All is forgiven. Papa worried. (Signed) Mother."
22. Remove the chassis and bolt
23. Uncertainties of the whether
25. The mighty one of old Rome
26. Laughs and music on Broadway @ $15.00 per
28. Family go-carts; capacity, seven
31. National Association of Millionaires
34. Cow catcher
36. Tongue twister: — seesaws down by the seashaw
37. Make mental movies starring the ego
39. A 1000-IQ-er, he thinks
42. Downtown Elkery
43. It's on the up and up (or down and down)
45. Having a developed underhand
46. Swiss holey of holeys
49. She dances by De Mille stream
51. Household help: obsolete
52. Before marriage she was this high to a grasshopper
53. He alone can answer "What's cookin'?"
57. When Dummy was told to go jump in the lake, here's how he was last seen
60. Trouser motif at Leavenworth
62. Put in a plug for a long line of light tripper-uppers
64. What you get from carrots and spinach
65. Something no wedding cake should be without
66. You spell eggs with this: 2 wds.
67. Kind of yx bird
68. Bro's pigtailed defender, admirer, and irritatress
69. Something for the birds
70. Six-months-old Junior's face after cereal

DOWN

1. If you're crafty, it's obtainable at a bargain sail
2. Necklace mermen give mermaids
3. O, throw the soprano what she's yelling for!: 2 wds.
4. He gives hundreds of dollars for miserable quarters
5. What you're at when you're at home at home
6. Hail, hail, the gang's all here
7. How Father Time gets by
8. Something you get in the eye
9. This has a mustache, a lot of blubber, is ten feet tall and seaworthy
10. Hangouts for good sailsmen
11. There's something humerus about this bone
12. The Rams failed to attain it in '76
15. More inclined for a harder fall
18. English Slave, Now Extinct
20. Proposed county seat for Davenport, Iowa
24. After a shocking blowout, they leave everybody in the dark!
27. The ginny Whitney
29. You've got to hit it on the head to drive a point home
30. A kind of Chinese chop
31. gnideceR chin?
32. Oriental babysitter
33. My first is attractive to women, my second is silent, my whole is from the Far North, poor dogs!
35. As the patriotic oculist said to the wise old Indian: "— can you see?"
38. Give him some rye and he sure feels his oats
40. Tin things in Bolivia
41. All Really Exist
44. Sambas of 1920
47. What ballplayers do in the spring
48. "The Light That Failed" was not the story about this man
50. One way to make present salary cover present cost of living
54. Hungry sword swallowers swallow these, too . . .
55. . . . and take these French delicacies for dessert
56. Hey, Dreamboat, your slip is showing!
57. Dog, turtle, canary, cat, goldfish
58. What Caesar became after his 61st birthday
59. Something found on a diamond
61. Mixed-up math
63. Many poor fish get caught in this

45 HARD CROSSWORD

ACROSS

1. Magna —
6. Stiffener
12. Frightened
18. Freight
23. Western shows
24. In —, privately
25. Full of small holes
26. Teem
28. Vacation that's not much of a change: 2 wds.
30. Groups of eight
31. Holder for ivy
33. Up to
34. Made public
35. Swindlers
37. Harvester
39. Garden tool
40. Defeat utterly
41. Enjoys
42. Thin
43. "Vanessa" composer
44. Yield
45. Luau drink
46. Irritated
47. Scandinavians
48. Hounded
49. Taj —
50. Worry about: 2 wds.
52. Matched
53. Device
54. Feudal estates
55. Eager
56. Get rid of
57. Granted
59. Frenzy
60. Placed at intervals
63. Charted
65. Barked shrilly
66. Heavy rains
69. Highway sounds
70. Befuddle
72. Hastened
73. Contrary
74. Adage
75. Off
76. Taper
77. Turned in for money
79. Sullen
80. In —, entirely
81. Actor Harrison
82. Wall paintings
83. Lamented
84. Indian dish
85. Till now: 2 wds.
86. Steep overhang
88. Criticized
89. Score
90. Facing
91. Voice quality
92. Accompanied
94. Massive
95. Looked for gold
96. Sweater fabric
98. Attracted
99. Emotionally
100. Obtaining by trickery
103. Imply
104. Active citizen
105. Experimental project
106. Mountain lakes
107. Old card game
108. Wall hanging
109. Blissful place
111. Dispute
113. Saucy
114. Legatee
115. Knocked down
116. Agreements
117. Vigor: slang
118. Punctuation mark
119. Author Fleming
120. Zeal
121. Istanbul natives
122. Luggage
123. Publication make-up
124. Economist
126. Explain
127. Texas-Louisiana lake
128. Imposing entrance
129. Square columns
130. Is guilty of
132. "Bonanza" star Greene
133. Wavy hair-do
135. Gaels
136. Carpentry joint
137. Hazardous
141. Chatter
142. Irritate
143. Styles
144. Look: slang
145. Greek letter
146. West Indian shrubs
147. Thin plank
148. Dumb mistake: slang
149. Asked the cost of
150. Exploit
151. Very small amount
152. Came crashing down: 2 wds.
154. Hot-water tank
155. Scope
156. Cudgel
157. Inoculations
158. Old-fashioned person
159. Mass meeting
160. Issued
162. Staffs of royalty
164. Aphrodite
165. Trite
166. Duplicates
167. Salons
168. Window squares
169. Affection
172. Prosecuted
173. Be ambitious
175. Reason
176. Reimbursed
177. Rhythm instruments
181. Gleaming
182. Trim, as trees
183. Deprived
184. Jacob's wife
185. Loafer
186. Be uncertain
187. Smallest amount
188. Lodestone
189. Unmanageable person
190. Masculine
191. Building wing
192. Handbag
193. Actress Lollobrigida
194. Family tree
196. Modern hostelry
197. Highway systems
199. Livestock
201. Fastened anew
202. Truthful
203. Watering hole
204. Army PX
205. Lump of earth
206. Multitude
207. Informed
209. Pennant
210. Large soup bowl
213. Assembles, as troops
217. Debase
218. Eden
219. Matures
220. "Square": slang
221. Say under oath
222. 6th Hebrew month
223. Stop right there!: 2 wds.
224. Least adulterated
225. Praises
226. Ancient Persian
227. Midwest State: abbr.
228. Squalid
229. Rhythmic
230. Catalogues
231. Latin dance
232. Effective
234. Service station
236. Selfish person: 4 wds.
239. Evening reception
240. Makes amends for
241. Pencil part
242. More recent
243. Gardening problem
244. Most fashionable
245. The "D" in FDR
246. Misplaces

DOWN

1. Get-up
2. Own up to
3. Genuine
4. Weight unit
5. Attacked
6. Made points
7. Yarns
8. Among
9. Crimson
10. Biscuit
11. Country outing
12. Ladles
13. Jaunty
14. Wiles
15. Caviar
16. Alienated
17. Abandoned
18. Covered
19. More competent
20. Noise from a den
21. Rifle or pistol
22. In a predicament: 6 wds.
23. Exhaust one's supply: 2 wds.
27. East Indian cedar
28. Scottish accents
29. Walker
32. Staggers
36. Sometime in the future: 2 wds.
38. Encourage
41. Black-and-blue
42. Filched: slang
43. Began to flower
44. Light boat
46. Wanders
47. Taste
48. — on, talked about incessantly
49. "Get spliced"
51. "Goofy": slang
52. Students
53. Broke open
54. Dark
56. Wastes time
58. Hoped
59. Absurd action
60. Acute
61. Might
62. Selfish purpose to promote: 4 wds.
63. Threaten
64. Wine bottle
66. Linger
67. Turkic tribesman
68. Cutlass
70. Actress, Lynn —
71. Poured
73. Husky
76. Porous vessels used in assaying
78. Vehicle for coasting
79. Moody
80. Trousseau item
82. Chops fine
83. Chief Justice, Earl —
84. Start (a meeting): 3 wds.
85. Melodies
87. Mountain lion
88. Looked 79-down
89. Coach
90. Cheaply metallic
93. Cover crop
94. Locks securely
95. Swamp
96. Chest of drawers
97. Celestial
99. Cues
100. Twists out of shape
101. Average
102. Reached: 2 wds.
103. Indian title of respect
104. Bravery
105. Small change: 2 wds.
106. Rhythm
110. Sprites
111. Slice
112. Vacuums
113. Redcap
115. Shackle
116. Relatives of the penny dreadful: slang
118. Nook
120. Barriers
121. Rich cake
122. Entrances
123. Counterfeited
125. Confuse
126. Legal excuse: hyph. wd.
127. Supply food
128. Mused
130. Novelist Buck
131. Equestrian
132. Spear
133. Lunatic
134. Disagreeable situation: 5 wds.
135. Fellows
137. Regular newspaper
138. Questionable: 3 wds.
139. Customary procedures
140. Located
141. Door parts
142. Descendants of ancient Egyptians
143. Advances
144. Openwork screen
147. Churlish ones
148. Fake
149. Iron Curtain country
150. Put on weight
152. Essay
153. Gift recipient
154. Robber
155. Established ceremony
157. Floor
159. Pursued: 2 wds.
161. Sir
163. Gist
164. Brag
165. Famous shepherdess: hyph. wd.
168. Hesitate
169. Non-flowering plant
170. Blemished
171. Holy
173. Deadly pale
174. Type of rock
175. Grossly stupid
176. Entertain
178. Slipper
179. Bulrushes
180. Troutlike fish
182. Livens up
183. Raillery
184. Area
187. Ghastly
188. Type of glove
189. Names
190. Thirty days
192. Baffling question
193. Web-footed bird
195. Respectable
196. Overgrown with lichen
198. Irrigate
199. His "hat's in the ring"
200. Complete
202. Antlers
204. Type of sweater
206. Aggressive salesmanship: 2 wds.
207. Braid
208. Scads: slang
209. Hairless
211. Turned upside down
212. Renew (a custom)
213. Declaim
214. Gets satisfaction for
215. Roomer
216. Vow
218. Deep ravines
219. Least polite
220. Cuban leader
223. Sharpened
224. Knights' aides
225. Summer fabric
226. — Carlo
228. Father
229. Walking stick
230. Mona —
231. Malicious gossips
233. Untruth
235. Quarrel
237. Lass: slang
238. — Tse-tung

Solution is on page 291

ACROSS

1. Hen's quarters
5. Ecologist's concern
9. Light blow
12. Annul
13. Castro's land
14. Fruit drink
15. Flower plots
16. Scent
17. Ignited
18. A couple
20. Chooses by vote
22. Thoroughfares
26. Cartoonist Capp
27. Wharf
28. Pay-stub "info"
33. Brewery output
34. Either's mate
35. Man's nickname
36. Lubricate
37. Fell back into illness
40. Bird of peace
41. Exist
42. Scholarly
44. "Skinflints"
48. Greek letter
49. Commotion
50. Tiny particle
52. Coconut tree
56. Countdown number
57. Split
58. N.Y. canal
59. Droop
60. Water pitcher
61. Ragout

DOWN

1. Baby bear
2. Undivided
3. Peculiar
4. Placard
5. Vehicles for small fry
6. Soggy soil
7. Woodwind
8. Wreath
9. Body powder
10. Mine entrance
11. Caresses
19. You and I
21. Actor Wallach
22. Shadowbox
23. Piece of bathroom flooring
24. Stagger
25. Paraguay's continent: abbr.
29. Savior
30. Midday
31. Donate
32. Toboggan
34. Run, as a machine
38. Mr. Lincoln
39. Overhead train
40. Window hangings
43. Near
44. Small rugs
45. Concept
46. Chantey or ballad
47. Pack away
51. Crude metal
53. Actor Carney
54. "Whopper"
55. Cat's "complaint"

ACROSS

1. Impulse
5. Rubbish
10. "Slowpoke"
11. Public address
13. Fencing move
14. "— the bullet," face a situation bravely
15. Mother
16. Since
17. Plot
19. Aries' symbol
20. However
22. Russian news agency
23. Carry on, as a war
24. Sacred
26. Tibia and ulna
27. Large crucifix
28. Sailors
29. Muscle
31. Frankness
33. Scarlet and wine
34. Immense
35. Encountered
37. First-rate
38. Shopping place
40. Spouse of 15-Across
41. Hence
42. Grasp
43. Detecting device
45. Very ugly
47. Are
48. Slight error, as of memory
49. Force

DOWN

1. New
2. Became a candidate
3. Fish spears
4. November event
5. Decorates
6. Proportion
7. Had lunch
8. Senor's consent
9. Reverent honor
10. Kill
11. Stout
12. Identifies
18. Applause
19. Payment to kidnappers
21. Long, angry speech
23. "A — to the wise . . ."
25. Solemn promises
26. Exchanged quips
28. Chore
29. Impudent
30. Draw back
31. Jack and joker
32. Meal
34. Worth
36. Sour; tangy
38. Lea sounds
39. Hack
42. Drill sergeant's word
44. Clamor
46. Prosecutor: abbr.

Solutions are on page 286

ACROSS

1. Zulu weapon
6. Narrow piece
11. Daché creation
14. Shipping container
15. Sports palace
16. Have a debt
17. June's flowers
18. Slang word for 11-Across
19. Lively, noisy
21. Utilize
22. Snare
24. Gets to one's feet
25. Exist
26. Robin —, famed outlaw
27. Noisy
28. Dictionary entry
29. Drains, as fat from gravy : 2 wds.
33. Pursue
35. Look angrily
36. Under the weather
37. Final
38. Sounds of pain
39. Urgent request
40. Gallery collection
41. Paint layers
42. Skirt fold
43. Small opening for a secret look
45. Appian Way

46. Maiden
47. "Oodles"
48. Paid notice
50. Revolve
53. Discover
54. Historic age
55. Incident
56. Skillet
57. Mistake
59. Dancer Dailey
60. Evade
62. Salary boost
63. Ancient
64. Hotel's prices
65. Knight's horse

DOWN

1. Scour
2. Writing that is not poetry
3. Relieve, as a pain
4. Consumed
5. Bring back to a former condition
6. Lettuce dish
7. Excursion
8. Sunset hue
9. At home
10. Grazing land
11. Bugle or antler
12. Deeply impressed
13. Golf mounds
20. Stenographic supplies

23. Fishing pole
24. Turns, as milk
26. Multitude
27. Bank businesses
28. Squander
29. Serving dish
30. Lubricated
31. Leaping insect
32. Off key
33. Applaud
34. Large rabbit

35. Objectives
38. Large deer
39. Frolic
41. Idle gossip
42. Gives thought to
44. Scheme
45. Stood for office
47. Ore pits
48. Got up
49. Challenged
50. Fix again
51. Football-shaped

52. Oversee, as a flock
53. Lose color
54. Cleveland's lake
56. Place
58. Destructive rodent
61. California city : abbr.

Solution is on page 287

"THE MOST"

From the two choices following each question, can you correctly choose which one is "the most"? 7 right makes YOU "the most"! Answers are on page 304.

What is the . . .

1. largest of the Great Lakes?   (a) Michigan   (b) Superior
2. world's largest city?   (a) Tokyo   (b) New York City
3. world's largest island?   (a) Ireland   (b) Greenland
4. world's largest lake (also called "Sea")   (a) Black   (b) Caspian
5. world's highest waterfall?   (a) Niagara   (b) Angel
6. oldest U.S. state?   (a) Rhode Island   (b) Delaware
7. world's highest mountain peak?   (a) Matterhorn   (b) Everest
8. oldest college in the United States?   (a) Yale   (b) Harvard

ACROSS

1. Rogue
6. Work hard
11. Alleges
16. Slow train
17. Artificial jewelry
18. Danger
19. Evade
20. Ceremonies
21. What a dove signifies
22. Poker kitty
23. Get up
25. 20th letter
27. Get it?
28. Birch or beech
30. Speak
32. Newest
34. Misplace
36. Face: slang
38. Behold!
39. "Hash mark"
42. Originated
44. Tempo
48. Chatter
49. Father
50. Mike's friend
52. Mingle
53. Pale purple
55. Set (a clock)

57. Frozen dessert
58. Drink slowly
59. — Gawain
60. Aged beer
61. Portable shelter
63. Famous
65. Mellowest
66. "Word" from the sponsor
68. Faucet
69. Drug: slang
70. Chattered
74. Quick
76. Whip
80. Fruit drink
81. Grow drowsy
83. Wandered
85. "Stretch the truth"
86. Parts in a play
88. Not sleeping
90. Burning
92. Penniless: slang
93. Parking timer
94. Ranted
95. Drain
96. Noblemen
97. Lock of hair

DOWN

1. Got some "shut-eye"

2. Red or blue
3. Sharp, as a pain
4. Demented
5. Excuse
6. Fairy
7. Body's middle part
8. Honored
9. Broke bread
10. Examination
11. Urgent request
12. Victory sign
13. Obliterate
14. Uses a kitchen utensil
15. Frozen rain
24. Trick
26. — Paso, Texas
29. The "Four Hundred"
31. Dust cloth
33. Child
35. Unwraps
37. Essay
39. Separated
40. Vestige
41. Black bird
42. Legal profession
43. "Oat-burner"
45. Likeness
46. Specks

47. Put forth
49. Station
51. Spring flower
54. Hubbub
55. Free (of)
56. Coat part
59. Divide
62. Actor Hunter
64. Roofing material
65. Went by car
67. Thicker
69. Frogmen
70. Dresses (oneself)
71. Worship
72. Under
73. Get along
75. Card game
77. Swarming (with)
78. Fathers
79. Obeys
82. Moist
84. Scoot
87. Piece (out)
89. Very small
91. Distant

Solution is on page 287

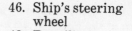
ACROSS

1. Rebuke
6. Not this
10. Provided with footwear
14. Thin cracker
15. Alleviate
16. Broad
17. — depth, thoroughly
18. Protection from attack
20. Smooth (out), as problems
21. Drunkard
23. Dispatch
24. Table linen
26. Rumor
28. Masculine
29. Underground vegetable
30. Considered
34. — bear, white animal
36. Ceremonies
37. Film, "The Three Faces of —"
38. At any time
39. Wanderer
40. On the ocean
41. Meadow
42. What George Burns puffs on
43. Make powdery
44. Veracious
46. Tresses
48. They use acetylene torches
51. Apparel
54. Free —, self-determination
55. Partake of the evening meal
56. Penniless
57. Letter carrier
60. 3.1416
61. Seasoning
62. Qualified
63. Stair post
65. Whirlpool
66. Meshy fabrics
67. Bird's chirp

DOWN

1. Rustling sound, as of silk
2. Eskimo boat
3. "— Thee I Sing"
4. Went first
5. Bureau
6. Very small
7. Round of applause
8. Beast of burden
9. Adolescent: hyph. wd.
10. Stealer: slang
11. Employ
12. Scent
13. Refuse to accept as true
19. Daring act
22. Striking dramatic scene
25. Alack!
27. Hindmost part
28. Measuring instrument
30. Competitor
31. Longs for
32. Divisible by 2
33. Lifeless
34. Animal hide
35. Above
36. Rascal
39. Certain infantry member
40. Desert like
42. Scorch
43. Chivalrous
45. Number of feet in 10 yards
46. Ship's steering wheel
48. Beguiling tricks
49. New Delhi coin
50. "Don't cry over — milk"
51. Church part
52. Leaping amphibian
53. "Ratted" (on)
54. Become limp
58. Mr. Lincoln
59. FDR's — Deal
64. The two of us

Solution is on page 287

STATE THE STATES

You needn't be a whiz at geography to play this geography game. Just follow the "addition" problems below and see how many you can make into States. Example: Actress Lupino+an exclamation would be IDA HO.

Answers are on page 304.

1. Actress Lupino+an exclamation
2. Modern+H+an electrical abbreviation+English county
3. A bird's bill+R+to inquire+A
4. Raw mineral+G+a preposition
5. Tint+a fuss
6. Doing laundry+a measure of weight
7. A man's nickname+cover snugly+Y
8. An original American+A
9. M+a preposition+a color+A
10. A woman's name+acreage
11. Mother+a preposition+E
12. W+part of "to be"+against+transgression
13. An unmarried girl+your and my+you and —, we
14. A woman's nickname+to disencumber+A
15. Minerva, for short+NE+a drunkard+A
16. Sick+a preposition+O+a form of "to be"
17. Just bought+a knitted fabric
18. R+a mortar trough+E+exists+country

CALCULATE A WORD

This puzzle is based on the idea that A is 1, B is 2, C is 3, and so on, with Z being 26; B + C would equal 5. Solving hint: If you take the sum of the given letters in each set below and subtract it from the total, you will get the sum of the unknown letters. Then you can determine which letters, when added together, will not only give you this sum but also will form an everyday five-letter word when written on the dashes provided. You may use a letter more than once in any word you form.

Example: CHASE would be given as C + __ + __ + S + E equals 36 or
3 + 8 + 1 + 19 + 5 equals 36.

Answers are on page 304.

A-1	N-14
B-2	O-15
C-3	P-16
D-4	Q-17
E-5	R-18
F-6	S-19
G-7	T-20
H-8	U-21
I-9	V-22
J-10	W-23
K-11	X-24
L-12	Y-25
M-13	Z-26

1. A + — + O + — + E = 43

2. — + R + — + I + T = 68

3. C + — + — + L + — = 36

4. — + — + A + — + D = 44

5. E + X + — + — + — = 55

6. — + — + O + O + — = 61

7. R + — + — + — + E = 79

8. — + H + R + — + — = 84

9. — + — + F + — + — = 38

10. — + — + — + — + W = 65

QUICK! WHO WAS IT?

Each of the following words or phrases should remind you quickly of some Biblical, literary, or historical character. To get 18 or more is excellent, 15 to 17 good, 12 passing.

Answers are on page 304.

1. Magic lamp
2. Excalibur
3. Hemlock
4. Kite
5. The Alps
6. Fountain of Youth
7. Golden Fleece
8. Trident
9. Cherry tree
10. Box of troubles
11. Winged feet
12. Coat of many colors
13. Pair of scales
14. The Mock Turtle
15. Mystic smile
16. Stratford-on-Avon
17. Trafalgar
18. Half Moon
19. "Cross of Gold" speech
20. Old North Church

ZIG ZAG

Fill your answers to the definitions into the diagram at the bottom of the page. The letters E (east), W (west), NW (northwest), NE, SW, etc., tell you the direction in which the letters must be written. The last letter of each word is always the first letter of the next word. The number to the left of the definition is the total number of letters in each word. To start you off, the first word is GREEN.

Solution is on page 311.

5	E	Color for St. Patrick's day
6	SE	1, 8, or 765
4	W	Soda flavor, — beer
5	NE	Hobo
5	W	Student
8	SE	Item in a cosmetic case
3	NE	Frontiersman Carson
5	NW	Add up to
4	SW	Final
6	NW	Crowd of people
10	E	Florist's building
5	SW	Roof edges
4	NW	Do the marketing
5	E	Flower part
4	SE	Small cube (of sugar)
6	W	Word of politeness
6	SE	Short trip, often done as a favor for another
8	NE	Follower of Jesus
3	NW	Have breakfast
4	SW	So
5	SE	Item at a playground
4	W	Compass direction
5	NW	Garbage
4	NE	Headgear
5	E	Shows to a chair
3	SW	Sorrowful
3	W	Homonym of "dew"
3	SW	Age
5	SE	Astray; wrongly
5	W	Muscular power
2	NE	You and I
3	SE	"Slippery" fish
5	W	Faithful
4	NW	Girl
4	E	Slender
5	NW	Fable's lesson
4	W	King of the jungle
5	SE	Birds' homes
5	SW	Word with "thunder" or "snow"
3	E	Angry
4	NE	Word in a letter salutation
4	SE	Wander
3	W	Damage
5	NW	Leases

2	SW	Baseball position between 2nd and third bases: abbr.
6	SE	Metal adhesive
3	W	Tear
3	NE	Tablet of paper
9	E	Adapt (a story) for a stage performance
4	NW	Send out; give forth
3	NE	"— the season ..."
5	SE	Frighten
3	W	Shade tree
4	SE	Army meal
6	W	No-school season
3	NE	Decay
3	SE	Funnyman Conway
5	W	Join together, as two companies
2	NW	Per: abbr.
8	E	Names officially, as to a position
3	NE	Use the eyes
2	SE	Actor Asner

(Continued in next column)

3-MINUTE QUIZ

by Al B. Perlman

Here's a quiz on some assorted subjects. See how many questions you can answer correctly, then turn to page 304 for the answers and scoring information. Only trivia experts will get the top score of 45 points.

1. The next time you run into one of those people whose opening greeting is always "Hey, whattaya know?" you can inform him (or her) that the Ob -Irtysh is a river 3,460 miles long and that it empties into the Gulf of Ob . (If you think I made that up, get out the almanac and look it up for yourself.) Anyway, here are some of the longest rivers in the world . . . and all you have to do is match each one up with the body of water it empties into.

1. Nile	_____	a. Gulf of Mexico
2. Amazon	_____	b. Gulf of Guinea
3. Mississippi	_____	c. Rio de la Plata
4. Yangtze	_____	d. Mediterranean Sea
5. Niger	_____	e. Yellow Sea
6. Parana	_____	f. Atlantic Ocean
7. Huang	_____	g. East China Sea

2. There's a place in the U.S.A. where, if you spread your feet apart and lean forward so your hands touch the ground, you'll actually be in four states. (If you don't know where that is, you'll also be in a state of confusion which makes it five.) As you face north, name the states where the following parts of you are in temporary residence.

   a. left arm: _____

   b. right arm: _____

   c. left leg: _____

   d. right leg: _____

3. Even if you're not a football buff, you probably know that the Rose Bowl is in Pasadena. (If you enjoy cluttering up your mind with a lot of facts really not worth knowing, Michigan defeated Stanford, 49 to 0, in the 1902 Rose Bowl game.) Anyway, here (as anybody can plainly see) is a list of cities. Name the Bowl associated with each.

   a. New Orleans: _____

   b. Jacksonville: _____

   c. El Paso: _____

   d. Miami: _____

   e. Dallas: _____

4. Here's a sequence of American Presidents, but somebody's name is obviously missing. Whose?

   Grover Cleveland, Benjamin Harrison, _____, William McKinley

5. You shouldn't have waited so long to apply for membership in your local Origami Society, because it just folded. Maybe you wouldn't mind explaining to the rest of us, though, just what *origami* is.

CROSS SUMS

NUMBER 6

In each of these Cross Sums, we have not filled in a digit combination. Instead, we have shaded one area in the diagram. If you need help starting the puzzle, the digit combination to go into that area is listed on page 320.

NUMBER 7

Solutions are on page 301

INTELLIGENCE CLOCK

The 20 problems of the Intelligence Clock are not difficult tests of knowledge, but you do have to be clear-headed and systematic to find your way from problem to problem as quickly as possible. In most cases, the solution of one problem depends on the solution of the one preceding it. You may not skip any questions, and all have to be answered in their logical order in order to make your time score valid.

Now, look at your watch and draw your starting time into the clock at top left of this page. Begin solving with problem 1; that problem will give you the number of the next problem to solve. When you have finished all the problems, draw your finishing time into the clock at top right of this page. Then, check your answers and your time score on page 305.

Remember, you're working against the clock, so you won't want to waste a minute!

1

There is a number between 30 and 40 which, when it is spelled out, has the same first and last letters. Now, reverse the digits of that number, spell out the new number, and the first and last letters will again be the same. This letter is the —th letter of the alphabet. Go to the problem indicated by this number.

2

Now, make better sense of the following sentence by substituting the words "question" and "marks" for the two words which obviously do not belong in this sentence:
BEFORE POPPING THE IMPORTANT PSYCHOLOGY MAN OFTEN PAINTS TIME.
The number of letters in the words between "question" and "marks" adds up to the number of the next problem.

3

Tell how many times the numeral 4 is required in numbering the pages 1 to 70 and you will have the number of the next problem.

4

Washington,
If I were in Rome,
  Berlin,
    France
I would be in Germany and the
  Europe
    French.
people would be English.
    Italian.

In the above sentence, only one of each set of choices makes the sentence a completely true statement. Cross out the incorrect ones and make a 3-letter word of the initial letters of the words not crossed out. Take this word to problem 19.

5

Which of the four E's below corresponds in every respect with the E on the black background? Go to the problem number shown above the correct E.

6

If flammable and inflammable mean the same thing, go to problem 15. If they have opposite meanings, go to problem 20.

7

If you were to first cut this triangle and rectangle all apart, following the lines shown, you would have a number of pieces when you had finished. The difference between the number of pieces in the rectangle and the number of pieces in the triangle will lead you to the next problem.

8

If B is larger than C, X is smaller than C. But C is never larger than B. Pick the only correct statement of the three below, and then go to the problem it leads you to. (a.) Therefore, X is never greater than B. (If correct, go to problem 13.) (b.) Therefore, X is never smaller than B. (If true, go to problem 16.) (c.) Therefore, X is never smaller than C. (If true, go to problem 19.)

The name of the city which was destroyed by the eruption of Mount Vesuvius was:

13. Naples 7. Palermo 6. Pompeii

The number of the correct answer is the number of the next problem.

How many sides excluding top and bottom, does the figure which contains the number 10 above have? Multiply your answer by 2 to find the next problem.

If you look at the United States flag you will see some familiar shapes. Two of these shapes enclose the number of your next problem.

Imagine a box full of steel balls. The diameter of all balls is 2½ inches. Open a flap in the box's bottom and the balls will fall out at the rate of 50 a minute. The opening is 9 inches long by 4½ inches wide. How many balls would fall out in a minute if the opening were 20 inches long and 2⅝ inches wide? The answer will lead you to the next problem unless it's the end!

One letter in the diagram below disturbs the logical order in which all the other letters are arranged. Which letter is wrong, and what letter correctly belongs in its place? When you have determined the *right* letter, find its numerical position in the alphabet, subtract 4 from that number, and get the number of your next problem.

If the wrong answer to the question "Which is the most populated country on earth?" is China, go to problem 17. Otherwise, go to problem 18.

(a) Books are to chapters as words are to —.
(b) When is to where as time is to —.
(c) Spots are to leopards as — are to zebras.
(d) Link is to chain as part is to —.

Fill in the answer to each of the incomplete relationships above, and one of your answers will suggest the design around the number of the next problem.

What is the word meaning half a half-dollar? Using this word to denote a percent, find that percentage of this problem number. The result is the number of your next problem.

The number of the next problem appears within a problem you have already solved on these pages. In fact, it appears twice, one above the other.

"The — should realize that the only difference between himself and the other party was nothing more than a plain tiff in the eyes of the court. Dismissed!" The word missing in the above paragraph can be found elsewhere in the same paragraph. The number of letters in the missing word, divided by three, leads to the next problem.

The word you brought to this question can be mixed with only one of these three groups of letters to form a new word (no proper nouns allowed):

CLC   ZEN   PHO

The shape indicated by the word you form encloses the next problem's number.

Just add the numbers in each of the two rows of figures below. The difference between their totals will be your next problem.

9,   7, 12, 28, 19, 31, 29, 13, 5, 14 =
17, 25, 12, 16, 3, 27, 18, 6, 11, 22 =

LOGIC PROBLEM 4

THE PATIENT'S BUSY MORNING

by Evelyn B. Rosenthal

A bored patient tried to amuse himself by counting the hospital personnel who came into his room one morning: three physicians (including the patient's own family doctor), a nurse, and a nursing student. From the following clues, can you find the full name of each and the order in which Pat and the others made their six visits?

NOTE: The family physician, the intern, and the resident are referred to or addressed as Dr.

1. Bob's visit was immediately preceded and followed by the nurse's two visits.

2. Dale's visit was after Ms. Ames's, but it was not the last.

3. Gold visited the patient more often than Evans did.

4. Sandy read carefully what the intern and Dr. White had already written on the chart that day.

5. The resident's visit was before both of Jill's visits; Dr. Fry's was after both.

Solution is on page 305

	Ames	Evans	Fry	Gold	White	order of visits 1 2 3 4 5 6	family doctor	intern	nurse	nursing student	resident
Bob											
Dale											
Jill											
Pat											
Sandy											
family doctor											
intern											
nurse											
nursing student											
resident											
order of visits 1											
2											
3											
4											
5											
6											

BUILD SCORE

The object of BUILD SCORE is to form 5-letter words for the highest possible score. You do this as follows:
In the diagram below, one letter of each word to be formed is given. Use the letters to the left of the diagram to form your words and score yourself according to the number value preceding each line of letters. You may use a letter as many times as you wish in forming your words. Don't forget to count the letter given in each line as part of your score. For example: On the second line, you would score 24 points for HAIKU, 31 points for PILAU or 42 points for BAYOU. Solve each line in this way. Words beginning with a capital letter, foreign words, slang, contractions, obsolete, poetic, and dialect words are not allowed.   Our score of 431 is shown on page 305.

POINTS	LETTERS
10—	B Y O
9—	L T U
8—	I X
7—	D R V
6—	E Q
5—	C S W
4—	J N
3—	A F K
2—	M P Z
1—	G H

DIAGRAM

1					B
2					U
3					I
4					L
5					D
6					S
7					C
8					O
9					R
10					E

COMEDY OF ERRORS QUIZ

Each paragraph below contains some literary reference—and also one or more errors pertaining to the literary work, the author, and the times in which he lived. You are indeed a bookworm to spot a total of 12 mistakes in all.
Answers are on page 305.

1. As William Shakespeare finished dictating the last page of his "Comedy of Errors," he told his typist to take the first train to London and deliver the manuscript to his publishers; and above all, not to forget to bring him back a carton of cigarettes.

2. While H. G. Wells was writing "Twenty Thousand Leagues under the Sea." he visited the first American nuclear submarine for details. He wrote "Around the World In Eighty Days" especially for the movies, and it was a smash hit.

3. Charles Dickens wrote "Oliver Twist," which was first published in a London magazine called Pickwick Papers. He also wrote "The Old Curiosity Shop," which was owned by Dombey and Son. His "A Christmas Carol" was written especially for Lionel Barrymore to recite during the holiday season.

4. The world's best-seller is the "Holy Bible." It was written in many books and by many authors. Moses was responsible for *Deuteronomy*, Daniel wrote the *Psalms*, Solomon, *Proverbs*, and John, the *Book of Revelation*.

DIRECTORY DILEMMA

Mr. Painter got the job of making a directory listing all the tenants in a commercial building. Unfortunately, when he had all the signs in place (as shown below) he realized he had gotten them all mixed up. But his assistant remembered that in each case the names of the owners sounded as if they had something to do with the businesses. Armed with this bit of knowledge, can you figure out how to rearrange the signs pictured below so that they will be correct? At the bottom of the page are listed the names of the various businesses, for your convenience. All you have to do is fill in the type of businesses on the dashes provided. Answers are on page 304.

BUILDING DIRECTORY

DUKE & LORD	CLEAN WATER COMMISSION
CANNON & GUNN	FINE FABRICS, INC.
GOLD & SILVERS	DOMESTIC EMPLOYMENT AGENCY
RIVERS & BROOKS	STEP-IN DANCE STUDIO
HUNT & FISCHER	BANG-UP WEAPONS, INC.
NICHOLS & BUCK	CAPE COD TOURIST BUREAU
WOOLEY & TARTAN	SMALL LOANS, INC.
HOUSEMAN & COOKE	GOSSIP COLUMN AGENCY
WYNTERS & SOMMERS	ROYAL ESCORT SERVICE
FINN & GILL	PRECIOUS METALSMITHS
KISS & TELL	SPICE FOR ALL SEASONS, INC.
LINDY & CHARLESTON	SPORTSMAN MAGAZINE

1. DUKE & LORD _____

2. CANNON & GUNN _____

3. GOLD & SILVERS _____

4. RIVERS & BROOKS _____

5. HUNT & FISCHER _____

6. NICHOLS & BUCK _____

7. WOOLEY & TARTAN _____

8. HOUSEMAN & COOK _____

9. WYNTERS & SOMMERS _____

10. FINN & GILL _____

11. KISS & TELL _____

12. LINDY & CHARLESTON _____

TANGLED JINGLES

Below you will find the first lines of three 4-line verses. The remaining three lines of each are tangled up with each other in the nine lines on the left below. Can you untangle them and "restore" the verses? Our "poetry" is printed on page 304.

They broke our secret code, today"

Are hailed by hostesses (no dishes!)

"Since I've absconded," so it read

I hope you're only idding-kay . . ."

(In fact, t'was but a note)

And by the cleaners . . . That's for sure

While "X" said, "Dear, oh, dear

"Please cancel out my vote"

On laps, a wee bit insecure

1. The treasurer's report was brief

_____

_____

_____ !

2. Those paper plates that sit "just so"

_____

_____

_____ !

3. The spy said, "To my great concern,

_____

_____

_____ !

ARROW MAZE 2

Starting at the S (start) and following the arrow leading out of that S, see if you can find your way to F (finish) in five minutes or less. When you reach a square that contains an arrow, you MUST follow the direction of that arrow. You may not simply go through a square that contains an arrow, and you may not change directions until you hit an arrow that tells you you may do so. When you reach a square that has two arrows, you may choose either direction. In this maze you MAY NOT retrace your own path although you MAY cross it.   Our solution is on page 314.

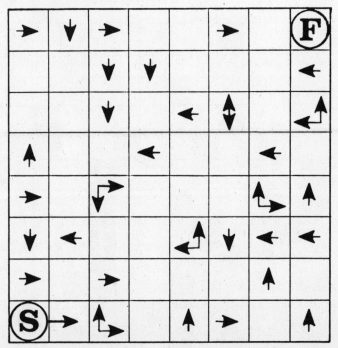

DEFINITIONS   WORDS

A. Author's
   income   214 180 50 97 230 153 67 7 162

B. Begone!:
   3 wds.   221 81 9 20 127 187 75 157 52 149

C. Like an ogre
   or fiend   13 144 212 93 30 183 41 205 161 240

D. In its scab-
   bard, as a   105 192 35 165 60 16 229 121 209 87
   sword

E. Type of TV
   antenna: 47 169 70 227 198 113 12 189 124 78
   2 wds.

F. Garden of the
   golden apples, 172 38 141 107 69 22 218 31 79 3
   in Greek
   mythology

G. Painstakingly
   slowly: 3 wds. 28 96 42 158 224 178 76 116 74 197

H. Author of
   "Kids Say the   175 36 130 216 108 236 58 164 29 136
   Darndest
   Things"

I. Specious
   reasoning   176 213 207 99 5 150 40 167 132

J. Basic dis-
   cipline in   54 173 112 1 234 95 190 215 133 170
   yoga

K. Take into
   custody   46 82 208 148 233 24 168 103 185

L. English
   coal city   44 225 146 64 206 98 10 160 34

M. Officiated at
   a race   120 202 94 147 128

N. Drill ser-
   geant's com-   186 14 57 129 238 156 33 106 85
   mand: 2 wds.

O. Got the
   hang of   53 226 126 181 84 71 217 152

P. Comparable
   to: 4 wds.   138 89 237 4 55 92 201 163 219 59

Q. Personal
   stake in a   68 135 184 17 100 37 228 73 223
   competitive
   venture: 21 115 88 155 196
   2 wds.

R. Emergency
   substitute   139 62 211 111 179 86 166 194 51 26

S. On —, well-
   balanced: 109 39 142 134 15 210 232 61 25 204
   3 wds.

T. Midday   143 195 19 2 90 117 239 122

U. Winningest
   coach in col-   43 193 102 203 18 188 83 114 123 32
   lege basket-
   ball history:
   2 wds.

V. Young
   informer   6 191 66 137 80 125 23 72 174 48

W. Mistaken:
   3 wds.   231 199 110 182 159 220 45 145 56 119

X. Native of the
   Western   8 101 131 140 171 63 222 77 177 49
   Hemisphere

Y. Religious
   philosophy   118 151 27 91 235 154 65 200 11 104
   which empha-
   sizes mental
   powers:
   2 wds.

1 J	2 T		3 F	4 P	5 I	6 V	7 A		8 X	9 B		10 L	11 Y	12 E		13 C	14 N	15 S	
16 D	17 Q		18 U	19 T	20 B	21 Q	22 F		23 V	24 K	25 S	26 R		27 Y	28 G	29 H	30 C	31 F		32 U
33 N	34 L	35 D	36 H	37 Q	38 F	39 S	40 I	41 C		42 G	43 U	44 L		45 W	46 K	47 E	48 V	49 X	50 A		51 R	52 B
53 O	54 J	55 P	56 W	57 N		58 H	59 P	60 D		61 S	62 R	63 X	64 L	65 Y	66 V	67 A	68 Q	69 F		70 E	71 O	72 V
73 Q	74 G	75 B		76 G	77 X	78 E	79 F	80 V	81 B		82 K	83 U	84 O	85 N	86 R	87 D	88 Q	89 P	90 T		91 Y	92 P
93 C	94 M	95 J	96 G		97 A	98 L		99 I	100 Q		101 X	102 U	103 K	104 Y	105 D	106 N	107 F	108 H	109 S	110 W	111 R	112 J
	113 E	114 U	115 Q	116 G	117 T	118 Y	119 W		120 M	121 D	122 T		123 U	124 E	125 V	126 O	127 B	128 M	129 N	130 H	131 X	132 I
	133 J	134 S	135 Q	136 H		137 V	138 P		139 R	140 X	141 F	142 S	143 T	144 C	145 W	146 L	147 M	148 K		149 B	150 I	151 Y
152 O		153 A	154 Y		155 Q	156 N	157 B		158 G	159 W	160 L	161 C		162 A	163 P	164 H		165 D	166 R	167 I	168 K	
169 E	170 J	171 X		172 F	173 J	174 V	175 H		176 I	177 X	178 G		179 R	180 A		181 O	182 W	183 C	184 Q		185 K	186 N
	187 B	188 U	189 E	190 J		191 V	192 D	193 U		194 R	195 T	196 Q	197 G	198 E	199 W	200 Y		201 P	202 M	203 U	204 S
205 C	206 L	207 I	208 K	209 D	210 S		211 R	212 C	213 I	214 A		215 J	216 H	217 O		218 F	219 P		220 W	221 B	222 X	223 Q
	224 G	225 L		226 O	227 E	228 Q	229 D		230 A	231 W	232 S	233 K		234 J	235 Y	236 H		237 P	238 N	239 T	240 C

DEFINITIONS   **WORDS**

A. Port or claret, e.g.: 2 wds.
32 171 95 140 189 79 20

B. Founded
156 107 200 163 153

C. Wink
53 77 29 176 115 23 201 123 16

D. "Procrastination is the art of keeping up with —": Marquis
199 43 89 76 9 162 125 83 134

E. Put in gear
211 168 170 150 38 181

F. Game played with small, flat disks: var. sp.
41 106 50 111 59 12 157 202 80
5 137 98

G. Secondary level of instruction: 2 wds.
69 28 6 193 17 116 206 64 36 133

H. Burst free of restraints
112 96 124 161 205 185 144

I. Meeting the usual standard, as of health: 3 wds.
2 183 121 139 71 204 145 155 65

J. Policies identified with FDR: 2 wds.
110 207 192 166 149 75 118

K. Fan; rooter
126 81 129 114 135 208 70 45 103 196

L. Goal of many pilgrims
151 212 186 105 175

M. Part of "IBEW"
34 3 25 56 94 97 210 159 104
67 147

N. Desire for food
142 90 188 131 10 24 158 55

O. Tell in detail
174 190 164 57 37 136 18

P. Anti-insect substance
148 173 180 160 63 108 33 141 14

Q. Mountain chain in Italy
58 27 62 101 138 4 143 86 47

R. Device found in cow barns
99 130 119 179 74 39 51 154 13

S. Mischievous action
46 8 60 85 109 26 73 169 194 146

T. Area receiving the greatest force of an earthquake
165 68 177 54 92 213 195 198 35

U. Diverging into two contradictory parts
102 15 93 42 178 72 22 82
203 49 127

V. A type of fungus growth
21 167 184 191 152 11

W. Extreme
128 7 30 52 87 44 182 66 120

X. A secretarial skill
88 19 187 132 113 197 100 172 1

Y. Removal, as from a threatened area
91 61 48 209 31 117 40 122 78 84

1 X	2 I	3 M	4 Q	5 F	6 G		7 W	8 S	9 D		10 N	11 V	12 F	13 R	14 P	15 U	16 C	17 G		18 O	19 X	20 A
	21 V	22 U	23 C	24 N	25 M	26 S		27 Q	28 G	29 C	30 W	31 Y	32 A	33 P		34 M	35 T	36 G	37 O	38 E	39 R	40 Y
	41 F	42 U	43 D		44 W	45 K	46 S	47 Q		48 Y	49 U	50 F	51 R	52 W	53 C	54 T	55 N		56 M	57 O		58 Q
	59 F	60 S	61 Y	62 Q	63 P		64 G	65 I		66 W	67 M	68 T	69 G	70 K	71 I	72 U	73 S	74 R	75 J	76 D	77 C	78 Y
79 A		80 F	81 K		82 U	83 D	84 Y	85 S	86 Q	87 W	88 X		89 D	90 N	91 Y	92 T	93 U	94 M		95 A	96 H	97 M
98 F	99 R		100 X	101 Q	102 U		103 K	104 M	105 L	106 F	107 B	108 P		109 S	110 J	111 F		112 H	113 X	114 K	115 C	116 G
117 Y	118 J		119 R	120 W	121 I	122 Y	123 C	124 H	125 D	126 K	127 U		128 W	129 K	130 R	131 N	132 X	133 G	134 D		135 K	136 O
137 F	138 Q	139 I	140 A	141 P		142 N	143 Q	144 H		145 I	146 S	147 M	148 P	149 J	150 E	151 L	152 V	153 B		154 R	155 I
156 B	157 F		158 N	159 M	160 P		161 H	162 D	163 B	164 O	165 T	166 J	167 V	168 E	169 S		170 E	171 A	172 X	173 P	174 O	175 L
176 C	177 T	178 U	179 R		180 P	181 E	182 W	183 I	184 V	185 H		186 L	187 X	188 N	189 A	190 O	191 V		192 J	193 G	194 S	195 T
	196 K	197 X	198 T	199 D		200 B	201 C	202 F		203 U	204 I		205 H	206 G	207 J		208 K	209 Y	210 M	211 E	212 L	213 T

Quotation is on page 308.
Word list is on page 312.

by **RUE MATHISON**

DEFINITIONS	WORDS

A. Composer of "The Student Prince" — 187 93 140 70 228 27 100

B. Complete; unmitigated: 3 wds. — 219 98 107 4 120 82 144 197 184

C. Forming a heap — 163 204 154 111 17 141 76 121

D. Make disparaging remarks about — 66 134 175 122 222 92 209 30

E. Specialist on a diplomatic staff — 71 181 85 168 226 147 40

F. British flag: 2 wds. — 206 115 14 97 178 43 165 124 72

G. "On the up and up" — 68 229 211 177 136 221 157

H. Moved around a central point — 193 110 60 162 126 5 81 52

I. Obliquely — 105 205 46 225 37 171 117

J. Best-cared-for; "spiffiest" — 22 128 195 216 61 49 123

K. Oklahoma in the 1930's, e.g.: 2 wds. — 180 114 21 146 58 132 214 8

L. Style of pants worn by men and women: hyph. wd. — 83 192 13 149 200 102 38 159 113 133

M. San Francisco Bay is one — 20 142 220 75 7 189 160

N. Miserly, ungenerous person: (slang) — 112 26 148 176 77 196 227 44 155 95

O. Technical "savvy": hyph. wd. — 33 166 150 194 131 190 9

P. Composed of diverse elements — 16 191 88 202 101 116 215 151

Q. Purified; made elegant — 109 78 145 36 198 63 170

R. Baubles, bangles, and beads — 224 108 1 186 153 42 167

S. Famous quadrennial event — 223 127 96 173 164 119 45 91

T. Mattingly, et al. — 210 65 138 15 212 53 29

U. A process for making steel: hyph. wd. — 137 208 34 169 3 79 183 118 48 217

V. Quantity, as of movie film — 106 172 51 203 86 188 59

W. Durante's "Mrs. —" — 161 152 80 199 31 125 12 182

X. State governed by a few persons — 139 201 156 24 130 213 55 185 11

Y. Word for people living in a Word X — 103 174 207 56 135 69 230 6 129

Z. Carry on; persevere: 3 wds. — 104 179 89 218 28 143 158 64

AA. Profound, as an analysis: hyph. wd. — 57 99 74 47 25 87 19

BB. First atomic-powered submarine — 94 32 84 18 41 67 23 54

CC. Make progress: 2 wds. — 62 2 50 90 39 73 10 35

1 R	2 CC		3 U	4 B	5 H	6 Y		7 M	8 K	9 O	10 CC	11 X	12 W		13 L	14 F	15 T	16 P	17 C		18 BB	19 AA
20 M		21 K	22 J	23 BB	24 X		25 AA	26 N	27 A	28 Z	29 T	30 D		31 W	32 BB	33 O	34 U	35 CC		36 Q	37 I	
38 L	39 CC	40 E	41 BB	42 R		43 F	44 N	45 S	46 I	47 AA	48 U	49 J	50 CC	51 V		52 H	53 T	54 BB	55 X	56 Y	57 AA
58 K	59 V		60 H	61 J	62 CC	63 Q	64 Z	65 T	66 D	67 BB	68 G	69 Y		70 A	71 E	72 F	73 CC	74 AA		75 M	76 C	77 N
78 Q	79 U	80 W	81 H	82 B		83 L	84 BB	85 E		86 V	87 AA		88 P	89 Z	90 CC	91 S	92 D		93 A	94 BB	95 N
96 S	97 F	98 B	99 AA	100 A		101 P	102 L	103 Y	104 Z		105 I	106 V	107 B	108 R	109 Q		110 H	111 C	112 N	113 L	114 K	115 F
116 P	117 I	118 U	119 S	120 B	121 C		122 D	123 J		124 F	125 W	126 H	127 S	128 J	129 Y		130 X		131 O	132 K	133 L	134 D
	135 Y	136 G	137 U	138 T	139 X	140 A	141 C	142 M	143 Z		144 B	145 Q		146 K	147 E	148 N		149 L	150 O	151 P	152 W	153 R
	154 C	155 N	156 X	157 G	158 Z	159 L	160 M		161 W	162 H	163 C	164 S	165 F	166 O	167 R		168 E	169 U	170 Q		171 I	172 V
173 S	174 Y	175 D	176 N	177 G	178 F	179 Z	180 K		181 E	182 W	183 U	184 B		185 X	186 R	187 A		188 V	189 M	190 O	191 P	192 L
193 H		194 O	195 J	196 N		197 B	198 Q	199 W	200 L	201 X	202 P		203 V	204 C		205 I	206 F	207 Y	208 U	209 D	210 T
211 G	212 T	213 X		214 K	215 P	216 J	217 U		218 Z	219 B	220 M	221 G	222 D	223 S		224 R	225 I	226 E	227 N	228 A	229 G	230 Y

DEFINITIONS   **WORDS**

A. Employee on a spread: 2 wds.
107 157 207 9 122 62 21 51 180

B. Rakishly fashionable
100 188 132 203 66 165

C. Brood, or feel keen regret: 4 wds.
19 96 83 193 151 144 166 57 32 109
120 133 101 7 45

D. Angry to the point of frenzy: 4 wds.
136 220 37 159 59 74 11 91
28 82 125

E. Do some tinkering on: 2 wds.
60 139 211 42 149 77 70 13 87 187

F. Outgoing waters: 2 wds.
10 31 141 169 206 108 63

G. "— In Arms," Roberts novel
20 215 39 170 76 142

H. Laughing uncontrollably: 2 wds.
146 99 26 214 106 56 8 46 75 175

I. Adds trimmings to
54 194 129 174 35 72 23 205
2 118 140

J. Agree completely (on): 4 wds.
79 192 130 86 102 167 61
38 117 162 52

K. — off, keep at a distance
58 190 143 25 204

L. Coming period of Christ's reign on earth: 2 wds.
115 156 105 185 64 29 43 176 210
18 1 80 95

M. Approaching failure: 3 wds.
24 199 186 173 98 168 222 84 154 111

N. Evangelist's command
182 128 4 69 216 48

O. Long, curved Turkish sword
196 33 158 112 15 92 178 221

P. Diminishing: 3 wds.
135 49 121 88 201 150 209 179 36

Q. Ancestral record: 2 wds.
147 198 85 71 30 110 126 152 183 5

R. International distress signal
68 131 97 217 195 171

S. Little sailboat
134 213 27 153

T. Arrogant: 3 wds.
104 67 208 160 202 55 181 163 78
16 116 155 94

U. Not too severe to be borne
93 14 197 148 219 177 34 73 161

V. Precede in time
47 113 189 44 12 123 137 212

W. — to, forbid with threats: 4 wds.
65 40 184 218 145 138 17 81 50
3 103 119 200 90

X. Miscellanea: 3 wds.
172 127 41 6 164 124
114 53 191 89 22

1 L		2 I	3 W	4 N	5 Q		6 X	7 C	8 H	9 A	10 F	11 D	12 V	13 E	14 U	15 O		16 T	17 W	18 L	19 C	20 G
21 A	22 X	23 I	24 M	25 K	26 H		27 S	28 D	29 L	30 Q		31 F	32 C		33 O	34 U	35 I	36 P		37 D	38 J
39 G	40 W		41 X	42 E	43 L	44 V		45 C	46 H	47 V	48 N		49 P	50 W	51 A	52 J		53 X	54 I	55 T	56 H	57 C
58 K		59 D	60 E		61 J	62 A	63 F	64 L	65 W		66 B	67 T	68 R	69 N		70 E	71 Q	72 I	73 U		74 D	75 H
	76 G	77 E	78 T	79 J	80 L	81 W	82 D		83 C	84 M	85 Q	86 J		87 E	88 P	89 X	90 W		91 D	92 O	93 U	94 T
95 L	96 C	97 R		98 M	99 H	100 B	101 C	102 J		103 W	104 T	105 L	106 H	107 A		108 F	109 C	110 Q	111 M		112 O
113 V	114 X		115 L	116 T	117 J		118 I	119 W	120 C	121 P	122 A		123 V	124 X	125 D		126 Q	127 X	128 N		129 I	130 J
131 R	132 B	133 C	134 S		135 P	136 D		137 V	138 W	139 E	140 I		141 F	142 G	143 K	144 C	145 W	146 H	147 Q		148 U	149 E
150 P	151 C	152 Q	153 S	154 M		155 T	156 L	157 A	158 O		159 D	160 T	161 U	162 J		163 T	164 X	165 B		166 C	167 J	168 M
169 F		170 G	171 R		172 X	173 M	174 I		175 H	176 L	177 U		178 O	179 P	180 A		181 T	182 N	183 Q	184 W	185 L
186 M	187 E	188 B	189 V		190 K	191 X	192 J	193 C		194 I	195 R	196 O		197 U	198 Q	199 M	200 W	201 P		202 T	203 B	204 K
	205 I	206 F	207 A	208 T		209 P	210 L	211 E		212 V	213 S	214 H		215 G	216 N	217 R		218 W	219 U	220 D	221 O	222 M

Quotation is on page 308.
Word list is on page 312.

by M. W. SMITH

DEFINITIONS   WORDS

A. Chilled cream-potato soup 218 57 119 135 99 73 143 13 197 69 211

B. Got around: 2 wds. 39 17 30 65 196 102 205 184 113 163 118

C. Comes to naught, as a plan: 3 wds. 71 9 125 43 109 16 36 156 216 98 81

D. The —: Washington, Oregon, and Idaho 202 155 112 186 26 150 168 58 198

E. Greek writers like Theognis of Megara and Solon: 2 wds. 5 114 35 175 180 62 84 45 105 145 115

F. "Techiness" 4 101 50 160 110 91 121 194 34 213 31 129

G. In this time 28 106 66 176 134 123 24 164

H. Presently: 3 wds. 61 77 128 104 136 14 209 93 172 190 159

I. Old King Cole summoned them: 2 wds. 107 75 126 220 46 64 189 178 166 6 80 33 157

J. "I blossom — when most you need me." Inscription for a fireplace, by T.A. Daly: 3 wds. 68 177 212 167 10 204 199 92 170 165 60

K. Petty lie, in Britain 103 83 90 153 183 47 200 139 22 40

L. In transit: 3 wds. 122 38 19 146 219 12 138 94

M. The Bastille, for one: 2 wds. 108 148 185 51 97 67 161 85 53 144 174 169

N. Legislator 88 21 116 154 162 132 42 141

O. Exams for occupational suitability: 2 wds. 96 44 59 117 203 127 52 142 187 8 131 208 82

P. Position of control: 2 wds. 20 25 70 149 137 78 130 214 140

Q. In *Courtesy*, Belloc says this is in courtesy: 3 wds. 193 124 15 48 147 191 2 210 86 56

R. Drowned a speaker's voice with derisive shouts: 2 wds. 120 201 87 23 49 11 181 27 173 54

S. Device used in brewing the "hot pot": 2 wds. 207 111 55 95 1 41 217

T. Here, and perhaps hereafter: 3 wds. 89 37 3 192 171 151 206 76 32 133 179 195 79 158

U. Restores to productivity 72 188 100 18 7 182 215 74 63 29 152

	1 S		2 Q	3 T	4 F	5 E	6 I	7 U	8 O	9 C	10 J	11 R		12 L	13 A	14 H	15 Q	16 C
17 B	18 U	19 L	20 P	21 N	22 K	23 R	24 G		25 P	26 D	27 R	28 G	29 U	30 B		31 F	32 T	33 I		34 F	35 E	36 C
	37 T	38 L	39 B	40 K	41 S	42 N	43 C		44 O	45 E	46 I	47 K	48 Q	49 R		50 F	51 M	52 O		53 M	54 R
55 S		56 Q	57 A	58 D	59 O	60 J	61 H	62 E	63 U	64 I	65 B		66 G	67 M	68 J	69 A	70 P	71 C	72 U		73 A	74 U
75 I	76 T		77 H	78 P	79 T	80 I	81 C	82 O		83 K		84 E	85 M	86 Q	87 R	88 N	89 T	90 K		91 F	92 J
93 H	94 L		95 S	96 O	97 M	98 C		99 A	100 U	101 F	102 B		103 K	104 H	105 E		106 G	107 I	108 M	109 C	110 F	111 S
112 D		113 B	114 E		115 E	116 N	117 O	118 B	119 A	120 R	121 F	122 L	123 G	124 Q	125 C		126 I	127 O	128 H	129 F		130 P
131 O	132 N	133 T	134 G		135 A	136 H	137 P		138 L	139 K	140 P	141 N	142 O	143 A	144 M		145 E	146 L	147 Q	148 M	149 P
150 D	151 T	152 U		153 K		154 N	155 D	156 C	157 I	158 T	159 H	160 F		161 M	162 N	163 B	164 G	165 J		166 I	167 J	168 D
169 M		170 J	171 T	172 H		173 R	174 M	175 E	176 G	177 J		178 I	179 T	180 E	181 R		182 U	183 K		184 B	185 M	186 D
187 O	188 U	189 I		190 H	191 Q	192 T		193 Q	194 F	195 T	196 B		197 A	198 D		199 J		200 K	201 R	202 D	203 O
204 J	205 B	206 T	207 S		208 O	209 H		210 Q	211 A	212 J		213 F	214 P	215 U	216 C	217 S	218 A	219 L	220 I	

DEFINITIONS   WORDS

A. Good grief!, e.g.
137 154 12 123 94 201 56 59 168

B. Cool off!: 2 wds.
172 2 79 214 90 28 138 142 101 66

C. Criminal lawyer: slang
7 194 27 127 180 80 38 97 161 206

D. Endless, or seemingly so
107 91 77 177 81 149 181 25 39

E. Composer of "Pomp and Circumstance": 2 wds.
156 217 88 208 45 200 203 37 220 70 117

F. Nothing special; ordinary: 4 wds.
128 125 171 106 111 152 32 210 35 116 199 162

G. Wet blanket
103 11 224 213 51 218 155 129 48 173

H. Stupid; stubborn
226 82 140 133 4 197 184 110 144 15 167

I. Speechify: 2 wds.
20 53 147 178 115 60 205 193 55

J. Basic and powerful
47 73 153 209 21 166 119 134 52

K. Uncle Tom's wife: 2 wds.
175 121 76 182 43 89 13 190 102

L. Domineering; expert
85 198 34 112 8 22 54 151 136

M. God's heavenly abode
83 23 131 42 174 93 225 126

N. Part of the wrist
84 74 100 36 10 135 159

O. Downhearted: 3 wds.
29 108 179 67 227 211 219 141 72 187

P. Push-ups, etc.
223 186 122 146 71 49 202 99 30 33 196 19

Q. November 1
40 143 61 212 188 148 216 165 69 57

R. Check in the earliest stage: 4 wds.
160 14 105 75 1 96 183 50 150 195 26

S. Fault or inadequacy
118 92 65 41 192 3 215 169 158 87 31

T. Violate a boundary
63 124 68 132 145 221 189 9

U. Play by Sutton Vane: 2 wds.
170 62 104 185 44 98 16 120 164 78 5 228

V. Don Quixote's steed
157 18 163 64 95 86 207 176 113

W. 1972 in the Chinese calendar: 4 wds.
204 58 6 114 130 191 17 139 46 222 24 109

1 R	2 B	3 S	4 H	5 U	6 W	7 C	8 L	9 T		10 N	11 G	12 A	13 K	14 R	15 H	16 U		17 W	18 V		19 P	20 I
21 J	22 L	23 M	24 W	25 D		26 R	27 C	28 B	29 O	30 P	31 S		32 F	33 P	34 L		35 F	36 N	37 E	38 C	39 D	40 Q
41 S	42 M		43 K	44 U	45 E	46 W	47 J	48 G		49 P	50 R	51 G	52 J		53 I	54 L		55 I	56 A	57 Q		58 W
59 A	60 I	61 Q	62 U	63 T	64 V	65 S	66 B		67 O	68 T		69 Q	70 E	71 P		72 O	73 J	74 N	75 R	76 K		77 D
78 U	79 B	80 C		81 D	82 H	83 M	84 N	85 L	86 V	87 S		88 E	89 K	90 B	91 D		92 S	93 M		94 A	95 V	96 R
97 C	98 U	99 P	100 N		101 B	102 K	103 G	104 U		105 R	106 F	107 D	108 O	109 W		110 H	111 F	112 L	113 V	114 W		115 I
116 F	117 E	118 S	119 J		120 U	121 K	122 P	123 A		124 T	125 F	126 M		127 C	128 F	129 G	130 W	131 M	132 T		133 H	134 J
135 N	136 L	137 A	138 B		139 W	140 H	141 O		142 B	143 Q	144 H		145 T	146 P	147 I	148 Q	149 D		150 R	151 L	152 F
153 J	154 A	155 G	156 E	157 V	158 S	159 N	160 R	161 C	162 F		163 V	164 U	165 Q	166 J		167 H	168 A	169 S	170 U	171 F	172 B	173 G
174 M	175 K	176 V	177 D	178 I		179 O	180 C	181 D	182 K		183 R	184 H		185 U	186 P	187 O		188 Q		189 T	190 K	191 W
192 S		193 I	194 C	195 R	196 P	197 H		198 L	199 F	200 E		201 A	202 P	203 E	204 W		205 I	206 C	207 V	208 E	209 J	210 F
211 O		212 Q	213 G	214 B		215 S	216 Q	217 E		218 G	219 O	220 E	221 T	222 W		223 P	224 G	225 M	226 H	227 O	228 U

NUMBER FILL-INS

In these puzzles, the numbers to be entered into each row across and each column down will form a numerical sequence with the numbers already in the diagram. For example, if you saw the numbers 5, ?, 15 already in the puzzle, you could figure out that the missing number is 10, and the sequence involves adding 5 to each number to get the next number. The sequences always increase from LEFT to RIGHT and from TOP to BOTTOM. See if you can figure out each sequence and fill in all the missing numbers.   Solutions are on page 319.

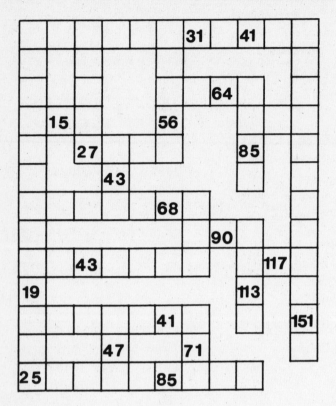

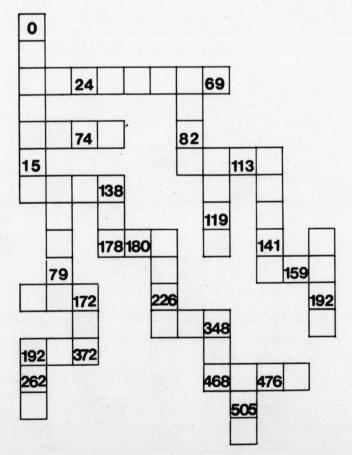

BOWL-A-SCORE CHALLENGER 4

In this bowling game your "pins" are the groups of letters below. In order to score a "strike," you must unscramble (anagram) the "pin" letters of each group and form one 9-letter word. The starting letter for each "strike" word is given. To score a "spare," rearrange the scrambled letters of each group into two words, with no letters left over. Words beginning with a capital letter are not allowed for either "strikes" or "spares." In forming your "spare" words, you may not simply split the "strike" word in two parts and use both exactly as they appear in the "strike" word. For example, FORE and FRONT would not qualify as a "spare" for the "strike" word FOREFRONT.

SCORING: Score 20 points for each "strike" and 10 points for each "spare." Perfect score (10 "strikes" and 10 two-word "spares") is 300.

Warning: This game is really tough! Only word bowling geniuses will score a perfect 300. The words we made are on page 309.

1. T
    R T   I **Strike** _____
    N O P   **Spare** _____
    I M   _____
    A   _____

2. L
    A A   A **Strike** _____
    E N E   **Spare** _____
    D I   _____
    T   _____

3. U
    S T   O **Strike** _____
    O O P   **Spare** _____
    K N   _____
    E   _____

4. C
    I A   I **Strike** _____
    T M I   **Spare** _____
    L P   _____
    E   _____

5. D
    B N   O **Strike** _____
    E E E   **Spare** _____
    I C   _____
    O   _____

6. W
    T U   B **Strike** _____
    E H K   **Spare** _____
    B C   _____
    A   _____

7. V
    R S   S **Strike** _____
    E G N   **Spare** _____
    C E   _____
    A   _____

8. V
    N R   V **Strike** _____
    E E L   **Spare** _____
    B E   _____
    A   _____

9. T
    R S   A **Strike** _____
    H I N   **Spare** _____
    A C   _____
    A   _____

10. Y
    R U   J **Strike** _____
    I I J   **Spare** _____
    C D   _____
    A   _____

FIGURE LOGIC 2

by L.G. Horsefield

Copyright 1989 by Bantam Doubleday Dell Publishing Group, Inc.

Solve Figure Logic by completing some simple arithmetic problems, which will enable you to move from clue to clue through the puzzle.

TO PROCEED: Look at the diagram at the bottom of the page and note that the number "15," answering clue 14-Down has been entered as a starting point. Your next step might be to 11-Down and then to another clue which mentions 11-Down. Continue solving by going from clue to clue as needed.

You might discover that, at times, you will not be able to complete an entire number at first; but you may be able, by logic, to determine what one or more of the digits must be. If you enter those digits into the diagram, they may help you solve other clues, and you can eventually return to the unfinished numbers and finally complete them.

CLUES ACROSS

1. Twice 3-Down
4. Digits of 1-Across reversed
7. Six times 10-Across
8. Same as 5-Down
10. Two less than 14-Across
12. 11-Down multiplied by 14-Down
14. One less than 11-Down
15. One-third of 4-Across
17. Nine times 20-Down
18. 15-Across multiplied by 16-Down
19. Same digit three times
21. Five times 24-Across
24. First two digits of 18-Across
25. Three hundred more than 27-Across
27. 32-Across divided by 5-Down
28. 2-Down plus 24-Across
29. Five times 14-Across
31. One-third of 25-Across
32. Three consecutive digits in order

CLUES DOWN

2. Twice 14-Across
3. Seven times 7-Across
4. Twice 12-Across
5. 9-Down divided by 10-Across
6. 1-Across minus 14-Across
9. Half of 3-Down
11. Two-thirds of 8-Across
13. 1-Across multiplied by 14-Across
14. One more than 11-Down
16. Seven times 24-Across
17. 16-Down plus 24-Across
19. 14-Across plus 19-Across
20. Three times 14-Across
22. Three times 11-Down
23. One thousand minus 4-Across
25. 2-Down plus 19-Across
26. Digits of 32-Across reversed
28. Five times 11-Down
30. Four times 11-Down

Solution is on page 294.

CODE-A-GRAPH

by Floyd R. Miller

Step 1

Start by solving the sentence below which appears in a simple substitution code—another letter of the alphabet has been substituted for the right letter. Look for clues in the coded sentence such as single-letter words which would be either A or I (see the introduction to Cryptograms, page 40, for further solving hints).

Step 2

Transfer the DECODED letters that have arrows above them into the boxlike spaces provided at the top of the diagram below. Write them in consecutive order: that is, as they appear in the decoded sentence. Do not rearrange them and do not skip any letters. REMEMBER: Only your decoded letters, NOT the original coded letters, are to be placed in the spaces at the top of the diagram. After you have placed the letters into their spaces, you will use them as a guide in completing a picture in the diagram.

Step 3

Each letter-number combination at the left of the diagram represents a dot in the diagram. For example, the first letter-number combination represents the dot where column W and row 7 intersect, and the dot where column W and row 14 intersect. You are to draw a line between these two dots. You will not be drawing one continuous line, as is the case in many connect-the-dot puzzles. When you have finished drawing lines between all the dots indicated by the letter-number combinations, you will complete a picture which is hinted at in the coded sentence you solved. We have entered some lines into the diagram which are not indicated by the letter-number combinations to give you a more complete picture.

GHA'PP KCLE NQIN CN'T I BCTS ZIL BQH BCPP

TIMS THZSNQCLD KHY I YICLG EIG, ILE QSYS'T

HLS NQCLD NQIN THZS OSHOPS IYS MSYG DPIE

NH QIMS OAN AO!

W7-W14

W14-A15

A15-T15

T15-D14

D14-D13

D13-T13

T13-T14

T14-A14

W1-W2

W2-A2

A2-F4

F4-U5

U5-Y7

Y7-G7

G7-H5

H5-V4

V4-M2

M2-W2

Solution of the coded sentence is on page 309.   Picture is on page 311.

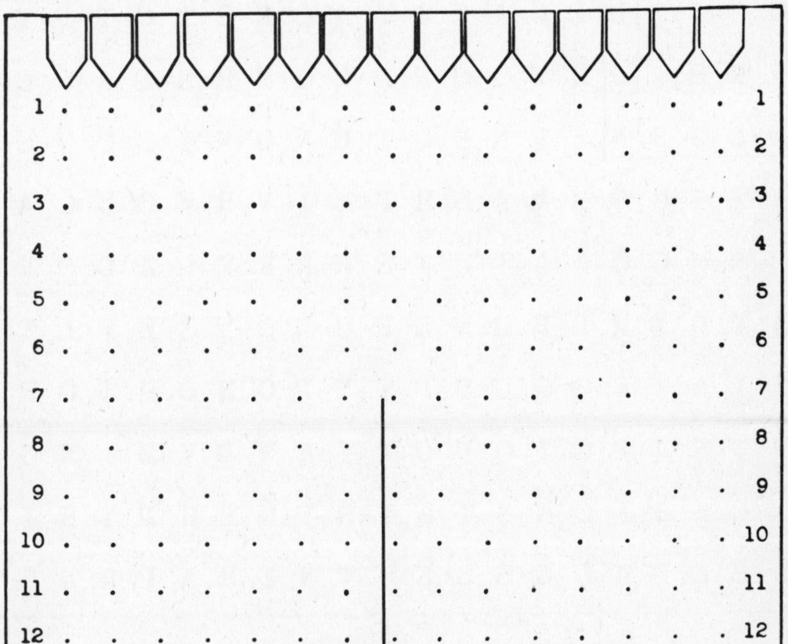

```
H C K R A M E P Y T R O I R E F N I E R
P A T U I S M O V E U P E V I R G U L E
A P N N R A T I V A S T E K C A R B O D
R I E U I N S E R T T R S P E U P M A E
G T D R S O R N R E Y C O P U Q O G W L
A A N I E S P O L I O P Y M U C G R P E
R L I N M O R N M L S T E O A E O Y R T
A S R A I S E U O A C K T V R N T E E E
P E B A C K S R C I S A L I G N T P C P
L N K O O N C L L C T P P F I E Y Y A Y
O D I R L L W A E I Y A O E S T O T P T
W N B A O D T O O R P N G M R S P A C E
E A G S N I F N D O T U N O E I L O N C
R T E C O M M A S H P E I V R W O D C A
C S M C O A A T C T S R R E E R A D O F
A T D X R L R O N E E U E D X S E Y L T
S I A K E O G U U P T N P O H O H T O H
E T S A P S I Q U O T Y A W P Y M I N G
T E H H L O N S T N I R P N E H P Y H I
S L E P A C S E S E H T N E R A P A R L
```

Solution is on page 301

WORD LIST

Align (‖)
Apostrophe (∀̇)
Asterisk (*)
Boldface type (bf)
Brackets ([ ])
Broken letter (×)
Capitals (caps)
Close (⌒)
Colon (⌃)
Comma (⋏)
Dagger (†)
Delete (ℒ)
Em dash (|H|)
En dash (|H|)
Hyphen (=)
Indent (→)
Inferior type (⊘)
Insert (∧)
Interrogation point (?)
Italic type (ital)
Let it stand (stet)
Lightface type (lf)
Lower case (lc)
Margin (⊐)
Move down (⊔)
Move up (⊓)
Paragraph (ℙ)
Parentheses (⟨⟩)
Period (⊙)
Push down (↓)
Quotation marks (∀̇∀̇)
Raise (⊓)
Roman type (rom)
Run on (run on)
~~Semicolon~~ (⌃)
Space (#)
Superior type (∀̇)
Virgule (/)
Wrong font (wf)

WORD LIST

Alcman

Apollonius

Aratus

Archilochus

Bacchylides

Callimachus

Corinna

Euphrion

Hesiod

Homer

Methodius

Nicander

Parthenius

Philetas

Pindar

Simonides

Stesicharus

Theocritus

Theognis

Tyrtaeus

Virgil

Xenophanes

```
W O F O J U Y E S U E A T R Y T C
O N I M E T H O D I U S E R O L O
P I W E M D S O E T R I S O D E R
C C O Q U I O V M A S L T R E J I
B A C C H Y L I D E S O H E K S N
P N L O R A O N S U R I E S U T N
S D S L L I I G I E S K O H E E A
I E W C I P A N S O H I C B E S L
M R M Q U M O N E K D O R S I I I
O A L P I L A S N O L E I D E C G
N W O P L E X C A I P E T D O H R
I M R O P A R T H E N I U S E A I
D O P R I S K C P U N I S T E R V
E A E U P H R I O N S A R A T U S
S W E X O A L Z N O M I N L A S U
O R K I L E T H E O G N I S O O K
P H I L E T A S X O R M I Z E R O
```

Solution is on page 301

MYSTERY DUO
by Sharon A. Winn

1. THE CASE OF THE *SANTA BARBARA* TREASURE

Bobo Swinson, that perennial optimist, bounded into Professor Prufrock's study, exclaiming, "Prof, you won't believe what I've gotten my hands on!"

Professor Prufrock laid aside the book he was reading, and asked mildly, "What is it this time, Bobo?"

Swinson waved a roll of parchment in front of the professor's face, "It's a map. A treasure map. I got it from an old Spanish sailor in B.J.'s Pub last night. It shows exactly where the Spanish galleon *Santa Barbara* went down in the Caribbean! It cost me $150, but if we can locate the wreck, we stand to make millions!"

"Ah, yes, the fabled *Santa Barbara*," the professor said. "If I remember rightly, the *Santa Barbara* went down somewhere southwest of the Bahamas in the mid-17th century."

"That's right," agreed Bobo enthusiastically, "and it was filled to the gunwales with gold and jewels." He looked dreamily off into space. "Just think, professor, I'm a millionaire."

"Hmmm . . .," Professor Prufrock said doubtfully. "Let me see the map."

"Okay, but it's very delicate since it's so old." Bobo carefully spread the map on the desk. The parchment was racked and discolored, and the ink was faded with age. "See here," Bobo said, pointing to a cross marked near the Bahamian Islands. "This is the place. The sailor said that the ship hung on a reef during a storm, and went down with all hands except the two men who made this map."

"Yes," Prufrock replied, picking up the map and scrutinizing it closely. The upper margin was dated 1556 with the name of the mapmaker, Salvador Gonzales, in faded script. The outlines of the land masses were dim, but recognizable. A legend read "Here be dragones" in the area of the Atlantic, and the sea lanes were marked with dotted lines. A large Maltese cross marked the spot where the *Santa Barbara* sank to the southeast of the Bahamas, with "*Santa Barbara*—fortie fathomes undere" scratched next to it in barely legible handwritting.

"Of course," Bobo said, "it's going to cost a lot of money to salvage it. I'll have to go down to the Bahamas and hire divers, and a salvage boat, but if you want to invest a couple of thousand, you'll be sure to get it back a hundredfold." He beamed at Prufrock. "After all, it's the least I can do for an old friend," he said magnanimously.

Prufrock rolled the map back up, and said, "Well, Bobo, though I appreciate your offer, I'm afraid that I couldn't invest in your undertaking. This map is a phoney, and you've lost your money. I'd suggest you have it framed and hang it on your wall. I have no doubt it will look very nice in your den."

"Phoney!" Bobo spluttered. "But, the sailor said it was found in an old sea chest in somebody's attic in Spain. It can't be phoney!"

Prufrock replied, in his mild voice, "But it is. I spotted two errors on it right away."

WHAT WERE THE TWO ERRORS PRUFROCK SPOTTED?

2. THE CASE OF THE CRYPTIC CLUES

"This is the fifth burglary in two weeks," Edge said grumpily, as he led Professor Prufrock up the walk to Ed Harrison's house. "And, the bad thing is that they have no rhyme or reason."

Prufrock stopped to admire an early hyacinth which was thrusting its aromatic blooms through a residue of snow. "What do you mean—no rhyme or reason?" he asked as he stooped to smell the flower's sweet fragrance.

Edge watched the portly professor inhale the flower's scent. "Well, the crimes don't make sense. First, the burglar robbed Joseph Saunders of a map he had gotten from the gas station. Next, he robbed Meister's Delicatessen, and this time he took some ice cream, plus all the cash in the register. Then, he robbed Icabod's Haberdashery, taking only a hat. After that, he robbed Yvonne Thibadeau's house; here he took her aspirin along with her priceless emeralds. But Ed Harrison, the used-car dealer, only lost a ladle, which was worthless. It just doesn't make any sense. It looks like this burglar just grabs whatever is handy when he breaks in."

He hovered over Prufrock as the elderly scholar gently touched the petals of the hyacinth, marveling at the satin smoothness of the flower. Grunting, Prufrock heaved himself to his feet, a formidable task considering his girth. He swayed slightly, regaining his balance, then asked, "Any suspects?"

"We've got five possibilities. All of them are kleptomaniacs who have been arrested before. There's Albert Morgan, and Mickey Ott, and Mark Swiggart, though he says he was out of town at the time of the Meister robbery. And, then there's Michael Smith and David Mitchel."

He started to walk toward the house again, saying, "And, each of them has been seen in the vicinity of at least one of the crimes. Morgan has been spotted at two sites, near the delicatessen and Harrison's house."

They entered the house and went into the kitchen where Harrison's ladle resided before it was stolen. The room had been left untouched since the crime was reported. As they walked into the room, Prufrock kicked a paper bag sending its contents skittering across the polished floor. Edge stopped, a perplexed expression on his face. "That's odd."

"What's odd?" the professor asked.

"This stuff in the bag. We've found the same assortment of things at the other burglaries. Look, here's some hairpins," he said, picking up a couple of metal objects. "And, there's a mirror, an acorn, an earring, some ink, lipstick and a comb. That's the same stuff we found at the Icabod and Thibadeau robberies."

Edge glanced up and saw that Prufrock was looking, with a strange expression on his face, at the bay window. Edge followed his gaze and saw something scrawled with lipstick across the glass panes. It read:

CLAIM HE THIS. M.

"I see he's left his dumb code," Edge commented. "The burglar leaves that same silly sentence at the scene of every burglary. It doesn't seem to mean anything though. Probably just the ramblings of a demented mind."

"On the contrary," Prufrock said in his mild voice. "It makes perfect sense. It's quite plain that this is the burglar's signature. And considering the four other sets of clues he's left, I suspect he **wants** to be caught. In cases of split personality, for instance, often one personality commits a crime and the other personality wants him to be caught. Anyway, you've got the burglar on your list of suspects. Now all you have to do is arrest him."

"I'll be happy to arrest him," Edge said, "but which one?"

WHICH ONE?

Answers are on page 309

CROSS SUMS

NUMBER 8

In each of these Cross Sums, we have not filled in a digit combination. Instead, we have shaded one area in the diagram. If you need help starting the puzzle, the digit combination to go into that area is listed on page 320.

NUMBER 9

Solutions are on page 301

SYLLABLE SAYING

The words that fit the definitions below can be formed by putting together the appropriate syllables from the list directly below. Cross off each syllable as you use it, as each one is used only once; no syllables are left over when the puzzle is completed. The number in parentheses will tell you how many syllables you need for each word. The number of dashes will tell you how many letters there are in each word. If done correctly, you will be able to discover a quotation by reading down (in order) the first letters and then the last letters of the words you have formed. To get you started, we'll tell you the first word is TAXI.   Answer is on page 309.

```
┌─────────────────────────────────────────────────────────────────────────────┐
│                            LIST OF SYLLABLES                                   │
│                                                                               │
│   bark    ci    cle    der    do    e    elf    em    fi    gan    graph    gurt    har    i  │
│                                                                               │
│   i    ic    ja    ju    lor    mas    me    mo    nal    New    nize    o    o    or    pa   │
│                                                                               │
│   Ro    sight    tai    tax    tel    ton    tow    un    ver    yo                          │
└─────────────────────────────────────────────────────────────────────────────┘
```

Definitions	Words
1. Cabby's vehicle	(2) _ _ _ _
2. Word on a health-food label	(3) _ _ _ _ _ _ _
3. To board a vessel	(2) _ _ _ _ _ _
4. Sir Isaac —	(2) _ _ _ _ _ _
5. Modern form of jujitsu	(2) _ _ _ _ _
6. Error of omission	(3) _ _ _ _ _ _ _ _ _
7. Dairy product, often flavored with fruit	(2) _ _ _ _ _ _
8. To transmit a message by wire	(3) _ _ _ _ _ _ _ _
9. Blend melodies together	(3) _ _ _ _ _ _ _ _
10. Small mischievous fairy	(1) _ _ _
11. Last, of a series	(2) _ _ _ _ _
12. — and Juliet	(3) _ _ _ _ _
13. Seaward pull of receding waves	(3) _ _ _ _ _ _ _
14. Spike of frozen water	(3) _ _ _ _ _ _
15. One who makes or repairs clothes	(2) _ _ _ _ _ _
16. Sleepwear with jacket and trousers	(3) _ _ _ _ _ _ _

67. KJL'SS OPQX UYGU APVPUV, GV G LVLGS
UYPQE, EPAH CSHGVLMH—PO QJU JQ UYH
GMMPAGS, UYHQ GU UYH XHCGMULMH.

68. BR NDX JCAJNG GPDH PD PLBTM QKRDVK NDX
GHKJM, PLK DPLKV RKCCDA ABCC QK HVKPPN
GXVK PD YKP LBG SDMK BT RBVGP.

69. PKYEILCEX, LI TLDD KT ECNSI, KTIBE IYAE
KYI IK VB PKDBSCDDX CE ISB BLADQ
PKAECEN DCNSI.

70. DXK MNPLIKQ CJDX DXK SBO CXP JZ SPJHS
HPCXKNK JH MVNDJUBIVN JZ DXVD XK UVH
HKEKN LK ZBNK CXKH XK VNNJEKZ.

71. QBE XLDY JT XLYCEK TDCKSXN XJ QLIN GSJ
VLE'X, GCXS NLTBXZ, BOBE UICOB XSBCI
VLIN.

72. JZBCBRN BL RTW JVR KI SWRRBGS HVWXBR
IKV JCC RTW TKOW VQGL LKOWZKXN WCLW
TBRL.—HJLWN LRWGSWC

73. AKJOAK QLHYBZAPJZ'H XROK-LTT VJO L NLW
XJTW QLH PJ KLP L PJLHPKW JZBJZ NKVJOK
AJBZA PJ NKW.

Solutions are on pages 306, 307

74. JLNPN RU TW XZTYNP WB CNPQ OZTQ SNWSVN
XNCNVWSRTY NQNUJPZRT BPWO VWWMRTY WT
JLN KPRYLJ URXN WB JLRTYU.

75. DY XAVB YZD YO ULBCLXXJYA, DTJAI YO
YDTLCX. JD'X WZD QJDDQL KYYU RYZ'QQ UY
PVDLCJAK QVXD RLVC'X OQYPLCX.

76. SREKRYNVS LE DLIR V XVPXRDDRN XTRXI;
KJOJYYJF LE V AYJOLEEJYS PJKR; KJNVS LE
VDFVSE YRVNS XVET.

77. G LCRD ZGE GVQCRDV BR: VTE'Y JBAAN!
VTE'Y LTAAN! LD'AD JDAD ITA G RJTAY
QCRCY. YGXD YCZD YT RZDOO YJD IOTLDAR.

78. FJWHW'V RSFJBRA LMQJ LSHW DHBAJFWRBRA
FJPR P TMTTEK, TMVFEBRA BARSHPRQW.

79. CLCKWN-CLCK HKXRKCW QS WZK HKQHMK LC
WZLG OQXMY JXK SQQMG, JCY WZK XKGW QS
VG JXK LC AXKJW YJCAKX LS LW LG FKXN
RQCWJALQVG.—WZQXCWQC OLMYKX

80. GRO VKVRP, SRHV LP XGJ SHHBAAVU, HGR IV
ZGUV PS GQQVGA LRVKLPGIEV IO G
HSZQVPVRP XLJPSALGR.

Solutions are on page 307

81. WP QDB HBZ PGGN QDBA PJWZF, KBAGEQ

QDBA NDBHZK OWEE KZJAMG ZD NGJZF.

82. XZH LHBKZ LFAZ LCND: "CY EBJ DZZQ F

NBBQ LEPXFHMZHCG GBPXFDCBD HB GBDYCQZ

CD, RFLLZH XJXXCZL FKZ FAA ZFKL."

83. NOXSGQA FOS UXLS BFZSOKSUWGA; AMFUU X

ZSUU TWI BMT? ZW NXGQ F OSFUUT YWWQ

WGS, TWI KIAZ F MIGQOSQ ZOT.

84. DVKXE BVK QGB OBUVDOVZESPGDQ GSH

NOVQH UHVUXH IOV EPQXPWH XHNNPZM IHXX

HZVKMO GXVZH?

85. LWGKTECHCDA YLQ VK FTJFKTPQ WKHMTCVKW

LH ENK HMCKDMK JZ LTTKHECDA ENK NXYLD

CDEKPPCAKDMK PJDA KDJXAN EJ AKE YJDKQ

ZTJY CE.—HEKFNKD PKLMJMR

86. PQRFOPXPSQ PX HPBF CDF OFQCPEFRF MDS

MGX CSHR CS WF OGJFLKH GQR EKC DPX

WFXC LSSC LSJMGJR.

87. EPHJVMAJO EJEEOPF, EOGCMLI ML VSP RGGO

EDPPKP, EDMLI EHRT SHOA-AGDIGVVPL,

CMFVAJO UPUGDMPF GA OHKB, OGLI-HIG

FJUUPDF.

88. TRXPOCPT VLLPRCTDE WQKNEN XOKLNN EDH

RXGH EL NEKCGH X TKHHP-WRQH EHXR CP X

VLLPTRLM MXGH.

Solutions are on page 307

Cryptograms continue on page 260.

KEY-LETTER SCORE 2

Copyright 1989 by Bantam Doubleday Dell Publishing Group, Inc.

Add any letter to each word below and then rearrange (anagram) all the letters to form a new word. HANDICAP: TRY TO REARRANGE THE LETTERS IN SUCH A WAY THAT THE SAME LETTER APPEARS AS THE FOURTH LETTER IN EACH OF THE 10 NEW WORDS. Plurals, proper nouns, and foreign words are not allowed. Place the new word onto the blank dashes. When all the new words are in place, circle the one letter that appears the most times in the fourth column. This is your key letter and you get 10 extra points every time it appears as the fourth letter in one of the new words. Score 5 points for each anagram you make. Our perfect solution of 150 points is on page 309.

Average score: 100 points   **Superior score: 120 points**

↓

A D O R N	1. _ _ _ _ _
T U N E R	2. _ _ _ _ _
S L A T E	3. _ _ _ _ _
L U N G E	4. _ _ _ _ _
C R U D E	5. _ _ _ _ _
L A D L E	6. _ _ _ _ _
U N T I L	7. _ _ _ _ _
T R A I L	8. _ _ _ _ _
S T R U T	9. _ _ _ _ _
T Y P E D	10. _ _ _ _ _

CODED CLICHES

Each two-word phrase in the left-hand column is a "disguised" form of familiar saying. See how good a detective you are by decoding each phrase and matching it with its proper cliche.   Answer is on page 309.

1. Dabbler's destiny

a. He who pays the piper may call the tune

2. Remunerator's right

b. Like mother, like daughter

3. Ruler's rule

c. There is honor among thieves

4. Hovel haven

d. Jack of all trades and master of none

5. Maternal model

e. Be it ever so humble, there's no place like home

6. Crock's criticism

f. Cleanliness is next to godliness

7. Soaping sanctifies

g. He that would govern others first should be master of himself

8. Criminal code

h. The pot calling the kettle black

ANAGRAM QUOTE

All you have to do to solve this puzzle is rearrange (anagram) the letters in each of the 21 4-letter words below to form 21 new 4-letter words. If done correctly, the initial letters of the NEW words, reading <u>left to right</u> in numerical order, will spell out a quotation.

Answer is on page 309.

1. MOAT
_____

2. DIAL
_____

3. CHIT
_____

4. EACH
_____

5. GRIN
_____

6. VANE
_____

7. REAL
_____

8. VEER
_____

9. RIDE
_____

10. AILS
_____

11. DIVA
_____

12. RAGE
_____

13. LOGE
_____

14. CONE
_____

15. VIED
_____

16. REAM
_____

17. NEAR
_____

18. EMUS
_____

19. SOUR
_____

20. MOOR
_____

21. NARY
_____

A-LINE-MENT

Write the names of ten states in the rows of the diagram (one name per row) ACROSS ONLY in such a way that the name of another state (not listed) will be spelled out in one of the columns (we won't say which one) reading down. The letters already entered in the diagram are there to help you determine which name goes in each row. HINT: Start solving by entering in the second row the only name containing the letter D which will fit in that row. You will notice that not all the boxes in that row are filled in. This holds true for every row: not all the squares of the diagram will be filled with letters. Continue solving in this manner until you have filled in all the names and discovered the eleventh one.

Solution is on page 311.

ARIZONA   MARYLAND

FLORIDA   VERMONT

IDAHO   WASHINGTON

IOWA   WISCONSIN

MAINE   WYOMING

MENU MATCH-UP

Match each of the foods in the right-hand column below with the location in the left-hand column that is most often associated with it.

Answer is on page 309.

1. Boston		a.	peach
2. Russian		b.	duck
3. French		c.	clam chowder
4. English		d.	sprouts
5. Spanish		e.	cream pie
6. Hungarian		f.	king crab
7. Idaho		g.	muffin
8. Georgia		h.	pastry
9. Manhattan		i.	rice
10. Irish		j.	dressing
11. Canadian		k.	pudding
12. Alaskan		l.	meatballs
13. Maine		m.	waffles
14. Peking		n.	broil
15. London		o.	toast
16. Brussels		p.	bacon
17. Danish		q.	stew
18. Swedish		r.	potatoes
19. Belgian		s.	lobster
20. Yorkshire		t.	goulash

NUMBER WORD STAR

All you have to do to solve this puzzle is complete the diagram using the letter/number combinations in such a way that the following two conditions are met: 1. the sum of the four numbers along each straight line equals 616; and 2. the four letters along each straight line spell out an everyday 4-letter word. This word may read either forwards or backwards. The letter/number combinations should be used just as they appear below; do not interchange them.

Solution is on page 309.

The missing letter/number combinations are:

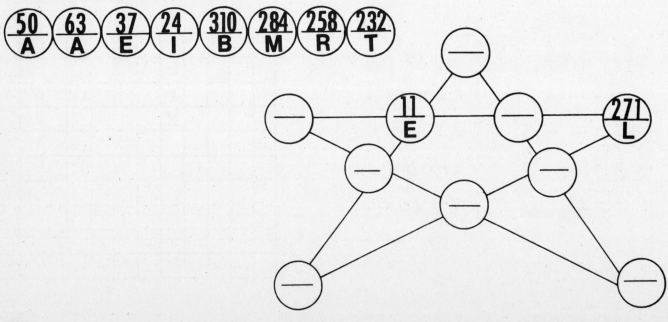

ANAGRAM WORD SQUARES

Word squares are blocks of words that read the same across and down. In other words, the first word across is the same as the first word down; the second word across is the same as the second word down, etc. Your job here is to anagram (rearrange) the letters of the words listed below into new words and then place those new words in the diagram in such a way that you will form word squares. Plural words are permitted.   Solutions are on page 320.

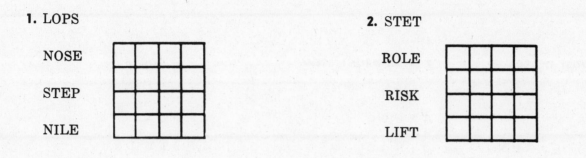

1. LOPS

NOSE

STEP

NILE

2. STET

ROLE

RISK

LIFT

LETTER, PLEASE

The numbers below stand for certain letters on the telephone dial. You will see that one number may stand for more than one letter—that is, 3 may be D, E, or F. By finding the correct letter for each number, you will have a quotation as an answer, which is shown on page 320.

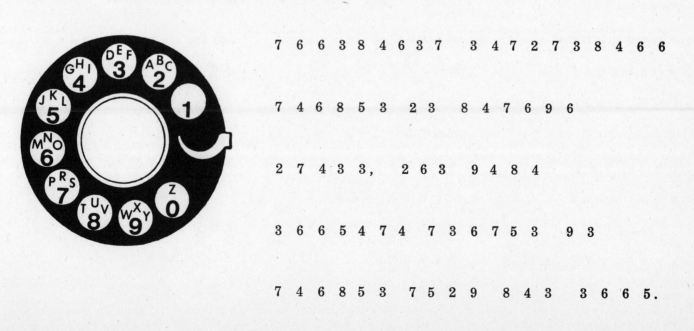

7 6 6 3 8 4 6 3 7   3 4 7 2 7 3 8 4 6 6

7 4 6 8 5 3   2 3   8 4 7 6 9 6

2 7 4 3 3,   2 6 3   9 4 8 4

3 6 6 5 4 7 4   7 3 6 7 5 3   9 3

7 4 6 8 5 3   7 5 2 9   8 4 3   3 6 6 5.

CRYPTOQUIZZES 4

A Cryptoquiz is a list of related words put into a simple code. You will find that one set of letters has been substituted for the correct letters of the words in each of the following lists. The title of each Cryptoquiz, and the example, will give you a hint as to what the disguised words may be. Then look for words which might betray themselves by their "pattern" of repeated or double letters. When you've identified a word, the known letters will help you to decode other words in that list. Remember that if G stands for M in one word, it will be the same throughout that Cryptoquiz. Each Cryptoquiz has its own code.   Answers are on page 310.

1. AT THE POST OFFICE

Example: Packages

N C J R Z N

Z K N C J S   Q J B P N

J X B K L B J R N

B X L T N C X B X P

    S X C C X B N

R K V X I   K B P X B N

"A J V C X P"

    Z K N C X B N

Z K N C J L X   R X C X B N

A T V P K A N

2. WATERFRONT SCENE

Example: Warehouses

G N S D Q

Q J N G Q

L H X J R D Q

Q S L C S H

K N Q J S D C S H

Q J N G M L D Z Q

P L H P G T L H B Q

T R H P Q J R D S C S H

Z D M   Z R X B Q

X L D P R

3. "S" FOODS

Example: Shrimp

J F D Z X T

J F D F Z C

J G C T F S Y

J G F Q Y R L L C

J G F N R N C K J

J F H J F Q R

J S F D D X G J

J L N F I K R N N C R J

J W H F J Y

J L R F A

4. BETTE DAVIS MOVIES

Example: All About Eve

P W C J Q D M Z F

N Q K Q X Q R

P W D T   H S G L M D I

N Z W D Q K

C M B,   H M I W J Q D

B W L G A   M C   L A Q

    D A S C Q

W   F L M R Q C   R S V Q

L A Q   O Q L D S V S Q P

    V M D Q F L

5. SEEN IN VARIOUS DESERTS

Example: Lizards

F X J F C

C K J H

N K N F S C

Y K C B C

N K D X T C

G K F F T X C J K Q X C

E K N Q   D S T X C

N K D E C B F X

N K G K M K J

M X O X F K F B Y J

6. ABOUT THE DIAMOND

Example: Pear-shaped

L C A

A F D U H S N C   K H M

X F D J C N M   A S Y C D F Q

I H D C   K F D Z W Y

F I D S Q ' N

    Z S D M X N M W Y C

B W H Y J   S Y   N W H M X

    F B D S K F

B F K C M N

N I F D E Q C

KEY POINTS 2

There are 7 key letters listed below. Add one of these key letters to each word below (using a different key letter for each word) and then rearrange (anagram) the letters to form a new word. HANDICAP: TRY TO REARRANGE THE LETTERS IN SUCH A WAY THAT THE KEY LETTER YOU HAVE ADDED APPEARS AS THE FOURTH LETTER IN EACH OF THE NEW WORDS. Plurals, words beginning with a capital letter, and foreign words are not allowed. Place the new words on the dashes provided (one letter per dash). When all the new words are in place, count 1 point for each letter in the new words and 5 points for each key letter that appears as the fourth letter in the new words.

Our perfect score of 77 points is on page 310.

Average score: 55 points   **Superior score: 66 points**

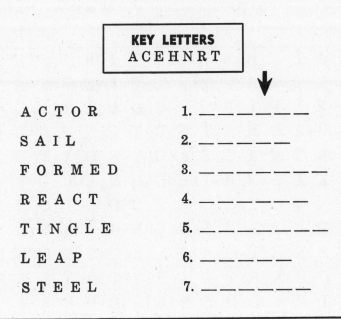

| KEY LETTERS |
| ACEHNRT |

ACTOR   1. _ _ _ _ _ _

SAIL   2. _ _ _ _ _

FORMED   3. _ _ _ _ _ _ _

REACT   4. _ _ _ _ _ _

TINGLE   5. _ _ _ _ _ _ _

LEAP   6. _ _ _ _ _

STEEL   7. _ _ _ _ _ _

NUMBERAMA

Can you discover the logical pattern of each number sequence and thereby discover the missing fifth number? For example, in row A, the missing number is 11, and this is how it is found:

$$6(+4)=10(-2)=8(+5)=13(-2)=11(+6)=17(-2)=15(+7)=22(-2)=20$$

A.	6	10	8	13	—	17	15	22	20	
B.	15	30	20	40	—	56	42	84	68	
C.	54	18	6	12	—	6	2	8	14	
D.	27	9	18	2	—	8	16	4	44	
E.	8	48	24	8	—	26	10	40	36	20
F.	37	63	7	35	—	35	7	39	13	
G.	7	21	28	17	—	38	61	34	3	
H.	57	62	75	15	—	32	8	11	24	8
I.	42	21	14	38	—	19	10	40	50	
J.	16	2	14	27	—	18	30	3	15	26
K.	2	58	36	20	—	63	59	57	56	

Answers are on page 310.

QUOTATION MAZE

Hidden in the diagram below is a quotation composed of 28 words. Here's how to find it: The letters of e
are in a straight line of adjacent letters reading either up, down, right, left, or diagonally. Do not skip letter
ing a word. The number of letters in each word is given below each dash at the bottom of the page. The last
each word of the quotation adjoins the first letter of the next word in the diagram, so your solution will be
uous line through all 28 words of the quotation. Beginning at START, draw a line through each word of the
as you find it in the diagram, and write that word on its dash. Work in order, from word to word, in the dic
solving, you will not cross any line you have already drawn, and once you have used a letter in the diagram
not return to it to form another word. We have started you off with "IT IS," the first two words, and entered
the correct dashes. You are now looking for a 3-letter word that adjoins the "S" of "IS." Solution is on pag
Remember: Each word is formed in a straight line, and no letter may be used more than once.

START ➤

```
B S A L E H E P S M T I R I P S L I
C G U I O A T Y W B T L U Z I A T M
P J K L P L U O T C O V F T T D I R
W D R A D N A T S R Y C N R U S C B
O C W T E J C E A O Y B O V T H E A
F T K A E V H I B D O M E R U T A N
W I R Q O T S C A T M C O L O N E A
A R D F Z E H I S I E H T F R D Y O
N T E E R T O A O L H C G S N O N I
D H G H A B I L I W T T O T S N R A
T R I M G L D E N L G B D R E W T D
E H O G G I S U C D N G R E F A P R
T U I L H S H B C T E X A N Z R L A
S A S O V E C A S P R M O G I D P W
I B E F S L R W I L T E O T O W S P
F G S A L S E O G T S L I H S E X U
A T L T D B F R O M Y T R S T I L L
D O I B W A N N E N R U A N I S E B
```

IT   IS

2	2	3	6	2	3
8	6	2	5	3	8
2	6	6	3	6	2
2	4	4	8	2	8
5	6	3	6		

WORD STAIRCASE

The answer to each definition below can be broken up into two or three words. Each Across word is part of a Down word and vice versa, forming a chain of words down the staircase. We have filled in the answers to the definitions of 1-Across and 2-Across to help you get started.

Solution is on page 311.

ACROSS

1. Couch
2. Residence
3. Actor, — Borgnine
4. Shade of red
5. Apportion
7. At the present
9. Writing in script
11. Text you're supposed to write in
13. Wading across (a river)
14. Bring into harmony
15. — to, plan on
16. — from, notwithstanding
17. Blood-giver
19. Nipped
21. National hymn
23. Baseball batting order
25. Saying farewell
26. Human being
27. Make oneself like the others
28. Inventor's protection

DOWN

1. An indefinite amount
2. "— Abe" Lincoln
3. Fur for royal garments
4. Red bird
6. Game related to bingo
8. Lasting for 24 hours
10. Knitting, needlepoint, etc.
12. Process of assembling dictionaries, novels, etc.
13. Chinese-cookie "filling"
14. Go to, as school
15. Not outdoors
16. Desert; leave unattended
18. Planet's path
20. Resident who rents
22. Skirt edge
24. Disturbing
25. Member of the clergy
26. Act on the stage
27. Happy and fullfilled

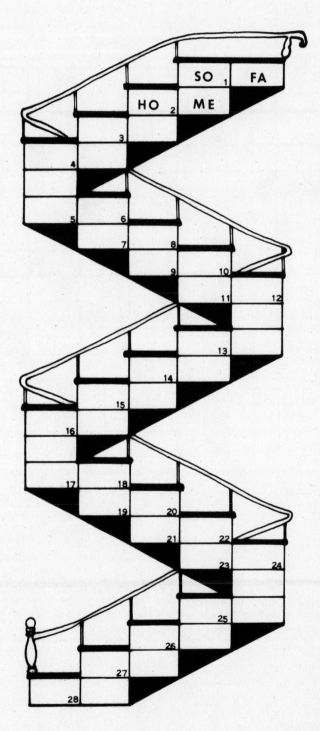

195

ACROSS

1. Brag
5. Sharp; sour
10. Detect
14. Tender feeling
15. Medicator
16. Boorish
17. Gem for October
18. Perform wrongly
19. Elevator-brake inventor
20. Town crier
22. Watch pocket
24. Aardvark's fare
25. Enthusiast
26. Lament
28. In search of
31. Feather scarf
32. Have one's say
35. Pleased
36. Keen intuitive power: 2 wds.
38. Diving bird
39. Funnyman Brooks
40. Attention-getting call
41. "Gunga —"
42. TV personality: 2 wds.
45. Jazz great Kenton
46. Actor Falk
47. Sound receptor
48. Florist's item
49. Cordial
51. Sal, for one
52. — and Tina Turner, singers
54. Unfavorable
55. Wet blanket: hyph. wd.
59. Akron product
61. New
63. Mrs. Chaplin
64. Plastic material
65. Watch over
66. Partaker (of)
67. Actress Lange
68. Supernumerary
69. Gull's kin

DOWN

1. Small splotch
2. Stride easily
3. Track shape
4. Plump: hyph. wd.
5. Madison Ave. denizen
6. Invent
7. Curvy letter
8. United Fund symbol: 2 wds.
9. Cleaning item
10. Sign for a 45-Down
11. Stop: 4 wds.
12. Valhalla host
13. "Dry run"
21. Impair
23. Domineering
26. Certain theater seat
27. Gibbon
28. Panting
29. Symphony instrument
30. Suffer for a misdoing: 3 wds. (slang)
31. Love letter: hyph. wd.
33. Cambodian
34. Man's nickname
36. Heavy swell
37. Barnyard-dweller
39. Biblical woman
43. Victory symbol
44. Short poem
45. Hit show, usually
48. Buddy
50. Scope
51. "Rigoletto" role
52. Have a "hankering"
53. About two lbs.
55. Actress, Deborah —
56. Actor Ferrer
57. "Humdinger": slang
58. Tall tale
60. Watch closely
62. Large tub

Solution is on page 287

FIND-A-WORD

Copyright 1989 by Bantam Doubleday Dell Publishing Group, Inc.

What is the longest possible word you can form from the letters of each of the 10 words listed below? You may not use any letter more often than it appears in the listed word and you must rearrange the order of some of the letters. You may not be able to use all the letters in your new word. Proper names, contractions, and foreign words are not permitted; but plurals are okay, and you may use any form of a word ("ed," "ing," etc.). To score yourself, count one point for each letter used in each of the words you form. We scored 66 points. Our list of words is on page 310.

1. LUSTER _____
2. VALISE _____
3. UNCLEAR _____
4. SALVAGE _____
5. LITIGANT _____
6. NEBULOUS _____
7. PERPETUAL _____
8. DROMEDARY _____
9. PROVIDENCE _____
10. MANIPULATE _____

ACROSS

1. Deception
5. Substantial
10. Seasons
15. Relentless; pitiless
16. Be an author
17. Court event
18. "Hunt and peck"
19. Sailors: slang
20. Weaver's device
22. Print measure
23. Propeller noise
25. Had a go at
27. To a —, exactly
28. Feel under par
30. Above
32. Phonograph needle-holder
33. Lectern
34. — of Nations, U.N.'s predecessor
36. Culmination point
38. Evergreen
39. Sticktight is one
40. Stage-set item
41. Geological discovery
44. Like "a bird"
46. Appear
47. Eliot or Poe
48. In the direction of
49. Artist's medium
50. Bewilder

52. Frosts
54. At bat
55. Search for
57. Bulb plant
58. "Moniker"
59. Cause to remember
61. Skillful
62. Play's division
63. Plus
64. Sermon's subject
65. Pint-sized
68. Best man's trust
70. Devotee
71. Spoken
73. Of course!
74. Unmatched, as a shoe or a sock
75. Smallest ones of 12-Down
77. Require
79. One
80. Sense
82. Round ones don't fit "square holes"
84. Lasso
86. Outdoor dining area
87. Depart
89. Challenges
90. What Rip Van Winkle did
91. Go in
92. Was in debt

DOWN

1. Impede
2. Short trip by plane
3. Once again
4. Belonging to me
5. Took an oath
6. Sphere
7. Tilt to one side, as a ship
8. That thing
9. Long for
10. Ornamental round nailhead
11. Actor, — Carney
12. Groups of newborn puppies
13. Stories
14. Glossy
15. One way to gain a base
19. Donate
21. Skirt border
24. 60 minutes
26. Inclined walk
29. Tag
31. Scarcer
33. Clear
35. Surmising
37. Intricate
38. Rival
40. Look furtively
41. Sly and wily
42. Bit of news

43. Mislay
44. Number of sides in a tetragon
45. Ready for harvesting
46. Hastened
47. Furrier's item
51. Hitchhiker's desires
53. Unkind
56. Finale
60. Order from the voters
61. Fender mishap
62. General's helper
64. Snarl
65. Prevaricates
66. Jumped
67. Ancient slaves
68. Frolics
69. Perfect model
70. Merriment
72. Ire
75. Public disturbance of the peace
76. Lovers' quarrel
78. Depict
81. Pup's bite
83. Seth's mother
85. Mine product
88. Half a 22-Across
89. Perform

Solution is on page 287

53 and 54 MEDIUM CROSSWORD

ACROSS

1. Hoodlum
5. Pounce (down)
10. Follow-up drink
12. Certain apartment: hyph. wd.
14. Overdecorated
15. Peculiar
16. Overhead train
17. Went first
18. Hoard
20. Mr. Lincoln
21. Small valley
23. Large vase
24. Arizona river
25. Hanker for
27. Helmsman
28. Freight weight
29. Sedan
30. "Lucky" number
33. Interfere: 2 wds. (slang)
36. Oh, woe!
37. Chart
38. Rime; frost
40. Kindled
41. Giver
43. Perish
44. Bovine
45. Long, long time
46. Unstable, in chemistry
48. Sure-footed
50. Made amends
51. Insurgent
52. Watched

DOWN

1. Sewing need
2. Manipulate
3. U.N. member: abbr.
4. Acquires
5. Pledged under oath
6. Walk through water
7. Antique
8. Stamp of approval
9. Indian village
10. Frigid
11. Give back
13. Skirt feature
19. Pay dirt
20. Be sick
22. Colorado park
24. Circumference
26. Charged atom
27. Too opportune
29. Mini-dome
30. Drawing room
31. Cure-all
32. Large tub
33. Prohibition
34. Antiseptic
35. Captured
37. Nickel alloy
39. Coarse grass
41. Relief, in Britain
42. Fixed charge
45. Recede
47. Lad
49. Myself

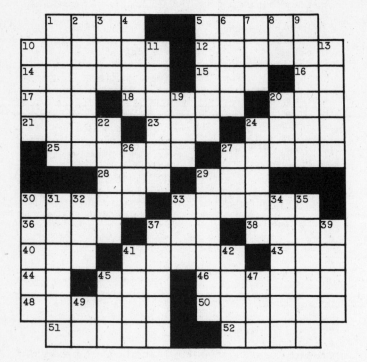

ACROSS

1. — mode: 2 wds.
4. Boutique
8. What person?
11. Vague
12. Have on
13. Food: slang
14. Investigates: 2 wds.
16. Little brook
17. Tears
18. Dish
20. Slyly malicious
22. Grab
23. Trimming
24. Bend
25. My: Spanish
27. Actress Gardner
28. Sword part
29. Forest god
30. Gracious!
31. Gay
32. Meat
33. Girl's name
34. Road divisions
35. Heavy nail
36. Candy flavor
37. Claw
38. Youngsters
42. Dollar bills
43. Story
44. Exist
45. Carmine
46. Cast off
47. However

DOWN

1. Paid notices
2. Falsehood
3. "Land of the free"
4. Pilfer: slang
5. Coop denizens
6. Feed-bag grain
7. Estate
8. Ashen
9. Cavity
10. "Wise" bird
13. Mania
15. Faction
19. Subsist (on)
20. Shut with force
21. Dark blue
22. Sullen
24. Gathers
25. Indication
26. Writing fluids
28. — song
29. Depict
31. Imprisons
32. Pool
33. Caught sight of
34. Moved in a line
35. Rational
36. 5,280 feet
37. Correlative
39. Exclamation
40. Before: poetic
41. Trap

Solutions are on page 287

DUPLEX CROSSWORD   by Gerard Mosler

Follow the same procedure here as you do when solving crosswords, except that in this tricky puzzle you will, in many instances, have TWO letters of the defined word to write into one box. As a help, you will find in a parenthesis, after each definition, the number of letters in the word that goes into the diagram. We have entered the answer to 1-Down as an example.

ACROSS

1. Dims (5)
5. Demolished (5)
9. Late statesman Stevenson (5)
10. Select members of a select group (5)
11. Eating places (6)
12. Easily bribed or corrupted (5)
13. Permits (4)
14. Beaver's contruction (3)
15. Utter (3)
16. Hobos (6)
19. Monk's title (3)
21. "Beware the — of March" (4)
22. Liquid measure (4)
25. Decayed (6)
27. More hackneyed (6)
28. Quiet (5)
29. Makes changes (6)
30. Boot parts (5)
31. Smaller (6)

DOWN

1. Canoe oar (6)
2. Dismounted (4)
3. Least fatty (7)
4. Titles for knights (4)
5. Renovate (6)
6. Immigrant (5)
7. Greek letters (5)
8. Put off (5)
14. Titles for women who have been knighted (5)
17. Enigmas (7)
18. Pixies (7)
19. Chilly crop killers (6)
20. Proportion (5)
23. Buries (6)
24. More concise (6)
26. Famed archer, William — (4)
27. Of great stature (4)

Solution is on page 287

Crazy Crossword

There are zany definitions in this Crazy Crossword, so please look out for traps. For example, 34-Down is "Ruffle the feathers," and the answer is RILE. The clues are sly, so be careful.

ACROSS

1. Dome doilies
5. The thing the lingerie salesman gave his gal
9. Funny l'il fellow
14. Association of Benevolent Invisiblizing Exeunters (for those who want to vanish into thin air)
15. Made in Moscow for world consumption
16. It would like for you to keep your trap shut
17. This has made suckers out of Americans
19. Man who rides around in a Fjord
20. Kute Dimpled Temptress (has anybody seen this gal?)
21. What you might do to those underfoot
23. A summery kind of riff
24. Their theme song is "Merrily we roll along!"
26. MacGlamorgals
28. Sneers at with a supercillious schnozz
30. Please do this, or else!
31. Tough Thomas (or so he sounds), the Perennial Penpusher
32. The Flat of the Land after April 15th
36. MacLingo
37. It takes a lot of these to make an Olympic team
38. Lie perfectly in the past
39. Massachusetts river that sounds like a place where Elks hang out
41. Sock-o material
42. Napoleoniclinks
43. Works in Washington: Republican
44. Folks who have any come out on top
47. Lily, the Lidmaker
48. Twisted eel
49. A knightly trip
51. When a crook can't beat it, he takes it
54. There is this thing about money these days: 2 wds.
56. Awe-fully respectful feeling
58. Glamorized girlesque show
59. retniW teknalb
60. No matter how you look at this, you probably had to give up something for it
61. Cover the mush with the sour milk of human unkindness
62. D.A.s the underworld of rats
63. Kind of port the Scotsman sent for

DOWN

1. Old-fashioned thing the boy and girl went woo-wooing on
2. How the footnote says "It's Biding In Ditto"
3. It ain't protocol to look one in the oral orifice: 2 wds.
4. Is it a pupil's job to do this?
5. Musical tick-tack-toers play on them
6. The Volcano Song: Be Brave, Young —!
7. A mite mixed up
8. "Dear Abbey: Does she or doesn't she?
          (Signed) —————"
9. Best thing to do for this disease is to forget it
10. A good cry in Hoo's Hoo
11. He once was the first to Finnish in the Olympics
12. This is the end of Bessie
13. Bamboo's cousins
18. It'll go hard with you, if you're this broke
22. These will throw light on any subject
25. Requested: Russian
27. Just dandy
28. Old-fashioned tannery
29. Package of Joy
30. Chief supports of the American railroads
32. Some people die and get their faces on money, he lives and gets his hands on it
33. Arizonian in California
34. Ruffle the feathers
35. tI t'nseod etiuq ekam esnes
37. Where Julius went for a dunkibus every diem
40. Go off, on, off, on, off, on, off, on, off
41. What the old-fashioned corset wearer made of the old-fashioned man
43. Toe dunkers
44. These animated fur coats came in three sizes, and had a series of dialogues with a small female
45. Funny man Steve who used to keep us up late
46. What people who didn't want to come to the party never seem to want to do
47. He beat an old-time heavyweight champ with his hand in a sling
50. 1/2ish
52. This is only skin deep
53. Oh, for the love of this guy!
55. Get the hint?
57. Puckette-sized pipsqueak

Solution is on page 287

ACROSS

1. Salaries
6. Couches
11. Bottle top
14. Decorate
15. Barter
16. Generation
17. "— each his own"
18. Have status
20. Inexperienced
21. Negative word
22. Before, to a poet
24. Keats or Yeats
26. Repair
28. Back part
30. Pitfall
32. Governs
35. Is in session
37. Abyss
39. Camp shelter
40. Member of a theatrical troupe
42. Train station
44. Eye inflammation
45. Keystone State: abbr.
46. Clock reading
48. Hurricane centers
50. — Paso, Texas
51. Terminate
53. Prepares (the way for)
55. Seaside
57. Uncommon
59. Performed
60. Pack away
61. Freezing rain
63. Departed
65. Healthy
68. Pub drinks
70. Fasten (down) securely
72. Perish
73. Box top
75. Parking area
77. Sketched
79. Mother
80. Expert
81. Unattached
83. Nominated
85. Marry
86. Endured
87. Garment for milady

DOWN

1. H2O
2. Worship
3. Depart
4. Blunder
5. Break off suddenly
6. Beef source
7. Word of choice
8. Distant
9. Resident of 54-Down
10. Drainpipe
11. Romantic lights
12. "Long, Long —"
13. Caress
19. Kindergartners
23. Where the sun rises
25. Recording ribbon
27. Cashew or pecan
29. Noisy uprising
31. Features of some organs
33. Step in
34. Fashion
36. Stumble
38. Plaything
40. Copycats
41. Feature of Venice
42. Satan
43. Trial
47. Like a "wet hen"
49. Exhibition
52. Feared intensely
54. Biblical garden
56. Had debts
58. Snakelike fish
60. Move slightly
62. Discloses
64. Lost color
66. Sour fruits
67. Directs
69. Chimney accumulation
71. ". . . — me your ears"
73. Statute
74. Frozen water
76. Also
78. 1941 declaration
82. Thus
84. "Dream Along with —"

Solution is on page 287

WORD ASSOCIATION

What one word do the four words in each group listed below suggest to you? For example, "Pump, beat, broken, valentine" would probably suggest "heart". Your answers may not always match ours, but be sure that each of your answers has some connection with every word in its group. **See page 310 for our answers.**

1. Ocean, brain, navy, permanent
2. Zoo, circus, farm, forest
3. Razor, grass, propeller, shoulder
4. Wave, mountain, cardinal, royalty
5. Song, movie, knight, book
6. Beads, piano, puppet, kite
7. Old jokes, ear, tassel, pone
8. Dandelion, wineglass, watch, pipe
9. Clam, egg, walnut, beachcomber
10. Piano, lock, code, music
11. Tree, teeth, words, hair
12. Measles, leopard, stains, ladybug

58 and 59 EASY CROSSWORD

ACROSS

1. Coconut tree
5. Woe is me!
9. Policeman: slang
12. Thought
13. Part of an egg
14. Miss Gardner
15. Stinging plant
17. Wrong-doer
19. Chinese drink
20. Anybody
21. Look at
23. Young dog
25. You and I
26. Animal fat
28. Preserve
31. Drink slowly
34. While
35. Gap or hole
38. You may not!
39. Four-poster
41. Inquires
42. Feedbag food
44. Paid notice
46. Snakelike fish
48. G.I.'s bed
49. Like a zebra
53. Nevertheless
55. Craving (for)
56. Amend or alter
59. Single item
60. Clock "info"
62. Always
63. Marry
64. Fruit pit
65. Close by

DOWN

1. Bowling club
2. Fruit drink
3. X, y, or z
4. Spouse
5. "Yes" vote
6. Behold!
7. Too
8. — milk, dieter's drink
9. Indian boats
10. Stove part
11. Peel
16. Lick up
18. Modern
20. Paddled for punishment
21. Thick slice
22. Comfort
24. Employs
27. Accomplish
29. Carpentry clamp
30. Half an em
32. Go —, enter
33. Fence part
36. Dad
37. Depart
40. Mended
43. Lively
45. Delve
47. Caustic agent
49. Display
50. Melody
51. Caresses
52. Great Lake
54. Level
56. Bright color
57. Salty expanse
58. Go wrong
61. Myself

ACROSS

1. Seaman's map
6. Came in second, in a race
12. Pilot's "O.K."
13. Rests
15. Avoid artfully
16. Map direction
17. Therefore
18. Become firm
19. Wipe out
21. For each
22. Snow-coaster
24. Deed
25. Unadorned
26. Hurry
28. Young zebras
29. Penalize
32. Like "Abe"
33. Warehouse
34. Signal system
35. Congressmen: abbr.
36. "Ain't — Sweet?"
37. Scraping sound
41. Election-winners
42. Sheen
44. Prevarication
45. Bone: Latin
46. 1976, for one
47. Worship
49. Breakfast nook
51. Big ship
52. Red-ink items
53. Youthful years

DOWN

1. Water —, salad plant
2. Wretched hut
3. Jr.'s marble
4. Barn color
5. Cedar or yew
6. Sermonize
7. Fewest
8. Church recess
9. Folding bed
10. Plural suffix
11. Wastelands
14. Most painful
20. Measles symptom
21. White-faced
23. Plumbing problems
25. Blunder: slang
27. Utility
28. Food fish
29. Sentence-ender
30. Knife or fork
31. Dozes
32. Farm implements
34. Odd jobs
36. Blackboard
38. Solo
39. Police-car "warner"
40. Equals
42. Acquires
43. Veteran sailor
46. Sure!
48. — out, fade away
50. I won't!

Solutions are on page 287

ACROSS

1. Rigid
6. Secret watchers
11. Lucid
16. Coil
17. Dirty spot
18. — out, paid
20. Disagreeable situation
21. "Snitch": 2 wds.
22. Survive
23. Noah's vessel
24. According to law
26. Guided trips
28. Fellows
29. Cultivate (the soil)
31. Brooks
32. Memorize
33. Desk items
34. Purloin
36. Go by plane
37. Trousers
38. Chain of mountains
39. Encounters
41. Hurl
42. Summon (up), as courage
43. Gathers leftover grain
45. Garden enclosure
46. Baseball ploy
47. Empty spaces
48. Sandy shore
49. Proposes as suitable
53. Shabby: slang
54. Instruct
55. Chants
56. Go to —, deteriorate
57. Aardvark's diet
58. Aspect
59. Massive
60. Foundation
61. Drink cooler
62. Take by force
63. Converses
64. Poetry
65. Most brazen: slang
67. Dowdy
68. El-Sadat's predecessor
69. Otherwise
70. Hazardous
71. Made a movie of
72. Pieces of paper
75. Leanings
76. Prove false
77. Gets the word
78. Sew temporarily
79. Tick-tack——
80. Pub game
84. Consumes
85. Weeps
86. Puddles
88. Smell strongly and unpleasantly
89. Actress Gardner
90. Kingdom
91. Floating wreckage

93. Hawaiian garland
94. Hairdo decorations
96. Under one's —, softly
98. Give up the occupancy of
100. Chooses
101. Knights' weapons
102. Makes happy
103. Searches for
104. Concluded
105. Hinder

DOWN

1. Soul
2. Excite amusement in
3. Vex
4. Autumn
5. Escaper
6. Odorous
7. Tugs
8. Aimlessly
9. Self
10. Condemn to punishment
11. Stir up vigorously
12. Permits
13. Addition to a house
14. Food
15. Retaliation for a wrong

16. Petty quarrels
17. Stable compartments
18. Becomes fermented
19. More compact
25. Presents
27. Solemn promise
30. Grieves
32. Door fastening
33. Fake jewelry
35. Like a sieve
37. Arrest: slang
38. Ladder parts
40. Print measures
41. Tranquility
42. Damp and close
43. Hurried look
44. Second mention of two
45. Banquet
46. Narrow beds
47. Nerve center
48. Beauty's prince, at one time
49. Smooth and lustrous
50. Thinly scattered
51. Flung carelessly
52. Guide
54. The things here
55. Ill-humored
58. Squeeze
59. Football players
60. Soil

62. Becomes limp
63. Flavor
64. Sound; well-founded
66. Shifts direction
67. Colors
68. Nothing
70. Look like
71. Examines by touch
72. Cuts the wool from
73. Villains: slang
74. Fit to be consumed as food
75. — out, jump from a plane
76. Acting family of note
78. Army VIPs: slang
79. Blew, as a horn
81. Tell
82. Seesaw
83. Heavens
85. Pennies
86. Location
87. Hoarded
90. Move to and fro
91. Ward (off)
92. Masculine
95. Honey-maker
97. Raced
99. Lion or tiger

Solution is on page 289

SCOREWAYS

Your goal in this game is to try to get the score shown in the circle above the diagram. Start at the arrow and follow the diagonal lines as if they were the path of a ball bouncing against a wall (the four sides of the diagram) or a barrier (the short, heavy lines within the diagram). Whenever you hit the wall or a barrier, you must change direction, and go in the direction of the line, as a ball would after it bounced. You may NOT go through a barrier. When you enter a circle, you score the number of points in that circle; when you come out of a circle, you may go in any direction EXCEPT the one you just came from (in other words, you may not retrace your path). Once you've entered a circle, you may not enter it again. The game is over when you enter a square, so try not to enter one until you have entered all the circles you can and collected those points. You may also add the points of the square you finally enter to give you your total score. We've traced the path to the first circle. Now you're on your own! REMEMBER: The game is over when you enter a square!   Our answer is on page 311.

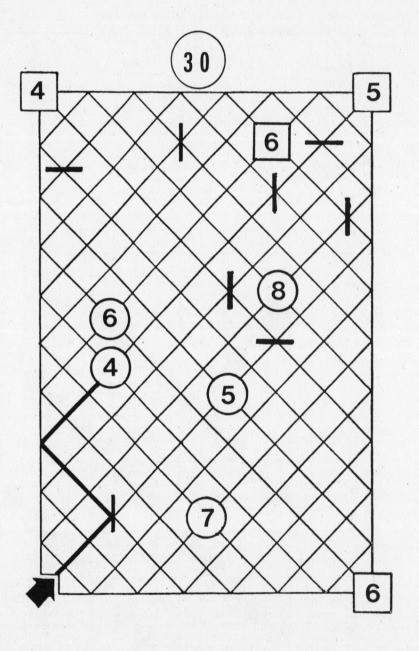

CREATIVE GREATS QUIZ

From the first-person thumbnail sketches given below of great people in the arts or sciences, can you identify each famous person described? Twelve correct is excellent, as this is a real toughie! Answers are on page 310.

1. Although I was trained for the ministry, I wrote over 100 books about impoverished boys facing overwhelming odds who persevered to win fame and fortune. I gave most of my fortune earned from these books to poor boys and died impoverished myself.

2. Now considered one of the greatest English poets and the best of the Romantic era, my poems were not well received by critics during my lifetime. I'm famous for a couple of odes I wrote, and also for my love letters to Fanny Brawne. I died of tuberculosis in Rome when I was only twenty-six years old.

3. I am an American novelist, a major figure in the history of the novel. My brother was a famous psychologist and theologian, and my father was one of the first millionaires in America. I became an American expatriate and spent the last part of my life as a British subject. Writers and critics respect me for my fastidious craftsmanship. I never married.

4. I created the memorable character Holly Golightly for my Broadway play about a famous jewelry store. I also wrote a book about one of the most cold-blooded crimes in recent years.

5. My real name is Charles Dodgson. Although I'm famous as the writer of wildly imaginative children's books about a little girl, my real specialty was mathematics.

6. I wrote over 2,000 poems during my lifetime, yet only seven were published, and these anonymously. Since my death, over 1,500 of them have been published. I led a strange life. I always dressed in white and practically never left my house or yard. Some people have speculated that I became a semi-recluse because of my love for a married man.

7. A master of counterpoint, I was a prolific composer of great musical works. I used each of the 24 major and minor keys and was the first composer to do this. I was also an accomplished violinist and organist—in short, I was a musical giant. In my private life, I married twice and had 20 children —a large family even for my day.

8. I am an artist of Spanish birth who spent many years living in France. I began my career as a traditional artist and gradually found my way into Cubism and the abstraction of the human form. I am considered to have been the most influential artist of the 20th century. The most comprehensive exhibit of my art ever mounted recently ended at New York's Museum of Modern Art.

9. I am a famous Viennese physician who never practiced internal medicine. The mind and emotions were my great interest, and I founded a whole new concept of medicine that was met with much opposition. I was forced to flee the Nazis in 1938, and my family and I moved to England. I died there the following year, an honored and respected man.

10. Though I am acknowledged as one of the masters of English fiction, I didn't begin learning this language until I was in my twenties. I once said "I write in English, think in French, and dream in Polish." My real name was Korzeniowski, and most of my books are about the sea.

11. I was a famous and unorthodox dancer whose private life was as well-known as my professional life. An American, I was acclaimed in London, Paris, and on the Continent. I died tragically at 49 when, while riding in an automobile, the long scarf about my neck caught in an automobile wheel.

12. An American poet, novelist, and critic and patron of the arts, I am a woman who for many years was an expatriate in Paris, where my salons were famous. My style of writing is unique and characterized by the use of words for their associations and sounds rather than for their literal meanings. I originated many famous phrases, among them "the lost generation."

13. I attained great success as one of the first writers of hard-boiled detective fiction. "Private eye" Sam Spade is the hero of some of my books.

14. I introduced many innovations into the American theater including masks for the actors, lighting effects, sound effects, and soliloquies. Although my plays were powerful and popular, I had an unhappy personal life. One cause of my unhappiness was my daughter marrying Charlie Chaplin.

15. I am one of the most famous actresses of all times, the illegitimate daughter of a Dutch Jewish woman. I, too, had an illegitimate son whom I adored, many lovers, and one brief marriage, but my life was the stage and I enjoyed overwhelming success in my work. Although I was French and spoke no English, the United States was the scene of some of my greatest triumphs.

VOCABULADDER

Copyright 1989 by Bantam Doubleday Dell Publishing Group, Inc.

Here are nine words for you to define by completing the sentence following each word. Do this by filling in the blanks with the proper words taken from the Word List at the bottom of the page. The numbers in parentheses before each dash indicate the number of letters in the word you are seeking. You will use all the words in the Word List. The pronunciation for each word to be defined is given in parentheses; when more than one pronunciation is given, each is correct. A heavier accent mark (') indicates the syllable that gets the heavier stress.

Answers are on page 310.

1. AESTHETIC (*ess-thet'-ick*) : _____ (9) to art and _____ (6) ; showing _____ (4) _____ (5).

2. BLASPHEMY (*blass'-fuh-mee*) : _____ (7) or _____ (12) _____ (6) or _____ (7).

3. CALUMNY (*cal'-um-nee*) : A _____ (5) and _____ (9) _____ (9) about a _____ (6) ; _____ (7).

4. DELINEATE (*dih-lin'-ee-ate'*) : _____ (5) the _____ (7) of ; _____ (6).

5. HIERARCHY (*high'-uh-rahr'-key*) : A _____ (5) of _____ (7) or _____ (6) _____ (8) in _____ (5) of _____ (4).

6. RANCOROUS (*rang'-curr-uss*) : _____ (4) of _____ (6) _____ (4) or _____ (6).

7. MAELSTROM (*mail'-strum*) : Any _____ (5) or _____ (7) _____ (9).

8. INCESSANT (*in-sess'-unt*) : _____ (10) _____ (7) _____ (8) ; _____ (8).

9. POTPOURRI (*po'-poo-ree'* or *pot-poor'-ee*) : A _____ (7) of _____ (5) _____ (6) _____ (6) and _____ (6) ; any _____ (6).

WORD LIST

4 Letters				9 Letters
full	order	petals	profane	malicious
good	taste	sketch	slander	sensitive
hate	trace	speech	violent	statement
rank		spices	without	whirlpool
		things	writing	
	6 Letters			
5 Letters	beauty			**10 Letters**
	bitter	**7 Letters**	**8 Letters**	continuing
dried	flower			
false	malice	mixture	arranged	**12 Letters**
group	medley	outline	constant	
large	person	persons	stopping	contemptuous

206

SKILL-O-GRAM 3

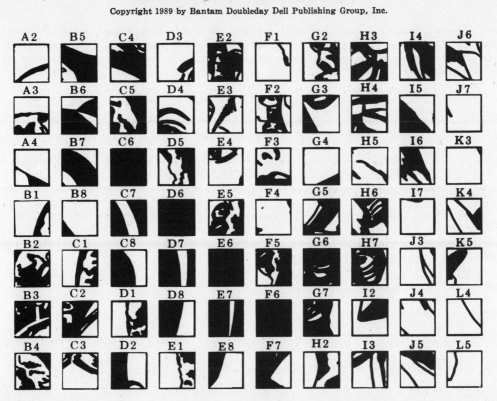

Each square above contains one part of a complete picture. Using a pencil or pen, you are to copy exactly what you see into the diagram below. Use the letter-number combinations as a guide, and draw exactly what is in each box above into the correspondingly numbered box below. Start with A-2, drawing in the box where Row A and Column 2 intersect: Then, draw in A-3, A-4, etc., and continue right through to the end. The result will be finished picture, as skillfully drawn as if by an artist. The artist's picture is shown on page 311.

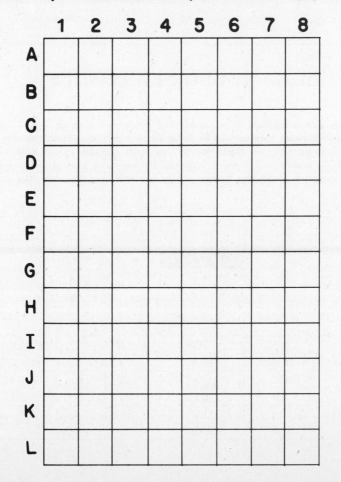

BAKER'S DOZEN

Did you know that a baker's dozen is 13 instead of 12 because, in olden days, bakers would be fined if they gave customers less than 12 items when they ordered a dozen? Thus, bakers would often add one more so as to be doubly sure. Other bits of not-so-well-known information are called for in this quiz. If you should answer even 6 correctly, consider it a good job.

Answers are on page 310.

1. Of what were the sides of Old Ironsides made?

2. A couple celebrating their tin wedding anniversary has been married how many years?

3. In a current survey by the *World Almanac*, who did American eighth-graders choose as their #1 hero?

4. What was Duncan Phyfe famous for making?

5. What would you call an animal with a bright-red nose, blue cheeks, and an orange-yellow beard?

6. What is unusual about this sentence: "No difficulty is too hazardous, or costly, if this is our aim, that finally mankind may stand up and ask 'Why'"?

7. Are true icebergs made of fresh or salt water?

8. Does the name "dandelion" have anything to do with jungle lions?

9. If they live in their homeland, of what nation are Basques citizens? Ukrainians? Flemings?

10. Is the air we normally breathe mostly composed of oxygen?

11. About how many pounds of sugar did the average American consume in 1987?

12. Who is "the Old Lady of Threadneedle Street"?

13. Which State's motto is *"Fatti Maschii, Parole Femine,"* meaning "Manly Deeds, Womanly Words"?

SCRAMBLED SENTENCES

There are two sentences composed of a total of 34 words in the diagram below, one word per box. Here's how to find them: The words already in the left-hand column are in their correct position in the sentences. The rest of the words are listed directly below the blank boxes, and those words are to be placed, in one order or another, into the boxes directly above. You must decide in which box a word belongs. If you have placed the words into their correct boxes, you can read the sentences by reading across the boxes. Note: a black box indicates the end of a sentence.

Answer is on page 310.

LAST				
TO				
BASEBALL		■		
BE				
AS				
IT'S				
AND				

	AN	BY	AMERICANS	PEOPLE
	SYMPHONY	THAT	THIS	TO
	YEAR	COUNTRY	STATISTIC	BASEBALL
	LIKELY	CONCERTS	WILL	SURVIVE
	THE	ALARMING	SOME	MAY
	VIEWED	MORE	BOTH	BUT
	GAMES		THAN	WENT

SHORT SCORE

Your object in this game is to get the lowest score possible while forming three words using the letter/number combinations below according to the following rules:

1. Each word must be at least 3 letters long. Words beginning with a capital letter, foreign words, contractions, obsolete, dialect, archaic, poetic, and slang words are not allowed, but plurals are okay.

2. You may use each letter/number combination only once per row.

3. To arrive at your score, add up the numbers that correspond to the letters of each word you have formed. If a word is 4 letters long or less, add 17 to the score for that word. If a word contains an asterisk (*), double your score for that word.

4. If your word contains an asterisk *and* is 4 letters long or less, double the score *first*, and *then* add the 17 points.

5. Enter the score for each word in the box provided to the right of each row of letters. Add the scores for the three words to get your total.

This is a game of strategy; you may discover you can get a better (lower) score on a shorter word even with the 17-point penalty, or you may do better using an asterisked letter.

Our lowest total for this game is 54 points. See if you come close to that; 55-60 points is a good score; 61-65 points is average. See page 310 for our answers.

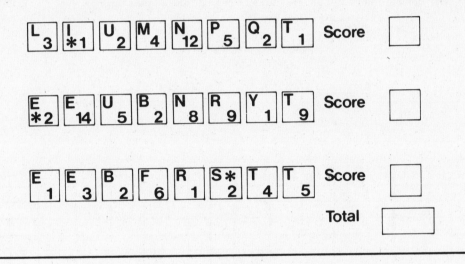

| L₃ | *1 (I) | U₂ | M₄ | N₁₂ | P₅ | Q₂ | T₁ | Score | ☐ |

| E*2 | E₁₄ | U₅ | B₂ | N₈ | R₉ | Y₁ | T₉ | Score | ☐ |

| E₁ | E₃ | B₂ | F₆ | R₁ | S*2 | T₄ | T₅ | Score | ☐ |

Total ☐

TIME FOR THE ASKING

"Good evening," said Professor Laremun, upon meeting Jane Renrael, a math student, in the campus coffee shop.

"Good evening, Professor," replied Jane. Seeing her wristwatch had stopped, she inquired, "Do you know what time it is?"

"Certainly," declared Professor Laremun. "If you add one-quarter of the time from midnight till now to half the time from now to midnight, you will have the correct time!"

Next morning when Jane entered the classroom late, Professor Laremun asked sharply, "Do you know what time it is?"

"Yes," Jane replied. "If you add one-quarter of the time from midnight till now to half the time from now till midnight, it will give you the correct time!"

Now—1. At what time did the Professor meet Jane in the coffee shop? 2. At what time did Jane enter the classroom?

Solution is on page 310.

LOGIC PROBLEM 5

Medical Convention   **by Lyn McConnell**

Dr. Green and four other physicians were among those attending a recent medical convention in Montreal. Each has a different type of practice, and they are all from different cities, among them St. Louis and San Francisco. From the clues below, can you determine each man's full name (one is Bill), his kind of practice, his wife's name, and the city he lives in?

1. The obstetrician and his wife entertained Bob and his wife, Kay and her husband, and Dr. Bennett at a cocktail party in their home on the last day of the convention.

2. Sally did not attend the convention with her internist husband because she is afraid of flying.

3. Anne is not Mrs. Brown.

4. Tom, who is not the psychiatrist, has never been to California.

5. Dr. Brown is not the surgeon.

6. The New York man—who is not the surgeon and whose first name is not Jerry—told Jane he thought her husband should have been an urologist instead of a G.P.

7. Mary and Tom's wife both hope to convince their husbands to visit Montreal again.

8. Dr. Jones wished his wife had attended the convention.

9. Anne, who is not Mrs. Jackson, had never met Jerry before the party.

10. Joe and his wife Jane are not from Chicago, nor is the man from Chicago the surgeon.

Solution is on page 313.

	Gr.	Ben.	Br.	Jo.	Jack.	Kay	Sally	Anne	Jane	Mary	ob.	int.	psych.	surg.	G.P.	St. L.	S.F.	N.Y.	Ch.	Mont.
Bill																				
Bob																				
Tom																				
Jerry																				
Joe																				
St. L.																				
S.F.																				
N.Y.																				
Ch.																				
Mont.																				
ob.																				
int.																				
psych.																				
surg.																				
G.P.																				
Kay																				
Sally																				
Anne																				
Jane																				
Mary																				

LOGIC PROBLEM 6

The Auto Repairs   by Frank W. Alward

One recent Friday morning, Ms. Cole and five other women brought their cars—among them, a Buick—into a local garage for different kinds of repairs; one needed to have its headlights adjusted. As it happens, all the repairs were completed that afternoon, but each at a different hour, varying from 1:00 to 6:00. From the following clues, try to determine each woman's full name (one first name is Sue), the make of her car, what type of repair it needed, and the hour at which the work on it was completed.

1. Ms. Noble's car was ready two hours after Ms. Stuck's.
2. The Chevrolet was ready three hours before Ms. McKay's car.
3. Jan's car, which is not the Dodge, was finished before Ms. Hobbs'.
4. The Plymouth was ready one hour after the radiator repair.
5. Ali's car was ready one hour before Ms. Innes's.
6. Ms. Stuck's car was ready one hour after Nan's.
7. The Dodge was ready one hour before the carburetor repair.
8. The tire was not done on the Ford.
9. The Olds was ready after the car which required an engine tune-up.
10. Nan's car was ready two hours before the brake repair.
11. Betty's car was ready before Marie's.
12. Ms. Noble's car was ready before 6:00.
13. Ms. McKay's car was ready one hour after the Plymouth.
14. The carburetor repair was completed two hours after Ms. Innes's car was ready.
15. Marie's car was ready before the Ford.

Solution is on page 314

	Ali	Betty	Jan	Marie	Nan	Sue	Buick	Chev.	Ply.	Dodge	Ford	Olds.	head-lights	rad.	carb.	tune-up	brakes	tire	1	2	3	4	5	6
Cole																								
Noble																								
Stuck																								
McKay																								
Hobbs																								
Innes																								
1:00																								
2:00																								
3:00																								
4:00																								
5:00																								
6:00																								
head-lights																								
rad.																								
carb.																								
tune-up																								
brakes																								
tire																								
Buick																								
Chev.																								
Ply.																								
Dodge																								
Ford																								
Olds.																								

THE DOT GAME

The idea here is to try to get as high a score as possible by sectioning off units of 5 or fewer squares in the diagram below. You may section off units going EITHER across OR down in a straight line; you may not go both across and down in the same unit, nor may you do diagonally. Try to section off your units so that you will get the highest score you can according to the scoring system given below. In order for a square to be included in a unit, it must be part of one of the combinations listed below.

Once you have used a square in a unit, you may not use it again in another unit; in other words, your units may not overlap. Each unit must consist of a line of adjacent squares forming one of the scoring combinations. We have already outlined one unit to get you started; note that this 4-square unit contains 1 quartet, which scores 20 points.

HANDICAP: When you have finished sectioning off as many units as you can for the highest score you can make, deduct 5 points from your total score for each square you did not include in a unit. Our solution, showing a score of 255 points, is on page 316.

SCORING

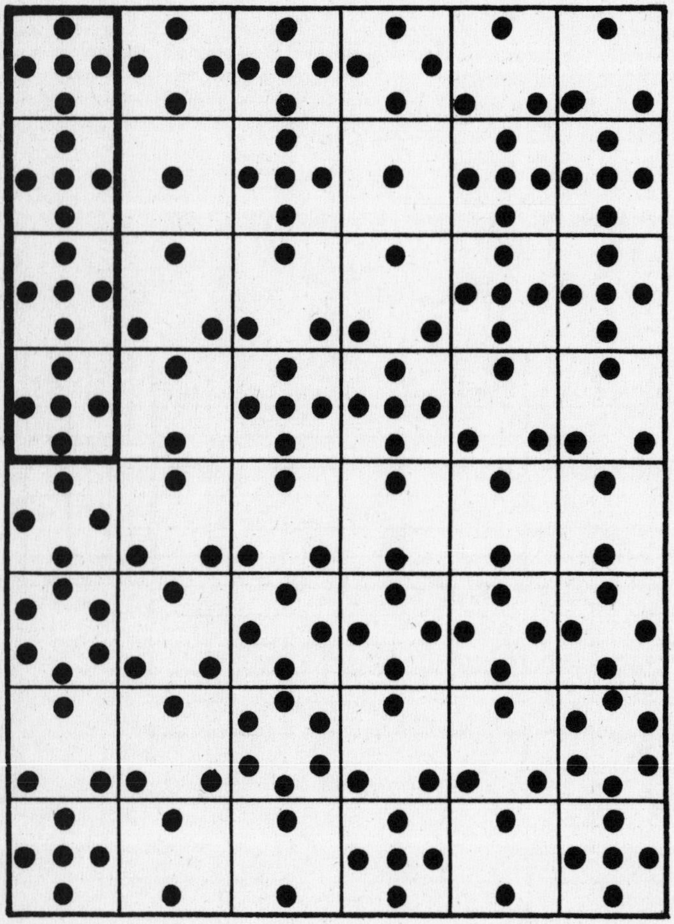

1 pair .... 5 points
(2 squares the same)

1 trio ....10 points
(3 squares all the same)

2 pairs in any order ....15 points

1 quartet ....20 points
(4 squares all the same)

4 consecutive numbers in any order ....25 points
(example: 2, 4, 1, 3)

1 trio plus 1 pair in any order ....30 points

5 consecutive numbers in any order ....35 points

Rate your game as follows:

250 or above: EXPERT SCORE
235 or above: EXCELLENT SCORE
215 or above: GOOD SCORE
195 or above: AVERAGE SCORE

TWENTY  QUESTIONS

Here's a score of questions on a variety of subjects. Don't expect to get too many right, but have fun guessing. Anything more than 10 answered correctly is a good job of quiz-taking. **Answers are on page 313.**

1. Who or what was G.B.S.?

2. On what island is Honolulu?

3. What ancient city was destroyed when Vesuvius erupted in 79 A.D.?

4. What are the endings of these "penny proverbs": "In for a penny..."; "A penny saved..."; "Penny-wise..."?

5. Is maple a soft or hardwood?

6. How many Tropics are there?

7. For whom are the Bermuda Islands named?

8. Is sterling silver pure silver?

9. When does the winter solstice occur in the northern latitudes?

10. What food was named for Sylvester Graham?

11. Was Abraham Lincoln the first Republican candidate for President?

12. What parliamentary rule ends debate and puts the measure under discussion to an immediate vote?

13. Whose historic raid took place at Harpers Ferry, West Virginia?

14. What is the world's largest man-made lake?

15. Who was the first king of all England?

16. What metal must be present in an alloy before it can accurately be called an amalgam?

17. A train leaves New York for Boston every hour of the day on the hour, and likewise one leaves Boston for New York every hour on the hour. The run is exactly six hours. If a train left Boston at midnight, how many New York-Boston trains would it pass en route?

18. What is jingoism, and how did the word come into being?

19. What four countries have common borders with Romania?

20. What is a funicular railway?

LADDERGRAMS 3   by IRENE R. HAYES

First, write the word that fits the first definition into space 1. Then drop one letter and rearrange the remaining letters to form the answer to definition 2. Drop one more letter, rearrange, and get the answer to definition 3. Put the first dropped letter into the box to the left of space 1 and the other dropped letter into the box next to space 3. When you have correctly solved the puzzle, the dropped letters in the boxes on the left and right, when read down, will spell out related words.   Solutions are on page 314.

1. DEFINITIONS

	1		2		3	
	4		5		6	
	7		8		9	
	10		11		12	
	13		14		15	
	16		17		18	

1. Short nails
2. Grocery bag
3. Pose a question
4. Mixture of yellow and red
5. Wrath; fury
6. Sounded (a bell)
7. Thaws
8. Allows
9. Affix (a time)
10. "Beauty and the —," children's story
11. Wagers
12. Abbreviation in a recipe
13. "Do unto — ..."
14. Dinah of TV
15. Stockings
16. City head
17. Navy's rival
18. Ewe's mate

2. DEFINITIONS

1. Fuzzy fruit
2. Hatteras or Cod
3. Pod vegetable
4. Express approval or admiration of
5. Couples
6. Seam mishaps
7. Plays (a drum)
8. Better than better
9. Adjust (a clock)
10. "Staff of life"
11. Grizzly or polar —
12. Exist
13. Window blinds
14. Noggins
15. Storage building
16. Hockey scores
17. Falls behind
18. Jolson and Pacino
19. Banquetlike meal
20. Has dinner
21. Occupied a chair

	1		2		3	
	4		5		6	
	7		8		9	
	10		11		12	
	13		14		15	
	16		17		18	
	19		20		21	

1	2	3	
4	5	6	
7	8	9	
10	11	12	
13	14	15	
16	17	18	

1. Sing, Swiss-style
2. Give (out) sparingly
3. Durocher of baseball
4. Oven-baked meat
5. Separate, as laundry
6. U.S. 66, and others: abbr.
7. Borrowed amounts
8. In addition
9. "Gal" of song
10. Took a swig of
11. Mend, as socks
12. Raced
13. Touch
14. One of the wee folk
15. Santa —, capital of N. Mex.
16. Concurs (with)
17. Shifting devices on cars
18. Old cloths

4. DEFINITIONS

1. Domesticated
2. Appointment
3. Summertime drink
4. Rome's country
5. Plane section
6. Height: abbr.
7. Palace
8. No longer fresh, as bread
9. Tardy
10. Owl cries
11. Inoculation
12. FDR's successor: abbr.
13. Flaws
14. Tire mishaps
15. Table seasoning
16. Combat zone
17. Dix or Bragg
18. To and —
19. Needle's "partner"
20. "Got the word"
21. Enjoy a book
22. 12-month units of time
23. Simple (to do)
24. One's chance to speak
25. Mark Twain's "The Adventures of Tom —"
26. Take an oath
27. Movie, "Star —"

1	2	3	
4	5	6	
7	8	9	
10	11	12	
13	14	15	
16	17	18	
19	20	21	
22	23	24	
25	26	27	

FIGURE LOGIC 3

by Evelyn Rosenthal

Copyright 1989 by Bantam Doubleday Dell Publishing Group, Inc.

Solve Figure Logic by completing some simple arithmetic problems, which will enable you to move from clue to clue through the puzzle.

TO PROCEED: Look at the diagram and note that the number "49," answering clue 29-Down, has been entered as a starting point. Your next step might be to 27-Down. Continue solving by going from clue to clue as needed.

You might discover that, at times, you will not be able to complete an entire number at first; but you may be able, by logic, to determine what one or more of the digits must be. If you enter those digits into the diagram, they may help you solve other clues, and you can eventually return to the unfinished numbers and finally complete them.

NOTE: A square of a number is the result of multiplying that number by itself.

CLUES ACROSS

1. Eleven times 5-Across
5. Two less than 10-Across
8. Same digits as 21-Across, rearranged
9. 4-Down plus 17-Across
10. 26-Down minus 19-Across
11. 19-Across multiplied by 20-Down
13. Consecutive digits, not in order
15. 9-Across minus 16-Across
16. First two digits of 3-Down
17. 15-Across minus 16-Across
19. See 27-Down
21. Consecutive digits in order
23. 20-Down plus 31-Across
25. Twice 15-Across
28. Thirty more than 30-Across
29. Thirty-five more than 14-Down
30. One-third of 10-Across
31. 19-Across multiplied by 27-Down

CLUES DOWN

1. Three times 28-Across
2. Consecutive even digits in order
3. 23-Across plus 31-Across
4. Twice 16-Across
5. Ninety less than 26-Down
6. Twice 29-Across
7. Four times 19-Across multiplied by 4-Down
11. Five more than 19-Across
12. One thousand more than 2-Down
14. Nine times 27-Down
18. Twice 3-Down
19. 9-Across multiplied by 19-Across
20. One-ninth of 31-Across
22. Seven more than 17-Across
24. Thirty more than 28-Across
26. Six times 9-Across
27. Square of 19-Across
29. One-ninth of 27-Down

Solution is on page 294.

SEVEN CLUES QUIZ

In each of the categories below you are given seven clues about a person, place, or thing. The idea is to guess what is being described in as few clues as possible. Since it's difficult to keep your eyes from jumping ahead, we suggest you use a piece of paper to cover the clues and slide it down as you reach each clue. As soon as you have a good guess, write it down on the line next to the clue that gave you the guess; BUT KEEP READING, ONE CLUE AT A TIME, to the end; you may be wrong and the following clues will probably help you. Write down your answer each time. When you have finished all six categories, check the answers on page 310; note the number of the clue where you first had the correct answer. Add up these numbers for your score (you are aiming for a low score). A score of 24 is outstanding, 28 is very good, 32 is good, and 35 is average.

A. LAND AREA
1. in North Africa ....
2. sirocco winds ....
3. Nile and Niger rivers ....
4. salt mines ....
5. 3,500,000 square miles ....
6. camel caravans and oases ....
7. world's largest desert ....

B. CITY
1. in Europe ....
2. in Italy ....
3. shipbuilding center ....
4. Murano glass is a product ....
5. St. Mark's Square ....
6. Bridge of Sighs ....
7. canals and gondolas ....

C. EVENT
1. annual event (except 1940, 1941, 1942) ....
2. awards ceremony ....
3. began in 1901 ....
4. prize consists of gold medal, money, and diploma ......
5. six prize categories ....
6. awards presented in Oslo and Stockholm ....
7. founded by dynamite inventor Alfred Nobel ....

D. PERSON
1. born 1881, died 1973 ....
2. painter, sculptor, graphic artist, ceramicist ....
3. leader of the School of Paris ....
4. "Rose Period" ....
5. cubism ....
6. "Blue Period" ....
7. born in Spain ....

E. LAND FORMATION
1. in Africa ....
2. in Tanzania ....
3. extinct volcano ....
4. two peaks—Kibo and Mawenzi ....
5. coffee and plantains grown on lower slopes ....
6. highest mountain in Africa ....
7. Hemingway wrote about it in "The Snows of —" .....

F. BODY OF WATER
1. in the U.S.A. ....
2. strait ....
3. four miles long, one to two miles wide ....
4. discovered in 1579 by Sir Francis Drake ....
5. links a bay and an ocean ....
6. mouth of the Sacramento and San Joaquin rivers ......
7. spanned by a bridge of the same name which links San Francisco and Marin County ....

Starting box: page 320
This Diagramless is 17 boxes wide by 17 boxes deep

ACROSS

1. Over
5. Paul: Spanish
6. Section of New York City
7. Standards
12. "— and inspired divinity"
13. Obloquy
14. Shuffle about leisurely
15. Social level
16. Devotee
17. Subject of a TV series: abbr.
19. London suburb
20. Ransacks
23. Seaport west of Algiers
24. Printer's mistakes
26. Mends
30. Unrefined but superior person: 4 wds.
35. Stuff or gorge
36. Trifling
37. Move
38. Plant resembling the yucca
39. Distraught
42. Dry, as wine
43. A Gabor
44. Elliptical
46. Show consideration for
49. Smooth sheer fabric
50. Vapors
52. Dexterous
53. Rather heavy
54. In a huff
55. Gourd fruit

DOWN

1. Turn aside
2. Qualified
3. Forerunner of the snowmobile
4. A Jones
5. Gait
6. Owns
7. Anything but a sure thing: 2 wds.
8. Harem room
9. Run the chance
10. "The hills are — . . . yet speak of God"
11. Merganser
12. Hermosillo's river
14. New Zealander
16. Took flight
17. Wild with fear
18. Pitcher's opposition
21. Brimless hats
22. Portico
23. Inducing sleep
25. Opposed to syn.
27. "In the know"
28. Jazz Age et al.
29. Concert highlight
31. Nonagreement
32. Uses the voice
33. Small orchard
35. Tree toad
39. African monkey
40. Eager
41. Victor Borge is one
45. Summit
46. Bout: hyph. wd.
47. Feeble
48. Alcott character
50. *Douloureux*
51. Pitfall
53. Extraordinary thing: slang

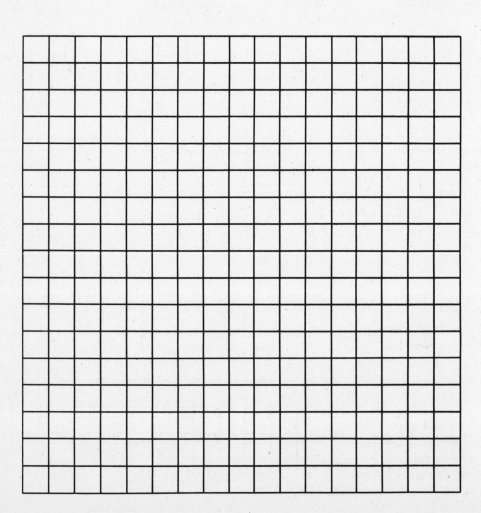

Solution is on page 292

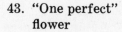
ACROSS

1. Purse item
5. In-between
7. Ceremony
11. Wintry spell: 2 wds.
13. Jot
14. Take a downward direction
15. Threaded nail
17. Interoffice note
18. Window glass
19. Tin Man's desire
21. Lab animal
22. Succor
23. Like steak tartare
24. Fortune
25. Essay
26. Pronoun
29. Tuber
31. Fair booth
33. Pipe diameter
34. Maneuver to gain a respite: 3 wds.
37. Mr. Mullins of the funnies
38. Holds on
39. Healing medicine
41. What is it?
42. Young fish
45. Infra-red device
46. Wager
48. Fish eggs
49. Pre-holiday time
50. Quadrangles
53. Immovable
54. Tangy sweet
56. Travelway
58. Country path
59. Upon
60. Standstill
62. Gas used in signs
63. Hiding place for an ace
64. Well-worn pants area

DOWN

1. Dungeon
2. Strange
3. State: abbr.
4. Cluster
5. Burrowing mammal
6. Dam
7. Player for Los Angeles
8. Say again
9. Love apple
10. Overact
11. Movie snack
12. Fruit-salad item
14. Carnival
16. Prepare for gifting
18. Butter serving
20. 25¢: 2 wds. (slang)
24. Bus money
26. Something dependable: hyph. wd.
27. Fodder grass
28. Mischief-maker
30. Jones and Swift
31. Wild plum
32. Depressed
34. Stately display
35. Manta
36. Cravat
37. Souvenir
39. Large gully
40. 1776, for example
42. Author Yerby
43. "One perfect" flower
44. Thus far
45. Dud: slang
47. Walked
51. Membership fees
52. Stem
53. Facade
55. Heavy weight
57. Paradise
58. Letter "sign-off"
61. Princess Radziwill

Starting box: page 320
This Diagramless is 17 boxes wide by 17 boxes deep

Solution is on page 292

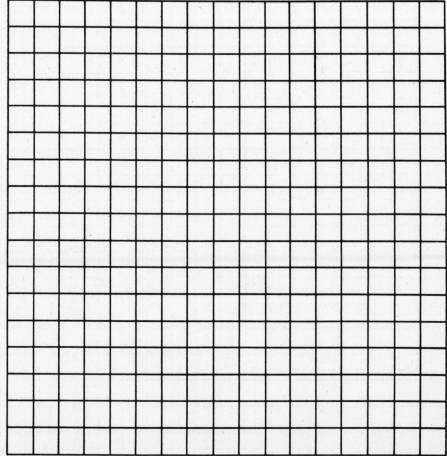

Starting box: page 320
This Diagramless is 19 boxes wide by 19 boxes deep

ACROSS

1. Thrash
5. Encourage
6. Capitol Hill product
9. Field deity
12. Clothe
14. "— Boy," Gainsborough painting
15. "King beater"
16. Dismantle: 2 wds.
20. Pronoun
21. Ignited
22. Used one end of a pencil
24. Teacher's flunkies
25. What a vacuum lacks
26. Jack Nicklaus, for one
28. Remove excess lipstick
29. Part of a mailbox
30. Charge per unit
33. Allow
36. Pond toy
37. Desertlike
38. Barbershop symbol
39. Order from a sentry
40. Revolves
41. Favorite flower since prehistoric times
42. Cleveland's lake
43. Itemize
44. Lawsuit
45. Day: abbr.
46. Summer drinks
47. Glazier's unit
48. Prepare copy
51. Fingerprinting fluid
52. Heflin or Johnson
53. Story
56. Finally: 2 wds.
59. Wedding vow: 2 wds.
60. — detector, polygraph
61. Ace for Nicklaus: 3 wds.
66. Number of a decapod's legs
67. Military force
68. Football and chess
72. Unusual
73. Flaw in some smiles
74. Rescue
75. Nursery item

DOWN

1. Flower-to-be
2. Miscalculate
3. Epoch
4. Would-be driver's worry
6. Dixie State: abbr.
7. Half a pint
8. Afternoon social
9. Go by
10. Dull pain
11. Require
13. Post-Christmas store sign
14. Wagers
17. Ditty bag
18. "The — McCoy
19. Threesome
23. Museum display
24. Poker kitty
26. It's passed at church
27. Decay
28. Measures of a hospital's size
29. Not liquid or gas
30. Fast
31. Get up
32. Adds dye
33. Unattached
34. Other
35. Between "ess" and "U"
36. Unadorned
38. Merry-andrew's stunt
39. U.S. Cabinet post: abbr.
40. Long narrow board
44. Sardine container
47. Dessert
48. Actress Gabor
49. Hyphen
50. Preposition
53. Very small
54. Commotion
55. Like summer days compared to winter days
56. Choir voice
57. Bound
58. — a hand
62. Fall behind
63. Historic period
64. Mischievous child
65. Direction
69. Disfigure
70. Female prototype
71. Witness

Solution is on page 292

ACROSS

1. Decant
5. Sybarite's delight
6. Turn informer: slang
9. Restaurant bill
12. Occupation; work
14. Dapper Dan
15. Edwin Markham's "The Man with the —"
16. Went —, went to extremes
20. Tourist stop
21. Zsa Zsa's sister
22. Richly deserved
24. A second time
25. "Butterflies — Free," recent movie
26. Detroit product
28. Double-runner
29. "War chariot"
30. Skip town
33. Cry of satisfaction
36. Beach grains
37. Declaim wildly
38. Had creditors
39. News; message
40. Was in a derby
41. Apply grease to
42. Nelson —, late singer
43. Word after grace
44. Rail or stilt
45. Time measure
46. Annoyance
47. Full gainer, for one
48. Diamond clubs
51. Pindar specialty
52. Potation
53. Supply station
56. Public discussion
59. Cotton State: abbr.
60. Ruined city on the Irrawaddy
61. Up and coming: 3 wds.
66. Pie plate
67. "Lend me your —"
68. Beelzebub
72. Member of a fraternal group
73. Watch closely
74. Agree (with)
75. Prof's concoction

DOWN

1. Little darling
2. Paddle
3. Home, to a Yankee abroad: abbr.
4. Refurbish
6. Polish
7. Ruckus
8. Canister contents
9. Slender
10. First-rate: 2 wds.
11. Stoop (over)
13. Uniform
14. Dead heat
17. Miss Arden
18. Not merely so-called
19. Accept the hazard
23. *Rojo*
24. Part of the Louisiana Purchase: abbr.
26. Gum drops or taffy
27. Moreover
28. Lawn requirement
29. Opposite of prompt
30. Picture border
31. Alençon and Cluny
32. "Everybody is wise after the —"
33. Knowing
34. Large group
35. Say further
36. Fountain favorite
38. Shade of green
39. Make a match
40. Uses the gavel
44. Auction offer
47. Homonym of "dough"
48. Bleat
49. Choir voice
50. Numerical suffix
53. Prohibits
54. Fatima's caliph husband
55. Back talk
56. Inscription on a coin
57. Depravity
58. Financial house
62. Aid for Lee Trevino
63. Forage
64. Cockney's "Present!"
65. Direction
69. Deadlock
70. Commercials
71. Hairdo protector

Solution is on page 292

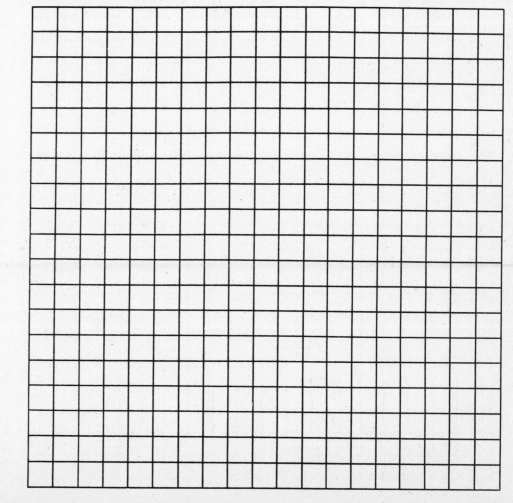

CHALLENGER
12 DIAGRAMLESS

Starting box: page 320
This Diagramless is 21 boxes wide by 21 boxes deep

ACROSS

1. Mowgli's mother
5. Edible root
9. Very old
11. Hebrew month
12. "... is a friend —"
14 Latvian city
15. Fine caviar
19. Issue (from)
21. Declare
22. "Zilch"
23. File for wood
27. Positive force, in Chinese philosophy
28. Author of "In His Own Write"
30. Terminal: abbr.
31. Crusoe's creator
34. Negative
37. Surgeon's arena: abbr.
39. Germans capitalize this
40. Lorry
41. Pater —
43. Nabokov title
46. Welcoming word
49. Cologne outcry
52. Sandal exposure
53. Primate of Madagascar
55. Herb Alpert's embouchure
57. Former Portuguese colony
58. Part of a trombone
62. Apian colony
63. Word of scorn
64. Op or pop
65. Young lamprey
66. Sound effect with tears
68. Heavyweight champ
69. Region in Israel
72. Desire
73. Word on a yard sign
76. Half of a half-and-half
77. New Testament trio
78. Actor Begley
79. With pleasure
83. Greek marketplace
85. Zoo category
86. Mood; frame of mind
90. Angers
93. Maritime displacement units
95. Set
96. Certain votes
97. Vocation
100. "Winnie-the-Pooh" character
102. Eastern priest
103. Drew close
105. In the —, alfresco
106. Waggish
107. Nurse
108. Builder's acquisition

DOWN

1. President Tyler's party
2. Mrs. Chaplin
3. Stripling
4. Don't move
5. Theda of the silents
6. Cut for television
7. Ready, willing and able
8. Refrain syllable
10. Arab League member
13. Mild oath
15. Source of fine scallops
16. Spacewalk: abbr.
17. Do a bank service
18. Pressing
20. "Darkness at —"
24. Shade of blonde
25. Canonized one, in Caen: abbr.
26. Golf term
28. Author Deighton
29. Poe avian's quotation
32. Word in a sentry's challenge
33. Possessive pronoun
35. Kin to "John"
36. Explosive
37. Canadian province: abbr.
38. Sara or Alice
42. Vend
43. Jolson and Smith
44. Moisture
45. Physicians' org.
47. Island of exile
48. Cash in Teheran
49. Turkish title
50. Trite humor: slang
51. Loathe
54. Bear genus
56. Greek letter
59. College League
60. Scottish river
61. Sea bird
67. Unit to measure hospital size
70. Hiatus
71. Inventor Whitney
73. Catch
74. I: Latin
75. Job for an electrician
77. Spoil
79. Boater or bowler
80. Overseas address abbr.
81. Quill, formerly
82. Shout
84. U.S.S.R. sea
87. Principal
88. Yearned
89. Mystery-writers' awards
91. Hurricane feature
92. Fast craft: abbr.
94. View: suffix
98. Sobeit!
99. Property
100. Throw things at
101. At liberty
102. Abraham's nephew
104. Louis XIV, e.g.

Solution is on page 292

CHALLENGER DIAGRAMLESS 13

ACROSS

1. Footwear item, now passé
5. Toynbee's Muse
6. Vaunt
10. Monarch, consort, ladies-in-waiting, nobles, et al.
11. Theater part
12. Targets for urban renewal
13. Open places on a musical staff
15. "None of woman born Shall — Macbeth"
16. Make up into a parcel
17. Powerful impulses
19. Be a success
21. Conform to rules
23. Minutes of court proceedings
27. Germany, Italy, etc., in World War II
28. Scads
30. Discarding
34. Permeate
35. Woodwind instrument
37. Native of Kraków
38. Heat-resistant glass
41. Central theme
43. Gauchos' footgear
44. Jewish month
45. New Zealand parrots
47. Minute, simple organism
49. Having little substance or strength
51. Turboprop, for one
52. Neophyte
53. Locale
54. Completely out of funds
60. Strike to produce a reverberant noise
61. Reddish brown
62. Cajun French, for one
65. Cotton processing machines
66. Squirrels' hoard
67. Long-limbed
68. Peeling
69. Dermis
70. "Uptight"
71. Choir member
72. — Acheson, late statesman

DOWN

1. Attila the Hun, "— of God"
2. Drop sharply and abruptly
3. Put on —, act "snooty"
4. Pre-kindergartner
6. Color of "my true love's hair"
7. Security item
8. S-shaped curve
9. Author, Nathaniel —
10. Mild cigar
12. Made fast
13. Whirl
14. What expectant fathers do in the waiting room
18. Herring's cousin
19. Culmination
20. Speech defects
22. Joyously unrestrained
23. Common Arab name
24. Equanimity
25. Interdiction
26. One who is of legal age
29. Bishoprics
31. Doctrine
32. Cozy corner
33. Went to work on: 2 wds.
36. Victory goddess
38. Coarse ground hominy
39. False gods
40. Hawaiian veranda
42. *Aficionado*
43. Expressing disapproval
46. Feign
48. Balmoral Castle's river
50. Woeful sounds
54. Leg part
55. Soviet news agency
56. Boat race
57. This "in good men is but knowledge in the making" (Milton)
58. Henry V and VIII
59. — chair, living room item
60. Verbose
62. Trim; cut
63. Citric or tannic —
64. Chinese secret society
67. How kings administer
69. Blackguard

Solution is on page 293

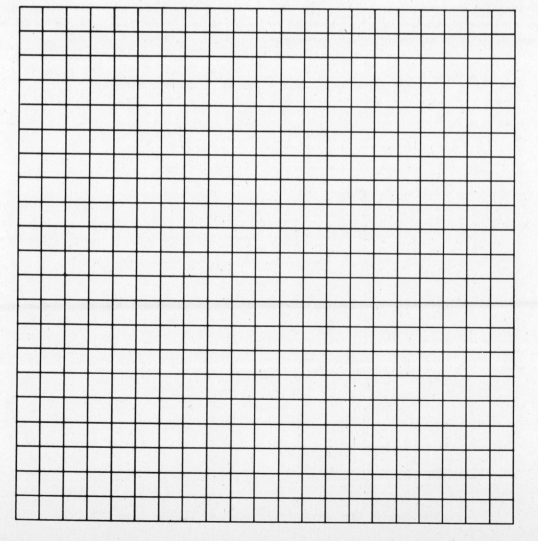

SPELL TO SCORE

The object of SPELL TO SCORE is to form 11 words by filling letters onto the dashes below, one letter per dash.

HANDICAP: Each word you form MUST begin with the starting letter (or letters) which is given below, and once a letter has been used (given letters included), you may not use that letter again in that word or in the word directly ABOVE or the word directly BELOW. For example, in the illustration below, ROCKY cannot be ROCKET because of the E and T in STAPLE, and PLATED cannot be PATROL because of the O and R in ROCKY.

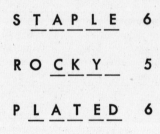

TO SCORE: Including the given letters, score 1 point for each letter in each word. Take an 11-point bonus if every letter of the alphabet appears at least once in your word list (include the given letters for this bonus). Subtract 5 points every time you cannot form a word containing at least 4 letters. Proper nouns and plurals are not allowed, nor are present-tense verbs ending in "s," such as "sings."

Average score: 55   Good score: 66   Perfect score: 77

Words	Points
1. N — — — — —	—
2. M A — — — —	—
3. Q — — —	—
4. P R — — — — —	—
5. S — — — — — —	—
6. J O — — — —	—
7. F — — — —	—
8. E M — — — — —	—
9. T — — — —	—
10. W A — — —	—
11. C — — — — — —	—

Our answer, showing a perfect score of 77, is on page 313.

LETTER COUNT

Copyright 1989 by Bantam Doubleday Dell Publishing Group, Inc.

The idea of Letter Count is to form everyday English words, Kriss Kross style, in the diagram at the bottom of the page using only the letters given in the graph below. Each letter in the graph has a numerical value which is determined by adding together the number of both the row and column in which the letter is found. For example: X is in the second row and the sixth column and therefore has a numerical value of 8; one of the E's has a value of 11, since it is the third row and eighth column (there are other E's and they will have different numerical values). In entering letters into the diagram, the numerical value of each letter must match the number of its square in the diagram. We have started you off by filling in the word "WHY" and crossing off in the graph the W with a value of 7, the H with a value of 13, and the Y with a value of 9. To solve, try out the various letter-number possibilities for the combinations of squares in the diagram, until you have determined the correct letters and words. Here's a suggestion: Fill in the letters with the highest and lowest numerical values first. It's a good idea to cross off each letter as you use it, since each letter is used once and only once. NOTE: There are no plurals or words beginning with a capital letter in this puzzle.

Solution is on page 313.

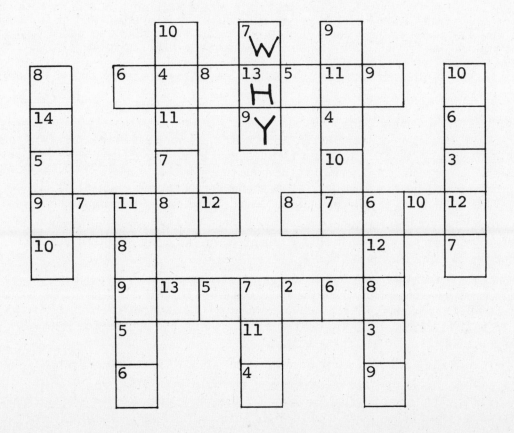

SOLICROSS
Trademark

The SOLITAIRE Word Game

PURPOSE OF GAME

The object of this game of word solitaire is to gain the highest score possible. To do so, you form words using letters from a predetermined list, placing them on squares of a specified value so that the words are formed both across (always from the left) and down (always from the top). This rule, and those following below, apply to the two Solicross games that appear on the opposite page.

HOW TO PLAY SOLICROSS

1. Write across on first line of DRAW COLUMN (on the opposite page) the first seven letters from the LETTER LIST. Indicate the last letter used from the list by a dot or a line (/).

2. Form a word using two or more of these letters. Names of people and places are not allowed, and only common English words may be used.

3. Place either BEGINNING LETTER or END LETTER of this word in the DIAGRAM on square indicated by a circle, filling in the other letters of this word either from left to right or from top to bottom (never from right to left, or bottom to top). Do not place letters on any blacked-out squares. Add up score (see 7 below) and enter in SCORE column. Scratch (/) in the DRAW column the letters used in the words.

4. Copy all unused letters of DRAW on the next line, adding enough letters from the LETTER LIST (in sequence) to bring next DRAW up to seven letters.

5. Form new words from each DRAW by adding one or more letters to an existing word to form a new word or words. All letters from any one DRAW must be used in only one row, either across or down. Only complete words may be formed. **Letters adjoining other letters must always form a word,** in crossword form.

6. Form new words by:
   a. Adding one or more letters to an existing word, at the beginning or end, or both. You may also form a new word by adding letters as connecting links between letters and/or words already in the diagram. Any additional new words formed by this move are, of course, added to your score. Even when you add an "s," "ed," "re," etc., to the beginning or end of an already existing word, this also counts as a new word in your score.
   b. Setting a new word at right angles to an existing word, incorporating one of its letters or adding to it.
   c. Placing a new word parallel to one you have already written in so that the letters adjoining also form words.

7. Score each time you complete one DRAW. Add together all numbers in the corners of the squares used to form or modify words. If a word has been changed by adding a letter or letters, count the entire word again. Two or more words formed at the same time are both counted; the square common to both new words is counted with each word. Words within words are not counted. Write your DRAW score in the SCORE column and your accumulated score at the bottom of the column.

8. If it becomes impossible to use any letters from a given DRAW, scratch all seven letters and subtract 25 points from your score for that DRAW. Bring down the next seven letters from the LETTER LIST and try to form your next word.

9. When the DRAW COLUMN is complete, the game is finished whether or not all the letters from the LETTER LIST have been used. If all the letters in the LETTER LIST have been transferred to the DRAW COLUMN, you may still continue to form words as long as you can. If at any time *all* the letters from the LETTER LIST are used up to form words, add 50 points to your score and count the game as complete.

10. When you **finish** the puzzle, the same word must not appear twice in the diagram.

11. There is no absolute answer, but **our games are shown on page 315.**
    When you have completed the game, you may play it again by making your own diagram and reversing the order of the letter list.

LETTER LIST

Z I M C A L R E M N A E T I A O E M S E C B N U V N P P A C
A L O L P Y L T O C J E Q B X H Y U R A E W K D E G S O F R

DRAW COLUMN	SCORE
TOTAL	

Our score: 387

SOLICROSS 2

LETTER LIST

R H A E C T R T A E H O S R C E L E T A C P R E E A S E R A
D N A T M O N I E W D T R A I Y A M G O R K E L R E N A I B

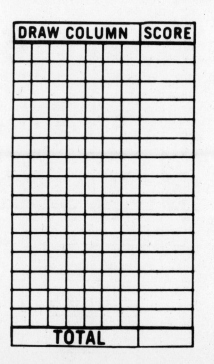

DRAW COLUMN	SCORE
TOTAL	

Our solutions are on page 315

Our score: 427

SOLICROSS 3

L A H M I C T I N B W O K Y T I B N T E V I G B D A A T R S
B R O I A Q P D C S O R F G I Z A L X O U S O M A R N I J E

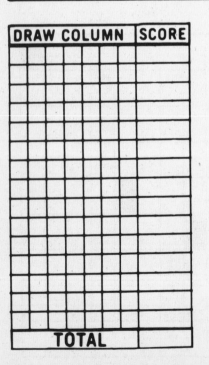

DIAGRAM

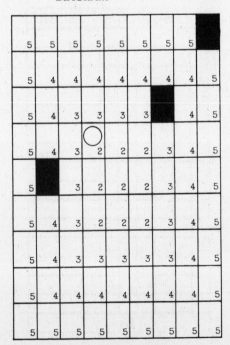

Our score : 424

SOLICROSS 4

P O A F D T R M R F O T O I C O L K W H E C E I F E S E M A
P T O H F E L A C W R N A S Y A T R E T L U M E B R T A U D

DIAGRAM

Our solutions are on page 315

Our score : 452

Copyright 1989 by Bantam
Doubleday Dell Publishing Group, Inc.

SOLICROSS 5

Y A N T O C R I Q P T A I W T O G Z N L S E R I N W O R E N
R A R S A T L E M U L O F Y P C U L V I Z S A J B R G E I D

DRAW COLUMN	SCORE

TOTAL

DIAGRAM

5	5	5	5	5	5	5	5	5
5	4	4	4	4	4	4	4	5
5	4	3	■	3	3	3	4	5
5	4	3	2	2	2	■	4	5
5	4	3	2	2	2	3	4	5
5	4	3	2	2	2	3	4	5
5	4	■	3	3	3	3	4	5
5	4	4	4	4	4	4	4	5
5	5	5	5	5	5	5	5	5

Our score: 362

SOLICROSS 6

F E N L A C O Z O T T U A D W S P E O G L O L P T A V I S R
G R O Q R A E W N Y M G I K X A V U H S O J O L R E P A E Y

DRAW COLUMN	SCORE

TOTAL

DIAGRAM

5	5	5	5	5	5	5	5	5
5	4	4	4	4	4	4	4	5
5	4	3	3	3	3	■	4	5
5	4	3	2	2	2	3	4	5
5	4	■	2	2	2	3	4	5
5	4	3	2	2	2	3	4	5
5	4	3	■	3	3	3	4	5
5	4	4	4	4	4	4	4	5
5	5	5	5	5	5	5	5	5

Our solutions are on page 315

Our score: 398

Quotation is on page 308.
Word list is on page 312.

by CATHERINE McFALL

DEFINITIONS	WORDS

A. Extreme fear of blushing — 172 91 21 37 159 195 190 137 19
— 45 176 89 116

B. Breach of law — 105 141 110 40 23 88 166 68 5

C. Part of the A.E.F. — 72 178 102 36 57 87 112 11 38 28
— 181 3 26

D. Arthur Hill TV co-star: 2 wds. — 125 138 76 155 56 171 177 51 100

E. During all four seasons: hyph. wd. — 135 84 167 122 66 158 150 94 79 20

F. Frank Sinatra, Jr., to his dad — 22 163 77 15 180 60 144 174

G. Crossbar for harness fastening — 173 13 191 189 111 142 29 43 109
— 146 74

H. Get a word in — — 136 98 161 186 59 99 80 24

I. Aramaic or Coptic, e.g. — 55 119 63 6 162 70 30 44

J. Fairy of Irish folklore — 65 103 32 75 179 140 113 143 2 184

K. Lacking in forethought — 61 8 129 96 18 196 4 50 118
— 71 148 185

L. Great wealth or prominence — 17 53 67 78 115 97 104 156

M. Easy; passive — 134 46 120 188 164 42 175 52 107 90

N. Congress which convened in 1877: hyph. wd. — 83 108 157 7 58 151 95 170 124 153

O. Morally uplifting — 9 165 121 130 49 106 81 12

P. Was conscience-stricken — 187 10 147 154 139 33 114 127

Q. Drama as a branch of art: 2 wds. — 25 35 64 152 132 82 47 54 183 149

R. Having made no will — 39 168 117 145 123 86 126 131 92

S. Path of a rocket — 34 69 160 193 16 73 182 169 85 31

T. Not sufficiently to meet requirements — 27 48 194 1 133 93 101 62 14 41
— 192 128

1 T	2 J	3 C	4 K	5 B	6 I		7 N	8 K	9 O		10 P	11 C	12 O	13 G	14 T	15 F	16 S	17 L	18 K	19 A
20 E	21 A	22 F	23 B	24 H	25 Q	26 C		27 T	28 C	29 G	30 I	31 S	32 J	33 P		34 S	35 Q	36 C		37 A
38 C	39 R	40 B	41 T	42 M	43 G	44 I		45 A	46 M		47 Q	48 T	49 O	50 K	51 D	52 M	53 L	54 Q		55 I	56 D
57 C	58 N		59 H	60 F	61 K		62 T	63 I		64 Q	65 J	66 E	67 L	68 B	69 S	70 I	71 K	72 C		73 S	74 G	75 J
76 D	77 F	78 L	79 E	80 H		81 O	82 Q	83 N	84 E	85 S	86 R	87 C	88 B	89 A	90 M		91 A	92 R	93 T	94 E	95 N	96 K
97 L	98 H		99 H		100 D	101 T	102 C	103 J	104 L	105 B	106 O	107 M	108 N	109 G		110 B	111 G		112 C	113 J	114 P
115 L	116 A	117 R	118 K		119 I		120 M	121 O	122 E	123 R	124 N		125 D	126 R	127 P	128 T		129 K	130 O		131 R	132 Q
133 T		134 M	135 E	136 H		137 A	138 D	139 P	140 J	141 B	142 G		143 J		144 F	145 R	146 G	147 P	148 K	149 Q		150 E
151 N		152 Q	153 N	154 P		155 D	156 L	157 N	158 E	159 A		160 S		161 H	162 I	163 F	164 M	165 O	166 B	167 E	168 R
	169 S	170 N		171 D	172 A	173 G	174 F	175 M		176 A	177 D	178 C	179 J	180 F		181 C		182 S	183 Q
		184 J	185 K	186 H	187 P		188 M	189 G		190 A	191 G	192 T		193 S	194 T	195 A	196 K

DEFINITIONS   **WORDS**

A. Symbolic figure seen on New Year's Eve: 2 wds.
22 132 42 174 105 166 52 187 7 89

B. The bane of Johnny Horizon
19 151 70 32 182 123 131 53 172 85

C. Steelmaking process: hyph. wd.
203 97 160 12 8 73 111 51 150 121

D. Traveled far and wide
129 50 100 165 40

E. Critically appraised
118 77 55 3 66 18 44 144 215

F. Childhood home of Jesus
54 188 72 139 155 103 81 124

G. Props for Spanish dancers
140 192 17 181 63 112 31 120 169

H. Last possible moment: 2 wds.
185 58 2 14 163 158 201
82 180 130 145 98

I. Passages through mountains
194 47 74 171 27 108 96

J. Persons of greater authority: hyph. wd.
195 29 208 94 107 177 11 128 46

K. Inventor of the elevator brake
206 142 79 10

L. Steles, statues, etc.
147 91 48 6 84 214 126 62 20

M. Horrified (at)
9 104 33 25 75 146

N. Meal on a stick: 2 wds.
41 117 170 90 141 30 122 106 76 133

O. Get-up-and-go
88 168 204 78 64 110 156 191

P. Taboo to certain people: hyph. wd.
114 49 92 189 178 152 212 173 200

Q. Informer, especially among children
38 157 138 56 134 15 93 125 190 86

R. Industrial problem-solver: 2 wds.
205 23 211 99 68 5 196 60 186
59 39 164 153 83 16 137

S. — to, un-mindful of
162 1 102 37 202 71 154 21 113

T. Accuracy; appropriateness
207 13 179 143 210 36 34 176 149

U. Pertaining to the whole Christian church
45 159 35 198 209 115 95 167 136 28

V. Birls
80 119 109 24 61 87 65 193

W. "Obstinacy and heat of opinion are the surest proof of —"
67 161 199 184 175 127 69 116 197

X. Usually calm and un-worried
57 43 183 135 4 148 101 213 26

1 S	2 H	3 E	4 X	5 R	6 L	7 A		8 C	9 M	10 K		11 J
12 C	13 T	14 H	15 Q	16 R	17 G	18 E	19 B		20 L	21 S	22 A	23 R	24 V	25 M	26 X	27 I		28 U	29 J	30 N	31 G
32 B	33 M	34 T		35 U	36 T	37 S	38 Q	39 R	40 D		41 N	42 A	43 X	44 E	45 U	46 J		47 I	48 L	49 P	50 D	51 C
52 A	53 B	54 F	55 E	56 Q	57 X	58 H	59 R		60 R	61 V	62 L		63 G	64 O	65 V		66 E		67 W		68 R	69 W
70 B	71 S	72 F	73 C	74 I	75 M		76 N	77 E	78 O	79 K	80 V		81 F	82 H	83 R	84 L	85 B	86 Q	87 V	88 O	89 A	90 N
	91 L	92 P	93 Q	94 J	95 U	96 I		97 C	98 H	99 R	100 D	101 X	102 S	103 F	104 M	105 A		106 N	107 J	108 I	109 V
110 O	111 C	112 G	113 S		114 P	115 U		116 W	117 N	118 E		119 V	120 G	121 C	122 N	123 B		124 F	125 Q	126 L	127 W
128 J	129 D	130 H	131 B	132 A	133 N	134 Q	135 X		136 U	137 R	138 Q	139 F	140 G	141 N		142 K	143 T	144 E		145 H	146 M	147 L
148 X	149 T	150 C		151 B	152 P	153 R	154 S	155 F	156 O	157 Q	158 H	159 U	160 C		161 W	162 S		163 H	164 R	165 D	166 A	167 U
168 O	169 G	170 N	171 I	172 B		173 P	174 A	175 W	176 T		177 J	178 P	179 T	180 H	181 G		182 B	183 X	184 W	185 H	186 R	187 A
188 F	189 P	190 Q	191 O		192 G	193 V		194 I	195 J	196 R	197 W		198 U	199 W	200 P	201 H		202 S	203 C	204 O	205 R
206 K	207 T		208 J	209 U	210 T		211 R	212 P	213 X	214 L	215 E										

by ELIZABETH B. WALLMANN

DEFINITIONS   WORDS

A. Lady's dressing gown — 141 69 36 106 151 13 118

B. Turn to one side; bend — 54 170 121 182 139 26 1

C. Tributary of the Missouri River — 50 91 180 8 160 135 19 79 107 173 72

D. Chivalry — 18 133 5 41 71 168 88 60 119 81 100 29

E. Overly emotional or demonstrative — 117 51 90 104 145 153 184 163

F. Goethe's scoffing fiend — 6 45 74 25 126 61 138 31 85 169 16 114 98 193

G. Takes on, as a task — 111 73 127 58 105 23 94

H. Mythical Greek egotist — 137 38 15 102 185 167 4 124 82

I. Master of an inn — 86 150 56 40 162 96 27 144

J. Adapting actions to expediency — 123 7 152 142 42 70 28 186 132 55 84

K. Doric or Ionic, e.g. — 57 34 164 115 22

L. Pre-school school — 158 11 191 148 64 110 131 101 76 44 175 53

M. Word with "jam" or "light" — 188 176 156 46 21 113 95

N. — case, luggage item — 172 97 35 59 147 129 187 2 78

O. Painstakingly exact — 30 149 177 125 68 47 165 80

P. Mixture of equal parts of milk and cream: 3 wds. — 128 146 10 178 20 159 92 62 134 48 32

Q. Capable of being understood — 75 39 66 3 103 181 190 112 89 14 122 166

R. Large, dangerous sea denizen — 24 161 143 99 174 67 52 120 189

S. Hard to deal with or please — 37 77 12 109 136 157 183 49 87

T. Opposite of deniable — 43 108 116 93 140 63 179 33 154 9

U. Wide open — 155 17 171 130 83 65 192

1 B	2 N	3 Q		4 H	5 D	6 F	7 J	8 C	9 T		10 P	11 L	12 S	13 A		14 Q
15 H	16 F	17 U	18 D	19 C		20 P		21 M	22 K	23 G	24 R	25 F		26 B	27 I	28 J	29 D	30 O		31 F	32 P
	33 T	34 K	35 N	36 A	37 S		38 H	39 Q	40 I		41 D	42 J	43 T	44 L	45 F	46 M	47 O	48 P	49 S	50 C
51 E	52 R	53 L	54 B	55 J		56 I	57 K	58 G	59 N	60 D	61 F	62 P	63 T	64 L	65 U	66Q		67 R	68 O	69 A
70 J	71 D	72 C		73 G	74 F	75 Q	76 L	77 S	78 N		79 C	80 O	81 D		82 H	83 U	84 J	85 F	86 I	87 S
88 D	89 Q	90 E	91 C		92 P	93 T	94 G	95 M	96 I	97 N	98 F	99 R	100D		101L		102H	103Q	104E	105G	106A
	107C	108T		109S	110L	111G	112Q	113M	114F	115K		116T	117E	118A	119D	120R		121B	122Q	123J	124H
125O	126F	127G	128P	129N	130U	131L		132J	133D		134P		135C	136S	137H	138F	139B	140 T		141A	142J
143R	144 I	145E		146P	147N	148 L		149O	150 I	151A	152J	153E	154T	155U		156M	157S	158 L	159P	160C	161R
162 I	163E	164K	165O	166Q	167H		168D	169F	170B		171U	172N	173C	174R	175L	176M		177O	178P		179T
180 C	181Q		182B	183S	184E	185H	186J	187N		188M	189R	190Q	191 L	192U	193F					

232

Quotation is on page 309.
Word list is on page 312.

by ELIZABETH B. WALLMANN

DEFINITIONS   **WORDS**

A. Incorrect

95 105 51 81 159 21 114 38 131

B. Herbage named for its growth pattern: 2 wds.

9 86 101 164 180 25 145 36 48 211

C. Cowboy hero created by Clarence Mulford: 2 wds.

127 23 52 97 15 192 35 68 136

3 89 118 41 148 60

D. Easy as pie

204 141 214 85 24 119 130 17 179 56

E. Principle of Couéism

137 195 112 33 74 50 102 154 11

124 208 188 169 199

F. Regard with suspicion

63 198 153 93 47 78 210 123

G. Young animal, esp. a horse

167 59 129 182 16 150 189 1

H. Lookout platform: hyph. wd.

13 207 142 157 191 79 30 108 113

I. Partial; unfair: hyph. wd.

146 29 110 170 163 18 128 67

J. Advocate of obedience to power

69 185 42 177 201 98 26 132 206

213 106 147 12

K. Doorsill

104 94 144 134 4 58 184 166 71

L. Topples; capsizes

77 27 122 2 196 116 138 175 149

M. Supreme Court Justice 1939-1962

172 155 53 91 99 34 143 83 19

217 62

N. Call to account; reprove: 3 wds.

186 65 165 10 202 49 176 75 31 55

O. Ragout

84 115 200 216 20 107 156 168 43 133

P. Spoke ambiguously

28 161 82 100 45 140 194 14 126

178 92

Q. High degree of skill

46 111 96 190 120 173 73 205 64 8

R. Position of tax official who rates real property

215 87 5 72 32 103 44 117 135

209 158 183

S. Instrument for determining distance: 2 wds.

39 7 109 160 88 193 125 66 151

174 76

T. Certain clothing and linens, collectively

57 70 171 162 197 139 40 181 212

U. Lukewarm; unenthusiastic

6 61 187 22 203 121 90 54 37

152 80

1 G	2 L	3 C	4 K	5 R		6 U	7 S	8 Q		9 B	10 N	11 E	12 J		13 H	14 P	15 C	16 G	17 D	18 I
19 M	20 O	21 A		22 U	23 C	24 D	25 B	26 J	27 L	28 P	29 I	30 H	31 N	32 R		33 E	34 M		35 C	36 B	37 U
38 A	39 S	40 T		41 C	42 J		43 O	44 R	45 P	46 Q	47 F	48 B		49 N	50 E	51 A		52 C	53 M	54 U	55 N
56 D		57 T	58 K	59 G		60 C	61 U	62 M	63 F	64 Q		65 N	66 S	67 I		68 C	69 J	70 T	71 K	72 R	73 Q
74 E		75 N	76 S	77 L	78 F	79 H	80 U		81 A	82 P	83 M		84 O	85 D	86 B	87 R	88 S	89 C		90 U	91 M
92 P		93 F	94 K	95 A		96 Q	97 C	98 J	99 M	100 P	101 B	102 E		103 R	104 K	105 A	106 J	107 O	108 H		109 S
110 I	111 Q	112 E		113 H	114 A		115 O	116 L	117 R		118 C	119 D	120 Q	121 U	122 L	123 F	124 E			125 S	126 P
127 C	128 I	129 G	130 D	131 A		132 J	133 O	134 K		135 R	136 C	137 E	138 L	139 T		140 P	141 D		142 H	143 M	144 K
	145 B	146 I	147 J	148 C	149 L	150 G	151 S	152 U	153 F		154 E	155 M	156 O	157 H	158 R	159 A	160 S		161 P	162 T	163 I
164 B	165 N	166 K	167 G		168 O	169 E		170 I	171 T	172 M	173 Q	174 S	175 L		176 N	177 J	178 P		179 D	180 B	181 T
182 G	183 R		184 K	185 J	186 N	187 U	188 E	189 G	190 Q	191 H		192 C	193 S		194 P	195 E	196 L	197 T		198 F	199 E
200 O	201 J		202 N	203 U	204 D		205 Q	206 J	207 H	208 E	209 R	210 F		211 B	212 T	213 J	214 D	215 R	216 O	217 M

DEFINITIONS   WORDS

A. Confused
___ ___ ___ ___ ___ ___
137 188 150 156 5 173

B. *Dernier cri:* 2 wds.
___ ___ ___ ___ ___ ___ ___ ___
88 22 187 67 179 74 110 171

C. With Word J, near our locality: 3 wds.
___ ___ ___ ___ ___ ___ ___ ___ ___ ___
155 138 42 199 126 29 17 172 101 184

D. Certain characters in a mystery plot
___ ___ ___ ___ ___ ___ ___ ___
66 148 114 209 87 194 106 107

E. Flower named for shape of its rhizomes
___ ___ ___ ___ ___ ___ ___ ___ ___
136 123 109 162 94 89 129 8 142

F. Minimally: 2 wds.
___ ___ ___ ___ ___ ___ ___
65 135 54 95 186 117 161

G. Barely begun; incipient
___ ___ ___ ___ ___ ___ ___ ___
168 57 77 108 210 166 176 202

H. Uncle Wiggily, e.g.
___ ___ ___ ___ ___ ___
83 45 39 119 103 178

I. "Chew the rag": slang
___ ___ ___ ___
104 2 25 115

J. See Word C: 3 wds.
___ ___ ___ ___ ___ ___ ___ ___ ___ ___
97 181 191 11 157 72 16 32 153 201

K. "—, out of mind": 3 wds.
___ ___ ___ ___ ___ ___ ___ ___ ___ ___
6 105 91 182 14 141 56 18 133 128

L. Titular heroine of a Christopher Morley novel: 2 wds.
___ ___ ___ ___ ___ ___ ___ ___ ___ ___
76 51 102 140 30 69 180 73 21 40

M. Variety of seals
___ ___ ___ ___ ___
165 146 37 27 24

N. Pulitzer-prize drama of 1932: 4 wds.
___ ___ ___ ___ ___ ___ ___ ___
177 46 198 53 3 152 139 185
___ ___ ___
112 23 4

O. "Happy is the — without a history": Beccaria
___ ___ ___ ___ ___ ___
98 131 195 19 200 59

P. Spritelike
___ ___ ___ ___ ___
64 145 50 38 70

Q. — after, painful awakening
___ ___ ___ ___ ___ ___ ___
154 60 75 211 78 204 58

R. Seneca called it the test of strong men
___ ___ ___ ___ ___ ___ ___ ___ ___
82 33 169 111 122 164 41 206 12

S. Forte of Mark Spitz
___ ___ ___ ___ ___ ___ ___ ___
132 84 62 207 49 174 159 99

T. The type of men who believe in luck: Emerson
___ ___ ___ ___ ___ ___ ___
190 147 205 85 15 13 124

U. Guiteau, Czolgosz, or Ray
___ ___ ___ ___ ___ ___ ___ ___
134 26 35 196 44 52 170 193

V. Hawthorne called them "earth's undecaying monuments"
___ ___ ___ ___ ___ ___ ___ ___ ___
130 116 120 175 93 143 90 149 158

W. Instruction for moving heavy, valuable object: 3 wds.
___ ___ ___ ___ ___ ___ ___ ___ ___ ___
100 48 197 55 167 163 118 125 144 113

X. Approximately
___ ___ ___ ___ ___ ___ ___
151 68 160 7 63 86 80

Y. Mistakenly: 2 wds.
___ ___ ___ ___ ___ ___ ___
189 127 71 61 121 203 208

Z. In good spirits; lively
___ ___ ___ ___ ___ ___ ___
96 92 192 10 81 34 183

AA. Graceful, piercing wit: 2 wds.
___ ___ ___ ___ ___ ___ ___ ___ ___
9 1 31 43 36 20 28 47 79

1AA	2I	3N		4N	5A	6K	7X	8E	9AA	10Z	11J	12R		13T	14K		15T	16J	17C	18K
19O	20AA	21L	22B	23N	24M		25I	26U		27M	28AA	29C	30L		31AA	32J		33R	34Z	35U	36AA
37M	38P	39H	40L		41R	42C		43AA	44U		45H		46N	47AA	48W	49S		50P	51L	52U	53N
	54F	55W	56K	57G	58Q		59O	60Q	61Y	62S	63X	64P	65F	66D	67B		68X	69L		70P	71Y
72J		73L	74B	75Q	76L		77G	78Q	79AA	80X		81Z	82R	83H	84S	85T	86X	87D	88B		89E
90V	91K	92Z		93V	94E	95F		96Z	97J	98O	99S	100W	101C	102L	103H	104I	105K	106D		107D	108G
109E	110B	111R		112N	113W	114D		115I	116V	117F	118W		119H	120V	121Y	122R	123E	124T	125W		126C
127Y	128K	129E		130V	131O	132S	133K	134U	135F	136E	137A	138C		139N	140L	141K		142E	143V	144W	145P
	146M		147T	148D	149V	150A	151X	152N	153J		154Q	155C	156A	157J	158V		159S	160X	161F		162E
163W		164R	165M	166G		167W	168G	169R	170U	171B	172C	173A		174S	175V	176G	177N		178H	179B	180L
	181J	182K	183Z	184C	185N		186F	187B		188A	189Y	190T	191J	192Z	193U	194D	195O		196U	197W
	198N	199C	200O	201J	202G		203Y	204Q		205T		206R	207S	208Y	209D	210G	211Q			

Quotation is on page 309.
Word list is on page 312.

DEFINITIONS   WORDS

A. Made a patsy of
155 3 68 27 129 176 36 47 218 56

B. Famous road in Italy leading to Rome: 2 wds.
74 17 2 46 108 158 110 94 90

C. Female swimmer
40 100 198 124 65

D. Nice to snuggle with
104 11 142 169 76 34 201 23 125 62

E. The —, Rome: 2 wds.
180 92 8 145 216 80 75 204 50
134 79

F. In plain words: hyph. wd.
197 102 57 174 5 78 85 182 132 205

G. The real McCoy
48 6 192 111 156 214 164 206 67

H. Flamenco dancer's prop
118 213 82 202 54 183 64 188

I. Proficiency: hyph. wd.
200 37 152 106 146 162 210

J. "Fessed up"
165 121 148 177 209 149 71 140

K. Unusual person or thing: 2 wds. (Latin)
45 211 181 28 221 61 135 35

L. Impose limits (on): 3 wds.
29 63 215 53 195 96 13 153
84 167 26

M. Discordant
52 193 72 186 1 127 83 60 220
117 33

N. Buttonholer or ruffler, e.g.
173 87 160 98 59 114 16 120 207 49

O. — Mountain, highest point in Maine
119 31 185 170 150 70 157 130

P. Workable
138 143 21 208 95 42 199 154 133
122 55

Q. Cut off; cease
184 189 58 4 144 219 171 166 139
44 97

R. Israelite judge
175 15 101 212 20 113

S. Stealthily: 2 wds.
51 136 99 25 116 179 194 19

T. Come-hither, as a look
161 105 10 81 187 217 93 39 22 196

U. Go-getter quality
86 190 147 137 41 66 128 159 30 12

V. Person driven from his native land
168 14 123 91 43 109 131 88 73 141

W. Shortcuts
178 69 38 151 103 126 24 112 89 9

X. 1956 Academy Award-winning actor: 2 wds.
191 203 18 107 172 77 163 32 115 7

	1 M		2 B	3 A	4 Q	5 F	6 G	7 X	8 E	9 W	10 T	11 D	12 U		13 L	14 V	15 R	16 N	17 B
18 X	19 S		20 R	21 P		22 T	23 D	24 W	25 S	26 L	27 A		28 K	29 L	30 U	31 O	32 X	33 M	34 D	35 K		36 A
37 I		38 W	39 T	40 C	41 U	42 P	43 V	44 Q	45 K	46 B	47 A	48 G	49 N	50 E	51 S	52 M		53 L	54 H	55 P		56 A
57 F	58 Q	59 N	60 M	61 K	62 D	63 L	64 H	65 C		66 U	67 G	68 A	69 W	70 O	71 J	72 M	73 V	74 B	75 E	76 D	77 X	
78 F	79 E		80 E		81 T		82 H		83 M	84 L	85 F	86 U	87 N	88 V	89 W	90 B		91 V	92 E	93 T	94 B	95 P
96 L	97 Q		98 N	99 S		100 C		101 R	102 F	103 W	104 D	105 T	106 I		107 X	108 B	109 V		110 B	111 G	112 W	113 R
	114 N	115 X		116 S	117 M	118 H	119 O	120 N	121 J		122 P	123 V		124 C		125 D	126 W	127 M	128 U	129 A	130 O	131 V
	132 F	133 P	134 E		135 K	136 S	137 U	138 P	139 Q	140 J	141 V	142 D		143 P	144 Q	145 E		146 I	147 U	148 J		149 J
150 O	151 W		152 I	153 L	154 P	155 A	156 G		157 O	158 B		159 U	160 N		161 T	162 I	163 X	164 G	165 J	166 Q	167 L	168 V
169 D		170 O	171 Q	172 X	173 N	174 F	175 R	176 A	177 J	178 W	179 S	180 E	181 K		182 F	183 H	184 Q		185 O	186 M	187 T
	188 H	189 Q	190 U	191 X		192 G	193 M	194 S	195 L	196 T	197 F	198 C	199 P	200 I		201 D	202 H	203 X	204 E	205 F	206 G
207 N		208 P	209 J	210 I	211 K	212 R		213 H	214 G		215 L	216 E	217 T	218 A	219 Q	220 M	221 K			

HI-SCORE

The purpose of this game is to make real words, which fit, Kriss Kross style, into the diagram given, using only the letters below. Use any of these letters as many times as you care to, even repeating them within a word. Each letter has a point count, and the words made with the letters should be everyday English words composed of the highest-point letters possible. For example, the word RATE would score 10 points. Proper nouns, hyphenated words, slang words or foreign words are not allowed. You may not use the same word more than once in the diagram.

When the diagram is completely filled with interlocking horizontal and vertical words, add up the number of points in this manner: Give each letter its value as indicated in the chart below. **COUNTING ACROSS ONLY**, add up the points for every box in every line. Count each letter only once. We scored 253 points; our solution, which will probably not agree with yours, is on page 314.

250 points or better is excellent   **225 to 249 points is good**
200 to 224 points is average

K	N	A	R	O	I	T	E	B	W
5	4	3	2	1	1	2	3	4	5

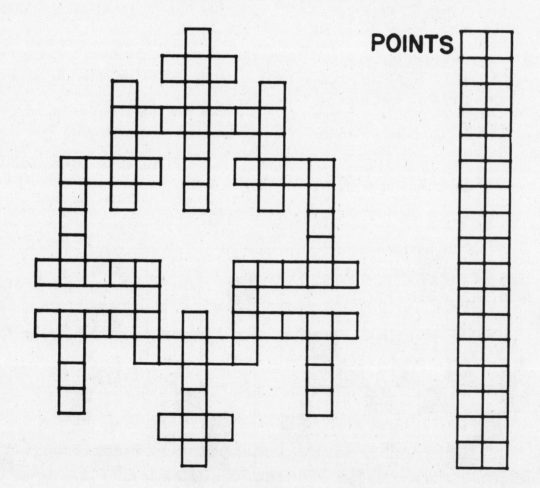

POINTS

TOTAL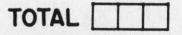

236

MAZE 2

Starting at the "S" (Start) near the top of the diagram, see if you can find your way to the "F" (Finish) near the bottom of the diagram. Our best mazer did it in only five minutes. Can you finish even faster? Solution is on page 316.

WORD ARITHMETIC 3

These are long-division problems in which letters are substituted for numbers. To solve the problem, determine the number value of each letter. When the letters in each problem have been arranged in order from 0 to 9 (using the line over the 0 to 9 for your letters), they will spell out a word or words.   Solution is on page 316.

1. 0 1 2 3 4 5 6 7 8 9

```
              Y O N
   RODS | S O O N E R
          D F N D
          N F S E
          R O D S
          F Y B N R
          Y S F Y F
            Y N I O
```

2. 0 1 2 3 4 5 6 7 8 9

```
            E A U
   RAN | S H I N E
         N I R
         L Q N
         R A N
         A E H E
         A L H N
           S U
```

3. 0 1 2 3 4 5 6 7 8 9

```
              N A T
   FIST | Y E A S T Y
          L T I F
          T L N T
          F I S T
          I F S M Y
          I M E S Y
            F M F M
```

4. 0 1 2 3 4 5 6 7 8 9

```
            A R M
   RAN | A L L O T S
         T O M A
         E N E T
         M R O T
         A A L S
         A I I R
           N S I
```

5. 0 1 2 3 4 5 6 7 8 9

```
            A I L
   ACT | P L I E R S
         P T C C
         I S I R
         A C T
         P R C S
         T A F T
           P A E
```

6. 0 1 2 3 4 5 6 7 8 9

```
            N U N
   FED | E X T R A S
         R D R U
         R U N A
         R X D D
         R D R S
         R D R U
           R
```

7. 0 1 2 3 4 5 6 7 8 9

```
            K I N
   GAL | R A K I N G
         A O N A
         R O K N
         R I G O
         K G L G
         K P O N
           N T A
```

8. 0 1 2 3 4 5 6 7 8 9

```
            R A Y
   AIL | C A R G O
         A I L
         S C G
         I Y U
         A C I O
         A A C A
           R R C
```

9. 0 1 2 3 4 5 6 7 8 9

```
            C O N
   ENDS | N O T I O N
          O U E I
          E C C R O
          E D N R U
          E I R C N
          E C I U D
            E C E I
```

WORD GRAPH

In this puzzle you are given a graph containing forty-eight letters which you will need to spell eight everyday 6-letter words. Each letter has a numerical value which is determined by adding together the numbers of both the row and the column in which the letter is found. For example Q is in the third row and the third column of the graph and therefore has a value of 6; one of the E's has a value of 8, since it is in the fifth row and third column (there are other E's and they will have different numerical values). Each series of numbers below the graph represents a word. The numbers in each series are in correct order, so that when the correct letter is substituted for each number, a 6-letter word will be spelled out. Your job is to discover the correct letter for each number by trying out the various letter possibilities for that number in the graph. Here's a suggestion: Work out the letters with the highest and lowest values first, and enter those letters above their numbers below. Cross off each letter as you use it, since each letter may be used only once. There are no plurals in this puzzle. Answers are on page 313.

	1	2	3	4	5	6	7	8
1	Y	O	P	T	L	E	R	O
2	U	E	I	S	M	Y	D	A
3	F	B	Q	P	N	T	T	N
4	L	R	E	B	D	Y	E	A
5	A	I	E	R	L	E	I	N
6	S	P	I	E	D	N	T	D

1.   7   4   8   10   6   11

2.   6   9   12   5   10   8

3.   8   7   10   3   13   9

4.   9   2   7   12   6   10

5.   5   8   13   4   11   9

6.   6   3   10   7   12   5

7.   7   11   5   9   14   8

8.   8   6   11   4   7   9

WHAT IS TIME?

That's a good question, but you won't have to answer it in this quiz. Answer as many of the questions below as you can, giving yourself the indicated points for each correct answer (check the answers on page 316). Evaluate yourself as follows: 76 points, perfect score (almost impossible!); 68-75 points, excellent; 58-67 points, very good; 48-66 points, good; 38-47 points, average.

1. If your plane could fly fast enough, would you be able to leave New York today and arrive in Los Angeles yesterday? *(2 points)*

2. The memory aid, "Spring forward, Fall back" is a reminder of what twice-yearly time event? *(2 points)*

3. What does the abbreviation E.T.A. stand for? *(2 points)*

4. We all know that in CASABLANCA Humphrey Bogart said, "Play it again, Sam." (Woody Allen even made a movie with that title.) As it happens, all of us are wrong. He said, "Play it, Sam." What song did Sam play? *(2 points)*

5. What famous scientific theory is largely based on the idea that time and space are interdependent, and who propounded this theory? *(2 points each)*

6. Fill in the missing word in each of these familiar sayings: (a) Time and _____ wait for no man. (b) _____ is the thief of time. (c) Time heals all _____. *(2 points each)*

7. If you were visiting a friend's yacht in the afternoon and you heard the ship's clock chime seven bells, what time would it be? *(2 points)*

8. What traditional figure is usually shown carrying a scythe or sickle? *(2 points)*

9. "To everything there is a season, and a time to every purpose under the heaven." These words come from which book of the Old Testament? (a) Psalms (b) Ecclesiastes (c) Job *(2 points)*

10. What well-known practice typing sentence includes the word "time"? *(2 points)*

11. Name two methods of keeping time other than clocks or watches. *(4 points)*

12. True or False? In this country daylight-saving time was first introduced during World War II in order to save fuel. *(2 points)*

13. As you are no doubt aware, the four chief time zones of the United States are Eastern, Central, Mountain, and Pacific. See if you can pick the right zone for the following twelve cities. HINT: There are three cities in each time zone. *(2 points each)*

a. Chicago, Ill.	g. Seattle, Wash.
b. Reno, Nev.	h. Cheyenne, Wy.
c. Detroit, Mich.	i. Phoenix, Ariz.
d. Salt Lake City, Utah	j. Cleveland, Ohio
e. Pittsburgh, Pa.	k. Juneau, Alaska
f. New Orleans, La.	l. Dallas, Texas

14. Match each quote about time in the left-hand column with its author in the right-hand column. *(2 points each)*

1. "Art is long, and Time is fleeting."	a. Thomas Paine
2. "Greater than the tread of mighty armies is an idea whose time has come."	b. Charles Dickens
3. "Time is but the stream I go a-fishing in."	c. Henry W. Longfellow
4. "You cannot fight against the future. Time is on our side."	d. William Gladstone
5. "Never before have we had so little time in which to do so much."	e. Victor Hugo
6. "It was the best of times, it was the worst of times."	f. Pablo Picasso
7. "Cowards die many times before their deaths."	g. Henry Thoreau
8. "These are the times that try men's souls."	h. William Shakespeare
9. "You can ask me for anything you like, except time."	i. Franklin D. Roosevelt
10. "I am only a public entertainer who has understood his time."	j. Napolean Bonaparte

UNIGRAMS

by Edg Duveyoung

To solve a Unigram, simply draw a line over the dotted figure so that you have completely retraced the figure, but without either *crossing* or *retracing* any line once you have drawn it. Remember: You should cover every part of the figure, but you MAY NOT retrace or cross your own path.

Our solutions are on page 316.

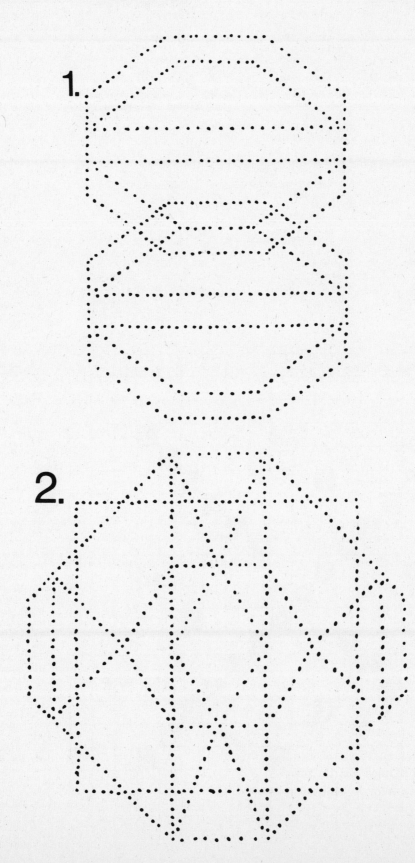

ACROSS

1. Ship's floors
6. Unit of illumination
10. Loop of a rope
15. Disk-jockey's bribe: slang
16. Tenor Mario
18. Skillful
20. Crew boss
21. Grandfather: French
22. Weight watchers
24. Obsolete word for "clumsy"
25. City in Georgia
27. Jostle (with the arm)
29. Arikara Indian
30. Set period
32. Parlor: 2 wds.
34. Chaff of grain
35. It "knits up the ravell'd sleave of care"
37. Portuguese coin
38. "Tetched"
39. Bedstead boards
40. Hemingway's "The — and the Sea,": 2 wds.
42. Places of learning
44. Gliding dance step
45. Choice item
47. Famous comic-strip dog
48. Cartoonist Day

49. British islands in the West Indies
52. Law degree: abbr.
53. Houses of worship
57. Funny
58. Pack down forcibly
60. Popular "health" food
62. Big ocean: abbr.
63. Currently discussed appellation for certain workers
66. One referred to namelessly: 3 wds.
68. Bronze: Latin
69. All-purpose
71. Furniture wood
72. Adjusted again
73. Introductions
75. For each
77. Alberta river: 2 wds.
79. Certain tosses, in playing marbles
80. Arrives
82. Emit noxious fumes
83. Go —, debark
86. Second largest Canadian city
88. Throngs
92. Boxer Patterson
93. Druggist's degree: abbr.
94. Necessities
96. Sailing vessel

97. Recounted
98. Tower of London display: 2 wds.
101. Spanish dollar
102. Pussycat's seagoing partner
103. One of Emerson's friends
104. B'nai —, Jewish fraternity
106. Pot cover
107. Not one of the two
109. Streisand portrayal
111. Spanish nobleman of the first rank
113. Venerate
114. Doctrinist group: French
115. Refuges
116. Cut, as lumber
117. Middle Ages worker
118. Bird call

DOWN

1. Maroon: 2 wds.
2. Site of the uvea
3. Stupor
4. Nicholas: German
5. Indonesian language
6. Synthetic materials
7. It occupies part of Hispaniola

8. "Steady" beau: 3 wds.
9. Chinese river
10. "Peck's —," movie of the thirties: 2 wds.
11. Dialect
12. Multiplied
13. Faucet word
14. Earths: Spanish
15. Eleanor or Dick
17. In a watchful manner
19. Handles
20. Soubriquet for a stout one
23. Meaning
26. Colorado Indians
28. Building plots
31. Ancient Egyptian city
33. Expression of approval: 2 wds.
34. White: French
36. Dan Rather and Gary Gates book (with "The"): 2 wds.
39. Restaurant "quickies": 2 wds.
41. Old Testament book: abbr.
43. Actor Holbrook
44. Butter-maker
46. Seascape paintings
48. Polo "inning"
49. Stadium shouter
50. Entertain
51. Banks, as money
53. — group, Grand Canyon geology division
54. Space between a vessel's bow and anchors
55. Anesthetic gas
56. Coin opening
57. Fellow
59. Sea: French
61. Sticky stuff: slang
64. Log-splitter's device
65. Flavor
67. — baby, recently born infant: hyph. wd.
70. Ade ingredient: 2 wds.
74. Famous silent screen comedian
76. Miss Jeanmaire
78. Tenth month, to early Romans: abbr.
80. Housekeeper's problem
81. Cheaper cut of meat: 2 wds.
83. Scottish river of song
84. Not so fast
85. Red-berried bushes
86. Odin's son
87. Central European river
89. "— you like to know?"
90. Small fishing boats
91. Fine English china
93. Communist sympathizer: hyph. wd.
95. Affront
98. Dear: French
99. Nostrils
100. — man, a nonentity
103. Muscle
105. Possess
108. Federal power producer (since 1933)
110. Middle: abbr.
112. Born

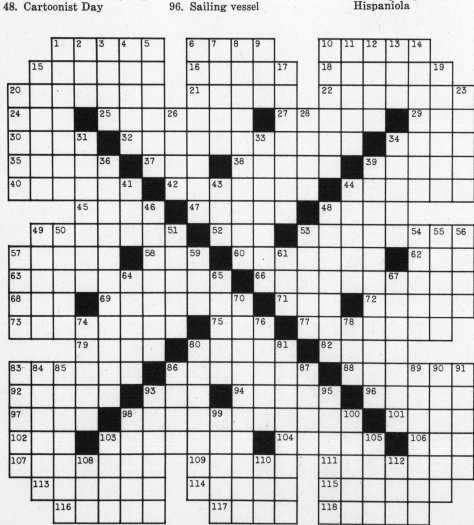

Solution is on page 289

ACROSS

1. Music for one
5. All our yesterdays make this
9. Quechuan
13. Alike — peas in a pod: 2 wds.
18. College course: abbr.
19. Give a wide berth to
21. Plaint from an alley
22. Shakespearean actress
23. Kurt Weill drama: 2 wds. (with "The")
26. Commingled
27. Save up for — day: 2 wds.
28. Art category
29. Member of dogdom
31. W.W. II post: abbr.
32. "Double fins": slang
34. Mexican halls
36. Segments of the foot
38. First zodiac sign
40. More grievous
42. Vouchsafe
44. One way to stand
47. Curtain-raisers: 3 wds.
50. One of the Three Musketeers
52. German exclamations
54. Taro root
55. Come to
57. Return blow
58. Aft
60. Revolver: hyph. wd.
64. Indian title
65. Soprano of note
67. Town west of Dayton
68. Less healthy-looking
70. Broad, stiff collars
72. Having pendants
74. Town near Lake Como
75. Melodious composition
78. Plantation house
80. Sharp stimuli
83. Singer, Ed —
84. Mart of a sort: 3 wds.
87. Uganda's neighbor
88. "Nine old —", the Supreme Court
89. Suit
90. Kind of cheese
92. Bristlelike organ
93. Follow
95. U.S. Navy captain: hyph. wd.
100. "Beat the —," be acquitted
101. 100th part of a rial
103. *Nipote* or *sobrina*
104. Blue jeans material
106. More logical
108. Keep within bounds
110. Greetings, in Granada
114. Symbol of diligence
116. Sly look
118. Dressed — nines, in one's best: 2 wds.
120. Assignor of property, in Civil Law
121. Sacred: comb. form
123. Rome: 3 wds.
126. Register
127. Deep freeze
128. Show scorn
129. Like — of bricks: 2 wds.
130. Intermediate, in law
131. Burmese demons
132. Nail containers
133. Do an office job

DOWN

1. Attacked: 2 wds.
2. Atelier pigment
3. Navigation aid
4. — thousand, rarity: 3 wds.
5. Certain paper used for wrapping food
6. Certain prayer
7. "Tea For Two," e.g.
8. Projecting points
9. Begem: poetic
10. Born: French
11. British ore truck
12. Stay for
13. Treelike
14. Salt, to a Parisian
15. Any new marvel: 3 wds.
16. "Wilful waste brings woeful —"
17. Hep or hip
20. Suzerain
24. January, in Jayuya
25. Ship's lowest deck
30. Man around the house
33. Gardener's purchase
35. Pacific treaty group: abbr.
37. Mind the baby
39. "Rain" character
41. Hindu peasants
43. *Bête* —, pet hate
44. Carson's predecessor
45. 4,840 sq. yds.
46. Cluster of stars in Taurus: 3 wds.
48. Of the hip joints
49. "Swipe"
51. Cookbook direction
53. Barbara and Monica
56. City on the Rhone
59. Very funny chap
61. Leaf aperture
62. White House designer
63. Continuously: 2 wds.
64. God, as the friend of man
66. Flatware piece
69. D-Day vessels: abbr.
71. Breathe in
73. Proud papa
75. — forward, presented oneself
76. Revise a law
77. Plane: French
79. Decorated anew
81. Shark of the Atlantic
82. Easy job: slang
85. Vanity cases
86. Scruffs
89. Tall, thin person
91. They make threats
94. "— *furtiva lagrima*," famous aria
96. Group who help turn flax into linen
97. A cutting
98. Tithes
99. Fit to be tied
102. Arikara Indian
105. Flathead catfish
107. Plant exudation
109. Office-wall sign
111. Olympic dweller
112. Ahead of the game: 2 wds.
113. Jule —, popular composer
114. Attention-getter
115. Lowest card in a pinochle deck
117. Portuguese gold coin
119. Robert —: 2 wds.
122. King Arthur's lance
124. Old campaigner
125. — it, run

Solution is on page 289

ACROSS

1. Bright green
8. Up and about
13. Bell's tongue
20. Castle in Spain, for example
21. Coast
22. She saves the day
23. River into Mobile Bay
24. Surfeited
25. Obvious
26. Dismaying
27. — manner, medical asset
29. Cut down
31. High, craggy hill
32. Geraint's beloved
34. Mammoth
35. Manufacturer
36. Scoff
37. Break bread
38. Viewed
39. Swift
40. Famous electrical inventor
41. Intellectual: slang
43. Thousand: French
44. Soothed
45. Send running
46. Type of spoon
47. Branches
48. "Hen tracks"
51. Twilled fabric
52. Hospital-staff member
56. Slur over in pronunciation
57. Future tour package: 2 wds.
59. Peggy or Michele
60. Church part
61. Caravel
62. Burden
63. Stone Age "pad"
64. "— pro nobis"
65. Cheat
69. Was granted membership: 2 wds.
70. Pertinent
72. Like Mr. Fixit
73. Good-looking
74. Smooth, in phonetics
75. Brahman or Kshatriya
76. "There's a Girl in My —"
77. Irritates
80. Predilection
81. Tedious delay: 2 wds.
84. Dewy
85. Flock of quail
86. *Père's* mate
87. Author of "The Fountainhead"
89. King of Israel
90. Heliacal
91. Plucky
92. Capri, for one
93. Lambkin's cry
94. Domesticated beast
95. Dutch Guiana
98. What Warren might call Shirley
99. Money-making process
101. Architectural style
103. Scurrilous
105. Hired
106. Wear away gradually
107. Rescue
108. Shaky
109. Anarchist
110. Factor

DOWN

1. Deleted
2. "Gone With The Wind" character
3. Eluding
4. Jewish title of respect
5. Fine steed
6. Gumdrop flavor
7. Tie: 2 wds.
8. Give, as homework
9. Ghost
10. Carry
11. Wrath
12. American tree: 2 wds.
13. Used tobacco
14. Pinch bar, e.g.
15. Jejune
16. Seed vessel
17. Religiosity
18. Elevate
19. Type of tire
28. Took to court
30. Migrant farm worker
33. Abase
35. Croquet stick
36. Icy
38. Alone: French
39. Oak or Blue —
40. Dravidian language
42. "The Battle Hymn Of The Republic" author
43. Playwright Connelly
44. Instances
46. Bounded
47. Theatrical entertainment
48. Mister from Madrid
49. Irish county
50. Try to outdo
51. Steeple top
52. Slender and leggy
53. Cheer up
54. Author Shute
55. Very small
57. Push along
58. Script style
61. Clambers (up)
63. Italian pals
65. Major industry
66. Pursuit plane
67. Precipitate
68. Pay (up)
69. High-liver's ailment
71. Asian mountain system
73. Zip —
75. Offhand
76. Love song
77. Eyelet
78. Salad greens
79. Put in proper order
80. Enameled metalware
81. Ancient people of Gaul
82. Unresisting
83. Animate
85. Tension-breaker
86. Writer Proust
88. Abandon
90. More prudent
91. Cicerone
94. Bank enclosure
95. Class-conscious individual
96. First homicide victim
97. Lady's slipper
100. Tit for —
102. Western state: abbr.
104. British actor, Alastair —

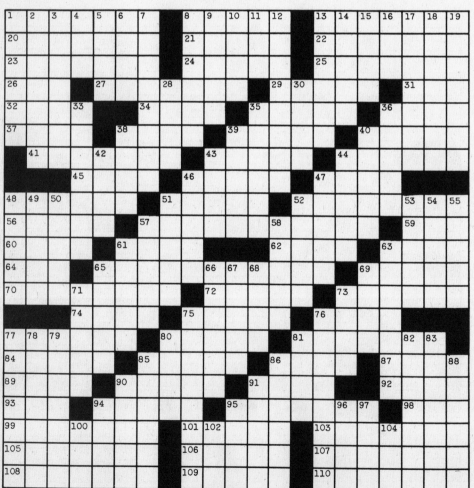

Solution is on page 289

by **HENRY and MARGARET TOPE**

ACROSS

1. Sports center in the Rockies
6. Dwell (on a subject)
10. Art cult
14. Negative electrified particle
19. Creator of Dr. Watson
20. On a trip
21. City on the Oka
22. Agricultural center in the Ukraine
23. Pride of Salt Lake City: 3 wds.
27. Japanese prince assassinated in 1909
28. Do the voice-over
29. False gods
30. Gypsy, to a gypsy
31. Barn owl genus
33. Appropriate
34. Circassian language
36. Tropical mimic bird
37. Incited (with "on")
39. Unmistakable
40. Grouchy one
42. Lined with mother-of-pearl
44. Mary Pickford's trademark
46. Service-station apparatus: 2 wds.
50. Deadly pale
51. Penetrate into every part
53. — lily
54. Import
55. Former
56. Church projections
58. What claques do
59. Pacific porgy
60. Badgerlike mammal
62. A source of formic acid
63. Ecclesiastical vestments
65. Snake's posture
67. Jewish or Arabic
70. Vice-squad job
71. Looked
74. *Cogito ergo* —
75. Cybill Shepherd was one
77. Part of "to be"
80. Gay tune
81. Newspaper edition
83. Chinese poet: 2 wds.
84. W.W. II sea scourge: hyph. wd.
86. Lena tributary
88. Espresso container
90. A Polynesian people
91. Jersey or Guernsey: 2 wds.
93. *Tía's* Parisian counterpart
94. Radio transmitter
95. Basic igneous rock
96. Biblical past tense for "cleave"
98. Immediately available: 2 wds.
99. Toadfish
101. See fit
103. Civil War general, Jesse Lee —
105. "Parlor pink's" leaning
108. Large body of water: abbr.
109. Indian thrush
110. "Paddy-wagon" passengers, sometimes
113. Labor abbreviation
114. Former member of the Supreme Court: 3 wds.

118. Noted English carmaker
119. Special card in canasta
120. Plumbago
121. Responses of ratification
122. Endeavor
123. Infinitive of 74-Across
124. Novelist Ferber
125. Gus Arriola cartoon character

DOWN

1. Word on a ticket
2. Dusky-black
3. Fourth of July festivities: 2 wds.
4. Hard, tough wood
5. Ramsay and Travers discovery
6. Animosity
7. Percipient
8. Morocco's capital
9. Magpie
10. Shula of football
11. Saudi —
12. Metric weight units
13. He is praised in 11-Down
14. Rainbows
15. Japanese dance drama
16. Rare bird: 3 wds.

17. Stew ingredient
18. Bellini opera
24. "A Boy — Sue"
25. In fact
26. Exclusive group
32. Monsters
35. Contrapuntal part music
36. Old Testament book
38. Opposite of specific
39. Canadian Indian
41. Mythical bird
42. Famed political cartoonist
43. Sailing
44. Pine fruit
45. Ally of John Bull: 2 wds.
47. "Deutschland — Alles"
48. All fizzed out
49. Lights-out signal
51. Peppery
52. He takes a rosy view
57. Grievous
61. Hebrew letter
62. Purpose
64. Ceremonial pipe
66. Minnesota's neighbor
68. South American armadillos
69. Thicket
71. Well-pleased
72. Girl's name
73. Prank

76. Buck's mate
78. Berne's river
79. Bustle
82. Immigrants
83. Narrow way
85. Commonplace
87. Corporal in Falstaff's "army"
89. The Mermaid, mentioned by Keats
92. Secret store
94. Sound to express contempt
97. — and fishes
98. Lake in central New York
99. Consecrated: French
100. Musketeer
102. Wastemaker
103. Quarreled
104. "— Frome," Wharton novel
106. Infernal fellow
107. Dressmaker's form
109. Weaver's reed
111. Man or Wight
112. Smoker
115. — Building, New York skyline feature
116. Seaman's assent
117. I love: Latin

Solution is on page 289

ACROSS

1. Men of Lhasa
6. Small flounders
10. Dismantle
15. Sect
19. Make joyful
20. Discharge
21. Rough
22. Irish battle cry
23. Act promptly: 5 wds.
27. Compass point
28. Trespasses
29. Short jazz figure
30. Hybrid fish
31. Shows displeasure
34. Feminine nickname
35. Make damp
36. Bring in enough to sustain momentum: 4 wds.
42. Dante's muse
43. Coney
44. Of the upper throat
45. Annual sports event: abbr.
48. Unit of length, in Greece
49. Rice dishes
52. Electrical-line accessories
54. Letter
55. Building beams: 2 wds.
56. Covering
57. "Canst thou live upon remembered —?"
58. Make, in Marseilles
59. Baseball play
60. Venetian magistrate
61. Compact receiver: 2 wds.
68. Rude fellow
69. Writer Waugh
70. Albatross
71. Tennyson's Arden, and namesakes
74. Psychoanalyst's topic
75. American capitalist
76. Bounder
79. Go to war: 3 wds.
81. More comely
82. Cry of triumph
83. Vulpine
84. Ancient stringed instrument
85. Singer, Diana —
86. Avid
88. World-wide standard: 3 wds.
92. Fur seals: 2 wds.
96. Stadium cheer
97. Old nautical cry
98. Silky-haired goat
99. Equine color
101. Brontë's "Jane —"
103. Sternward
106. Do a fruitless job: 4 wds.
111. Made a hole in one
112. Unicorn fishes
113. Negative reply: 2 wds.
114. Velocity
115. French "summers"
116. Faculty of perception
117. Small branch
118. Ruler of the underworld

DOWN

1. Permits
2. Word of lament
3. Thackeray's middle name
4. Consumed
5. Harden
6. Death
7. Sobeit!
8. Parts of aprons
9. Barnyard enclosure
10. One with a split personality, for short
11. Not kosher, in Judaism
12. Dennis the Menace's dog
13. Ceremonial response: 2 wds.
14. Classified ads
15. Telephones
16. Submarine: hyph. wd.
17. English philosopher
18. Subway fare
24. Narrow strip of land: abbr.
25. Family group
26. Pithy saying
32. Choose
33. Dweller in Sir Thomas More's fictional land
34. P.O.'s concern: abbr.
35. Deer of china: hyph. wd.
36. Retained
37. American Indian
38. Ships' lanterns
39. Louts
40. "Krazy Kat's" friend
41. One of the seven sins
45. Greek goddesses' high crowns
46. Seaman's hooded jacket of old
47. South African fox
50. Wading bird
51. Gull genus
52. Foot of verse
53. Trivial, in England
56. Panaceas
58. Three Stooges' forte
59. Philippine knives
61. Of a musical sound
62. "The crow makes wing to the — wood"
63. Crane operator's assistant
64. Self-esteem
65. Gloomy
66. Operatic part
67. Bee genus
68. Wagers
72. Land of the Magyars
73. Roman slave and gladiator
74. Author Gardner
75. Cut deeply
76. Pondered
77. Attention-getter
78. French engraver
80. Mr. Fortas and others
81. Actress, Nina —
85. Mirthful
87. Old Siamese coins: var. sp.
89. Brilliantly colored fish
90. Centipede
91. With: French
92. Ancient people of Iran
93. Decree
94. Harmonize
95. Textured fabrics
99. Bestow abundantly
100. Spanish cheers
101. "Rubáiyát" adverb
102. Abominable Snowman
104. Vanish
105. Spreads to dry, as hay
107. Dollar bill
108. Canadian province: abbr.
109. Close-grained wood
110. Health resort

Solution is on page 289

ACROSS

1. Set right; improve
5. Byzantine-type dome
11. One Russian symbol: 2 wds.
18. Of the cheekbone
19. Overlook
20. U.S. citizen
22. Resort city in Colorado: 2 wds.
24. — City, in Texas
25. "Exodus" hero
26. Dreams
27. Snack
28. Name in Genesis
29. Coined
31. Compass point
32. Old Norse poem
33. Dropsy
34. — fixe, obsession
35. Trolley sound
37. Judged
38. New Deal agency: abbr.
41. Substituting (for)
43. Brooks or Torme
44. Feminine suffix
45. Forty-—
47. River in Minnesota: 2 wds.
49. City in New York
50. Coin of India
51. Building wings
52. Sound of an awkward dive
56. 1950 Nobel Prize author
58. Flow
59. Outside: comb. form
60. Author of "I'll Cry Tomorrow"
61. Son of Zeus and Hera
62. "Cat on — Tin Roof": 2 wds.
64. Burns, for example
66. Preposition
67. Cry of the unsated
68. Pewter coin
69. Extinct bird
70. Actor's substitute: hyph. wd.
73. Feed the kitty
74. Army reserve group: abbr.
76. Old French measure
78. See 67-Across
79. Pennsylvania city near Pittsburgh
81. Locale in a story
82. D-Day vessel: abbr.
85. Pig — poke: 2 wds.
86. Expressed contempt
87. Clique; coterie
88. Air-raid warnings
90. Pulsate
91. College exam
95. County in Missouri (its seat is Houston)
96. Pronoun
97. Wood sorrel
100. Woolly
102. Cloche and toque
103. Contents of a seidel
104. Book of Psalms
106. Rolled tea
107. Tenant ousters
109. City in Minnesota: 2 wds.
111. City in Ohio
112. All about
113. Sports contest
114. Tells
115. Noted U.S. publisher, 1854-1925
116. Cape Cod decor

DOWN

1. City in Iowa
2. Comedienne May
3. Slangy negative
4. Group of oxen
5. Small tastes
6. Smiling broadly
7. Marriage, for one
8. — Lakes, in New Hampshire
9. Units of energy
10. In medias —
11. Hialeah attraction
12. "Ham it up"
13. Proofreader's mark
14. Sign at hit shows
15. Harangue
16. Where Plato taught
17. Aida's lover
18. River in Ohio
21. Tuaregs
23. Modern Caesar
27. Botch
30. Illinois town
32. Declaim vehemently
33. Lampreys' kin
36. Cloth made of flax fibers
37. Adherent of natural religion
39. Dream: French
40. Sea east of the Caspian
41. Horned viper
42. Illinois city
43. Fines
45. Nerve cell
46. Extra leaf
48. Bread spread
49. Pasture grass
52. City in Illinois or Indiana
53. City in Kentucky
54. Garb
55. Ring up
57. Singer from Brooklyn: 2 wds.
63. Biblical verb
64. Tobacco and lumber town in Virginia: 2 wds.
65. Vessel for riding the rapids
68. Across: prefix
69. Animated-cartoon hero
71. Hardy girl
72. Noun suffix
75. O
77. Terminus
79. Wags
80. Standard
82. Cut with a machine tool
83. Meat-cutter's tool
84. Woven fabric
89. Scalawag
90. Dissertations
92. Snowshoe
93. City in Georgia
94. Lowest amount
96. Basse-—, capital of Guadeloupe
98. Dear: Latin
99. Solo
100. Tennis term
101. "Stormy Weather" composer
103. — neck, dress feature
104. City in Indiana
105. Shipshape
108. Airlines company: abbr.
109. Aswan or Sennar
110. Blvd.

Solution is on page 289

67 EXPERT CROSSWORD

by HENRY and MARGARET TOPE

ACROSS

1. Shenanigans
7. Berlin coin
14. Prance about
20. Win back
21. Large wardrobe
22. 1968 Oscar film
23. It's hard to live within this, today
24. Green woodpecker: 2 wds.
25. With discretion
26. Senator Hatfield
27. "— el Bul Bul Ameer"
29. Blanche of the silents
31. Tatter
32. Large cursorial bird
33. Louisiana style of cookery
34. Composer of "The Merry Widow"
35. Palo —, site of Stanford U.
36. Question again
38. Fundamental principle
39. Actress, France —
40. Unproductive, as land
41. Son of Enoch
43. Very low marks
45. Fainthearted
48. Medusa's tresses
50. Waters down
54. Of transportation and supply
56. Dancer, Ruth St. —
58. Biblical queen
59. Hideous giants
60. Long-nosed animal
62. Obtain piecemeal
64. Aries
65. Leather: French
66. Amusement park attraction: 2 wds.
68. Soprano in "La Bohème"
69. Haunch
70. New York's governor
71. Postoffice machine
72. Raise trivial objections
73. What corps need
75. French star, Alain —
77. Constituent of igneous rocks
79. The Evil One, to Mohammedans
81. Removes a ship's deck
83. Sacred birds in old Egypt
84. Some food shops, for short
86. Miss Myerson
87. Economist Smith
88. Vatican residents
91. Casaba, for one
93. Lone card, in bridge
98. Rosary prayers
99. Not so many
100. Hemlock
101. Former UN agency
102. Indigene: abbr.
103. Month of the Jewish year
104. Leading the league: 2 wds.
105. Slight
106. Continual uproar
108. Tale of chivalry
111. Rumanian border city
113. Salt-yielding mineral
114. Kitchen utensil
115. Symbol chart on a map
116. Ejected
117. Sibyl
118. Incidents

DOWN

1. First reader
2. Change a title
3. Accumulate, like bank interest
4. Alcove
5. Kara —, desert, in Turkmen S. S. R.
6. Chewing-gum flavor
7. Forgive
8. Title for Lilli Marlene
9. Rousseau novel
10. *Persona — grata*
11. Little bite
12. Rainbows
13. Golly!: 2 wds.
14. Shrink timorously
15. Landed
16. Force: Latin
17. Too-too
18. Tell
19. Stingray genus
28. Star of constellation Eridanus
30. Alleviated
33. Love pat
34. Fraught
35. Bayberry trees
37. Saint Francis —, "Apostle to the Indies"
38. Thirteen: 2 wds.
39. The "man without a country"
42. Wheel spokes, for example
44. Competitor
45. Certain hats
46. Arch
47. Winner at Actium: 31 B.C.
48. Affrighted
49. Second —, clairvoyance
51. Flourishes
52. Light cotton fabric
53. Imaginative comparisons
55. Roman road
57. Lies dormant
61. Jimmy user
63. Weird
66. Deadly
67. Declines, as in power
68. Wise saying: French
70. Quotes
72. Dark blue
74. 66-Across, et al.
76. Secy. Brennan's post
78. Highest roof timber
80. *Serge de —,* denim
82. Perfumes
85. "— Folly," Alaska
87. Part of A. D.
88. Tennis great, — Gonzales
89. Fiji island
90. Leaves of a corolla
92. Poe's "rare and radiant maiden"
94. Buries
95. He won more votes than Pres. Hayes: 1876
96. Far East
97. Tribes on the move
99. Discharged
100. — *chance,* good luck
103. Memorandum
105. Dressing spice
107. With: German
109. Actress West
110. Melody
112. Race (a motor)

Solution is on page 289

ACROSS

1. What's-its-name
6. —-Jersey, large red hog
11. Golf club
16. Pedestrian
17. Rory —, name of 3 Irish rebel chiefs 300 years ago
18. Gives a wide berth
20. Common term: 2 wds.
22. Unsteadier
24. Verb suffix
25. Means of access
26. "Every believer is God's —"
28. Social
29. King of gray
30. Liqueur flavored with caraway seeds
32. Bridge of —, Venice landmark
33. Rare bargain
34. Ransack and plunder
36. Conductor Caldwell
38. Purchase terms: abbr.
39. Regional flora and fauna
40. Back-seat driver's word
42. — Hall, New Jersey university
44. Hugh Carey, to New Yorkers
46. Kind of black tea
48. Keep a subscription
50. Nor'easter
51. Figuratively, trouble: 2 wds.
54. Football's Gabriel
56. Night prowler
60. Wane
61. Heads: French
63. Hand on
65. Jericho had them
66. Go on the gad
68. Litter-collector: 2 wds.
71. Popular song of the twenties
72. Author of "The Dance of Life"
74. Indulge
75. The "muscle boys": hyph. wd.
77. Rocky point
78. Convince of: 2 wds.
80. Curve of the ninth degree, in math
82. "Tickles pink"
84. The art of weaving
86. Sponsorship
88. Female water sprite
89. Schedule
93. Bush
95. British government bond
98. In a group of
99. Slow boat: slang
101. Bulls: Spanish
103. Mother-of-pearl
104. No place for a big fish
105. North Dakota city
107. Therapeutic substances
109. School subject, for short
110. Kilim or Sumak
111. What 1976 events will be in 2076
113. "The perfume of heroic deeds"
114. Passable: hyph. wd.
115. Part of 39-Across
117. Resort areas depend on this: 2 wds.
120. Tittering laugh: hyph. wd.
121. Clout of a sort
122. Fellows who draw up the rear: 2 wds.
123. Altair and Deneb
124. Suit card
125. Transplanted

DOWN

1. No-tackling version of a certain sport: 2 wds.
2. Water the lawn
3. Native of: suffix
4. Father of Indira Gandhi
5. Makes neat
6. Toddler's opposite
7. Labor union: abbr.
8. *Chambre* or *sala*
9. Fragrant root used in perfumes
10. Sir — Hardwicke
11. Property guardian
12. Witch's brew
13. Figure (out): slang
14. American soldiers
15. Back number
16. Archaeologist's item
19. Taken care of: 2 wds.
20. Gains information
21. Tibetan priests
23. Important airfield equipment
27. Eager
30. Be persistent: 2 wds.
31. Word from a procrastinator
33. Stoker
35. City in the Ukraine
37. Really and truly: 2 wds.
39. Downstairs
41. Charges
43. Where Hercules slew the lion
45. Large container
47. Fore-and-aft rigged sailing vessel
49. Name in baseball's Hall of Fame, Edward A. —
51. Toast word
52. One-half denier
53. Second showing
55. Word in a Norman Mailer title
57. Wardrobe: 2 wds.
58. Set quotas
59. Nicholas, Ivan and Peter
62. Where Pago Pago is
64. Sana's country
67. Cloth remnant: 2 wds.
69. Corn meal cakes
70. Expressing end or purpose
73. Influential Chinese family
76. 37th U.S. President and family
79. Gesture of greeting
81. Former Hollywood restaurant
83. Actress Lollobrigida
85. Paintings by a French postimpressionist
87. Foolproof: hyph. wd.
89. He directed "It Happened One Night"
90. Measure
91. Winter underwear
92. Member of a litter
94. Cold Adriatic winds
96. Prayer
97. Pretend: 2 wds.
100. Phone stalls
102. Fort of Civil War fame
105. Jim Ryun is one
106. Cavalry subdivision
108. Middle, in law
111. Sunken fence
112. City on the Colorado River
114. The —, unchanged
116. Got together
118. — tape
119. Singer Ames, et al.

Solution is on page 289

69 EXPERT CROSSWORD

"INTERROGATIVE"

by EUGENE T. MALESKA

ACROSS

1. Room
6. Interweaves
12. Door sign
16. Angry: slang
18. Scold: 2 wds.
19. Renaissance swords
22. Hit show of 1924: 3 wds.
24. Reese of baseball
25. A continent: abbr.
26. Comforts
27. Sabatini's "Captain —"
29. FDR creation: abbr.
30. Hebrew "alpha"
32. Passover feast
33. Mississippi-basin soil
34. Vex
35. Turkish soldier in the reserves
37. But: Latin
38. Has on
39. Seek water with a rod
40. Villain's cry
42. Fastens with a rope
44. Molly's radio husband
45. Janitors' concern
49. Fragment
50. Black snake
51. Scorch
52. Congou or jasmine
54. Noun suffix
55. Wad of bills
58. Cleave
59. Dilate
61. Joke of a sort
62. Needle case
63. *Aficionado's* cry
64. Part of Macbeth's question: 4 wds.
67. Capital group for defense: abbr.
68. Oil-yielding beans
70. Resembling: suffix
71. Shrieked
72. "Skiddoo"
73. Side receiving odds: 2 wds.
75. Umbrella part
76. Gad's son
77. Republic east of Ghana
78. Eurasian chain
79. Composer Franck
81. Packer of a sort
83. Soils
85. Stated without proof
87. Boston nickname
88. Sharpened
89. Utmost extent
90. Hands
92. Capital of Morocco
96. Poetess Lowell, et al.
97. Delay
98. Cut
100. Cattail or pickerelweed
101. Hillbilly's mother
102. Miss Liberty's light
103. Hearth item
105. Sermon subject
106. More's perfect island
108. E.B. Browning sonnet: 5 wds.
111. Smudged
112. One result of colonialism
113. Far from strict
114. Colleen
115. Beveled out
116. Like 106-Across

DOWN

1. Branded
2. Exactly suitable
3. Electrical units, for short
4. Mackerellike fishes
5. Roman officials
6. Antedates
7. Brewery product
8. Is out of sorts
9. U.N. labor body: abbr.
10. Tough material used in bookbinding
11. Dress designers
12. Pumpkin, squash, etc.
13. Secondhand
14. Sault — Marie
15. Speech exercise: 4 wds.
16. Take an oath
17. Arctic base
20. Cherry-colored
21. Mariner at Pribilof Islands
23. Nobleman's younger son
28. W.W. II intelligence unit: abbr.
31. Small French hackney coach
33. Suspicious: slang
34. Playwright Sherwood
36. Agency dealing with mortgages: abbr.
38. Confused query: 4 wds.
39. Haggle
41. Poker payments
43. Makes less viscous
44. Rooter
45. On the other side of
46. National Military Park in Tennessee
47. Nursery-rhyme query: 4 wds.
48. Church caretakers
50. New York hockey team
53. Grapevine parasite
55. Plant or horn
56. "Gil Blas" author
57. Religious reader
60. Succor
61. True-blue friend
64. "Where —," Stassen book: 2 wds.
65. Type of medieval literary work
66. Poetess Sitwell
69. Alaskan auks
72. "— Mater," noted hymn
74. Overhead railways
75. Colophony
79. "Won't you —, Bill Bailey?": 2 wds.
80. Repaired
82. Capek play
83. Private eye: slang
84. Shade of red
85. "Catfish" Hunter, for one
86. Printer's assistant
89. Small ape
91. — oil, used in cologne
93. Four pecks
94. Peregrine
95. Doctrine
97. Burdens
98. Nocturnal noise
99. Straggled
102. Foulards
103. Take — view of, regard unfavorably: 2 wds.
104. State bird of Hawaii
107. School-community group: abbr.
109. Another FDR creation: abbr.
110. Aunt: Spanish

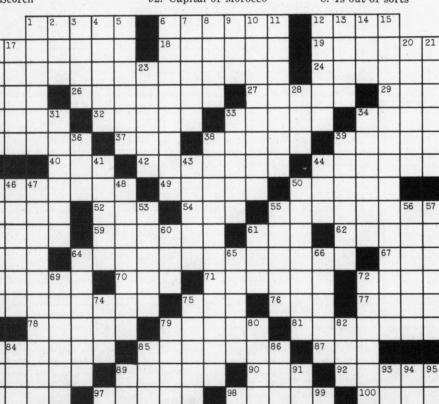

Solution is on page 290

ACROSS

1. Foolish
5. Insignificant
10. Dear: Italian
14. Honey: pharm.
17. Went astray
19. Do penance
20. Saroyan boy
21. Palm leaf
22. Speaking indirectly: 4 wds.
26. Scottish river
27. Sheer fabric
28. Palatine garb
29. Friendless fellow
30. Concern of Portia
31. *Ici*
32. Dispatched
33. Fruit of the ash
36. Semester
37. Playwright-composer Harbach
38. Legume
41. Gather
42. Lands
44. Map
45. "The Music Man" hero
46. Small error; fault
47. Lab bottle
48. Framework
49. Fixed quantity
50. Loathsome
51. Feel for
52. Lave
53. "Zorba" locale
54. United
55. Corpus
56. Italian producer
57. 1944 Nobelist in physiology
58. Charles' —, the Big Dipper
60. Panamanian liner
62. Preposition
63. Burned a bit
65. Like pelage
66. Colewort
68. Italian cleric
71. Tired out: 2 wds.
72. Mephitic
73. "007"
74. Rugged cliff
75. — poem, symphonic poem
76. Padraic —, Irish poet
77. Oats, in Scotland and Ireland
78. Beldame
79. Musical composition
80. Himalayas, to fliers
81. Beach: Spanish
82. Late actor Novarro
83. Aerialist's security
84. Camera part
85. Horse's gait
86. Late
87. Perjured oneself
88. Small talk
89. *Bifteck*
91. Engages beforehand
93. Jai-—
94. Name for Simon Templar
95. City in Oklahoma
98. Betty Smith novel: 5 wds.
102. New Deal agency
103. Inner Hebrides island
104. Rousseau book
105. Fix firmly
106. Son of Jacob
107. Captured
108. Not *au courant*
109. Trim

DOWN

1. Unfinished business of a sort
2. Zone
3. Brawl
4. Vietnamese holiday
5. Thaumaturgy
6. European country
7. Tipperary stream
8. Yoko —, Mrs. John Lennon
9. News agency
10. "Mooch"
11. Greek river
12. Cheer-leader's shout
13. Egg dish
14. Get on
15. Other
16. The Cowardly Lion
18. Varied
23. "A Doll's House" heroine
24. Average
25. *Pro — publico*, for the public good
30. Billiard shot
31. Achilles' —
32. Marvel (at)
33. Broadside
34. Violently
35. Ice-cream flavor: 2 wds.
36. Salver
37. Andrew Jackson: 2 wds.
38. Respighi tone poem (with The) : 3 wds.
39. Upper echelon
40. Change
42. Greedy
43. Nickname for New Haven, Connecticut: 3 wds.
44. Songstress Page
45. She wrote "Lummox"
48. Cautious
51. Water hole
52. Council
53. Chair material
55. French adverb
56. Island off Aden
57. Fabergé's medium
59. Zodiac sign
61. Clown: slang
63. Repressed: 2 wds.
64. Flee to wed
67. Mozart Donna
69. Forgot the period: 2 wds.
70. Middleman
72. Lost's partner
73. Marina sight
74. Ceiling flaw
76. Run!: 2 wds. (slang)
77. Coagulate
78. Inventive one
81. Spoke well of
84. As if
85. Easing of relations
86. Western city
87. Navigational device
88. Conceal
89. Sobol or marten
90. See 71-Across
91. Scop
92. Great Barrier Island
93. Italian river
94. State of agitation
95. City in Oklahoma
96. Man of many colors
97. Before: prefix
99. Baby-talk word
100. "— Big Girl Now:" 2 wds.
101. Undressed hide

Solution is on page 290

KRISS KROSS 11—SMALL, BUT OH MY!

Expert solving time: 22 minutes
Your solving time:

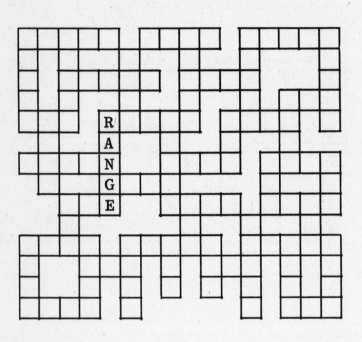

3 Letters	Ante	5 Letters
Act	Cage	Agent
Age	Cart	Caged
And	Crag	Cater
Arc	Dart	Crate
Cad	Dear	Eater
Eat	Earn	Grade
Ere	Edge	Grand
Erg	Erne	Greet
Ern	Gene	Racer
Err	Near	Range
Eta	Need	React
Gat	Rant	Reata
Red	Tang	Redan
Tee	Tear	Trade
4 Letters	Tend	Treed
Acne	Tern	

KRISS KROSS 12—WORD FUN

Expert solving time: 23 minutes
Your solving time:

First word across is listed on page 320

4 Letters	Attic	6 Letters
Arts	Cheri	Ethnic
Axil	Cramp	Heeled
Coop	Crimp	Hustle
Ecru	Haven	Leaven
Exit	Helen	Reline
Ioni	Ketch	Remake
Mash	Latin	Rustle
Mass	Loins	Sample
Noon	Match	Simmer
Omni	Niche	Simple
Pend	Plumb	Solder
Pond	Satin	Stylus
Shop	Sours	Topple
Stop	Style	
Suns	Three	
Yams	Thyme	
5 Letters	Tiara	**Solutions are on**
Asset	Tribe	**page 294**

CHALLENGER KRISS KROSS 13—TIME STUDY

Expert solving time without using a starting word: 40 minutes
Your solving time:
First word across is listed on page 320.

3 Letters

Ada
Aga
Ala
Ana
Ava
Baa
Boa
Eva
Fra
Sea
Via

4 Letters

Alba
Alta
Area
Aria
Asia
Cora
Data
Etta
Lola
Mesa
Nora
Pika
Rita
Soda
Toga
Vera

5 Letters

Aroma
Drama

Mamma
Mania
Manna
Melba
Omega
Opera
Parka
Plaza
Terza (rima)
Theda
Villa

6 Letters

Africa
Alaska
Alpaca
Armada
Asthma
Azalea
Banana
Camera
Canada
Cinema

Corona
Eczema
Egeria
Enigma
Galata
Luella
Mimosa
Nevada
Plasma
Rebena
Retina

7 Letters

Algebra
Arietta
Arizona
Bohemia
Cholera
Dilemma
Jamaica
Liberia
Madonna
Malaria

Melissa
Replica
Spatula
Stamina
Veranda

8 Letters

Bacteria
Hysteria
Insomnia
Marianna

9 Letters

Guerrilla
Incognita
Tarantula

Solution is on page 293

KRISS KROSS 14—WORD WORKOUT

Even with "TERRAIN" entered into its correct place in the diagram, it took the expert 38 minutes to solve this Kriss Kross.
Your solving time:

4 Letters

Alan
Alle
Amid
Dell
Earn
Etui
Inti
Itea
Lett
Line
Maar
Mile
Name

Rani
Rent
Rite
Tame
Taxi
Till
Tilt

5 Letters

Acids
Admit
Anile
Denim
Deter

Diene
Eclat
Ideal
Inlet
Latin
Liege
Liter
Lurid
Medal
Meter
Miami
Nadir
Nitid
Ratal

Tiers
Tiler
Treat
Trill

7 Letters

Aliment
Amateur
Dantean
Dilemma
Distant
Entente
Entrain
Eremite
Imitate
Inertia
Initial
Iranian
Iterate
Lantern
Lectern
Limited
Martial
Minaret
Mineral
Musical
Nitrate
Nitrile
Raiment
Redness
Remnant
Retrial
Tendril
Terrain
Trammel

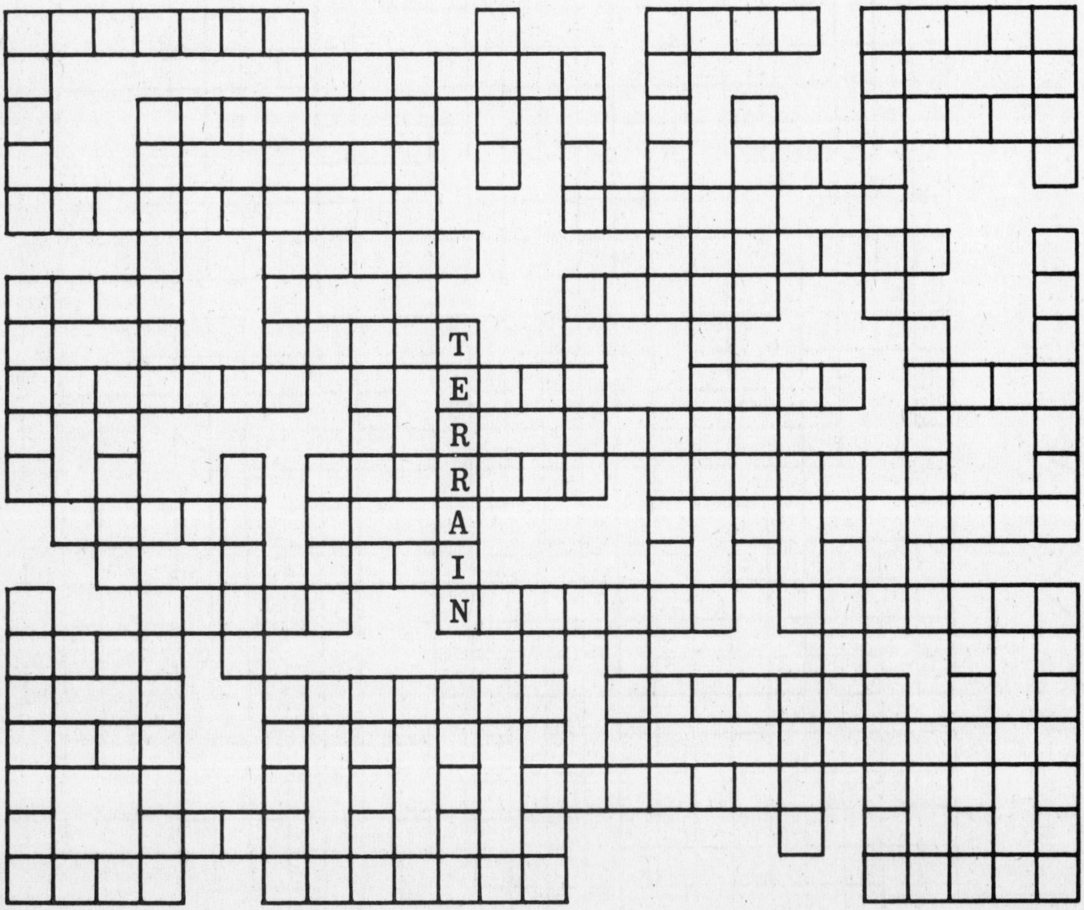

Solution is on page 293

Expert solving time without using a starting word: **86 minutes**
Your solving time:
First word across is listed on page 320.

5 Letters

Salvo
Scorn
Seals
Serra
Shame
Shirt
Sisal
Situp
Skate
Slang
Slash
Slide
Slits
Smees
Sneer
Snips
Snore
Spars

Spook
Stamp
Stash
Stoic
Stops
Storm

6 Letters

Samson
Sashes
Sateen
Scheme
School
Search
Season
Sedate
Seiner
Senate
Sensor
Shaker

Simmer
Single
Slaves
Slowly
Solemn
Sporty
Spurns
Stereo
Strain
Strait
Stress
Strums
Sugary
Sunset

7 Letters

Sadists
Sassoon
Screech
Serious

Settler
Sharpen
Singlet
Sinners
Sissies
Sisters
Slanted
Slicers
Smarter
Sourish
Spanish
Spasmic
Spirals
Spouses
Stammer
Stashed
Strafed
Stretch
Suppers

Solution is on page 293

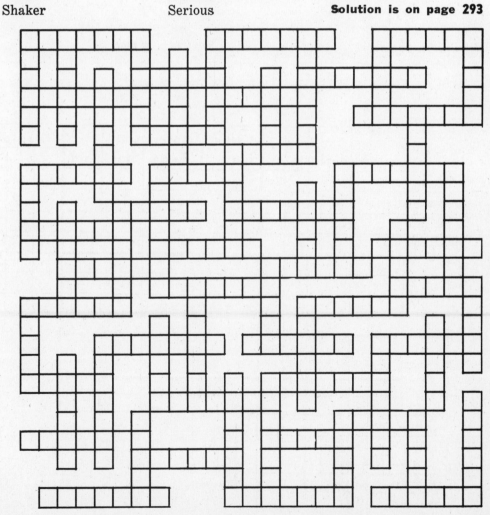

LOGIC PROBLEM 7

The Telephone Calls   **by Randall L. Whipkey**

On George G. George's last telephone bill, there were four long-distance collect calls listed, one from each of his four children, all of whom are away at college (one attends Columbia University). No two calls took the same amount of time, and no two cost the same. From the clues that follow, can you deduce the school each attends, his or her class, the length of the call each made, and how much each call cost?

NOTE: The charges have no relation to actual telephone rates.

1. Linda's call was twice as long as the junior's.

2. John isn't the sophomore.

3. The senior's call cost twice as much as the one made by Mike, who did not make the longest call.

4. The Georgia Tech student's call was twice as long as the freshman's.

5. The shortest call also cost the least.

6. The Ohio State student's call cost twice as much as the longest call, which was made by the Stanford student.

7. Karen's call cost $3.00.

8. The senior does not attend Stanford.

9. The total cost of the four calls was $10.50, with none costing less than $1.00.

10. Mike doesn't attend Ohio State.

11. The four calls totalled 54 minutes in length.

12. The lowest rate for any of the calls was 10¢ per minute.

Solution is on page 317

LOGIC PROBLEM 8

SUMMERSET MALL   **by Randall L. Whipkey**

Summerset Mall is a two-story shopping area containing twenty stores, including a men's clothing shop. The mall is designed so that there are five stores on the north side of the first floor numbered 101, 103, 105, 107, and 109 consecutively from east to west and five stores directly opposite them on the south side numbered correspondingly 100, 102, 104, 106, and 108 from east to west; the second floor layout is the same, the stores numbered 201-209 on the north and 200-208 on the south. From the clues that follow, can you deduce the name (one store is Rose's) and kind of store in each mall space?

1. The five stores occupying the first floor on the north side are (not necessarily consecutively) Gray's, Niven's, Dailey's, the bake shop, and the leather-goods shop.
2. The sporting-goods store is directly upstairs from Forrest's.
3. The shoe store is directly above Ogden's Cosmetics.
4. Dailey's is next door to the music store.
5. Baker's is in 204.
6. Mitchell's is directly above Queen's, which isn't the leather-goods store.
7. Of the following eight stores, these pairs are as far apart as possible: Jackson's and the florist's shop; Alden's and the ice-cream parlor; Troop's and the pet store; and Holden's and the music store.
8. Kelly's is next-door to both Palmer's and Mitchell's Gift Shop.
9. Smith's is directly opposite the music store.
10. Troop's isn't in 108.
11. The toy store is in 106.
12. Jackson's isn't on the first floor.
13. Baker's isn't the shoe store.
14. The florist's is opposite the art store.
15. The children's clothing store is directly above the women's clothing store.
16. Alden's is directly upstairs from Gray's.
17. Neither Niven's nor Dailey's is the florist's.
18. The leather-goods store isn't in 105.
19. The jeweler's is next-door to both Cramer's and the cheese shop.
20. Egan's, which isn't the toy store, is next door to Long's.
21. The furniture store, which isn't Holden's, is directly opposite the restaurant.
22. Inman's isn't the cheese shop.
23. The stationery store isn't Jackson's.

Solution is on page 318

Instead of the usual solving chart (which would be of little help in this particular Logic Problem), below is a diagram of Summerset Mall. As you determine the location, type, and name of each store, enter the information in the appropriate space.

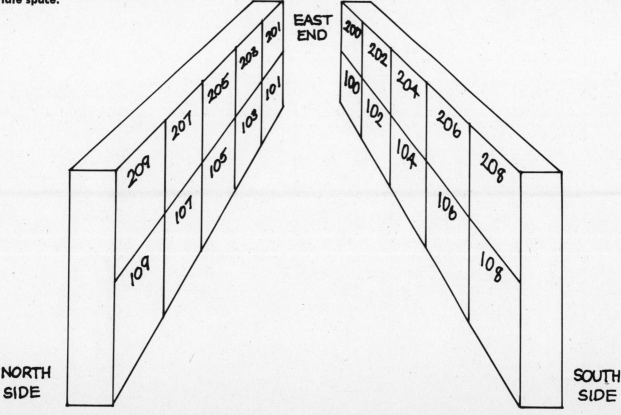

RECTANGLE LOGIC

Each of the three rectangles shown at the top of this page can be constructed from the pieces directly below them. Your task: To figure out how these lettered pieces should fit together, jigsaw fashion, in order to form each rectangle; no fair using scissors! As a rectangle is a symmetrical figure, your solution could be a mirror image of ours, shown on page 317.

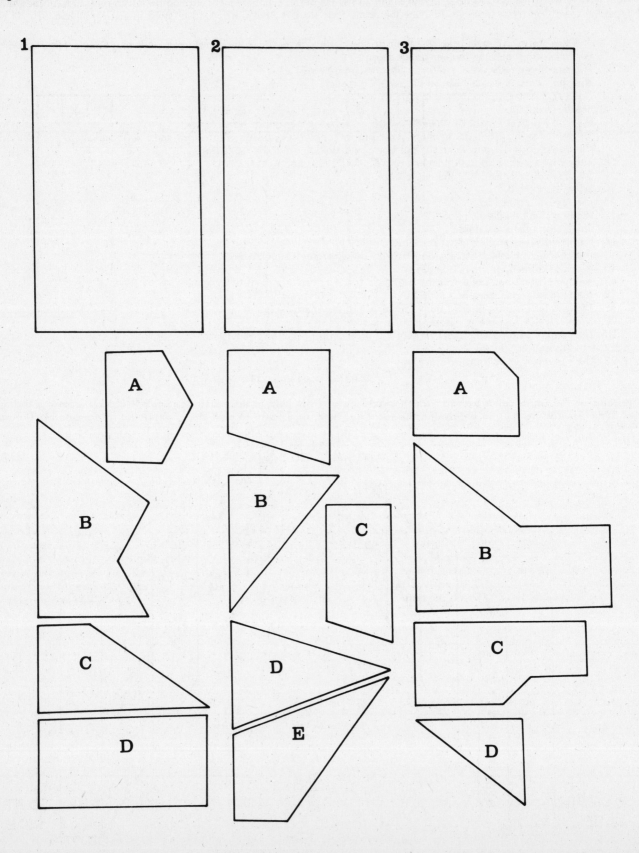

NUMBER PLACE

In this puzzle, your job is to place a number into every empty box so that each row across, each column down, and each small 9-box square within the large square (there are 9 of these) will contain each number from 1 through 9. Remember that no number may appear more than once in any row across, any column down, or within any small 9-box square; this will help you solve the puzzle. The numbers in circles below the diagram will give you a head start—each of these four numbers goes into one of the circle boxes in the diagram (not necessarily in the order given).

Solutions are on page 319.

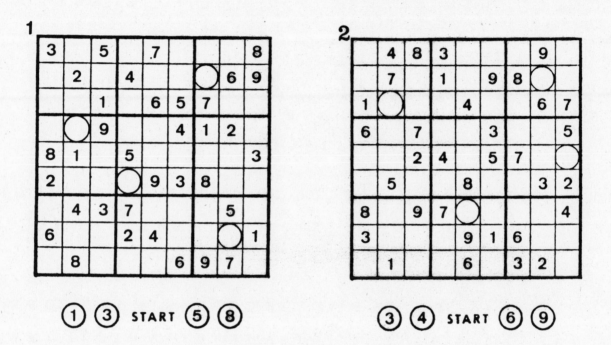

LETTER PATHS

Each letter square below contains five 5-letter words, scrambled, but all beginning with the same letter of the alphabet. For example, in No. 1, all the words in that letter square begin with "M" (but not the same "M"; there is a different "M" for the beginning of each word). Locate the words by moving in any direction from letter to adjoining letter, without skipping over any letters. Use each letter only once. Draw a continuous line through the letters as you form your words, touching each letter only once. You may not cross the line you have already drawn. It doesn't matter which word you start with, as long as you find all five words.

Solutions are on page 319.

1

R	R	O	N	I
R	A	M	M	A
Y	T	O	L	R
M	T	M	M	U
O	U	S	T	Y

2

G	U	E	V	E
U	A	A	U	V
R	S	V	L	A
I	V	O	V	U
L	E	W	T	L

3

N	B	Y	O	N
O	U	K	B	U
T	L	N	E	S
A	B	R	C	B
Y	R	E	B	H

Cryptograms begin on page 40.

89. G EHLGA ADRZE AP NP XLDRZN G SLHIPZ'I

XGJO RI SGA RA.

90. B FQOX SZ FNPYTJC MYSVJ ZOSY KNJ ZXQJ

GOPKJM "JTH SZ MQYYJO" PT KNJ BQKQYT

MVC.

91. CRWTDHKT OVES NGJAW JN DHE LEDDMVL

VSVRJL'N ARJBYVE, WTV KECMVAEHJW'N

NUHJEW JN VOVX UHJBYVE.

92. ANR DKIR FRX HGGF PC K SPH WZA CZWIPHR

IKHD SBKXPFQ HKFL XRKBL CRKHRF NGHR.

93. EGOH ZGKVSGHADMK GZIK TYHKSEB

YHEHJKHU TYDZ YHKWYJGPGPR SJPUK, ZJPB

LYGRSWEB VDEDYHU EHJAHK UJPVHU JLDMW

MIDP DMY EJFP.

94. QLIHLJMDQ, YLHI IEJZFFWLM CNZHL ENDWX

ODJXI DEJSII HNL IXQ'I FWAL FAWWLHZP

FSDJM, HNLP LJDILM HNLO.

95. GHNLRGM QDXKU UQHXRGM QHTK LDADTVHPU

NH ZHPT LKDJNL NLDG SKRGM UPTTHPGVKV

SZ SKJJRMKTKGN GHGUQHXKTU.

CHALLENGER

96. KGXM UPNLULBGY PQPJUVJ, XVRJVXDM

RGYVXH TPJLWBLN BGJXPAL VRLJ-DVDFRGX

QGRYPJLH UWNGJA PGN HMVK.

Solutions are on page 307

97. CJPZS CDKSP UDSM VGDN DK MDCS RGSSM.

DRWSGNBMS, NWP UD CDMR ZBV ZJKXM TJGGP

ZGJKTWSM?

98. MUKAV: UDG HQY HQAZ UKK KRUGI DGEZ

JSSKBIUJHEG RKA SQASBPMUJISGM UDJU

PQYDU HGUUGA HG JUUAQHBUGZ UK J EJAV.

99. IKE'M TS ISZSGASI TX CKCVFJU JCCFJVBS;

GM ASSUB NGMY MYS NGEI.

100. GH YR IPBXU WBLV QRV JXX VZPLR WPQQRAL

PE J VARJUCGXX, VZRN'U QAGEU JE JYHBX

XPV PH IPAE.

101. KBTVDT LMFKAL YBMMCKCQ KCTVFDL

BEFDT FSK CBLMCKD NFBLMEVDC NBSLVDT

SDMFEQ AVLCKP.

102. ATHCHAHEV AQRRLC NMTC VJ MRIJEE HC

ENLMIU.

103. BYIZF EHKVZMRQ: OYQ FRH QYPK Y CMXK

AKZZKI URIJ UWRVK BIRQHQOMYZMRQ MVQ'Z

OWYQSKJ LF IKPRXYA RC CRHI AKZZKIV?

YQVUKI: EHKHK.

CHALLENGER

104. VWH-BNKX IZVFIXMBVZF KDNSBDNS SV OZXDH

MDS XPXZ OXDB FVTZHVTLG; IZVWVSLXH

CXZKXSBDBNVS IZVHTMXF BGNF CWDPVZ.

Solutions are on page 307

105. G KGV KYMR MZXEZ QBM RBKZ RW JZGXV
GJKWMR ZEZXL RXGPZ OYR
HZVMYXZ—HXBRBHM HWKZ XZGPL-KGPZ.

106. PSBWLAGDGUU LU JFG UVKJMG PBRWBRDQG
JFG ALSMGJ UFGXU VHSD JFG KBVJRM FGGM
JFRJ QBVUFGU LJ.

107. N HONKZ WSXWYS UXGYT NKTSST UDYY
HOSNI DGHXLXJNYS NKVGIDKUS
"QISUZUXLWSKVS."

108. IBHQ CQB P KPK HBE JDDK LMDOCPIPHQ
MTIDR ZBHZDMHPHQ RLDDK; HBF P RECHK
CHK RECMD CQJCRE FJDH ZCMDIDRR LDBLID
KMPOD RB SCRE.

109. SWTSBW SRZGJH WBGYUJTEV HYE ZB YSUGN
CBVHWJZBC YV ZBJEQ YCBSU JE UKB YWU TA
UWBYUJEQ UKB SRZGJH YV JA UKBN YWB
ETU NTRW WBGYUJTEV.

110. GYBWIS YTSQHWS MPPIF PTDGZFRYFC HOPB
FXRPTDRMRX VYWVPDF YMDPB GP GYF QPPT
XYZVGD RT Y BYWYB FNPPW DBYN.

111. LZBXWY, OCQBE IBVBOPI BR PDQW ECOO
OBRP OBUP XOGTTGZVI BR YWP EDZU TBOO
IWBRP.

112. "BTTXTGRB," MLPUGCXV FRFX TPGV BTJPC;
"BNXF," MPGFJXUXV XRQLJ JXFPUC.

Solutions are on page 307

113. ZE Z XZKXHDGH, ENH NZTXGKLHK WQG LHE
PI ZOE EQ XH Z DZKXQS DQOW QJ TZSW
QENHKI.

114. QIL ZXSM QYVLT Y ZYQI; QILE X TLL IXG
KHBXEJ TQSYXJIQ QF QIL NHFQILTHXEL QF
MSB IXGTLHK.

115. ULCH GDVZLEU UGM VZH YLRJY'U ELDYZ;
VZHM WGJ'V QRJX VRCH VL TERVH VZHRE
UVDQQ, PDV LVZHEU WGJJLV PH FELSRQRW
DJSHUU VZH FEHUUDEH RU VHEERQRW.

116. FVNX N WZBNANHX ADMHR CA XVB TBLLU
ZNMJVXBL DS TNHU KVCZRLBH NA XVBU
KVNAB XVB QLCJVX SZNAVBA DS ZCJVXHCHJ
QMJA.

117. DGFO OWLIGFRC AWLFL DORF FOBV REB, HW
WHB ARH IWLLGJCV JB GCC RF BRLB.

118. ZKCDGRK CBDTZL GXBLY MTVQKQRYY HZBS
MCXDQR VLGC TZDDN HZSVQN.

119. QNMR KVXXZ RCQQM PYVF FJKZCPCBXZH
ZJHNVJQ JFLRCHRXJHXV PYV LJMHYVJQ
BYQQXKCJHX BRYVJQX.

120. GRMLSQ'Y SXVA ZKLGMH: ZQRLMXPLC DXCB
PCKDQSY WSKD XG RZLGBRGVQ RCKGWYXBQ
VKLGMSH SKRBY.

Solutions are on page 307

FORM-A-WORD

Work Form-A-Word as follows:

1. Form the longest single word you can from the letters on the first line of the diagram (leaving enough letters to enable you to form a word on the second line). Scramble the letters as you please to form the word.

2. Mark off the letters used, and write the word on line 1 (to the right of the diagram).

3. Then drop each unused letter down to the next line if the box directly beneath the letter is completely blank. If it isn't, the letter is lost. Black boxes in the diagram are there so that you cannot bring down the letters directly above them if those letters are unused. In forming a word, you may use all the letters in a line even though they may be separated by black boxes.

4. Work each line this way; but do not form plurals, words beginning with capital letters, or words of less than 3 letters.

5. If a word cannot be formed, drop all the letters you can to the next line and continue playing.

6. Score 1 point for each letter used and subtract 5 points for each line without a word.

    NOTE: In order to get a perfect score, every letter in the diagram must be used.

    Average score: 44   Good score: 48   Perfect score: 58

    Our list of words, which may not agree with yours, is on page 314.

SCORE

#													
1	L	A	N	T	E	L	G	Y	R	D	E		
2			■					■					
3		W		R		E		L		A			
4	R		A		C		I		M		E		
5		E		V		E		A		S			
6	A		R		B	■	C		E		A		
7		I		E		A		R		M			
8	G		A		K		N		I		S		
9		E		Z		M		A		N			
10	I		■			L		E		■		K	
11		N		A		D		I		T			

TOTAL

THE CENTER SPELLS IT

First, think of a four-letter word which answers the definition in column I. By adding a letter to the center of that four-letter word, you'll form a five-letter word which answers the definition in column II. Write the center letter of the word in Column II on the dash provided in column III. If done correctly, the letters in column III, reading down, will spell out a familiar expression. Answer is on page 317.

I	II	III
1. Close (a door)	Sudden, loud outcry	_____
2. Butterfly's "cousin"	December, August, or February	_____
3. Ceased living	Cut into tiny pieces	_____
4. Recover (something lost)	An evil spirit	_____
5. Party giver	Lifting device	_____
6. An entrance or exit	Giver, as of blood	_____
7. Price paid	Land along the sea	_____
8. Part of a plant below ground	R2D2 or C3P0 from "Star Wars"	_____
9. Rescue	Medicinal ointment	_____
10. Small body of water	Unit of weight equal to 16 ounces	_____
11. Practice boxing	Piece of asparagus	_____
12. State of deep and prolonged unconsciousness	Punctuation mark used to indicate a pause	_____
13. Fail to win	Not form-fitting; baggy	_____
14. Halt	Bend or lean forward	_____
15. Extreme anger	"Home on the —"	_____

SHOPPERS' SPECIAL

How much do you know about shops, shopping, and shop words? You've got real shopping know-how if you can answer six of these questions. Ten correct answers make you shopper par excellence! Answer is on page 317.

1. To get tonsured, you would go to a a. millinery shop b. barber shop c. boot shop
2. A napoleon would be bought in a. a bakery b. an antique shop c. a florist's shop
3. To fill a prescription in England, you would go to the shop of a. a draper b. a chandler c. an apothecary
4. Which of these items would you be most apt to find in a millinery shop? a. a gambado b. a puttee c. a toque
5. A haberdashery is a shop for a. men b. women c. infants
6. "Nation of Shopkeepers" is a nickname sometimes applied to a. France b. Germany c. England
7. Shoppers looking for needles, thread, or pins would go to the a. ideas department b. notions department c. browsing department
8. A shop in which union membership is required of the employees is a. a closed shop b. an open shop c. an indifferent shop
9. The British ironmonger's shop is the same as our a. auto-repair shop b. laundry c. hardware store
10. A shoplifter is a person who a. manages shops b. steals from shops c. advertises shops

---

CIRCUS ENIGMAS

The verses below describe two circus "personalities." Each line of each verse gives you a clue to one letter of the missing word. Can you discover the two words? Answers are on page 317.

1.
My first letter's in *train*, but not in *car*;
My second's in *rope* and is also in *bar*;
My third is in *llama* and also in *goat*;
My fourth is in *top hat*, but never in *coat*;
My fifth in *excitement* and also in *fear*;
My sixth in *gazelle*, but is never in *deer*;
My seventh in *audience*, also in *me*;
My whole makes a circus a fine thing to see.

2.
My first is in *cage*, but is never in *door*;
My second in *lion*, but never in *roar*;
My third is in *lemonade*, also in *sweet*;
My fourth is in *peanuts*, but never in *treat*;
My fifth is in *horses*, but never *bareback*;
My sixth is in *candy* and also in *sack*;
My seventh is in *pony* and in *antelope*;
My eighth is in *tent*, but is never in *rope*;
My whole is an animal stronger than man,
Who has, among children, many a fan.

WORD LINK

Copyright 1989 by Bantam Doubleday Dell Publishing Group, Inc.

This puzzle is not as hard as it may look. The words to go into the diagram, Kriss Kross fashion, are listed below in capital letters. The word or words in parentheses after each capitalized word are those words which will cross or connect in the diagram with that capitalized word. The words in parentheses are listed in the EXACT ORDER that they cross the capitalized word. Here's how to go about solving:

1. We have started you off with ARSON. Look at ARSON in the list and you will see that the words *onlooker* and *lonely* will cross or connect with ARSON.

2. We have shown you where to put LONELY. Remembering that the words in parentheses are in order, you should be able to figure out where the word ONLOOKER must go.

3. Proceed entering words in this manner until you have completed the puzzle. It's a good idea, by the way, to cross off BOTH the capitalized word and all places where that word appears in parentheses.

4. Keep in mind that there will always be a space of one or more boxes between each word in the diagram.

ANON (*Raymond, Tonto*)
ARGON (*Congo*)
ARSON (*onlooker, lonely*)
BONBON (*Oberon, only*)
BONE (*goner, yonder*)
BONNET (*session, seton, tongue*)
CONFER (*consent, Oberon*)
CONGO (*cotton, argon*)
CONSENT (*confer, second, Teton*)
COTTON (*Congo, onset, none*)
EBONY (*one, lonely*)
GONER (*bone, iron*)
ICON (*iron*)
IRON (*icon, goner*)
LONDON (*lonely, Raymond*)
LONELY (*arson, tongue, London, ebony*)
MONSTER (*onlooker, sonnet, Raymond*)
MORON (*Raymond, Tonto, noone*)
NONE (*sonnet, cotton*)
NONSENSE (*onion, session, seton*)
NOON (*Teton, Orion, onion*)

NOONE (*moron*)
NOTION (*yonder, onset, Orion*)
OBERON (*bonbon, confer, second*)
ONE (*tongue, ebony*)
ONION (*nonsense, Ontario, noon*)
ONLOOKER (*Orion, monster, arson*)
ONLY (*bonbon, yonder*)
ONSET (*notion, sonnet, cotton*)
ONTARIO (*second, Teton, onion*)
ONTO (*Tonto*)
ORION (*noon, onlooker, notion*)
RAYMOND (*monster, anon, moron, London*)
SECOND (*consent, Ontario, Oberon*)
SESSION (*nonsense, bonnet*)
SETON (*nonsense, tonic, bonnet*)
SONNET (*onset, none, monster*)
TETON (*consent, Ontario, noon*)
TONGUE (*bonnet, one, lonely*)
TONIC (*seton*)
TONTO (*onto, anon, moron*)
YONDER (*only, notion, bone*)

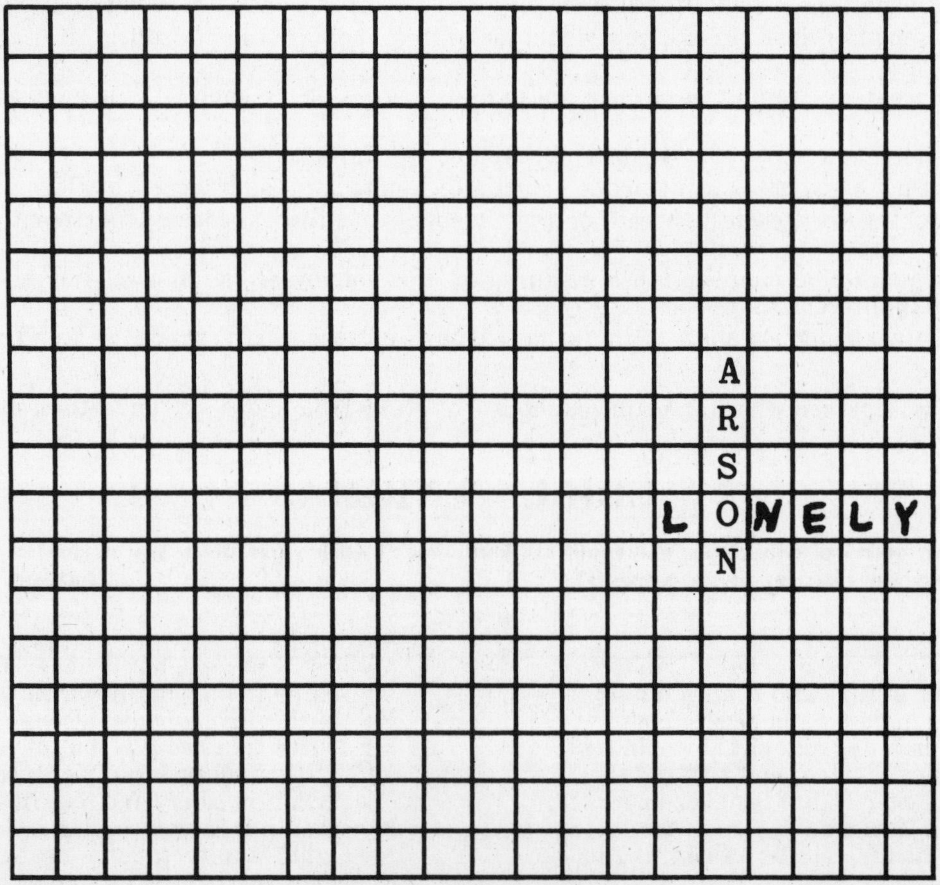

Solution is on page 318

TANGLEWORDS

DOUBLE ''L''

Tanglewords is like a Word Search (see pages 26 and 27), but in reverse. In this puzzle, the diagram contains blank squares into which YOU write the missing letters, completing the diagram as you fit the 28 words into their correct places. Circled letters already entered are the starting letters for one or more words (in fact, any letter may be part of more than one word). Beginning ONLY with a circled letter, fill in each word in a straight line forwards, backwards, up, down, or diagonally. Words may overlap or cross in any direction, but no square, black or white, may be skipped over. Black squares are "stops"; do not go through a black square as you fill in a word. (You may, however, pass between the connecting points of two black squares, as with WALLPAPER, which has been filled in to start you off. When all the words are entered correctly, there will be one letter in every white square.

Solution is on page 319.

All	Dill	Llama	Skull
Alloy	Fall	Mull	Tall
Ball	Frill	Pulley	Toll
Ballet	Gullible	Quill	Twill
Call	Hallucinate	Roller	Valley
Cello	Hello	Scroll	Wallpaper
Collect	Ill	Silly	Yellow

LETTER CHOICE

The object of Letter Choice is to use all the letters (except those circled) in the diagram below in spelling out seven everyday words of three or more letters each.

TO SOLVE: Each word you form MUST begin with one of the circled letters heading the columns in the diagram. The second letter of the word must be one of the letters in the column headed by the circled letter with which you began the word. The third letter must be chosen from a column HEADED BY THE SAME LETTER USED AS THE SECOND LETTER of your word. Continue selecting your letters in this fashion. Thus, the fourth letter must be selected from a column headed by the third letter; the fifth letter from a column headed by the fourth letter, etc. Choose your letters carefully: not all the letters in the diagram have a corresponding circled letter heading a column. Therefore, if you pick a letter that does not head a column, you cannot continue forming that word.

For example: Notice how the word MONTH could be formed in the sample diagram. Starting with the circle M at the top of the sixth column, find the O in that column. Then locate the N in the column headed by the O, the T in the column headed by N, and the H in the T column. Notice also that there is no column headed by the letter H; therefore, you can go no further (you could not form the word "monthly" for example).

While forming your words, you do not have to keep going until you come to a letter that does not head a column; you may stop at any point. For instance, you could form the word TIME (starting with the circled T, finding the I in the T column, the M in the I column, and the E in the M column).

SAMPLE

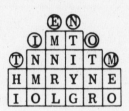

Since you may use each UNCIRCLED letter only once, cross out each letter as you use it. Do NOT cross out any of the circled letters, as you will need them to start other words and to locate other letters. Once you have crossed out all the letters in a column, however, you may not use the circled letter heading that column for either starting new words or continuing other words. NOTE: You will not necessarily use every circled letter to start a word and you may use a circled letter to begin more than one word.

TO SCORE: Score 1 point for each letter in the words you form including the first letter. The more letters used, the better your score. Remember, form everyday words; neither proper nouns nor words of less than three letters are allowed. WARNING: To get a perfect score, all the uncircled letters must be used.

Average score: 30   Good score: 35 to 40   Perfect score: 45

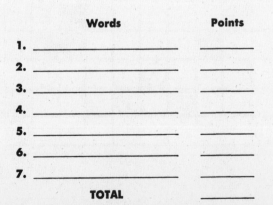

Words	Points
1. _____	_____
2. _____	_____
3. _____	_____
4. _____	_____
5. _____	_____
6. _____	_____
7. _____	_____
TOTAL	_____

Our answer, showing a perfect score of 45, is on page 317.

CROSS SUMS

NUMBER 10

In each of these Cross Sums, we have not filled in a digit combination. Instead, we have shaded one area in the diagram. If you need help starting the puzzle, the digit combination to go into that area is listed on page 320.

Copyright 1981 by Dell Publishing Co., Inc.

NUMBER 11

Solutions are on page 320

3-D DRAWINGS

Here's a puzzle designed to test your ability to "see" around the corner into a third dimension, all the while staying on a two-dimensional piece of paper. Shown below are both top and front views of three different buildings. Can you make a drawing showing how each of the three would look if viewed from the right-hand side?

Our drawings are shown on page 318.

1   **Top View**

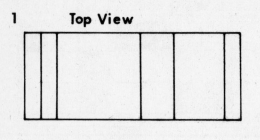

Front View

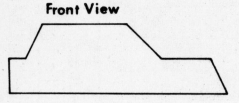

2   **Top View**

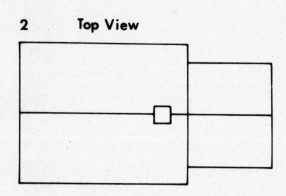

Front View

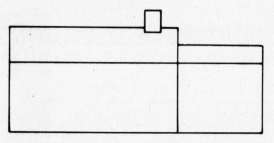

3   **Top View**   **Front View**

LETTER CHASE

Copyright 1989 by Bantam Doubleday Dell Publishing Group, Inc.

Solve Letter Chase as follows:

1. Choose letters from the Letter List to complete the words started below. Always proceed from left to right in choosing letters, and cross off letters as you use them. Do not double back in the Letter List once you've begun to select letters for any word and do not rearrange their order in any way once you've selected them. Letters must be selected in the same order as you use them in each word, but they do not have to appear together in the Letter List. The crossed-off letters may not be used again.

2. Formed words must be at least three letters long, but do not form any word by adding more letters than there are blank dashes.

In this puzzle, for example: ST ____ ____ ____ could be STY, STAR, STILL or STRAY (among others).

3. Form only common English words. Words beginning with a capital letter, obsolete or foreign words, and plurals are not allowed.

SCORE: Give yourself 5 points for each word formed, plus 1 point for every one of the letters in the formed word, including the letters given. Subtract 10 points from your total score for every word that can't be formed. A score of 70 points is passable; 80 points is average; 90 points is good; 100 points is perfect. NOTE: To get a perfect score, all the letters must be used.

LETTER LIST

A R I L E C A K R O C E D A N L R A I E L V U N E O T M L N E B Y

WORDS	POINTS
1. R O __ __	____
2. A __ __ __ __	____
3. V A __ __ __	____
4. B A __ __ __ __ __	____
5. H __ __ __	____
6. C L __ __ __ __	____
7. T __ __ __ __ __	____
8. L E __ __ __	____
9. D O __ __	____
10. S T __ __ __	____
TOTAL	____

Our answer, showing a perfect score of 100, is on page 315.

BOWL-A-SCORE CHALLENGER 5

Copyright 1989 by Bantam Doubleday Dell Publishing Group, Inc.

In this bowling game your "pins" are the groups of letters below. In order to score a "strike," you must unscramble (anagram) the "pin" letters of each group and form one 9-letter word. The starting letter for each "strike" word is given. To score a "spare," rearrange the scrambled letters of each group into two words, with no letters left over. Words beginning with a capital letter are not allowed for either "strikes" or "spares." In forming your "spare" words, you may not simply split the "strike" word in two parts and use both exactly as they appear in the "strike" word. For example, FORE and FRONT would not qualify as a "spare" for the "strike" word FOREFRONT.

SCORING: Score 20 points for each "strike" and 10 points for each "spare." Perfect score (10 "strikes" and 10 two-word "spares") is 300.

Warning: This game is really tough! Only word bowling geniuses will score a perfect 300. The words we made are on page 319.

1. R   **Strike**
    S S   **A** _____
    G T I   **Spare**
    A E   _____
    N   _____

2. M   **Strike**
    E E   **B** _____
    T B A   **Spare**
    R R   _____
    O   _____

3. U   **Strike**
    T T   **A** _____
    R S T   **Spare**
    I N   _____
    A   _____

4. P   **Strike**
    E L   **P** _____
    C E E   **Spare**
    A B   _____
    A   _____

5. R   **Strike**
    M O   **M** _____
    E L M   **Spare**
    A D   _____
    A   _____

6. Y   **Strike**
    R T   **A** _____
    I R R   **Spare**
    A B   _____
    A   _____

7. T   **Strike**
    L N   **C** _____
    E I L   **Spare**
    E E   _____
    C   _____

8. U   **Strike**
    T U   **U** _____
    M M T   **Spare**
    I L   _____
    A   _____

9. R   **Strike**
    M O   **A** _____
    I L L   **Spare**
    A D   _____
    A   _____

10. T   **Strike**
    S S   **D** _____
    E I M   **Spare**
    D E   _____
    A   _____

CHALLENGER SECTION

The following Challenger Section is intended for solvers who are seeking an out-of-the-ordinary solving experience. The puzzles that follow were especially constructed and edited with intent to offer a true challenge to solvers, no matter how sharp their solving skills may be.

In this Section such helps as "2 wds.," "hyph. wd.," and "slang" following definitions have been omitted. However, in the spirit of fairness, foreign words and abbreviations are so designated.

"CLUES TO AMUSE AND CONFUSE"
by EUGENE T. MALESKA

ACROSS

1. Between Ali and au rhum
5. Near-perfect report card
10. This Mme. told de *tales*
15. DEF predecessor
18. *Late* cousin of *etc.*
19. Not so long
20. Caesar's planet
21. *Love*-filled Pope
23. "— boy!"
24. 2/nd
26. Area, *if in* Morocco
27. Atlas display
29. What inspired Watt
30. Jeffersons' followers
32. Items for Arnie Palmer
34. Cuban export
36. "Sweet — love" (Tennyson)
37. Encountered *on train*
39. *Adlai* becomes a lama
40. Non-paper tissues
41. Happify
42. Knightwear
44. Ford or Lincoln
46. Frivolous and conceited: German
49. Man in Indiana
50. Petal's neighbor
51. —bury steak
53. Horse-race Ridge
54. Palindromic Burmese
55. Drive back but not forth
56. Harpists on high
58. Blanc fellow
59. Court-to-court order
61. ⁹⁄₁₀
63. Takes — view
64. Certain Asians
65. Spooky lake?
66. :
70. George White's were the talk of the town
74. "What is so — as a day in Jan.?"
75. Certain tree devotees
76. French river *namer*
77. Sitter's creation
78. Intro to "Rhythm"
80. Encirclers
81. Songs for singles
82. Between go and kite
83. Louts
85. Xanthippe
86. "The Lath Time I — Parith"
87. Son of *Norma*
88. Lot, karma, and doom
90. Site of HST's cradle
93. B-complex components
95. Advanced $ & ¢
97. Wriggler sniggler
98. Shrew with 32 reddish-brown-tipped teeth
99. ?
101. Man good enough for Godunov
104. Least colorful
107. DLI + DLI
108. Esool
111. Singer Adams
112. Half of a pair to wear
113. No place to walk!
114. First half of a course on insects
115. Hemp for a cloudless dayy
116. Short pathways
117. Grating berries
118. Like newly sown lawns?
119. Burned up the road

DOWN

1. Sun or moon follower
2. *Taut* little island
3. Arbatsun, in baseball
4. Zip
5. AWOL beginner
6. Cockney instrument
7. Cockney's salutes
8. After so and before ever so
9. Hallows, Star, and About Eve
10. Family tree of Saint Emma
11. Gumshoe, *etc.*
12. Odor, not a Napoli
13. Berger, the breadwinner
14. He was bairn in Scotland
15. Cooke who concocted "America"
16. Day, summer, Father, etc.
17. Known: French
22. Two jaws and a lever
25. Bellow, not a roar
28. Kind of Ranger
31. "— Be Seeing You," song of Capri
33. P M P K N S
35. After-dinner drinks
37. Glue it again
38. Mr. Dale of Sherwood Forest
39. Find M for Murder here
40. Tiaras, tiaras, tiaras
43. Monkey's uncles
45. Wings for Nero's A.F.
47. Word with for and more
48. *All* or *O* composer
50. Study course for *marines*
51. Backward *Anne's* medicinal leaves
52. Planes' radar systems
55. Medium for hams
56. Coat torn? Sew its —
57. Pearl's spurners
60. A world revolution
61. "— a Moray," song for 97-Across
62. Letter from London
64. Do a cuddle-up
66. Beddy-bye
67. Moor destroyer
68. Sort, sort
69. She's worth 2¢ in India
70. A room, *alas!*
71. Lal
72. Advice to Macduff
73. 9 in., 9 in., 9 in.
76. Gazelle that produces some *mohair*
79. *Tin stars'* subways
81. Get Brown moving
82. Anonymous
84. Armstrong's "one small" one
87. Avis' first name
89. Worker on galleys
91. Makes the suit suit
92. Anthropology *dame*
94. "— 'orse comes hin," Cockney bettor's wish
95. Item in Diogenes' *palm*
96. Emmy's older brother
97. Pound the poet and others
100. Fishy melody-a
102. Lawrence Welk's first count
103. How Kyle learned in school
105. Kind of cure
106. Big shoe size?
109. Tuck's partner
110. Land near Gomorr.

Solution is on page 290

ACROSS

1. Heavy block of wood
6. Eject in a stream
11. —-sided, tall and slender
15. Suitable
16. Dishevel
17. Imprison hastily
19. Smiles broadly
23. Calcium oxide
24. Sound a horn
25. Nag
26. Victorian medallion for Indian notables: abbr.
27. French friend
28. German historian (1854-1928)
30. Up
31. Home
32. Stupid
34. Bracing
36. Receive
37. Resting place
38. Attain
40. Harbor barge
42. Lively
43. Short distance
45. Pronoun
46. — system
47. Make good use of
51. Decimal base
52. First-rate, as success
55. He wrote "Over the Rainbow"
56. Canvasses
58. Decorate, as silver
59. John —, author of "The Beggar's Opera"
60. Guys
61. Agree
63. Brace
64. Function
65. Coquettishly
66. Languish
67. Move furtively
68. — beard, seaweed
70. Unit of measure
71. Extravagance
73. Sensational
74. Ugly smile
76. Slight
77. Woman's name
79. Councils of elders
81. Establish
84. China blue
85. — beetle, weevil
86. Dispirited one
88. Setline
90. What sometimes "have it"
91. — ginger, herb
93. Equality
95. Card game
96. Spenserian heroine
97. Weighty
99. Widespread
100. Draw
101. Talks
105. Certain officers
106. Alarm
107. Free
108. Sheer
109. Pythagoras' "perfect number"
110. Word from the host

DOWN

1. Cry of surprise
2. Oilstone
3. Hoists
4. Helen Porter Mitchell's stage name
5. One rank below bishop
6. "Shake a leg!"
7. Kentucky bluegrass
8. Yelp of pain
9. Member of the wedding
10. Ninth grader, usually
11. Segment
12. Prank
13. Copy
14. Fire-fighters
15. Ignition device
17. Storage box
18. Group
19. Flower
20. Chemical compound
21. Secret watcher
22. Championship
28. Jelly ingredient
29. With justice
31. "— ruleth safely but he that is willingly ruled"
33. Dignitaries' accessories
35. Tasty dish
37. English author (1882-1956)
39. Langshan
41. Element with atomic weight of 118.69
42. Have — for, consider superfluous
44. Showing staring surprise
46. Don't move
47. Erstwhile Acadian
48. Came into being
49. Rest soundly
50. Coward's namesakes
52. Underworld abode
53. Nabs
54. Spins
57. Willy —, rocket expert
58. Concomitant of "bill"
61. "Crime and Punishment" heroine: var. sp.
62. Kids' idea of a splendid clubhouse site
63. Hat assembler
65. Objet d'art
67. Irritated
69. Fits snugly
70. Cape —, Massachusetts
72. Haggard heroine
74. Shore
75. Clever conversation
77. Cancel
78. Author Trilling
79. Pertaining to certain Asian silk-makers
80. Combining form meaning earnest
82. Quality
83. One kind of saw
85. Ponders (over)
87. Leaf through rapidly
89. Big name in Louisiana
91. Titter
92. Cupboard
94. River rising in Wyoming
97. Flurry
98. Tower, as a mountain
100. — majesty
102. 5-centime piece
103. Actress, Mary —
104. Stolen

Solution is on page 290

ACROSS

1. Mr. Milquetoast
7. Contour-making machine
13. Pounding tool
19. Assert without proof
20. Man in *una plaza de toros*: Span.
21. Native of Nevada
22. They figure in many a Victorian novel
24. Birds of the hawk family
25. Exclamation of discovery
26. Pearl Buck heroine
27. Poured oil on
29. Company, in Paris: abbr.
30. Military "lights out"
32. Cars
34. Stingy
35. Greek "I"
36. Seat of the Krupp works
38. —*avis*, unusual person
39. Bestowed
40. Noise (about)
41. Middle part: var. sp.
43. "I — for you and balsam"
44. Hippodromes
45. Egyptian earth god
48. Contended
49. Encircled
50. "Love all, — a few"
51. R.L.S.'s "— With a Donkey"
53. Varsity man
55. England's "West Point": abbr.
58. Warm hues
59. Lounges
60. Vigilant
62. Oxfords have them
63. Cape —, California
65. Moved to reverence
66. Installs in office: var. sp.
69. Irregular
70. Forage crop
72. Six, in Venice
73. Period of ten years
75. More terse
76. Poet's preposition
78. Assist feloniously
79. Frost creation
80. Bitter vetch
81. Senility
83. Epic poetry
84. Brittle candies
86. Verse form used by Horace
87. City on the Hudson
88. Scottish Highlander
89. Alcor and Enif
93. Skates or torpedoes
94. Refection
95. Seasoner of hides
97. Seed covering
98. Prairie State: abbr.
99. Competitions
101. She threw the Golden Apple
103. Chinese pagoda
104. — Head, Hawaiian headland
106. Father Barber's clan
109. Groups of nine
110. Forty-—, gold-seekers
111. Melancholy: French
112. Dignified
113. Stamp-moistener
114. "— Resartus," Carlyle work

DOWN

1. Author of "Answered Prayers"
2. Honolulu greetings
3. Certain sailboats
4. — *annum*, by the year
5. Prefix meaning "soil"
6. Staggers
7. Criterion
8. Scalding
9. Girl's name derived from Ariadne
10. Latin-American laborers
11. Late conductor Rapee
12. Don Quixote's mount
13. More wan
14. Old-fashioned oath
15. Member of the Upper House: abbr.
16. Wycherley comedy of 1675
17. Former White House aide Baldridge
18. Places on a throne
21. Bristles
23. Ophelia's brother
28. Field of crystallized snow
31. Parched, in Paris
33. Kern's "All The Things You —"
35. Angers
37. At no time
39. Follower of Juliette Gordon Low
40. German name for Moravia's capital
42. Olden star, — Asther
43. Holds up to public ridicule
44. Altars: Latin
45. Declares formally
46. Stoat
47. Victor Herbert operetta
49. 1937 play by Odets
50. Type: Spanish
52. Waistcoat
53. Pro and —
54. Departed
56. More submissive
57. Venomous snakes
59. — majesty, treason
61. Alleviate
63. Kind of engineer: abbr.
64. Ideology
67. Axiom
68. Head: French
70. Greek god of war
71. Moves laboriously
74. French pastries
75. Hot-water tanks
77. Builder of a famous St. Louis bridge
79. False show
81. Mocks
82. Iridescent
83. He was: Latin
84. Presidential nickname
85. Depot: abbr.
87. Cares for
88. Meter-readers
90. Sculptor
91. Venetian bridge
92. Killer
94. *Haut* —, high society
95. Person in a kind of pool
96. Dissensions
99. Ulster
100. Small piece of fabric
102. Poet Teasdale
105. — *culpa*
107. South American country: abbr.
108. Russian village

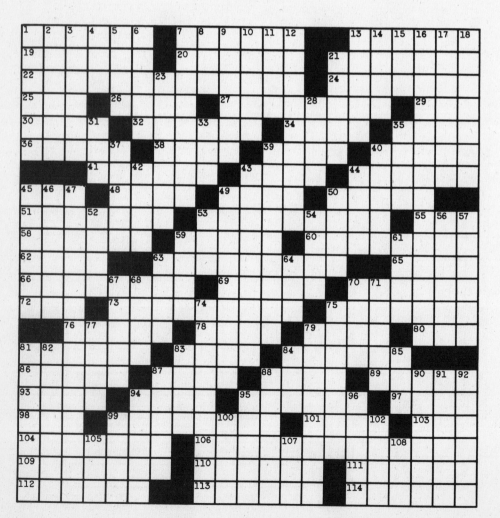

Solution is on page 290

ACROSS

1. One of the "three B's"
5. Youngsters
9. Put under control
14. Kern favorite
17. Israeli port
18. South Seas romance by Melville
19. Immature seed
20. Broadway attraction
21. Noah's son
22. Pupil, in paris
23. John —, American artist
24. Movie house: Spanish
25. French article
26. Italian painter known as "Il Soiaro"
27. Suez Port
28. Grammatical separation
30. Arm of the sea
32. Stephen Douglas' sobriquet
35. Trimming
36. Fly alone
37. Didactic novel by Dr. Johnson
40. She played "Florence Nightingale" in the movies
42. City in Nigeria
43. Author of "Quentin Durward"
44. Greek vowel
45. Bowling area
46. Perennial National League powerhouse
47. Iranian coin
48. Peccadillo
50. Remained fast
51. City on the Dnieper
52. Swindles
53. Painter known as "Lo Spagnuolo"
54. Oriental apricot
55. Britain-hater
57. The 50: abbr.
58. "Small stuff"
60. Secret police
61. Suggest for consideration
65. Twaddle
66. "Kicked up a row"
68. Visibility reducer
69. Street Arabs
72. State: French
73. Takeout
74. Box-office lure
75. Entertain
76. Cymric god of war
77. It was lost "for want of a nail"
78. Red-orange color
79. Plea at sea
80. African gazelles
82. Go in quest
83. Worst
84. Merchandising label
86. Reductions
87. Confusion; jumble
88. China and its neighbors
90. Herring's "cousin"
93. Theater district
95. Chief Buddhist center of ancient Japan
96. Deduce
98. California's Big —
99. Gudrun's husband
100. Indian corn
102. In the air
103. One-third of a Caesarian report: Latin
104. Tissue
105. Cutting tools
106. An O'Grady
107. "Picnic" playwright
108. Marmee's prettiest
109. Lacks
110. — code
111. "Now he belongs to the —"

DOWN

1. Swiss city: alt. sp.
2. "The miseries"
3. Disheartened
4. Skirt feature
5. Child in Maeterlinck's "The Blue Bird"
6. In —, miffed
7. Argumentative people
8. Bishopric
9. — sauce
10. Effective advantage
11. Problem for Perry Mason
12. Man of Yale
13. Zahnarzt
14. "— Mother," famous painting
15. "— soit qui mal y pense," motto of the Order of the Garter
16. Uses credit
18. Conway —, former film star
20. Embarrassing outbreak
26. With brightness
27. WW II battle site
29. Western Bat
31. Tried to persuade
33. Charged particles
34. "The Ballad of Reading —"
38. On
39. Bombay garb
40. Old Testament book after Micah
41. Resin
42. Steady, when on an even one
43. Citizen of old Baghdad
46. Baltic seaport
47. British naval officer who captured Gibraltar
49. Clear the field
51. Unites
52. Public fund
53. Article of virtu
55. Amends
56. Small bottle
59. Author of "Trinity"
61. Boy in Congress
62. Musical hit in 1931
63. Skyrockets
64. Wading bird
66. Arrange in a new way
67. Discoverer of Sandwich Islands
69. Convulsive effort
70. Love in Spain
71. Melodiously
74. Hardware item
76. Burn to a cinder
77. Pharaoh after Rameses I
78. Houston athlete
81. Padded footstool
82. Ancient capital of Elam
83. Remove
85. "As You Like It" role
86. Touch gently
87. Mario Puzo subject
89. Took it easy
91. Chocolate sweet
92. American Indians
93. Polynesian chestnut
94. Columnist's tidbit
97. Word with cone or gay
101. U.S. humorist
102. Textile screw pine
103. Roman way

Solution is on page 290

ACROSS

1. Bridges and Brummell
6. Stitched
10. German composer
15. Contract item
16. Asian capital
17. Heebie-jeebies
19. Bargaining and compromise
21. Considering everything
23. Linesman's call
24. Rocklike
25. Popular column topic
27. Zodiac sign
28. Typical of: suffix
29. Close thing
30. Poem divisions
31. Hurried
32. Place for convalescing
34. Set
35. Founder of British India
36. Heckles
37. Forthright
38. Large beetle
39. Finger or Great
40. Process, as sea water
41. Certain prep course
42. Velodrome vehicles
43. Launch-pad structure
44. Fowl
45. Weather in Genesis
46. Hateful
47. NASA routine
51. Danube tributary
52. Pops' home
53. Props (up)
54. Swiss canton
55. Helicopter
57. — scholar
58. Attempt
59. Afterwards
60. — McBoing Boing, cartoon character
61. Blocks
62. Dreaded
64. "I'm losing my —!"
65. Bird's-eye view
66. Dealt
67. Actress Jens
68. North Dakota city
69. Slackening device
70. Chandler's Marlowe
71. Guide
74. Potholes' kin
75. Frankfurter: var. sp.
76. Long and slender
77. Sorrow
78. One in charge: abbr.
79. Ramshackle place
80. Cotton flannel
81. Hebrew letter
82. Soiled, in a way
84. Famous surgeons
88. Without exception
89. Place for sports
90. Very bad
91. Two of a kind
92. Not one
93. "Cabaret" director

DOWN

1. Tunic
2. Like the San Andreas Rift
3. Indian rice
4. Handling
5. Basketball tries
6. "Rain" heroine
7. Geraint's wife
8. In the bag
9. Stingy
10. U.S. president
11. — Island, former immigrant station
12. Radar image
13. One: German
14. Actuality
15. Singing group
16. Divide
17. Squandered
18. Short- —
20. Moves around
22. Let down
26. Bit of gossip
29. Rear-view mirror hangings
30. Hoax
31. Burned
33. Keepsake
34. Speed
35. What muscle-men compare
37. Bowdler was one
38. Hags
39. Chinese weight
40. Small fish
41. Did a "cats and dogs" routine
42. Soft cheese
43. Old term for relished
44. Considerable
46. Covered
47. Famed prep school
48. Neil Simon comedy (with "The")
49. Does a Christmas chore
50. His —
52. Check-casher
53. Marine decapod
56. Medicine-chest supply
57. French impressionist
58. Condescend
60. Worker on a ship
61. — Bono
62. Loaded (with)
63. White House locale
64. New Orleans athlete
65. At once
66. Conditions
67. Climb
68. Liturgical headdress
70. Wisdom units
71. Brazilian dance
72. Michener novel (with "The")
73. Jittery
75. In one piece
76. Daft
79. Hit hard
80. Textile processor
83. School group: inits.
85. Macaw genus
86. Uncle: Spanish
87. Males

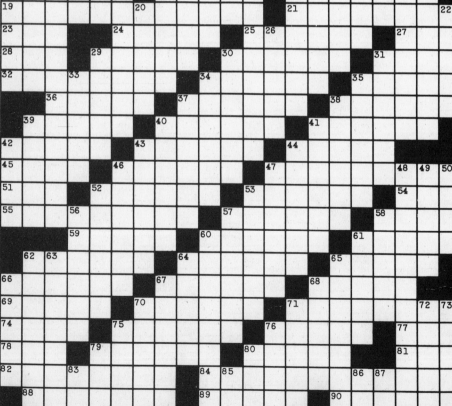

Solution is on page 290

ACROSS

1. *Start of the Split-Quote*
8. Biblical source of the Split-Quote
13. Mortar troughs
17. Commercial centers
18. Muse of astronomy
20. Hebrew religious caste
22. Ranches, out West
23. Economize
24. Armenian capital
25. Extra-innings situation
26. Tulle
27. West Coast nine
29. Adjective suffix
30. City on the Oka
32. Israeli statesman, — Eshkol
34. Louvre name
35. Shield border
36. Bremen's river
38. Form of music
40. Chip for the pot
41. W.W. I battleground
42. By way of
44. Travel (on one's way)
46. Long, adventurous journeys
49. Gives admittance to
53. Classifies
56. Stone paving block
57. Beast that slew Adonis
58. — Mahal
60. These sometimes get crossed
62. Tool for boring mine shafts
66. Creative work
67. Joshua's co-spy
69. Traffic-court revenue
71. Wrathful
72. *Middle of the Split-Quote*
76. Goliath, to David
77. Let
78. A two on a par-four hole
79. Chemical suffix
80. Ancient king of Persia
82. Area in R.W. Service's poems
84. Sand's "*Elle et —*"
85. Service points
86. Michael Romanov, e.g.
88. Korean capital
90. Far from flippant
92. Snapped
96. Famous name in fashion
98. Droop
99. Adenauer, "*Der —*"
100. Lamp-to-be, often
103. Exactly
105. Gentle heat
109. Birthday mail
110. Andy and Min
111. Risky business: abbr.
113. Mother of Helen of Troy
114. "— Yankee Doodle Dandy"
115. Crackle
118. Priest's vestment
120. Shepherded
121. Chaise —
123. Spectrum analyzer
124. District in Rome
126. "Whodunit" awards
127. Become a pensioner, perhaps
128. Brother of Electra
129. Fish dish
130. Hold back
131. *End of the Split-Quote*

DOWN

1. Present, as a gift
2. Part of H.R.E.
3. Binges
4. Affliction
5. Land of the Peacock Throne
6. Castro
7. Wine-company employee
8. Supreme Court members
9. London's Marble —
10. Island in San Francisco Bay
11. Churchill's word for Russia
12. Ape or monkey
13. Possessive
14. Egg: comb. form
15. Variegated
16. He found Livingstone
19. Amazon native
20. Native of Riga
21. Makes a debut
28. Sleep, food, etc.
31. Crowbar
33. Promise
35. Tasty mollusks
37. Washington Irving character
39. —-how
43. Perfume base
45. Beach find for the coffee table
47. Thus far
48. Workers' weapon
49. Subsided
50. Lunar or solar halo
51. Author, Willa —
52. Sauce for *pasta*
54. Small combo
55. Good judgment
59. Product from calves' feet
61. Flower leaf
63. Theater synonymous with vaudeville
64. Makes up (for)
65. Most recent
67. Indian pony
68. Large pill
70. Musical transition
73. Let forth
74. Stirred
75. Cover-up name
81. Word with Pedro or Jose
83. Night, in Nice
85. Gabriel or Raphael
87. Ziegfeld production
89. Hot water vis-à-vis jar tops
91. Inform (on)
92. Insincere; superficial
93. In fashion
94. Eccentric
95. Depressing influence
97. Converse, mod style
101. Treated maliciously
102. Will subject
104. Brew receptacle
106. *Jai alai*, in Spain
107. Short poem
108. Salad-bar morsel
110. French stoneware
112. Type of cigar
115. Some pound dogs
116. Dismounted
117. Moved swiftly
119. Form, as a storm
122. Moll or doll
125. Where Beersheba is: abbr.

Solution is on page 290

279

ACROSS

1. To the —
7. Artist's chalk
13. Develop
18. Weep
19. Destination of wasted money
20. Typical small town
22. Beyond description
24. Threat of a sort
25. Function
26. Poser
27. At the moment of
29. Curb or restraint
30. The ones indicated
32. — line
33. Menu item
35. Passepartout's employer
36. "— Western Eyes," Conrad novel
38. Rely upon
40. Velvety cloth
41. Cob's mate
43. Mme. Schiaparelli
45. Head of a religious house
46. "Snake eyes"
47. Inadmissible testimony
49. Display vanity
51. Arias
53. Let loose
54. Relates at length
55. Coddled
58. Scottish fare
59. Fire lights
60. Parts of a musical instrument
61. Gypsy word for gentleman
62. Os
63. Station initials
65. Hammer head
66. Take advantage of
67. Rustic
68. Crib
69. Behold: French
70. Bailiff's command
72. *Frite*
73. Wisconsonite
74. Ship's cable hole
75. Person obsessed
76. Valiant
77. Honey buzzard
78. At the masthead
80. Climb (a pole)
82. Common contraction
83. Like legumes
84. Foot
86. Get around
88. Dinghy accessories
89. Snappish
90. Rabelais' — of Lanterns
92. Bristling
96. Revolution time in Russia: abbr.
97. Standard of cheapness
98. Symmetrical
100. Through the medium of
101. Sure thing
103. An act whose consequences can't be foretold
107. German
108. Resort
109. Now
110. Building part
111. Adolescent
112. Perceives

DOWN

1. War vessel
2. Loan
3. "Ich dien" is one
4. Interjection
5. "Spare to us our friends, — to us our enemies"
6. Dog in "The Wizard of Oz"
7. Man of high rank
8. When one wishes
9. Item lost by "my dame"
10. Craggy hill
11. Familiar shape
12. Brought about
13. A "three wood"
14. Shofar
15. Author of "The College Widow"
16. Cooperate wholeheartedly
17. Pulver and others
19. Hardships
21. Light anchor
23. Immensely
28. Sorehead
31. "— Serenade"
33. Essences
34. Having similar qualities
35. Papal garment
37. Uncharged
39. Deliberate "leaks"
40. 13th Century family of travelers
41. Pennsylvania Senator (1897-1921)
42. Be full of envy
44. Shock
47. Brouhaha
48. Diocese
50. Moon valley
52. Exclamation indicating a slip
54. Repaired a 9-Down
55. In good —
56. Oxford features
57. Tenfold
59. Improvident one
60. Pegasus and Bucephalus
63. Camp furniture
64. Ill-nourished
65. Less svelte
67. Soporific
69. W, in Hebrew
71. Gets as a consequence
72. It shows a picture of Grant
73. Algerian seaport
75. Iamb
76. Use distractive methods on
77. Fruits
79. Conversation, they say
81. A U.S. capital city
83. Speak in favor of
85. Hooray!
87. Remove
89. Thin and metallic
91. Gather in rows
92. George Eliot's real name
94. She turned men into swine
95. They're usually double, rarely triple
97. Couturier
98. Ex-Yankee pitcher, Johnny —
99. Interjections
102. Oklahoma Indian
104. What G. W. didn't and Pinocchio did
105. She had "Three Faces"
106. — Basilio

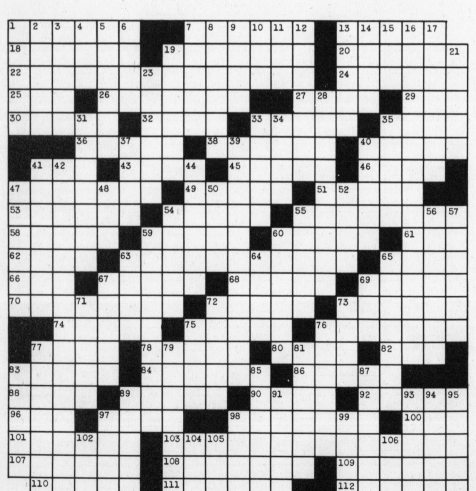

Solution is on page 290

ACROSS

1. Soothing agent
5. Substandard language
10. Fen
15. Eliot novel, "— Bede"
19. Mother of Prometheus
20. Novelist, Meyer —
21. "Tear a passion to tatters"
22. Throw a — to
23. Split
24. Author Jong
25. Tall, ornamented cap
26. Tittle; trifle
27. Line from Bliss Carman's "Spring Song"
31. Glutinous
32. Resplendence
33. Speak in a shrill and reedy voice
34. Father superior's jurisdiction
37. Lacy item
38. Newly married man
42. Baseball's MVP in '51, '54 and '55
43. Pollute
44. Homer scholar, Andrew —
45. Owl's call
46. Came to rest
47. Went after a pitch
48. Arch fellow
49. Sales pitches
51. Kind of touch
53. Abates
55. "I could unfold —"
56. Organic covering
57. Gum from a sapodilla
58. Cube root of twenty-seven
59. Gloom
60. Rebel
61. Back: comb. form
63. Put up with
66. Mediterranean region
68. Bridge call
72. "You're pulling —!"
73. Make jubilant
74. Storyteller
75. Misses Faye and Ghostley
77. Compete
78. Fragrant evergreen
79. Look toward
80. Parisian's "dream"
81. Brother of Seth
83. Enticed
84. Military corpsman
85. Railroad bridges
87. Long-billed bird
88. Sideboard display
89. Scene of an action or activity
90. Of the ear
91. Trapper's trophy
92. Burns' description of his wife
100. Wording
101. African oases
102. Lifeless
103. Vanity case
104. Basso's forte
105. Alpine crest
106. Remove in thin layers
107. Mr. Foxx of TV
108. Deteriorates
109. Gather ye rosebuds while —
110. Of bodily tissue
111. Captain Hook's henchman

DOWN

1. Brewery yeast
2. On a cruise
3. Connection
4. "Necessity is the mother of invention": Latin
5. One of Snow White's friends
6. Composer Anderson
7. Tel —
8. Congratulatory phrase
9. Growling
10. Recollection
11. Accord
12. Senator from Delaware
13. Increase
14. North Atlantic catch
15. Plato's definition for man
16. Means of access or egress
17. Reverse: prefix
18. Farina
28. Coffeehouse offering, in *Roma*
29. Shed feathers or horns
30. Gibbon
34. Behind, nautically
35. Misrepresent
36. Sell for
37. Intimidate
38. Kind of hard roll
39. "Do — a Waltz?"
40. Hill, in Italy
41. A sight —
43. Scintillate
44. Picador's weapon
47. Persian tiger
48. Tailor's measurement
50. George C. Scott role
52. Dense smoke
53. Mewl or pule
54. Reminiscent of a Roman philosopher's works
57. Storage hamper
60. Advantage
62. Pervasive atmosphere or quality
63. Don Adams role
64. U.S. President
65. Extant
67. "Little people"
68. Radium emanation
69. Costume jewelry
70. Miss Arnaz
71. On end
74. Aroma
76. Save
78. Potter
82. Apiary materials
83. Dodecanese island
84. Dissolve
86. Poetic contraction
87. Actress, Ruth —
88. Wobble
90. Writer Loos
91. Gem, in Venice
92. Vega or Procyon
93. Leander's lass
94. Sartre's "No —"
95. The same: Latin
96. Well-being, of old
97. News brief
98. Photographer's subject
99. French Nobel-prize writer

Solution is on page 291

ACROSS

1. Big show
7. Clown
12. Certain freshman
17. Seeds for bread
18. Exhausts
20. Makes allusion (to)
22. *Ex mero motu*
24. Recite like a cantor
25. Mass, e.g.
26. "Syndicate" member
27. Swan song
29. Accountant's word
30. Mono-
31. Desperation diet
32. Colorful board
33. Superlative suffix
34. Passage in a sawmill
36. Title word
38. What ILGWU members do
39. Relative of a chapter
40. — miss
41. LCI's
43. Vilify
45. Reminder of an old hurt
47. Flavor
49. Meal
51. Touching
55. Circumscribe
57. Doorstops
59. Prayer start
60. Mooning sounds
62. Take up again
64. *Cum* —
65. On one's toes
67. Brainwear
70. Word for Joan of Arc
71. Most ancient of the Greek gods
73. Goody
74. Timidly
76. Humorously, a hairpiece
77. Overcharge
79. Textile fiber
81. Us
83. More risqué
85. Fermented milk drink of Southern Russia
87. Its mascot is the goat
88. Bridge term
90. See 49-Across
92. "Post Office" item
95. Army chaplain
97. Diminish the beauty of
98. Greek "X"
99. "Humboldt's Gift" author
101. Responsive cry
102. Cleanse
105. Learning
107. 100 square meters
108. Negative correlative
109. Ermine
110. Solving aid
111. Broadway group
112. Headwear
114. Short-lived sensation
117. Drop off
118. Bird dog
119. Lathe operators
120. Shallow display drawers
121. Spent
122. Assagais or jereeds

DOWN

1. Attended
2. One under another's aegis
3. Path
4. Impress deeply
5. Caller's direction
6. Needles
7. Prompted
8. Dos Passos trilogy
9. Nikola —, American electrician and inventor
10. Routine
11. These are held by the House of Rep.
12. Comparison-shop
13. Penitent period
14. Salamander
15. Keep alert
16. Hemingway
17. Channing
19. Caresser
21. Begin earnestly
23. Numbers game
28. Fighting
31. Woody Allen works
32. Daisy's love indicator
33. Road surface
35. Alluvium
37. Auxiliary verb
39. Assayer's cup
41. Mentally quick
42. Abduct
44. Moisture
46. Hard —, diligent
48. Shooting star, e.g.
50. Tiresomeness
51. Steal
52. Opening-night call
53. Cause for an appeal case, perhaps
54. Sound from the insect world
56. Peevishly sensitive
58. Swamp plant
61. Movie bargain
63. Very offbeat
66. Maize
68. Danny or Sammy
69. Anode symbol
72. Musical work
75. U.S. native, to the world
78. Detective-story writer Wahlöö
80. Family member
82. Pin down
84. Stomach
86. Sound from the fans
89. Morning prayers
91. Fatuous
93. Defame
94. Classifiers
95. These indicate the boss of a family
96. Sum
99. Concoct
100. Resists impairment
102. Entertains
103. Paris annuity
104. Name akin to Peggy
106. Dispossesses
109. Bewildering
110. Golfer Middlecoff
111. O'Neill's Miss Christie
113. Feather scarf
115. German article
116. One end of a famous trail: abbr.

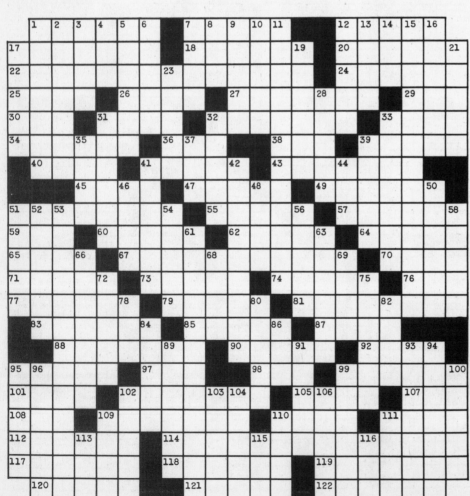

Solution is on page 291

"QUOTATION"
by EUGENE T. MALESKA

ACROSS

1. Famous park in Vienna
7. — a ghost
13. Puzzle
18. Antedate
19. Grieg character
20. Man wanted
22. *Start of a well-known quotation*
25. Port near Haifa
26. On — with
27. Of sound
28. Vex
29. Company: French abbr.
30. Ancient Greek land
32. One of the Channel Islands
33. Snooze
34. *Vidi*
36. Prying people
38. Sevier Lake product
40. Refuse
41. Disengage
43. Packs
45. "Cousin" of NATO
47. Defect
49. Rathskeller mug
51. Farm asset
55. Theoretical
59. Part of Q.E.D.
61. *Continuation of the quotation*
62. Businessman's group: abbr.
63. Cry of disgust
64. Foamed
66. Street sounds
67. Snarl
69. Author of the quotation
72. To laugh: French
73. Leper
75. Part of 45-Across
76. Wind spirally
78. Nebraska's neighbor: abbr.
79. Lightly sarcastic
81. Noted Fitzgerald
82. Judaea
84. Sneering
86. Tea
89. Kafka character in "The Trial"
90. Scenite
92. Thick
94. Brings to bear
98. Justifiable claim
101. Roman optimist's word
103. Discriminate
105. Bottom
106. Ellipsoidal: prefix
107. Bard of yore
109. Underdone
110. Spoil
111. Leonine feature
113. Strains to lift
115. Lorna Doone's man
117. Vessel for flowers
118. *End of the quotation*
122. Kind of vinegar
123. Little 'un
124. Makes manifest
125. St. Laurent feature
126. Ropelike filament
127. Bombastic orator

DOWN

1. Exact
2. Shangri-La
3. *Ne plus ultra*
4. Alphabet letter
5. Miss Millay
6. Recommence
7. Revere and Adams
8. *Enero to Diciembre*
9. *Wagon-* —, sleeping cars
10. Character of a people
11. Hippodromes
12. Fruits of ash, elm, etc.
13. Larboard
14. Pronoun
15. To-do
16. Miss May
17. Loose overcoat
18. Unruffled
21. Tearful
23. Guardian of Crete
24. Leg ornament
31. Mottle
35. Egyptian nationalist party
36. Whodunit hero
37. Lottery
39. Source of poi
40. Academic title
42. Liz Taylor role, for short
44. Very sweet: var. sp.
46. Name on a labor act
48. Isle of —, S. England
50. Reputation
52. Three-team vehicle
53. Bested on the track
54. Mail again
55. Of the people for whom England was named
56. Yellow
57. River
58. Odd job: dialect
60. Edward —, Blackbeard
64. Airtight
65. Drivel
68. Froggy
70. Seaweed
71. Soprano Farrell
74. Puerto —
77. Bobcat
80. Machine parts
83. Gladly
85. Fell into disuse
87. "Humdinger"
88. Made into a steep slope
91. Flees
93. Eldritch
95. Fanciful tale
96. Kitchen gadget
97. Accent
98. Punctuation mark
99. Puts to use
100. — CXVI, source of the quotation
102. Part of USSR
104. More flushed
108. One of the Fondas
112. Nervous
113. Chinchilla
114. Egyptian oasis
116. Tebaldi or Callas
117. Outlet
119. Girl in a song
120. Hands
121. Mrs. Gump

Solution is on page 291

CROSSWORD 2

```
SKY  CODE  SLIM
PIE  OVEN  LADE
ITS  MEW  PIPES
NETHER  TAN  AS
    EAT  RANGE
TART  MOST  LED
HID  SEATS  BAY
ERA  PACE  TORE
   YOUTH  SOW
DO  FRY  ENTRAP
ABAFT  BAA  ORE
MOLE  GASP  OIL
PEER  ONES  MAT
```

CROSSWORD 3

```
ALL  WRAP  HAS
NEE  HARE  ROLL
DISCOVER  AWAY
   SOLE  FAILS
ALONE  JOINS
SINK  CURRY  PA
IFS  RUMMY  CUB
AT  GULPS  POLE
   WISPY  COMET
   RIDER  SOUP
CUED  IGNORANT
ALLY  TOIL  COO
BED   SOPS  TWO
```

CROSSWORD 4

```
GARB  RIPEN  COMB
OBOE  EVADE  ALEE
MALL  LONGWINDED
ATLIBERTY  BOATS
DESTINY  BINS
    TATTOOED  TOP
POOLS  OPUS  DIDO
EAVE  TWITS  EMIR
SHED  RENO  SPENT
OUR  CAREFREE
   TEAM  SOANDSO
SMART  SCOUNDREL
TAKESAPART  SAVA
ALEC  CARTE  OMEN
GIST  TRESS  NARD
```

CROSSWORD 5

```
FEW  PAPER  CAW
ALE  ERODE  LIE
NIL  AID  CRIME
   CORE  BOOM
STOW  SCRIBBLE
COMES  HALE  EL
APE  TRITE  PAD
TI  HAIL  DRIVE
SCRAMBLE  USER
   ALMS  RENT
SPITE  PAW  ODD
HOD  RAISE  LYE
YES  STEER  SEW
```

CROSSWORD 6

```
LEFT
ARIA  STAB
MILL  POLO  RIB
PEEK  UPTODATE
   TORSO  ORAL
   CURT  WELL
   BORE  ONLY
LURK  AWAY
OGRE  EATEN
PLAYBALL  DASH
EEL  ASIA  OLEO
   GETS  USES
         TOME
```

CROSSWORD 8

```
COCA  MAUL  SHAME
ALAS  ACRE  CIGAR
DICKERING  ADAGE
SOO  ADD  APT  TIC
   PERI  ICE  SECT
ASHEN  ANYONE
COOL  BIS  PARROT
TON  VOLUBLY  EMU
STYLES  LEE  SPIN
   EXTRAS  PORTS
SCUD  OAR  TAXI
PAN  ANT  SOW  MOP
ADDER  INCULPATE
TREAT  NEAR  SNOW
SERRY  GENS  IDES
```

CROSSWORD 9

```
PLUM  STEMS  THIN
LANE  TREAT  WADE
OMIT  OIL  ADORES
WET  HUM  DRY  EAT
   EDIT  TREES
ODDER  FOE  SALTS
PA  NEAREST  PORT
ERR  DIE  SEA  TIE
REAR  REVEALS  BE
ASTER  DAD  BARED
   DEPOT  RUDE
AGO  ARM  HAM  TOP
PARADE  TAG  TIME
EVER  SHORE  AREA
DESK  SENDS  PENS
```

CROSSWORD 11

```
BIRD  BOARD  SLAW
ODOR  EIDER  LOPE
ALLY  ELOPE  EASE
RELISH  ALINED
   COIL  SMOG
DESERVE  PUSHOFF
AXE  TED  APE  VIA
RID         ANT
ELA  HAS  SEA  LIT
DENMARK  EMBASSY
   ARMY  TILT
DAGGER  NEEDED
ROAN  ELITE  AURA
ANTE  SATIN  SAIL
MEET  TWEET  ELSE
```

CROSSWORD 12

```
CHAT  NORM  CALF
HOLE  ARIA  CAVIL
EASE  PENT  ABASE
FRONTPAGE  TOILE
   AWED  RATTLES
FRIGID  SILL
LADEN  STALEMATE
AVER  SHALY  AGED
TEASPOONS  BRING
   LORD  DEMOTE
GALLANT  LENA
AFOOT  SHIFTLESS
MIDGE  TAME  ALTO
URGED  OLEA  DAUB
TEES  POST  ENDS
```

CROSSWORD 13

```
LIFT  MEG  WISH
ODOR  AXE  AREA
VERY  RIM  SEEM
EAT  ART  AT
   UGLY  FLEAS
FINAL  PIE  UPS
ORAL  HOT  ASIA
ROT  OAT  BITTY
   NEEDS  PURR
   ME  BOY  APT
LAMP  FLU  GLUE
ABET  RUT  AILS
DENY  YES  SALT
```

CROSSWORD 14

```
NAP  SLAM  SPOT
OIL  CORE  PILE
DROPOUT  BLADE
   TOLD  PAIN
RATED  CARTOON
ITEM  CURES  DO
GOD  FORTS  TOO
IN  SILLY  FURS
DESTROY  DENSE
   TIER  SEEN
PLANS  CONTEST
RING  SALT  LIE
ODDS  ONES  SPA
```

CROSSWORD 16

```
VERDI  RAGE  WILL
IDIOM  OVER  IDEA
SNOWMOBILE  NEAT
EAT  OWED  STAVE
   BRER  STEELER
CURRANT  NEAR
ORIEL  FLOE  SLIP
AGRA  BROWN  TARO
LEEK  LOOP  GAMIN
   TEAS  USELESS
RASHEST  DENE
ARIEL  IDLE  PEP
RANI  ANTIFREEZE
ERIC  LIEN  AWARE
RACE  BERG  LEGAL
```

BIBLE CROSSWORD (17)

```
WOMAN SHED SELF
ALONE TAKE EVOL
FISTS OPEN LIVE
EVE  TEN  YELLED
REST WEST  WE
   WOE HOT RAMS
WAGON HEROD  TOP
ARR EYO CLE ERE
RIE SOUTH  ERRED
ESAU  USE  FRO
   NO EATE TRES
SHOWER  AWE  ASE
LEVI ADAM NOISE
ORES CARE OWNER
WERE EYED SEEDS
```

CROSSWORD 18

```
TREATS  CAMEL
HOLLOW  ARENA
CEASE  ARRESTS
RARE  TRUE  SET
ITS  HOME  WARS
ME  TIPS  BAG
ERRORS  CARESS
    ERE  HARM  IN
PILE  ROSE  ONE
ODE  LINE  WINE
SEASIDE  PALER
EASES  SHAVER
SLEET  TOWERS
```

CROSSWORD 19

```
     PEA    SPOT
   COALS    CAME
  BOTTLES   ARIA
WARS   WALLETS
ERR  STEWED
BEE  HAD  MET
 SCRAP  MODES
  TIP  CAN  NAY
  DELAYS  ACE
GLADDER   INKS
RAIL  DESERTS
ACRE   DARES
BESS    GAS
```

CROSSWORD 20

```
MOWS ASHEN ADDA
AMIE NOOSE SEAN
GETTHEUPPERHAND
INSTALLS  ALLAY
    LIES  AIDE
SEERS  ESSAYIST
PERRY TAPIR  DEO
ERIS WAVES  PEER
AGE LOREN RAADS
SESSIONS  BILLY
   ENDS  ROAM
NAIVE  CONTESSA
UNDERTHEWEATHER
MOOR EIDER TORA
BALE LEEDS OPAL
```

CROSSWORD 21

```
STORES SOPS BAT
ARRIVE IDLE LIE
NO PEP LEAP ADE
DUG RAGE NIECES
APED LAND ASK
LEMON SCAN STEW
SOS EYES OWE
ASCENTS STOPPED
PEA EACH SUE
TAPS ROAM PATCH
EEL WRAP LORE
FASTER BRIM TEA
IRK AERO NOW AT
LEI SEAR GROUSE
MAN ELMS SENSED
```

CROSSWORD 22

```
MOP SPOIL STAMP
ILL LEASE TOTAL
SEA EAT THEN TO
TOTTER STOP DEW
  TOP SLEW PASS
STEM DEAR LOT
TAR SOAP CARESS
AL SLOT FACE HE
BETTER DARE POT
  RED WINS PAWS
SLAW PIGS FIR
MAP BEDS TREATS
IT SORE DIE SUE
LEMON SHARE ONE
ERASE TAMED LED
```

CROSSWORD 24

```
WET SLOTS CRY
IRE CANOE LIE
TRAPEZE ADOPT
ANY ALAS
SPIRE AD WEEP
TANK GROWN XI
RUN PROBE NIL
IS RAISE POLO
PESO ME CADET
POKE HEN
SHADE FEATURE
AID POEMS SAY
WEE THESE EWE
```

CROSSWORD 25

```
FOG SHOUT SKY
OWL HARSH PIE
REALIZE RAIDS
NINE COLT
DECAY CONTEST
OVER CAMEO HE
NOD DATES TON
OK RIVET ROWS
RECOVER WORSE
AVID COOP
TIRED COMMENT
IRE EVADE DUE
PAT SIREN ONE
```

CROSSWORD 26

```
MAPLE BOMB FADE
ALLAN OPAL ONES
COAST OUTOFSTEP
ANY ROTS WATERY
WEASELS LORE
  TOAD BEVERAGE
SPRAT HIVES SEE
LAIR FINER STAR
ARC SINGE CARRY
BEKINDTO SAGO
  NAGS DURANTE
REFUGE SENT AIM
OVERSTATE OVULE
BITE EDAM NITER
SLED DOGS SASSY
```

CROSSWORD 29

```
BREAD SLIP MATS
RINSE TALE IDOL
ODD NEEDLE SODA
WEST RAY PAT AT
  HEAL LED DYE
HOTELS SADDLE
EVE MELTS SEATS
RENT DIETS GRIP
ORDER NESTS ERE
  ENAMEL ROARED
MAD GAS BINS
AD HER HAD HOSE
SOLO ROUSES MAY
TREE EDGE ALIVE
SETS DEED GATES
```

CROSSWORD 30

```
TIGHT SWAP MESA
ALLOY PICA EVIL
BLUEPRINTS TERM
USE HACK SCENES
  SOME SPORT
TIPTOP CHOPSUEY
ASHEN GLORY ARA
SLOW TAUNT GLOW
KEN BRINE PULSE
STEALING BRAYED
BLUES TEEM
ABOARD SEAM IRE
LOOM OPENMINDED
ALTO URGE SALAD
ETHS TOOT EMERY
```

CROSSWORD 32

```
PRAISE  THEWS
RAGDOLL LAUGHED
ITALY OVATE IRA
MERE BOAST STIR
  ROOST ORIENT
CAPSULE TOUGH
ALL TEETH GHOST
STAG SNOUT TUPI
TOILE DENEB SUE
  NAVES DEEPEND
SPARED HENNA
EASE GLORY TUBA
AND DIODE SENOR
TEASING DWINDLE
LYING  EXTOLS
```

CROSSWORD 33

```
PEEP GRIME SHE
DEBAR LACES LID
ADORE ORE SLIDE
TAN DIVE SEAMEN
EL WIRE PANT
PACE HATCHETS
SPURT PUREE ROE
LARD CANTS WANE
ITS PORTS LOSES
THEORIES HERE
PENS BEAK RE
STRESS BIND MAY
PRUNE PAT ELATE
AID NOISE RISES
TOE TREES SETS
```

BIBLE CROSSWORD (34)

```
THAT HEADS BID
HATE ANGEL MADE
EDEN STONE ABLE
TO EN ESTEEM
AT PUR SPIES E
BRIBES SAID AD
AARON THINE AN
GREW BRING ELSE
AS TAUNT CROWN
IT UTTE WARNED
N EARTH LEG ER
DIVINE DO ES
EVER RAISE TOIL
BERS ERRED INTO
TRY DEEDS REST
```

CROSSWORD 35

```
SPRIG BRAID
CARAFE RAINED
ELAN TOANDFRO
SUM PEWIT LIP
AT HAVEN JADE
REFUTES DAMES
AMEN FAME
BACON GIVESUP
AVER TAXIS SI
LOU FATED MEN
SUPPOSED SOFT
ACTOUT URANUS
HOTLY PETAL
```

CROSSWORD 36

```
GLIB HID DAWG
LENA ATE EVIL
OATS SEMINOLE
WREST MATINEE
ROAD GEM
DECORATOR GAG
IRON RUG WERE
DAM DEBUTANTE
BID EAVE
ASSURED PERIL
REPLEVIN LACE
CRAG ICE ETON
HERE LET TEND
```

CROSSWORD 38

```
STEWS PROMPT
PIXIE LIBERAL
ATONE ONETIME
RAT ROWDY SID
SNIP YES SONG
ESCAPED LUNGE
LIZ KIN
SEVEN DEDUCTS
OVER RIP PART
BAN DAVIT LIE
EDIFICE ALIVE
RECOVER PACED
DEPART SPOTS
```

CROSSWORD 39

```
FARM ATTACK
TABOO CORDONS
ASSET CRYSTAL
THE OBEY EVA
TIN RUN BESET
LOCO OTTER
ENERGY EDICTS
BASIN CARL
BOAST COS PEA
EGG FIRM SAY
ELASTIC ARISE
REVIVAL RAZOR
SEDATE THEN
```

CROSSWORD 41

```
RASP CALEB WHIP
ORCA AVINE HONE
CROWSNESTS ISLE
COW PART TATTER
OWLCARS DIGESTS
HAY BORNE
SPARK WAG ELIOT
PERI HORSESENSE
IRES UMBER PLAN
LITTLEBEAR HAGS
ELEMI ARR PAYEE
ABETS PUN
HAWSERS TURTLES
ENISLE DORS ENE
RILE CARRIECATT
OLLA TWIST UVEA
DEAL SEPOY BERT
```

CROSSWORD 42

```
BEGAN STREW AWL
AROMA HOUSE BAA
LIE PROMISE ASK
MESS OVEN PASTE
LATE RICHES
ROTATE GLINT
ALIKE BRING GAY
SIDE GRAND HOPE
HOE TRADE TOWEL
PRIDE DIRNDL
AGREED CUPS
LOANS SOAP EDIT
TUG STAGGER ACE
AGE EAGLE OFTEN
RED SPEED BEAST
```

CROSSWORD 43

```
PAGES POOLS COT
ACORN ARROW ADO
IT ROBS ERE NET
NOR WETS DEAD
TRIP GOOD TRIES
SEA RUES TENT
STEALS PATH STY
OH REAL LIES EL
ARE SLOT RETIRE
PORT TORE LAD
SWEAT TART ROWS
CROP PAIL LIP
HUT AIR SNAP DO
USE SLATE SEWER
MAD TENOR SPENT
```

CRAZY CROSSWORD (44)

```
SCARE MEOW MUG
KOREA OLGA PALO
IRONS BALLERINA
FASTED PERSONAL
FLEE IFS UNUM
REVUE SEDANS
NAM LASSO ESAU
IMAGINE SMARTIE
HALL STAIR SLY
CHEESE AGNES
MAID NEE CHEF
PLUNGING STRIPE
EXTENSION HALER
TIER ONEE APTER
SIS NEST MESSY
```

CROSSWORD 46

```
COOP SMOG TAP
UNDO CUBA ADE
BEDS ODOR LIT
TWO ELECTS
STREETS AL
PIER EARNINGS
ALE OR ED OIL
RELAPSED DOVE
BE LEARNED
MISERS ETA
ADO ATOM PALM
TEN TORE ERIE
SAG EWER STEW
```

CROSSWORD 47

```
URGE TRASH
SNAIL ORATION
LUNGE BITE MA
AS SCHEME RAM
YET TASS WAGE
DIVINE BONES
ROOD TARS
BRAWN CANDOR
REDS VAST MET
ACE MARKET PA
SO HOLD RADAR
HIDEOUS EXIST
LAPSE DINT
```

CROSSWORD 48

S	P	E	A	R		S	T	R	I	P		H	A	T
C	R	A	T	E		A	R	E	N	A		O	W	E
R	O	S	E	S		L	I	D		S	P	R	E	E
U	S	E		T	R	A	P		S	T	A	N	D	S
B	E		H	O	O	D		L	O	U	D			
		W	O	R	D		P	O	U	R	S	O	F	F
C	H	A	S	E		G	L	A	R	E		I	L	L
L	A	S	T		M	O	A	N	S		P	L	E	A
A	R	T		C	O	A	T	S		P	L	E	A	T
P	E	E	P	H	O	L	E		R	O	A	D		
			L	A	S	S		M	A	N	Y		A	D
R	O	T	A	T	E		F	I	N	D		E	R	A
E	V	E	N	T		P	A	N		E	R	R	O	R
D	A	N		E	L	U	D	E		R	A	I	S	E
O	L	D		R	A	T	E	S		S	T	E	E	D

CROSSWORD 49

S	C	A	M	P		S	W	E	A	T		A	V	E	R	S
L	O	C	A	L		P	A	S	T	E		P	E	R	I	L
E	L	U	D	E		R	I	T	E	S		P	E	A	C	E
P	O	T		A	R	I	S	E		T	E	E		S	E	E
T	R	E	E		U	T	T	E	R		L	A	T	E	S	T
			L	O	S	E		M	A	P		L	O			
S	T	R	I	P	E		B	E	G	A	N		T	I	M	E
P	R	A	T	E		D	A	D		P	A	T		M	I	X
L	A	V	E	N	D	E	R		R	E	G	U	L	A	T	E
I	C	E		S	I	P		S	I	R		L	A	G	E	R
T	E	N	T		N	O	T	E	D		R	I	P	E	S	T
			A	D		T	A	P		D	O	P	E			
G	A	B	B	E	D		R	A	P	I	D		L	A	S	H
A	D	E		N	O	D		R	O	V	E	D		L	I	E
R	O	L	E	S		A	W	A	K	E		A	F	I	R	E
B	R	O	K	E		M	E	T	E	R		R	A	V	E	D
S	E	W	E	R		P	E	E	R	S		T	R	E	S	S

CROSSWORD 50

S	C	O	L	D		T	H	A	T		S	H	O	D
W	A	F	E	R		E	A	S	E		W	I	D	E
I	N		D	E	F	E	N	S	E		I	R	O	N
S	O	T		S	E	N	D		N	A	P	E	R	Y
H	E	A	R	S	A	Y		M	A	L	E			
		B	E	E	T		R	E	G	A	R	D	E	D
P	O	L	A	R		R	I	T	E	S		E	V	E
E	V	E	R		R	O	V	E	R		A	S	E	A
L	E	A		C	I	G	A	R		G	R	I	N	D
T	R	U	T	H	F	U	L		H	A	I	R		
			H	A	L	E		W	E	L	D	E	R	S
A	T	T	I	R	E		W	I	L	L		S	U	P
P	O	O	R		M	A	I	L	M	A	N		P	I
S	A	L	T		A	B	L	E		N	E	W	E	L
E	D	D	Y		N	E	T	S		T	W	E	E	T

CROSSWORD 51

B	L	O	W		A	C	E	R	B		S	P	O	T
L	O	V	E		D	O	S	E	R		R	U	D	E
O	P	A	L		M	I	S	D	O		O	T	I	S
B	E	L	L	M	A	N		F	O	B		A	N	T
			F	A	N		B	E	M	O	A	N		
A	F	T	E	R		B	O	A		S	P	E	A	K
G	L	A	D		S	I	X	T	H	S	E	N	S	E
A	U	K		M	E	L		H	E	Y		D	I	N
S	T	E	V	E	A	L	L	E	N		S	T	A	N
P	E	T	E	R		E	A	R		P	E	O	N	Y
		H	E	A	R	T	Y		G	A	L			
I	K	E		B	A	D		K	I	L	L	J	O	Y
T	I	R	E		N	O	V	E	L		O	O	N	A
C	L	A	Y		G	U	A	R	D		U	S	E	R
H	O	P	E		E	X	T	R	A		T	E	R	N

CROSSWORD 52

S	H	A	M		S	O	L	I	D		S	A	L	T	S
S	T	O	N	Y		W	R	I	T	E		T	R	I	A	L
T	Y	P	E		G	O	B	S		S	H	U	T	T	L	E
E	M		W	H	I	R		T	R	I	E	D		T	E	E
A	I	L		O	V	E	R		A	R	M		D	E	S	K
L	E	A	G	U	E		A	C	M	E		F	I	R		
		B	U	R		P	R	O	P		F	O	S	S	I	L
F	R	E	E		S	E	E	M		P	O	E	T		T	O
O	I	L	S		P	E	R	P	L	E	X		I	C	E	S
U	P		S	E	E	K		L	I	L	Y		N	A	M	E
R	E	M	I	N	D		D	E	F	T		A	C	T		
		A	N	D		T	E	X	T		L	I	T	T	L	E
R	I	N	G		F	A	N		S	A	I	D		Y	E	S
O	D	D		R	U	N	T	S		N	E	E	D		A	N
M	E	A	N	I	N	G		P	E	G	S		R	O	P	E
P	A	T	I	O		L	E	A	V	E		D	A	R	E	S
S	L	E	P	T		E	N	T	E	R		O	W	E	D	

CROSSWORD 53

		T	H	U	G		S	W	O	O	P		
	C	H	A	S	E	R		W	A	L	K	U	P
O	R	N	A	T	E		O	D	D		E	L	
L	E	D		S	T	O	R	E		A	B	E	
D	A	L	E		U	R	N		G	I	L	A	
	D	E	S	I	R	E		P	I	L	O	T	
		T	O	N		C	A	R					
S	E	V	E	N		B	U	T	T	I	N		
A	L	A	S		M	A	P		H	O	A	R	
L	I	T		D	O	N	O	R		D	I	E	
O	X		E	O	N		L	A	B	I	L	E	
N	I	M	B	L	E		A	T	O	N	E	D	
R	E	B	E	L		E	Y	E	D				

CROSSWORD 54

A	L	A		S	H	O	P			W	H	O
D	I	M		W	E	A	R		C	H	O	W
S	E	E	S	I	N	T	O		R	I	L	L
		R	I	P	S		P	L	A	T	E	
S	N	I	D	E		S	E	I	Z	E		
L	A	C	E		C	U	R	V	E		M	I
A	V	A		F	O	R	T	E		P	A	N
M	Y		J	O	L	L	Y		P	O	R	K
		S	A	L	L	Y		F	O	R	K	S
	S	P	I	K	E		M	I	N	T		
N	A	I	L		C	H	I	L	D	R	E	N
O	N	E	S		T	A	L	E		A	R	E
R	E	D		S	H	E	D		Y	E	T	

DUPLEX CROSSWORD (55)

P	A	L	E	S		R	A	Z	E	D
A	D	L	A	I		E	L	I	T	E
D	I	N	E	R	S		V	E	N	A	L
L	E	T	S		D	A	M		S	A	Y
		T	R	A	M	P	S			
F	R	A		I	D	E	S		P	I	N	T
R	O	T	T	E	D		T	R	I	T	E	R
S	T	I	L	L		A	L	T	E	R	S
S	O	L	E	S		L	E	S	S	E	R

CRAZY CROSSWORD (56)

W	I	G	S		S	L	I	P		A	B	N	E	R
A	B	I	E		H	A	T	E		M	O	U	S	E
L	I	F	E	S	A	V	E	R		N	O	R	S	E
K	D	T		T	R	A	M	P	L	E		M	I	D
		H	O	O	P	S		L	A	S	S	I	E	S
S	C	O	R	N	S		R	E	M	I	T			
H	A	R	D	Y		T	A	X	P	A	Y	E	R	S
E	R	S	E		T	R	I	E	S		L	A	I	N
D	E	E	R	F	I	E	L	D		L	I	S	L	E
			E	L	B	A	S		W	A	S	T	E	S
B	A	L	D	I	E	S		D	A	C	H	E		
E	L	E		C	R	U	S	A	D	E		R	A	P
A	L	A	C	K		R	E	V	E	R	E	N	C	E
R	E	V	U	E		E	M	I	R		L	E	N	T
S	N	E	E	R		R	I	D	S		F	R	E	E

CROSSWORD 57

W	A	G	E	S		S	O	F	A	S		C	A	P
A	D	O	R	N		T	R	A	D	E		A	G	E
T	O		R	A	T	E		R	A	W		N	O	T
E	R	E		P	O	E	T		M	E	N	D		
R	E	A	R		T	R	A	P		R	U	L	E	S
		S	I	T	S		P	I	T		T	E	N	T
A	C	T	O	R		D	E	P	O	T		S	T	Y
P	A	T	I	M	E		E	Y	E	S		E	L	
E	N	D		P	A	V	E	S		S	H	O	R	E
R	A	R	E		D	I	D		S	T	O	W		
S	L	E	E	T		L	E	F	T		W	E	L	L
		A	L	E	S		N	A	I	L		D	I	E
L	I	D		L	O	T		D	R	E	W		M	A
A	C	E		L	O	O	S	E		N	A	M	E	D
W	E	D		S	T	O	O	D		D	R	E	S	S

CROSSWORD 58

P	A	L	M		A	L	A	S		C	O	P
I	D	E	A		Y	O	L	K		A	V	A
N	E	T	T	L	E		S	I	N	N	E	R
			T	E	A		S	O	M	E	O	N	E
S	E	E		P	U	P		W	E			
L	A	R	D		S	A	V	E		S	I	P
A	S		O	P	E	N	I	N	G		N	O
B	E	D		A	S	K	S		O	A	T	S
		A	D		E	E	L		C	O	T	
S	T	R	I	P	E	D		Y	E	T		
H	U	N	G	E	R		R	E	V	I	S	E
O	N	E		T	I	M	E		E	V	E	R
W	E	D		S	E	E	D		N	E	A	R

CROSSWORD 59

C	H	A	R	T		P	L	A	C	E	D
R	O	G	E	R		R	E	P	O	S	E	S
E	V	A	D	E		E	A	S	T		S	O
S	E	T		E	R	A	S	E		P	E	R
S	L	E	D		A	C	T		B	A	R	E
			R	U	S	H		C	O	L	T	S
P	U	N	I	S	H		H	O	N	E	S	T
E	T	A	P	E		C	O	D	E			
R	E	P	S		S	H	E		R	A	S	P
I	N	S		G	L	O	S	S		L	I	E
O	S		Y	E	A	R		A	D	O	R	E
D	I	N	E	T	T	E		L	I	N	E	R
L	O	S	S	E	S		T	E	E	N	S	

CROSSWORD 1

CROSSWORD 7

CROSSWORD 10

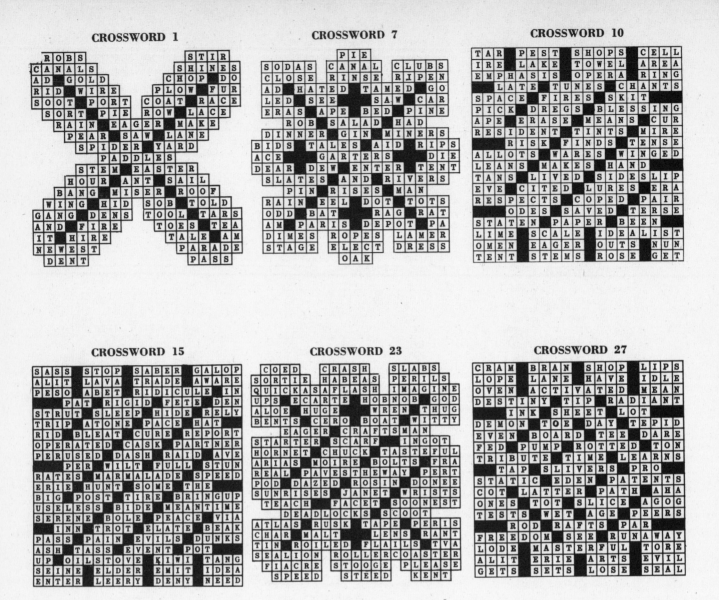

CROSSWORD 15

CROSSWORD 23

CROSSWORD 27

CROSSWORD 31

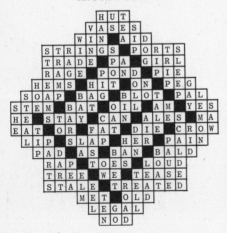

CROSSWORD 37

CROSSWORD 40

CROSSWORD 60

CROSSWORD 61

CROSSWORD 62

CROSSWORD 63

CROSSWORD 64

CROSSWORD 65

CROSSWORD 66

CROSSWORD 67

CROSSWORD 68

CROSSWORD 69

CROSSWORD 70

CROSSWORD 71

CROSSWORD 72

CROSSWORD 73

CROSSWORD 74

CROSSWORD 75

CROSSWORD 76

CROSSWORD 77

CROSSWORD 78

```
BALM  SLANG  MARSH  ADAM
ASIA  LEVIN  EMOTE  BONE
RENT  ERICA  MITER  IOTA
MAKEMEOVERMOTHERAPRIL
    ROPY  GLORY  PIPE
ABBACY  DOILY  BENEDICT
BERRA  TAINT  LANG  WHOO
ALIT  SWUNG  WAG  SPIELS
FINISHING  WANES  ATALE
TEGUMENT  CHICLE  THREE
    MURK  ARISE  NOTO
STAND  LEVANT  REDOUBLE
MYLEG  ELATE  RACONTEUR
ALICES  VIE  CEDAR  FACE
REVE  ABEL  LEDON  MEDIC
TRESTLES  HERON  TEASET
    SITE  AURAL  PELT
SHEISAWINSOMEWEETHING
TEXT  WADIS  INERT  ETUI
ARIA  ARETE  SCALE  REDD
ROTS  YEMAY  TELAR  SMEE
```

CROSSWORD 79

```
SPLASH  CUTUP  PLEBE
CARAWAY  USESUP  REFERS
ATONESPLEASURE  INTONE
RITE  HOOD  LASTACT  NET
ONE  FAST  PALETTE  MOST
LOGWAY  THE  SEW  CANTO
NEAR  BOATS  TRADUCE
SCAR  SAPOR  REPAST
PATHETIC  LIMIT  WEDGES
OUR  SIGHS  RENEW  LAUDE
ATIP  THINKINGCAP  MAID
CHAOS  TREAT  SHYLY  RUG
HOLDUP  RAYON  YOUANDME
RACIER  KEFIR  USNA
NOTRUMP  FEAST  KISS
PADRE  MAR  CHI  BELLOW
AMEN  DETERGE  LORE  ARE
NOR  MINIVER  CLUE  ANTA
TURBAN  NINEDAYSWONDER
SNOOZE  SETTER  TURNERS
TRAYS  WEARY  SPEARS
```

CROSSWORD 80

```
PRATER  PALEAS  POSER
PRECEDE  ANITRA  OUTLAW
LETMENOTTOTHEMARRIAGE
ACRE  APAR  SONANT  RILE
CIE  ELIS  SARK  NAP
ISAW  SNOOPS  SALT  DENY
DETACH  STOWS  SEATO
FLAW  STEIN  TRACTOR
ACADEMIC  ERAT  OFTRUE
NAM  OUGH  SPUMED  TOOTS
GNAR  SHAKESPEARE  RIRE
LAZAR  TREATY  COIL  KAN
IRONIC  ELLA  HOLYLAND
CYNICAL  PEKOE  LENI
NOMAD  DENSE  EXERTS
CASE  SPES  SECERN  FOOT
OVO  SCOP  RARE  MAR
MANE  HEAVES  RIDD  VASE
MINDSADMITIMPEDIMENTS
ALEGAR  PEEWEE  EVINCES
STYLE  STRAND  RANTER
```

JUMBO CROSSWORD (28)

```
CUSH  SHAD  HART  SLED
MASHER  STEPUP  RISEUP  SHORED
SOMEONE  TORTOISESHELL  HOARDED
HOP  ENSNARE  LAM  DIEDOWN  INA
ODOR  ATONE  LEFTIST  PARRY  SCOT
TIRES  ODD  COKE  SLAB  DOT  STATE
SEESTARS  COWER  SARAH  PELLETED
RETIRE  LAMED  MOLES  REELED
ILK  FARED  PAS  SLAPS  GEL
LOVE  BAYOU  CASTS  BRAWL  TAME
NEVE  NOCOMPARISONBETWEEN  RAMP
ENE  LOREN  PLAN  MALA  NAVAL  TEE
AIR  ABET  TAINT  PIERS  TIME  IRA
RELAYED  FENCE  LAITY  SEMINAR
SNIVEL  MINCE  PAL  KNEAD  SORELY
TEAR  PUREE  PAROL  GALES  NEED
CLOSET  FARMOUT  DEFEND
AFFAIRS  GINA  SNUB  REARCAR
LOOKSEE  FAZED  EGRET  AMPOULE
TARGET  DRIZZLE  DENSITY  SPELLS
IKE  ONE  IDA  TAT
LISSOM  SKITTER  GRADERS  PARITY
NEAREST  STOLE  LURES  EPITOME
GENESEE  ELLA  ASIS  DONATED
GARAND  DESIRED  SHAKEN
HOBO  BLOOD  NOTES  SPITE  YEAR
SECOND  SOLID  NED  PLACE  BRACES
CARAFES  NOSED  SLACK  BEARCAT
ORE  IMPS  ROBED  WEAVE  BRAT  EGO
USA  ROOTS  BANE  ERNE  PLUME  DEW
RATE  SOUTHERNCONFEDERACY  FENS
YELP  KNEED  YARDS  RAISE  RUST
AIL  TRAIT  DAY  RIVET  SER
PEPPER  EVERT  LEVER  FEARED
PASSEDUP  ENURE  SAVES  DECLINES
ACTED  BED  TEEN  TOUR  SEA  METAL
SKID  CYNIC  DECEASE  SPASM  RIDE
SEM  HARDPAN  ASP  REALTOR  REP
ERASURE  INONESELEMENT  EVIDENT
STONED  NOMORE  ELOISE  DECALS
EGGS  NEWS  DANE  DENY
```

JUMBO CROSSWORD (45)

```
CARTA  STARCH  SCARED  CARGO
RODEOS  CAMERA  POROSE  ABOUND
BUSMANSHOLIDAY  OCTETS  PLANTER
UNTIL  AIRED  CROOKS  REAPER  HOE
ROUT  LIKES  SKINNY  BARBER  CEDE
RUM  RILED  SWEDES  HUNTED  MAHAL
STEWOVER  PAIRED  GADGET  MANORS
AVID  DUMP  AWARDED  FUROR
SPACED  MAPPED  YIPPED  TORRENTS
HONKS  BEWILDER  SPED  BALKY  SAW
AWAY  CANDLE  CASHED  SURLY  TOTO
REX  MURALS  WAILED  CURRY  SOFAR
PRECIPICE  PANNED  TALLY  TOWARD
TONE  ESCORTED  BULKY  MINED
BOUCLE  LURED  HOTLY  WANGLING
SUGGEST  VOTER  PILOT  TARNS  LOO
ARRAS  HEAVEN  CONTROVERSY  PERT
HEIR  FELLED  PACTS  OOMPH  COMMA
IAN  FERVOR  TURKS  GRIPS  FORMAT
BUDGETEER  SOLVE  CADDO  PORTAL
ANTAS  PERPETRATES  LORNE
MARCEL  CELTS  MITER  DANGEROUS
JABBER  CHAFE  MODES  GANDER  PSI
ANILS  BOARD  BONER  PRICED  FEAT
MITE  TOPPLEDOVER  BOILER  RANGE
BAT  SHOTS  FOGEY  RALLY  EMITTED
SCEPTERS  VENUS  BANAL  DITTOS
ROOMS  PANES  FONDNESS  SUED
ASPIRE  CAUSE  REPAID  CASTANETS
SHINY  PRUNE  BEREFT  RACHEL  BUM
HALT  LEAST  MAGNET  TERROR  MALE
ELL  PURSE  GINA  PEDIGREE  MOTEL
NETWORKS  CATTLE  RETIED  HONEST
OASIS  CANTEEN  CLOD  HOST
POSTED  BANNER  TUREEN  MARSHALS
LOWER  GARDEN  RIPENS  CORNY  VOW
ADAR  HOLDIT  PUREST  LAUDS  MEDE
ILL  SORDID  CADENT  LISTS  CONGA
TELLING  GARAGE  DOGINTHEMANGER
SOIREE  ATONES  ERASER  LATTER
WEEDS  NEWEST  DELANO  LOSES
```

SKILL-O-GRAM 1

HEXAD PUZZLE

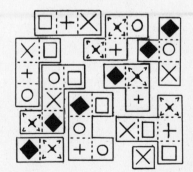

DIAGRAMLESS 1

```
LEAD FORK OFF
IDLE OMEN DOE
AGES RIDE OLD
RESPECT EARL
ONE SLY OR
STAND HAS TWO
TOLD RUG FEET
ELL HAT BONDS
ME MUG FAR
ROAR MARGINS
LAW LOAD EDIT
ATE ERIE TONE
YES DENS SLEW
```

DIAGRAMLESS 2

```
WAITS
DESTROY
RISK OWED
POET HO SAW
NEST PUP MAT
ERE GIN AISLE
AM WANDERS LA
RIDES RAM HEM
STY WET CATS
SEW AD MARS
DIPS WARM
GATHERS
NEEDY
```

DIAGRAMLESS 3

```
CHAR
HOLE BOLT
ELLA AMOR FIBS
FLED CASA IDOL
SOY KNEW GENE
WEB OLDHAND
SOAR NEAT
PREFERRED
TIES TRIM
SQUINTS GIG
OURS CHAD RAP
RIGA HIRE DATA
ADEN ERIN ACHE
STAY FLEA
TERN
```

DIAGRAMLESS 4

```
VAST
HISS ABHOR
CACHE TURRET
JOLIET TEMPO
ACTEDUP WEIR
BOER PIG INNS
SAD QUEST
GULCH
QUELL HIM
SOUL YAP GENE
ARAL TELLALL
SERIN ROOTED
HARBOR TROUT
DELVE HEMP
LEAP
```

DIAGRAMLESS 5

```
PIT SPOT
CONE PLAID
TURNADEAFEAR
NOTE COAT RIOT
OUR HERE ROE
DRAW HYMN
TEPID FEE
EDUCE EVADE
NEW DELAY
AWAY YELL
RAG TAKE SAY
TRIP OMIT VOTE
PLAYWITHFIRE
EVENT ELSE
EASY RYE
```

DIAGRAMLESS 6

```
AWL MAR
LEI SHADE
LLB MORAL
MALE AUTRY
WON RUSS
RAP LATHERY
TMEN DATE HOE
RISE EGO MOOD
AMI APER ELKO
PEDDLER WAD
ERIN RAN
EBONY DEER
DANCE ELA
ALTER NID
MIO TAY
```

DIAGRAMLESS 7

```
DAB
PALE
DEVIL
ARIEL
WITNESS SOHO
TAM CROW
SCARY OBOE
CALLITQUITS
OVAL HURTS
PORE SAG
EYED YES MAAM
CONGA
URGED
FARE
FLY
```

DIAGRAMLESS 8

```
PAST
PABLO
HARLEM NORMS
SACRED ODIUM
MOSEY CASTE
FAN FBI KEW
LOOTS ORAN
ERRATA PATCHES
DIAMONDINTHEROUGH
SATIATE PALTRY
STIR SOTOL
MAD SEC EVA
OVATE SPARE
NINON STEAMS
ADEPT PORTLY
IRATE
PEPO
```

DIAGRAMLESS 9

```
COMB
MEDIUM RITE
COLDSNAP ATOM
FALL SCREW MEMO
PANE HEART RAT
AID RAW FATE
TRY SHE POTATO
STALL BORE
PLAYFORTIME
MOON WAITS
REMEDY YES FRY
LAMP BET ROE
EVE YARDS FAST
MINT ROUTE LANE
ONTO DEADLOCK
NEON SLEEVE
KNEE
```

DIAGRAMLESS 10

```
BEAT
URGE ACT PAN
DRESS BLUE ACE
TAKEAPART SHE
LIT ERASED
PETS AIR
PRO BLOT
SLOT RATE LET
BOAT ARID POLE
HALT SPINS ROSE
ERIE LIST CASE
WED ADES PANE
EDIT INK
VAN TALE
ATLAST IDO
LIE HOLEINONE
TEN ARMY GAMES
ODD GAP SAVE
TREE
```

DIAGRAMLESS 11

```
POUR
EASE RAT TAB
TRADE DUDE HOE
OVERBOARD INN
EVA EARNED
ANEW ARE
CAR SLED
TANK FLEE AHA
SAND RAVE OWED
WORD RACED LARD
EDDY AMEN BIRD
DAY PEST DIVE
BATS ODE
ALE BASE
DEBATE ALA
AVA ONTHERISE
TIN EARS SATAN
ELK EYE SITE
TEST
```

DIAGRAMLESS 12

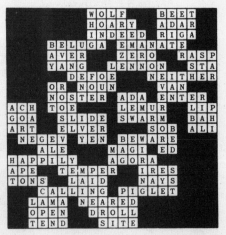

```
WOLF BEET
HOARY ADAR
INDEED RIGA
BELUGA EMANATE
AVER ZERO RASP
YANG LENNON STA
DEFOE NEITHER
OR NOUN VAN
NOSTER ADA ENTER
ACH TOE LEMUR LIP
GOA SLIDE SWARM BAH
ART ELVER SOB ALI
NEGEV YEN BEWARE
ALE MAGI ED
HAPPILY AGORA
APE TEMPER IRES
TONS LAID NAYS
CALLING PIGLET
LAMA NEARED
OPEN DROLL
TEND SITE
```

DIAGRAMLESS 13

KRISS KROSS 1

KRISS KROSS 4

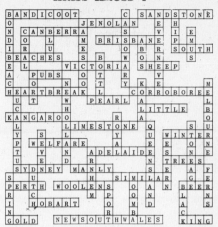

KRISS KROSS 5

KRISS KROSS 6

KRISS KROSS 10

KRISS KROSS 13

KRISS KROSS 14

KRISS KROSS 15

KRISS KROSS 2

KRISS KROSS 3

KRISS KROSS 7

KRISS KROSS 8

KRISS KROSS 9

KRISS KROSS 11

*Word list is
on page 302*

KRISS KROSS 12

FIGURE LOGIC 1

FIGURE LOGIC 2

FIGURE LOGIC 3

SKILL-O-GRAM 2

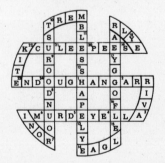

CIRCLE BACK

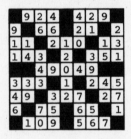

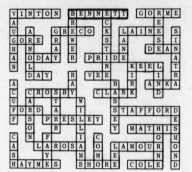

PICTURE THAT!

1. Building a dream house; 2. catching a cold; 3. dressing a chicken; 4. on the house; 5. walking on air; 6. raising the roof; 7. holding a candle to; 8. cutting a rug.

CHANGELINGS 1

1. DASH, mash, mast, malt, SALT. 2. FEED, fend, find, bind, BIRD. 3. NEWS, sews, sees, seem, stem, ITEM. 4. PORE, pone, pond, pend, rend, READ. 5. STEP, seep, sees, sues, suns, sung, RUNG. 6. POUR, pout, lout, loot, loon, loin, lain, RAIN.

WHAT'S WRONG?

1. run, ?; 2. sunny, comma after Southwest; 3. Some, students, history; 4. Either, two, is, quite, dependable; 5. swimming, prefers, winter; 6. Affect, disposition?; 7. , "I believe rain."; 8. Principal, principals, their; 9. all together; 10. School, Park?

JOHN WHO?

1. John Barrymore; 2. John Steinbeck; 3. John Alden; 4. John Hancock; 5. John L. Sullivan; 6. John Wayne; 7. John Rolfe; 8. John Smith; 9. John Philip Sousa; 10. John Tyler; 11. John J. Pershing; 12. John Wesley; 13. John James Audubon; 14. John L. Lewis; 15. John H. Glenn, Jr.

MIRTHFUL MISQUOTES

1. "Rome wasn't built in a day." 2. "People who live in glass houses shouldn't throw stones." 3. "Where there's a will there's a way." 4. "Time heals all wounds." 5. "If at first you don't succeed, try, try again." 6. "Absence makes the heart grow fonder." 7. "Black is the color of my true love's hair." 8. "Too many cooks spoil the broth." 9. "If the shoe fits, wear it." 10. "The meek shall inherit the earth."

A BEELINE FOR YOUR BUS LINE

Your street runs in a curve which you cut off by walking in the direction indicated.

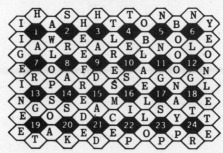

EYE SPY

The pattern with the stars (which is the second one from the left in the bottom row of box 1) is the pattern Mr. Carlton picked and is the one missing from box 2.

LADDERGRAM 1

```
1.
H  LEASH   SALE   SEA    L
A  ALIENS  LINES  LENS   I
R  GRAPES  PAGES  PEAS   G
B  BOOTHS  HOOTS  SOOT   H
O  MOTELS  MELTS  ELMS   T
R  BEARS   BASE   ABE    S
```

```
2.
V  CARVE   RACE   ARE    C
O  ADORE   READ   ADE    R
Y  YOUTH   THOU   HOT    U
A  IDEALS  SLIDE  SLED   I
G  KINGS   INKS   KIN    S
E  BEETS   BEST   TBS.   E
S  SERVES  VERSE  EVER   S
```

```
3.
S  WASPS   PAWS   ASP    W
U  AMUSES  SEAMS  MASS.  E
M  METALS  TALES  LETS   A
M  HERMIT  THEIR  HIRE   T
E  OTHERS  SHORT  ROTS   H
R  PEARL   LEAP   ALP    E
Y  MARY    ARM    MA     R
```

```
4.
F  SHIFT   HITS   'TIS   H
A  CANOE   ONCE   CEN.   O
I  DUTIES  DUETS  TEDS   U
T  STAVES  VASES  SAVE   S
H  HEARTS  TEARS  STAR   E
F  FINDERS DINERS REINS  D
U  HOUSE   HOES   SHE    O
L  GALLON  ALONG  LOAN   G
```

FIND THE SENTENCE

Words crossed out, in the order of the instructions given: 1. ice, Nicholas, placed, can, evacuate; 2. appointment, evaporate, important, stop; 3. minimum, significant, thermometer, possess, cheese; 4. on, in, an, no; 5. hat, his, the, and; 6. while, tasted, lasted, are, these; 7. live, lasted, look, let, last; 8. while, these, tried, helps, never; 9. as, or, at, is, us; 10. seedy, system, years, yes, yeast; 11. fortunate, incapable, Austria, designated, burlesque; 12. nation, noun, neon, nomination, numeration.

Sentence: Some books are to be tasted, others to be swallowed, and some few to be chewed and digested.

PINWHEEL 1

```
I H A S H H T T O T O N B N Y
I A I W R E A L E B N O L E
G L R A E R L N O O
E R O A F D E S A G N L
I P A S E A G N E
N G O S A M I L A T E
E T A K E D E P O P R E
```

(numbered 1–24)

TRIANGLE TANGLE

ABC, ABD, ACD, ABE, ADE, AFH, AFJ, AHJ, AKM, AKO, AMO, APQ, APR, AQR, AST, ASU, ATU, APE, ARE, BCE, DCE, BED, BEP, DER, EGH, EGI, EHI, ELM, ELN, EMN, EPQ, EPR, EQR, KLP, NOR, FGP, IJR.
```
```

CRYPTOQUIZZES 1

1. Seven Dwarfs, prince, the hunter, stepmother, poisoned apple, kiss, princess. "Mirror, mirror on the wall," forest animals. 2. oxfords, sandals, boots, loafers, moccasins, clogs, wing tips, pumps, wedgies, slippers; 3. out!, strike three!, play ball!, safe!, fair ball!, balk!, foul ball!, you're out of the game!, time out! 4. candle, flashlight, flash bulb, neon sign, lantern, beacon, lamp, torch, chandelier, spotlight; 5. President, governor, judge, district attorney, councilman, congressman, mayor, comptroller, senator. 6. coffee, Rio de Janeiro, Brasilia, jungles, Sugar Loaf Mountain, Sao Paulo, Portuguese language, rain forest.

NUMBER SQUARES

1.

15	27	21	17
33	5	11	31
9	29	35	7
23	19	13	25

2.

480	508	506	486
502	490	492	496
494	498	500	488
504	484	482	510

ARROW MAZE 1

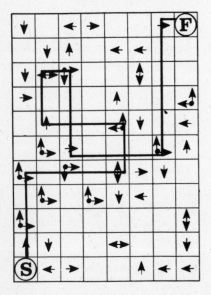

FAMOUS AMERICANS QUIZ

A. Thomas Jefferson; B. John Adams; C. Aaron Burr; D. John Paul Jones; E. Alexander Hamilton; F. Patrick Henry; G. James Madison; H. Noah Webster.

WHAT DO YOU SAY?

1. lie down and roll over; 2. overheated house; 3. wagon wheel; 4. down by the river; 5. clams on the half shell; 6. A for effort.

FIGGERITS 1

1. Great deeds are usually wrought at great risk. 2. A wise man is out of the reach of fortune. 3. The truly generous are the truly wise. 4. No one has ever drowned in his own perspiration. 5. Time is the most valuable thing a person can spend. 6. The time to face the future is the present. 7. He that rises very late must trot all day. 8. Hope is the dream of a waking man.

FUN WITH FACTS AND FIGURES

1. 31
2. $31 + 24 = 55$
3. $55 - 26 = 29$
4. $29 + 9 = 38$
5. $38 + 3 = 41$
6. $41 - 35 = 6$
7. $6 \times 6 = 36$ (once, from, who, cookies, rolls)
8. $36 \div 2 = 18$
9. $18 - 1 = 17$ (number is misspelled)
10. 17

WHAT'S THEIR LINE

1. b; 2. d; 3. a; 4. b; 5. d; 6. a; 7. b; 8. d; 9. c; 10. b.

CHANGELINGS 2

1. TALL, till, tilt, lilt, LILY; 2. PULL, pill, will, wild, weld, WEED; 3. CALL, cull, curl, curs, ours, OUTS; 4. SHORT, shore, score, scope, slope, slops, STOPS; 5. HEAT, peat, pent, pant, pane, pave, WAVE; 6. BRAVE, grave, grape, gripe, grips, grins, gains, rains, RAIDS.

BIBLE QUIZ

1. Rebecca (at the well); 2. Eve; 3. David; 4. Methuselah; 5. Moses; 6. Jacob; 7. Delilah; 8. Solomon (scales of justice).

VOCABULARY QUIZ 1

1. The woven edge of cloth which prevents raveling; 2. stone or metal disc used in hurling contests; 3. poetic word for "silent", "quiet"; 4. grain-threshing instrument; 5. main part of the shock or impact; 6. beguiling or coquettish trick; 7. to behead; 8. showy and cheap; 9. usual practice or habit; 10. a military governor of Japan who, until 1868, exercised absolute rule.

QUOTATION PUZZLES 1

1. All sorts of things and weather
   Must be taken in together
   To make up a year.
2. What this country needs is less public speaking and more private thinking.
3. There is no strong performance without a little fanaticism in the performer.
4. Modesty is the gentle art of exhausting your charm by pretending not to be aware of it.
5. A good business manager hires optimists for salesmen and a pessimist for credit manager.
6. Hope is unwinding a piece of knotted string that you suspect will not be long enough anyway.

LOGIC PROBLEM 1

From clue 3 Pablo and Pedro are, in one order or the other, the Lopez and Rodriguez boys. From clue 5, Pedro's last name is Rodriguez and Pablo's is Lopez. The Sanchez boy, from Honduras, is not Carlos (clue 2) or Juan (clue 6); he is Felipe. Carlos' last name is not Diaz (clue 7); it is Hernandez, and the Diaz boy is Juan. Pedro Rodriguez is not from Flores (clue 4), La Palma (clue 5), Danli (clue 7), or Managua, Nicaragua (clue 8); he is from San Jose, Costa Rica. The Sanchez boy is from Honduras (clue 2). Neither the Lopez boy (clue 1) nor the Hernandez boy (clue 8) is from Managua, Nicaragua, so Juan Diaz is. Pablo Lopez is not from Danli (clue 1) or La Palma (clue 5); he is from Flores. He isn't from El Salvador (clue 6), so he is from Guatemala, while Carlos Hernandez is from El Salvador. Carlos is not from Danli (clue 7), so he is from La Palma and Felipe Sanchez is from Danli. To summarize:

Juan Diaz, Managua, Nicaragua
Carlos Hernandez, La Palma, El Salvador
Pablo Lopez, Flores, Guatemala
Pedro Rodriguez, San Jose, Costa Rica
Felipe Sanchèz, Danli, Honduras

WORD ARITHMETIC 1

	0	1	2	3	4	5	6	7	8	9
1.	P	L	A	S	T	I	C/B	O	X	
2.	H	A	L	F/P	R	I	C	E	D	
3.	G	U	N/H	O	L	S	T	E	R	
4.	F	I	N	G	E	R/B	O	W	L	
5.	H	U	M	B	L	E/W	A	I	F	
6.	B	L	A	C	K/N	I	G	H	T	
7.	L	I	F	E/O	N/M	A	R	S		
8.	B	U	C	K	E	T/S	H	O	P	
9.	R	I	G	H	T/P	L	A	C	E	

THREE LITTLE WORDS

1. gag, tin, her; 2. don, man, ice; 3. mar, one, sty; 4. ran, err, age; 5. sag, ten, had.

WORD STEPS

1. PERSON, SONnet, NETwork, WORKshop, SHOPPER, (PERSON); 2. PITFALL, FALLout, OUTside, SIDEarm, ARMPIT (PITFALL). (*Other solutions are possible.*)

CATEGORIES 1

Lebanon, England, Thailand, Spain, Turkey, Romania, Austria, Venezuela, Egypt, Luxembourg. (*Others are possible.*)

NAME GAME

eagle, goose, quail, raven, robin. (*Others may be possible.*)

PYRAMID

a, am, ram, ramp, tramp

SILLY DILLIES 1

1. oil well; 2. rock and roll; 3. foot of the bed; 4. spotlight; 5. shutterbug; 6. bighorn sheep.

CRYPTOQUIZZES 2

1. seal, sheep, skunk, snake, sparrow, squirrel, stork, swallow, swan, sea lion; 2. tugboat, yacht, sailboat, glass-bottomed boat, ferry, freighter, motorboat, canoe, steamboat, houseboat; 3. nut-brown, snow-white, dapple-gray, ruby-red, bottle-green, robin's-egg blue, baby-blue, midnight-blue, pea-green, lemon-yellow; 4. scissors, chisel, hatchet, carving knife, cleaver, scraper, pruning shears, nail clipper, pocketknife, sickle; 5. El Paso, San Francisco, Orlando, Pueblo, San Diego, Buffalo, Toledo, Sacramento, Reno, Amarillo; 6. Lady Macbeth (*Macbeth*), Juliet (*Romeo and Juliet*), Bianca (*The Taming of the Shrew*), Cordelia (*King Lear*), Calpurnia (*Julius Caesar*), Ophelia (*Hamlet*) Desdemona (*Othello*), Cleopatra (*Antony and Cleopatra*), Hermia (*A Midsummer Night's Dream*), Portia (*The Merchant of Venice*).

PRESTO-CHANGO!

1. yellow, green, blue; 2. lamp, bulb, shade; 3. poet, rhyme, verse; 4. lion, den, roar; 5. phone, ring, bell; 6. pitch, ball; out; 7. knob, dial, radio; 8. drum, beat, band; 9. stage, play, acts; 10. chess, move, board.

(*Other answers are possible.*)

RED-WHITE-AND-BLUE QUIZ

1. Red Sea; 2. White House; 3. blueprints; 4. blue-plate special; 5. white lie; 6. redcoats; 7. Red Cross; 8. blue ribbon; 9. *White Christmas;* 10. whitecap; 11. once in a blue moon; 12. red carpet; 13. Bluegrass State; 14. blueblood; 15. Red Square; 16. white flag; 17. redwood; 18. redbreast; 19. white elephant; 20. out of the blue; 21. red herring; 22. blue-chip; 23. whitewall; 24. white sale.

CATEGORIES 2

1. LANGUAGES: Latin, Arabic, Norwegian, Greek, Ukrainian, Armenian, German, English, Spanish; 2. BLOSSOMS: begonia, lily, oleander, sagebrush, sweet pea, orchid, marigold, sunflower; 3. SALTWATER: shark, albacore, lobster, tuna, whale, anchovy, turbot, eel, ray.

HIDDEN VEGETABLES

1. radish (ext*ra dish*es); 2. spinach (*spin a chi*lling); 3. artichoke (*tart I choke*); 4. beet (*be et*ernally); 5. corn (politi*c or n*ot); 6. onion (Bost*on I on*ly); 7. pepper (*pep, per*sonality); 8. bean (*be an*swered); 9. carrot (*car, rot*ary); 10. eggplant (*egg, plan to*); 11. potato (s*pot a to*tal); 12. pea (ap-*pea*rs); 13. cabbage (*cab, bag*el); 14. turnip (*turn I p*assed); 15. tomato (a*tom a to*ugh).

PICTURE PERFECT?

1. no picture on wall; 2. slats on window are vertical; 3. stove dial and outlet positions are reversed; 4. no pie in oven; 5. no handle on oven door; 6. knobs on bottom cabinet are lower in B; 7. socks not in A; 8. no pocket on apron; 9. apron strings are longer; 10. earrings are double in B.

STARGRAM 1

1. inward; 2. anthem; 3. outcry; 4. consent; 5. hairpin; 6. forgave. Mystery Name: Tim Conway

SOME PUMPKINS

"Pumpkin" stands for hand.

TRAVEL FRACTIONS

1. 1/3 PEN (P) + 2/3 ARM (AR) + 1/4 IRON (I) + 1/3 SUN (S) = PARIS.
2. 1/2 NEST (NE) + 1/5 WHEEL (W) + 1/5 YACHT (Y) + 2/5 ORGAN (OR) + 1/4 KITE (K) = NEW YORK.
3. 1/2 FLOWER (FLO) + 1/6 RABBIT (R) + 1/3 EAR (E) + 1/4 NAIL (N) + 1/2 CENT (CE) = FLORENCE.
4. 1/2 BELL (BE) + 1/5 RADIO (R) + 1/2 MUFF (MU) + 1/4 DESK (D) + 1/5 APPLE (A) = BERMUDA.

VOCABULARY QUIZ 2

1. hyperbole: "hypogenous" describes substances or organisms that grow on the lower surfaces of other things, such as spores on the undersides of some fern leaves; 2. prescribed: "proscribe," as it is commonly used, means to forbid the practice of (an activity); 3. otologist's: an orologist is someone who studies mountains; 4. jewelry: a chatelaine is an ornamental chain or clasp worn at the waist by women (with keys or a purse attached); 5. vortical: "vitriolic," as it is commonly used, means caustic or bitter; 6. colloquy: a colliery is a coal mine and its accompanying buildings; 7. obsequious: "ignominious" characterizes something as shameful or disgraceful.

FIGGERIT WORD LISTS 1

1. drudgery, Walker, tourist, Steeler, daughter, Saturday, Haggard; 2. thrift, fashion, measure, cartoons, Moscow, tweeter, foursome; 3. rogues, sweetly, Yule, through, Auntie, treaty, Greta; 4. private, winners, notion, hinders, sorehead, in season, Powers; 5. lining, proven, tomatoes, Paulette, Highness, balance, smashed; 6. truth, free time, Stein, cutter, feathers, Porter, hunts; 7. Larry, starved, Melville, starter, lathered, history, mustard; 8. profit, Grandma, Peking, Mathis, wharf, woodsman, meander.

BODY ENGLISH QUIZ

1. calf; 2. eyes; 3. foot; 4. arms; 5. ears; 6. heart; 7. ribs; 8. elbow (or shoulder); 9 legs; 10. head; 11. hands; 12. "hip."

WORD S-T-R-E-T-C-H

1. stubby (6); 2. arresters (9); 3. formless (8); 4. dispelled (9); 5. partition (9); 6. sensatory (9); TOTAL: 50.

STAR SCRAMBLE

1. doughy; 2. commit; 3. ribbon; 4. heroic; 5. import. Bonus word: orchid.

PICTURE REBUS

three—re=the; sun—n+pretzel—tzel+dime—di=supreme; tee—e+stem—em=test; loaf—la=of; goose—se+d=good; man+n+zeroes—zo=manners; pins—pn=is; two—w=to; spout—so=put; cup—c=up; wig—g+thorn—orn=with; s+dome—d+bow—w+donkeys—onke=somebody's; badge—ge=bad; ones: The supreme test of good manners is to put up with somebody's bad ones.

BOWL-A-SCORE CHALLENGER 1

STRIKES: 1. governess; 2. postulate; 3. playhouse; 4. sculpture; 5. appendage; 6. makeshift; 7. austerity; 8. hackneyed; 9. pseudonym; 10. panegyric. SPARES: (*Other combinations are possible. Score full credit for them as long as they are correct.*) 1. gross, even; 2. oust, petal; 3. soupy, hale; 4. pulse, curt; 5. paged, nape; 6. thief, mask; 7. tray, suite; 8. heady, neck; 9. money, spud; 10. crying, ape.

DOVETAILED WORDS

1. turnip, retain; 2. chorus, evolve; 3. anyway, design; 4. beckon, liable; 5. propel, affirm; 6. summit, salary; 7. within, indigo; 8. garage, render; 9. mutiny, hectic; 10. ornate, veneer.

SPELLATHON

aorta, cadet, caned, carat, cased, caved, cease, cedar, ceded, dated, eased, eaten, ended, evade, orate, quart, quota, quote, raced, radar, rated, raved, raven, rotor, sated, saved, sedan, squad, squat, tease, tenet, torte, toted, trace, trade, vaned.
Less frequently used words: aedes, cacao, carte, decan, enate, oaten, ratan, saran, tarot, tetra, trave.

LETTER SWITCH

1. Keep true to the dreams of thy youth. 2. It is only when men begin to worship that they begin to grow. 3. Throw a lucky man into the sea, and he will come up with a fish in his mouth. 4. When we have not what we love, we must love what we have. 5. The race is not to the swift, nor the battle to the strong. 6. If you would be wealthy, think of saving as well as of getting.

SHARED LETTER QUIZ

1. A; 2. D; 3. F; 4. N; 5. O; 6. R; 7. S; 8. T. Anagrammed, the letters spell out STANFORD.

WORD LIST FOR WORD SEARCH 4

apples, artichokes, avocado, banana, beans, beets, cabbage, cantaloupe, carrots, celery, corn, cucumber, dates, eggplant, figs, garlic, grapes, green beans, herbs, lemon, lettuce, limes, mango, mushrooms, nuts, okra, onions, oranges, papaya, parsley, parsnip, peach, pears, peas, peppers, pineapple, plants, plum, potato, prunes, pumpkin, radishes, rhubarb, rutabaga, scallions, spinach, squash, tomato, turnip, watermelon, yams.

DEFINITIONS OF TRUCKERS' LINGO IN WORD SEARCH 5

1. apply brakes 2. speeding driver 3. cab without trailer 4. road rules 5. state trooper 6. arrogant driver 7. trailer shipped by air 8. 2-axle assembly 9. cargo trailer 10. unhitch trailer 11. small 2-cycle engine 12. driver's seat 13. reckless driver 14. drive without cargo 15. low-powered truck 16. tire 17. small warehouse tractor 18. trailer sent by ship 19. open-bodied truck 20. odd-job driver 21. trip instructions 22. bad driver 23. lowest gear 24. independent trucker 25. power unit 26. rush cargo 27. old-model truck 28. driver 29. log book 30. low trailer for heavy loads 31. mechanic 32. small yard tractor 33. pickup and delivery 34. small cab with big trailer 35. trailer loaded on train 36. cab-trailer power cable 37. turnpike 38. connect cab to trailer 39. "danger" flares 40. hit the brakes 41. bad tire 42. full truck assembly 43. small trailer 44. tires 45. pass a vehicle 46. park 47. diesel exhaust pipe 48. unload 49. driver's helper 50. tachometer 51. new driver

FIGGERITS 2

1. The ignorant man adores what he can't understand. 2. A wise man will learn much from his enemies. 3. Anger is always worth less than it will cost you. 4. A liar won't be believed when he tells the truth. 5. Water and people must move or become stagnant. 6. A simple apology will not erase unkind words. 7. You cannot teach a crab to walk a straight line. 8. The unexamined life is a life not worth living.

NOTED WOMEN MATCH

1. Louisa May Alcott; 2. Edna St. Vincent Millay; 3. Mary Roberts Rhinehart; 4. Susan Brownell Anthony; 5. Grace Kelly Grimaldi; 6. Martha Jane Canary; 7. Gypsy Rose Lee; 8. Marie Sklodowska Curie; 9. Clare Boothe Luce; 10. Cornelia Otis Skinner; 11. Margaret Chase Smith.

LADDERGRAMS 2

1.				
C	CABLES	BALES	SEAL	B
H	HEARTS	STARE	EAST	R
I	MAINE	AMEN	MAN	E
L	LITTLE	TITLE	TILT	E
L	BLAZER	ZEBRA	BARE	Z
Y	SAWYER	SWEAR	WARS	E

2.				
K	KITES	SITE	TIE	S
N	WINTER	WRITE	TIRE	W
I	LASSIE	SALES	LASS	E
T	EARTH	HARE	HER	A
T	SITTER	TRIES	RISE	T
E	BEETS	BEST	TBS.	E
D	DRAPES	SPARE	PEAS	R

3.				
S	FASTER	AFTER	FEAR	T
T	BUTTER	BRUTE	BERT	U
U	ARGUE	GEAR	AGE	R
F	FLAKES	LEAKS	ALES	K
F	FEAST	EATS	SAT	E
E	EASY	SAY	AS	Y
D	BEADS	BASE	ABE	S

4.				
H	SHAMED	DAMES	ADES	M
O	OMITS	MIST	MTS.	I
M	MOUNTS	SNOUT	OUST	N
E	SCORED	CORDS	RODS	C
M	SCREAM	ACRES	CARS	E
A	PETALS	SLEPT	LETS	P
D	DIALS	SAIL	ALS	I
E	LEASED	DEALS	LADS	E

SILLY DILLIES 2

1. Cross over the bridge; 2. Head over heels in love; 3. Shrinking violets; 4. Raising Cain; 5. Wet behind the ears; 6. Tea time; 7. Someone's (some 1's) on the phone; 8. Running around in circles; 9. Scattered showers; 10. It's all over town.

THINKING THINGS THROUGH

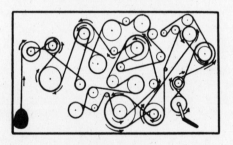

STARGRAM 2

1. shotgun; 2. beehive; 3. foghorn; 4. halfway; 5. pigskin; 6. send-off; 7. bellhop.
Mystery Name: Peggy Lee

WORD HUNT

Basin, boiler, book, broiler, cake knife, can, canister, cooker, corer, cup, dish, fan, fork, freezer, griddle, grill, jar, jug, kettle, knife, ladle, mixer, mug, opener, pan, plate, platter, pots, rack, roaster, saucer, scoop, sifter, sink, skillet, spoon, squeezer, teapot, timer, tin, toaster, tray.

HIDDEN FABRICS

1. satin (_sat in_); 2. linen (_line never_); 3. gingham (_Edging ham_); 4. nylon (_any longer_); 5. velvet (_travel veteran_); 6. denim (_garden I manage_); 7. chiffon (_much if fondue_); 8. muslin (_slam us line_); 9. wool (_two olives_); 10. calico (_Erica, licorice_); 11. rayon (_crayons_); 12. silk (_tonsil kept_); 13. cotton (_cot tonight_).

CAN YOU SPOT THE ODD ONES?

1. 3 and 5.
2. The leftmost dancer in the second row, and the fifth from the left in the third row.

SWITCH FIVE

1. throw, threw, shrew, shred, sired, sided. 2. chord, chore, shore, share, spare, spade.

QUOTATION PUZZLES 2

1. Liberty can never flourish in any nation where there is no popular education.
2. There will never be a system invented which will do away with the necessity to work.
3. Every great advance in science has issued from a new audacity of imagination.
4. How often do the events that determine our lives seem obscure when viewed from close up.
5. Better translate something from another language than compose some original nonsense.
6. Follow the middle course again and again and by repetition it becomes a fixed habit.

LETTER LINK 1

	V	
K I	R	E
L O	N	B
T G	F	

(_Other solutions are possible_)

PATCH QUOTE

The discovery of what is true and the practice of that which is good are the two most important objects of philosophy.

WORD INSERT

1. straining; 2. tribune; 3. polite; 4. ballet; 5. maiden; 6. heated; 7. douses; 8. growing; 9. market; 10. heighten.

SHAKESPEARE OR THE BIBLE?

1. Psalms 55:21; 2. Hamlet; 3. Hamlet; 4. Mark 3:25; 5. Numbers 32:23; 6. Luke 12:19; 7. Henry IV, Part I; 8. Henry VIII; 9. Corinthians II 13:12; 10. Song of Solomon 8:7.

WORD SEARCH 1

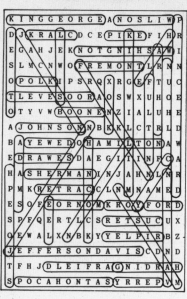

WORD SEARCH 2

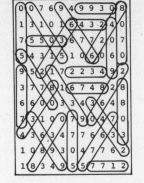

WORD SEARCH 3

Word List is on page 303.

WORD SEARCH 4

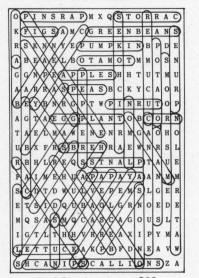

Word List is on page 298.

WORD SEARCH 5

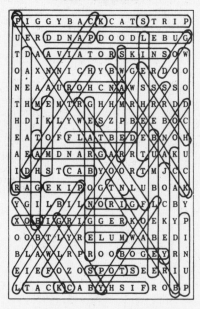

WORD BASEBALL

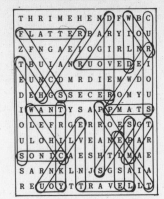

WORD SEARCH 8

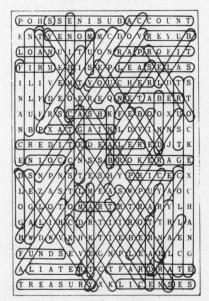

WORD SEARCH 6

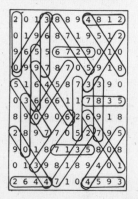

WORD SEARCH 7

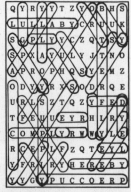

Word List is on page 303.

WORD SEARCH 9

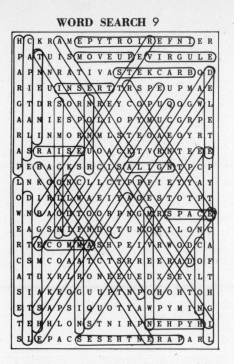

WORD SEARCH 10

FIT-IN

R	O	D	S		H	A	R	M		H	A	Y
E	D	I	T		O	L	E	O		A	R	E
S	O	M	E		D	E	F	R	O	S	T	S
T	R	E	E	S			A	S	K			
			R	E	F	U	S	E		O	N	E
T	O	W		L	O	S	T		A	R	E	A
U	P	H	I	L	L		E	N	T	E	R	S
N	E	A	T		L	A	N	E		S	O	T
A	N	T		T	O	S	S	E	S			
			L	A	W			D	A	T	E	S
C	H	O	O	S	E	R	S		L	I	V	E
O	I	L		T	R	I	O		A	M	E	N
O	D	D		E	S	P	Y		D	E	N	T

PATCH PUZLE

P	I	G		S	L	O	W		S	H	O	P
A	C	E		H	A	R	E		T	O	N	E
L	E	T	T	U	C	E		A	R	E	A	
		A	T	E		P	E	N	S			
S	W	A	N	S		W	A	N	D	E	R	S
T	A	L	K		F	I	N	D	S		O	H
A	G	E		P	I	P	E	S		S	U	E
G	O		D	A	R	E	S		L	O	S	E
E	N	T	E	R	E	D		R	I	D	E	R
		R	A	T	S			T	O	M		
O	P	A	L		C	A	B	B	A	G	E	
D	I	C	E		S	O	L	E		D	A	Y
D	E	E	R		O	W	L	S		D	Y	E

(Other solutions are possible.)

HEXAGON HUNT

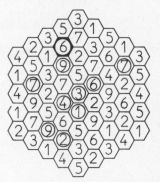

CROSS SUMS 1

CROSS SUMS 2

CROSS SUMS 3

CROSS SUMS 4

CROSS SUMS 5

CROSS SUMS 6

CROSS SUMS 7

CROSS SUMS 8

CROSS SUMS 9

ALPHAGRAM

ALIEN, RIGID, VAGUE, CANDID, PRESS, SOMEBODY, ESTATE, THORN, JUNIOR, REPRIMAND, SHAMPOO, COLONIZE, PROVOKE, OUTWIT, BORAX, ANKLE, APOLOGY, EYEBROW, FLATTEN, BOBCAT, SQUELCH, PROGENY, DISTRESS, READY, CANARY, RECENT

FIGGERIT WORD LISTS 2

1. stranger, headache, nonsense, trainer, mountain, awaited, hunted; 2. marches, William, manners, Sharon, Miller, wife, Curie; 3. Sawyer, sweaters, Hollow, Atlantic, ghosts, tiny, guilty; 4. televise, wobbled, teller, heather, blunder, health, Winters; 5. Braves, complete, ganders, strangle, tomatoes, Power, Mount; 6. pinkies, swallow, tangled, laundry, Monday, senior, poodle; 7. blackens, Chicago, caraway, Caroline, Sonata, truth, butter; 8. Texas, flavors, white lie, funnies, liniment, gold mine, Shining.

LOGIC PROBLEM 2

The Parks boy isn't the first baseman, outfielder (clue 3), shortstop, or pitcher (clue 7), so he is the catcher. He is Bobby, and the pitcher was chosen by the Cougars (clue 4). Andy and the Mason boy are the infielders (clue 1). The pitcher chosen by the Cougars is not Donny (clue 6) or Chad (clue 7), so he is Eddie. The Ogden boy, who is neither Eddie (and, therefore, not the pitcher) nor the outfielder (clue 8), must be one of the infielders, so he is Andy (clue 1). He was not picked by the Leopards (also clue 1), and neither was Chad (clue 2), or Bobby (clue 3), so Donny was. The Mason boy is not Donny (clue 1), so he is Chad, and Donny is the outfielder. Donny's last name isn't Land (clue 6), so it is Nabors, and Eddie's is Land (clue 6). Chad is not the shortstop (clue 7); he is the first baseman, and Andy is the shortstop. Andy Ogden was not picked by the Jaguars (clue 2) or Panthers (clue 5); he was chosen by the Lions. Bobby was picked by the Jaguars and Chad by the Panthers (clue 9). In sum:

Eddie Land, pitcher, Cougars
Chad Mason, first base, Panthers
Donny Nabors, outfield, Leopards
Andy Ogden, shortstop, Lions
Bobby Parks, catcher, Jaguars

HOURGLASS WORD PUZZLE

1. END (E-N from HEARTEN, leaving HEART, D from SCARED, leaving SCARE); 2. GALE (G from SONG, leaving SON, A-L from ALLOW, leaving LOW, E from SCARE, leaving SCAR); 3. SLOWS (S from SCAR, leaving CAR, L-O-W from LOW, S from SON, leaving ON); 4. CARTON (C-A-R from CAR, T from HEART, leaving HEAR, O-N from ON); 5. HEARING (H-E-A-R from HEAR, I-N-G from GIN, rearranged).

FIGGERITS 3

1. A flow of words is not proof of great wisdom. 2. Gardens are the purest of all human pleasures. 3. Proverbs are the unwritten laws of morality. 4. To rejoice in another's fortune is to share it. 5. He who forsees troubles suffers them twice over. 6. You can't get rid of a bad temper by losing it. 7. Skill to do can really only come from doing. 8. If you would speak pungently, speak briefly.

WHAT'S ZAT?

1. ZAT is D. In this case, Zat is a circle with one dot inside and one dot outside.
2. ZAT is C. In this case, ZAT is a figure which has all of its corners sectioned off, with a figure or figures in the center which match its own shape; the number of figures in the center is equal to the number of sectioned-off corners that are black.
3. ZAT is B. In this case, ZAT is a picture of two shapes, one laid on top of the other, with a dot at the center of the plane of overlap.
4. ZAT is C. In this case, ZAT is a figure with 1, 2, or 3 central lines, with identical figures on one side (or on the top side), and other (but identical to each other) figures on the other (or bottom) side; the number of figures on *each* side is double the number of center lines.
5. ZAT is E. In this case, ZAT is two consecutive letters of the alphabet touching each other; the letter which comes first in the alphabet is the larger of the two.

BOWL-A-SCORE CHALLENGER 2

STRIKES: 1. insecurity; 2. placidness; 3. originally; 4. wavelength; 5. intramural; 6. mendacious; 7. chronicler; 8. metaphoric; 9. heathenism; 10. tripartite.
SPARES: (*Other combinations are possible. Score full credit for them as long as they are correct.*) 1. cruise, tiny; 2. clasp, dines; 3. laying, roil; 4. twelve, hang; 5. natural, rim; 6. anode, music; 7. horn, circle; 8. poetic, harm; 9. anthems, hie; 10. titter, pair.

WORD LIST FOR KRISS KROSS 9

4 Letters: shin, hind, dial, alto, toil, oily, your, urge, gear, earl, life, eyed.
5 Letters: frost, stake, taken, enter, terse, serve, verse, sever, every, yodel.
6 Letters: sacred, credit, editor, torrid, riddle, leaven, avenge.
7 Letters: entrust, trustee, steeple, pleases, session, oneself, selfish, fishing, shingle.

BUILD-A-WORD

1. pathological; 2. lithograph; 3. habitable; 4. artistries; 5. patented; 6. wagonload; 7. tomorrow; 8. behemoth; 9. faraway; 10. maladies.

TWO FOR EACH

1. c, f; 2. h, d; 3. e, g; 4. g, j; 5. a, c; 6. j, i; 7. f, b; 8. b, e; 9. i, a; 10. d, h.

ANAGRAM ANTICS

1. florist; 2. butcher; 3. surgeon; 4. doorman; 5. dentist; 6. cashier; 7. janitor.
Answer: furrier

LOGIC PROBLEM 3

The number 1 record is not by Countto Five, Gotta Good Beats (clue 1), Sparkle Band, Smythe Brothers (clue 2), Diamond Needles (clue 3), or Group of Wrath (clue 4), so the Foo-ManChoose have the number 1 hit. Then, the group recording for Avocado Records has the number 2 hit and the Group of Wrath number 3 (clue 4). Neither the Countto Five, Gotta Good Beats (clue 1), Smythe Brothers (clue 2), nor Diamond Needles (clue 3) have the number 2 record on Avocado's label, so the Sparkle Band does. The Foo-ManChoose then are on the Sol label (clue 2). Neither the Gotta Good Beats (clue 1), Diamond Needles (clue 3), nor Smythe Brothers (clue 5) have the number 4 hit, so the Countto Five does. Therefore, the Group of Wrath (the number 3 hit group) is on the Nadir label, and the Gotta Good Beats have the number 5 song (clue 1). By clue 5, therefore, the Smythe Brothers have the number 6 record, and the number 7 sound is on the Heart label; the latter is by the Diamond Needles. The Smythe Brothers (the number 6 hit group) are not on Trolley (clue 3) or Speck Records (clue 5); they are on the Jemm label. The number 5 hit by Gotta Good Beats is then on the Trolley label (clue 3), with the Countto Five on the Speck label. In sum, this week's Super Seven are:

1. FooManChoose, Sol Records
2. Sparkle Band, Avocado Records
3. Group of Wrath, Nadir Records
4. Countto Five, Speck Records
5. Gotta Good Beats, Trolley Records
6. Smythe Brothers, Jemm Records
7. Diamond Needles, Heart Records

CRYPTOQUIZZES 3

1. apartment, house, studio, penthouse, loft, beach house, cottage, furnished room, bungalow, chalet. 2. tent, sleeping bag, first-aid kit, knapsack, field glasses, flashlight, rope, compass, pocket knife, canteen. 3. ranch, saloon, corral, cookhouse, bunkhouse, adobe, stable, smokehouse, hotel, church. 4. liftoff, launch, spacewalk, command module, rocket stages, lunar orbit, splashdown, debriefings, spacesuits, weightlessness. 5. don't call us, we'll call you, maybe tomorrow, another time, come back, perhaps later, try next week, not right now, some other day, stop in again. 6. Bunker Hill (Mass., 1775), Boston (Mass., 1775-1776), Concord (Mass., 1775), Ticonderoga (N.Y., 1775), Yorktown (Va., 1781), Princeton (N.J., 1777), Long Island (N.Y., 1776), Brandywine (Pa. and Del., 1777), Saratoga (N.Y., 1777), White Plains (N.Y., 1776).

CRYPTIC PLACES
Mineral Point, Wisconsin

The lead-mining industry which created this town is inactive now. However, a few century-old stone houses on Shakerag Street, built by Cornish miners, are restored and kept open to visitors.

WORD ARITHMETIC 2

```
        0 1 2 3 4 5 6 7 8 9
 1. S P E C I A L / T O Y
 2. M O N A R C H I S T
 3. P L A Y W R I G H T
 4. W H I R L / A B O U T
 5. G E L A T I N O U S
 6. W A L N U T / D E S K
 7. K I D / T R O U B L E
 8. M A T C H / B O X E S
 9. T I N Y / C H E R U B
10. C L O T H E S P I N
11. T H E / S A N D B O X
12. C I T Y / G A R D E N
13. P I N K / G L O V E S_
14. L A R G E / C H I M P
15. B I G / L U N C H E S
```

ANTONYMS QUIZ

1. b; 2. c; 3. a; 4. d; 5. b; 6. a; 7. c; 8. a; 9. d; 10. c.

LETTER INSERT

1.

C	A	B
L	I	E
O	D	E
T	E	N

2.

R	A	N
U	S	E
S	E	A
T	A	R

WORD LIST FOR WORD SEARCH 3

curious, stamp, power, row, wild, devour, road, driver, recess, scuff, flatter, reach, hut, tedious, sonic, chew, want, tricky, you, uncle, event, travel, lamps, sets, sharp, poem, mat, treat, time, else.

WORD LIST FOR WORD SEARCH 7

ally, apply, butterfly, buy, comply, cry, defy, deny, dry, dye, eye, fly, fry, guy, hereby, lullaby, lye, occupy, outcry, ply, preoccupy, pry, rely, reply, rye, shy, sky, sly, spry, spy, stupefy, sty, supply, try, why, wry.

BOWL-A-SCORE CHALLENGER 3

STRIKES: 1. contracted; 2. appetizing; 3. reactivate; 4. infraction; 5. soundtrack; 6. festoonery; 7. shenanigan; 8. tourmaline; 9. dishabille; 10. achromatic.

SPARES: (*Other combinations are possible. Score full credit for them as long as they are correct.*) 1. accent, trod; 2. ate, zipping; 3. attire, cave; 4. contain, fir; 5. actors, dunk; 6. soften, yore; 7. gains, henna; 8. outran, mile; 9. hills, abide; 10. chaotic, ram.

VACATION FROM VEXATION?

1. The old woman in "The Old Woman in the Shoe;" 2. Snow White in "Snow White and the Seven Dwarfs;" 3. "Rumpelstiltskin;" 4. Beauty in "Beauty and the Beast;" 5. Aladdin and his wonderful lamp from one of the tales in "Arabian Nights;" 6. "Little Miss Muffet;" 7. The piper in "Pied Piper of Hamelin."

FIGGERIT WORD LISTS 3

1. promise, part-time, dogwood, sniffles, snowman, forward, on foot; 2. Angeles, purple, parents, murder, flashes, Seattle, dash out; 3. wolves, marbles, western, portrait, uniforms, printer, harshly; 4. sitter, Johnson, cheerio, Foster, trains, roaster, serious; 5. forever, Whistler, without, fumbles, reforest, secures, shores; 6. glad rags, lobby, midget, Autry, fiction, opening, tease; 7. cranky, dollar, Molly, Dorado, moisten, Caroline, golf; 8. Yankee, fingers, banked, powdery, politely, future, slip out.

CROSS NUMBERS

A				B			
5	8	4	10	6	9	2	13
9	7	1	2	8	3	4	96
3	6	2	20	7	5	1	3
42	7	10		55	8	9	

C			
7	1	8	56
6	5	2	32
9	4	3	33
9	24	12	

"THE MOST"

1. b (Superior, 31,800 square miles; Michigan, 22,400 square miles; Huron, 23,000 square miles; Erie, 9,910 square miles, Ontario, 7,600 square miles); 2. Tokyo, with a population of 10,686,660 people, New York City's population is 8,085,000 people; 3. b, covering an area of 840,000 square miles. Ireland is 31,829 square miles; 4. b, covering 169,000 square miles. Black Sea is 164,000 square miles; 5. b, (in Venezuela) 3,212 feet high; Niagara, at its tallest on the Canadian side, is only 158 feet high; 6. b, the first of the Original 13 States, Rhode Island was the 13th; 7. b, at 29,028 feet high, the Matterhorn is 14,690 feet high; 8. b, founded in 1636; Yale was founded in 1701.

STATE THE STATES

1. IDA + HO = IDAHO; 2. NEW + H + AMP + SHIRE = NEW HAMPSHIRE; 3. NEB + R + ASK + A = NEBRASKA; 4. ORE + G + ON = OREGON; 5. COLOR + ADO = COLORADO; 6. WASHING + TON = WASHINGTON; 7. KEN + TUCK + Y = KENTUCKY; 8. INDIAN + A = INDIANA; 9. M + ON + TAN + A = MONTANA; 10. MARY + LAND = MARYLAND; 11. MA + IN + E = MAINE; 12. W + IS + CON + SIN = WISCONSIN; 13. MISS + OUR + I = MISSOURI; 14. FLO + RID + A = FLORIDA; 15. MIN + NE + SOT + A = MINNESOTA; 16. ILL + IN + O + IS = ILLINOIS; 17. NEW + JERSEY = NEW JERSEY; 18. R + HOD + E + IS + LAND = RHODE ISLAND

DIRECTORY DILEMMA

1. Royal Escort Service. 2. Bang-Up Weapons, Inc. 3. Precious Metalsmiths. 4. Clean Water Commission. 5. Sportsman Magazine. 6. Small Loans, Inc. 7. Fine Fabrics, Inc. 8. Domestic Employment Agency. 9. Spice for All Seasons, Inc. 10. Cape Cod Tourist Bureau. 11. Gossip Column Agency. 12. Step-In Dance Studio.

HOW WELL DO YOU FOLLOW DIRECTIONS?

1. DIAMONDS
2. G I A M O N D S
3. G I L S O N D S
4. G I L S R O R N D S
5. O G I L O S R O O R N D O S
6. O G I L O S R O O I R N D O S
7. O G I L O S R O B O I R N D O S
8. O G I L O S R O B O S I R N D O
9. O G I L O S R O B O S T I R N D O
10. O G I L O S R O B O S T I R F N D O
11. O G I R L O S O B O S T I R F N D O
12. O G I R L O S O B E S T I R F E N D O
13. O G I R L O S O B E S T F R I E N D O
14. A O G I R L O S O B E S T F R I E N D O
15. A GIRL'S BEST FRIEND

CALCULATE-A-WORD

1. adore; 2. trait; 3. child; 4. grand; 5. exile; 6. brook; 7. route; 8. throw; 9. defer; 10. renew.

QUICK! WHO WAS IT?

1. Aladdin; 2. King Arthur; 3. Socrates; 4. Benjamin Franklin; 5. Hannibal or Heidi; 6. Ponce de Leon; 7. Jason; 8. Neptune; 9. George Washington; 10. Pandora; 11. Mercury; 12. Joseph; 13. Justice or Libra; 14. Alice; 15. Mona Lisa; 16. Shakespeare; 17. Lord Nelson; 18. Henry Hudson; 19. William Jennings Bryan; 20. Paul Revere.

THREE-MINUTE QUIZ

1. a. 3; b. 5; c. 6; d. 1; e; 7; f. 2; g. 4. Score 1 point for each; 10 points if you got them all.
2. a. Utah; b. Colorado; c; Arizona; d. New Mexico. Score 2 points for each one and 10 points for all four.
3. a. Sugar Bowl; b. Gator Bowl; c. Sun Bowl; d. Orange Bowl; e. Cotton Bowl. Score 2 points for each correct answer; 15 for all five correct.
4. Grover Cleveland (the only President to serve two nonconsecutive terms) 5 points.
5. Origami is a technique of folding paper into decorative or representational forms. 5 points.
   40-45 points excellent
   30-39 points good
   20-29 points average

TANGLED JINGLES

1. The treasurer's report was brief
   (In fact, t'was but a note).
   "Since I've absconded," so it read,
   "Please cancel out my vote!"
2. Those paper plates that sit "just
   so"
   On laps, a wee bit insecure,
   Are hailed by hostesses (no dishes!),
   And by the cleaners . . . That's for
   sure!
3. The spy said, "To my great concern,
   They broke our secret code, today!"
   While Agent "X" said, "Dear, oh,
   dear,
   I hope you're only idding-kay . . .!"

WHAT'S THE NAME?

1. Robert; 2. Samuel; 3. Walter; 4. Henry; 5. Thomas; 6. James; 7. Margaret; 8. Richard; 9. Francis; 10. Harry.

INTELLIGENCE CLOCK

1. Thirty-eight, eighty-three; the letter is "e", the 5th letter of the alphabet, which leads to problem 5.

5. The only E that corresponds in every respect is No. 16, so on to 16.

16. Quarter. 25% of 16 is 4, so 4 is the next problem.

4. Rome, Europe, Italian. The letters form the word I R E, which is to be taken to problem 19.

19. I R E, when mixed with C L C, will yield the word "circle". The number of the problem enclosed in a circle is 7.

7. The number of pieces in the rectangle is 18, while there are 16 pieces in the triangle. The difference in amounts is 2, so 2 is the next problem.

2. The sentence should read "Before popping the important question, man often marks time." MAN OFTEN has 8 letters, so 8 is the next problem.

8. (a) is correct, and even if you didn't work this out, problems 16 and 19 have already been done. So the next problem is 13.

13. The wrong letter is the N in the 4th column, 3rd row of the diagram. Reading across, one letter is omitted between each letter given; reading down, two letters are omitted between each letter given. The correct letter should be M, the 13th letter of the alphabet. Subtract 4 from 13 and you get 9, the number of the next problem.

9. Pompeii is the city which was destroyed by Mount Vesuvius, which takes you to 6.

6. They mean exactly the same, taking you to 15.

15. a. letters, b. place, c. stripes, d. whole. Stripes are around 11, so that is the next problem.

11. The familiar shapes are stars, and 20 is enclosed by two stars, so on to 20.

20. The top row add up to 167, the bottom row to 157; the difference between them is 10, so 10 is next.

10. The figure has 7 sides. That number, multiplied by 2 gives you 14, the next problem.

14. China is the most populated country, with almost 900 million people. Since the answer is right, go to problem 18.

18. The missing word is "plaintiff", which has 9 letters. 9 divided by 3 takes you to problem 3.

3. 17 4's are needed, so the next problem is 17.

17. The number is 12, which appears twice in problem 20, so next problem is 12.

12. If the steel balls are all 2½ inches in diameter, not even one could fit through an opening that was only 2⅜ inches wide.

TIME SCORE

24 minutes or less
You are clear-headed and logical, a marvelous person in an emergency, for you are not disconcerted when time is a factor. You are a winner in most things you tackle, and mathematics is probably your forte.

25—29 minutes
Above average, but with a little more care you could probably have done better. You may have worked too hard at trying to beat the time score. Are you the kind of person who simply has to win?

30—34 minutes
About average. Perhaps in your daily life, attention to speed and methodical procedures are not important. In any case, you are not a competitive person and you do not care to take games too seriously.

35 minutes or more
This is below average and, if you were not interrupted several times, you are probably somewhat impetuous and inclined to jump to conclusions. Generally you do not do well in tests against time.

LOGIC PROBLEM 4

Since five people made six visits, one person made two; this was the nurse (clue 1), Jill Gold (clues 3, 5). Neither Bob (clue 1), Dale (clue 2), nor Jill (clue 5) made the first visit or the last. Since Sandy did not make the first visit (clue 4), Pat did, and Sandy made the last. Ms. Ames is not Dale or Sandy (clue 2) and must be Pat—and as a "Ms." rather than "Dr." must be the nursing student. From clues 1 and 5, then, the second visitor was the resident, Jill Gold made the third and fifth visits, Bob made the fourth, and Dr. Fry is Sandy and made the fifth visit. The resident is Dr. White, Bob is the intern, and Sandy Fry must be the patient's own doctor (clue 4). By elimination, Dr. White's first name is Dale and Bob is Dr. Evans. In sum:

1: nursing student Pat Ames
2: resident Dale White
3: nurse Jill Gold
4: intern Bob Evans
5: nurse Jill Gold
6: patient's doctor Sandy Fry

BUILD SCORE

1. blurb (45); 2. bayou (42); 3. alibi or rabbi (38); 4. broil (44); 5. blood (46); 6. buoys (44); 7. toxic (40); 8. outdo (45); 9. tutor (44); 10. butte (43). TOTAL: 431 points.

COMEDY OF ERRORS QUIZ

1. Shakespeare did not dictate, had no typist, no trains, and no cigarettes at that time (4 errors); 2. Jules Verne wrote both books; he didn't write for the movies; there were no nuclear submarines (first one launched in 1954) in Welles' day (he died in 1946) (4 errors); 3. "Dombey and Son" and "Pickwick Papers" were also books written by Dickens; "A Christmas Carol" was written in 1843 and Lionel Barrymore was not born until 1878, so Dickens could not have had such plans for it (3 errors); 4. David wrote the Psalms; Proverbs is traditionally ascribed to Solomon, though now it is generally regarded as a composite work (1 error). Total errors: 12.

1. Many folks keep on believing they're living within their means even if they need to borrow money to do it.

2. Each time I think I've graduated from the school of experience, some expert comes along and adds another course.

3. When you're fleeing temptations, be perfectly certain you don't leave behind a forwarding address.

4. There are several rules to help you gain success but only one certain rule for failure—try pleasing everybody.

5. One of the finest reducing exercises is walking—especially when it leads you right on past the refrigerator.

6. At election time, people try to learn what the candidates stand for while politicians want to learn what the people will fall for.

7. I know that loan sharks will usually be around troubled waters.

8. Years ago, men climbed the ladder of success one rung at a time. Today, they demand an escalator to be furnished by the government.

9. The head, like the stomach, is most easily infected with poisons when it is empty.

10. Anybody who believes television has destroyed conversation certainly does not have a telephone bill to pay.

11. My cash reserve is becoming very much like the old gray mare—not what it used to be.

12. Autumn lit bittersweet tapers to burn on the hilltop.

13. Love, like fresh paint, makes things beautiful wherever you spread it, but merely dries up when it isn't used.

14. Some abstract art is certainly proof that many things are often not as bad as they are painted.

15. The pretty crescent moon is a golden comma separating day and night.

16. Now that we have subcompact cars, back-seat drivers have been forced to move up front.

17. Marriage: that glorious institution held together with two books —cook and check.

18. Every king springs from a race of slaves, and every slave has had kings among his ancestors. (Plato)

19. A perverse satirist once remarked humorously, "The truth is never as black as it is painted nor as white as it is whitewashed."

20. Perhaps the public highways would be safer if we left the cars alone and inspected the drivers every year.

21. Laughter is a song rippling like a stream—running swiftly with the wind around a happy dream.

22. The greatest feats are not performed by strength; most often they are the result of very patient, careful, and constant perseverance.

23. It's a very wise person who knows what not to say—provided he doesn't say it.

24. Spiritualists are usually neither pessimists nor optimists—just happy mediums.

25. Success is certainly relative. The more of it a man may have, the more of them he'll find he has.

26. A play is like a cigar. If it is a failure, no amount of puffing will ever make it draw—if a big success, everybody wants a box.

27. Of all the billions of snowflakes that fall each winter, it's hard to believe that there aren't at least two alike.

28. There are three ways you will get something done: do it yourself, hire someone, or forbid your kids to do it.

29. Sometimes I believe the world would be much better off if we had had fewer so-called improvements.

30. Don't ever let the best you have done so far be the standard for the rest of your life.

31. The dog is called man's best friend because he offers no advice, never tries to borrow money, and hasn't any in-laws.

32. One of the best things about having an attic is that you don't have to clean it all out to make room for your car.

33. If our government used a little more pruning and a little less grafting, we might have a little more prosperity.

34. It would be great if everyone could have a second chance, but life doesn't promise man any such thing.

35. Freedom of the press is something that is really guaranteed only to those persons who own one.

36. Could people call the long-winded after-dinner speaker "gust of honor"?

37. When some individual becomes conscious that he is ignorant, he has made a start toward obtaining knowledge.

38. Sometimes what the reasoning mind would shut out, the love-ruled heart allows to enter.

39. We reach up sinewy arms of custom and tradition to choke today and impede tomorrow.

40. Some of our Washington interpreters of laws can always be trusted to take many perfectly good ones and interpret the common sense out of them.

41. Long and curious speeches are about as fit for dispatch as a regal robe with a long train is for a race.—Francis Bacon

42. Tiptoes of opposition often turn into a sound of stampede.

43. Self-discipline can be as satisfying to you as indulgence.

44. Contrary to what we all once accepted on faith, oil seems to have become a principal cause of troubled waters.

45. The fellow who always declares that he's nobody's fool probably has his suspicions.

46. Wouldn't you say it's apparent that today's taxation with representation isn't so hot, either?

47. There is not much fun in medicine; still there is really a good deal of medicine in fun.

48. It could be a good idea to call pirate ships the "thugboats."

49. Americans have more food to eat than people in any other country in this world—and more types of strict diets to discourage them from eating it.

50. I think that a man's brain originally is only a small, barren attic, and we stock it with what we choose.

51. Because you have the power of speech, it doesn't necessarily follow that you have a talent for conversation.

52. It is extraordinary to what an expense of time and money people will go in order to get something for nothing.

53. There are two expressions for which you need no translation. One is the smile of a child; the other is the wag of a small puppy's tail.

54. When a guy hasn't a good leg to stand on, he will most likely concoct a lame excuse.

55. It is quite a lot better to debate a question without settling it than to settle a question without debating it.

56. I see dark feathers of dusk drifting down to the earth tonight.

57. They say the average taxpayer works five months out of each year for the government. We doubt the paid federal workers do much better.

58. Pray ne'er a tear may dim the eye that time and patience cannot dry.

59. If nobody cared at all for you and nobody cared about me, and if we all stood alone in the battle of life, what a cold, dreary old world this would be.

60. When you growl all day, naturally you feel dog-tired at night.

61. Worry is an old fellow with bended head, carrying a load of feathers which he believes is lead.

62. Taxation's madly growing—it obviously never wanes; to find more new ways of taxing, our leaders tax their brains.

63. The guy who will not economize may eventually have to agonize.

64. Prudent advice to tourists: When in underdeveloped countries, don't drink the water; in developed countries, don't breathe the air.

65. The wind is a fiddler wailing outside our kitchen door in the inky blackness of this night.

66. My political ideal is a democracy. Everyone should be respected as an individual, but no one idolized. —Albert Einstein

67. You'll find that visits, as a usual thing, give pleasure—if not on the arrival, then at the departure.

68. If you always stop to think before you speak, the other fellow will be pretty sure to get his joke in first.

69. Mountains, at fall of night, often turn out to be molehills in the early morning light.

70. The problem with the guy who is going nowhere in particular is that he can never be sure when he arrives.

71. Men talk of taking flights to Mars who can't, with safety, even drive their cars.

72. Ability is the art of getting credit for all the home runs somebody else hits.—Casey Stengel

73. George Washington's cure-all for a bad cold was to eat a toasted onion before going to bed.

74. There is no danger of very many people developing eyestrain from looking on the bright side of things.

75. To snap out of depression, think of others. It's but little good you'll do watering last year's flowers.

76. Yesterday is like a cancelled check; tomorrow is a promissory note; today is always ready cash.

77. A wise man advised us: Don't hurry! Don't worry! We're here for a short visit. Take time to smell the flowers.

78. There's nothing much more frightening than a bubbly, bustling ignorance.

79. Ninety-nine percent of the people in this world are fools, and the rest of us are in great danger if it is very contagious.—Thornton Wilder

80. Any event, once it has occurred, can be made to appear inevitable by a competent historian.

81. If you but feed your faith, surely your doubts will starve to death.

82. Pet store sale sign: "If you need a good sympathetic companion to confide in, basset puppies are all ears."

83. Friends are like watermelons; shall I tell you why? To find a really good one, you must a hundred try.

84. Could you say hypochondriacs are those people who dislike letting well enough alone?

85. Advertising may be properly described as the science of arresting the human intelligence long enough to get money from it.—Stephen Leacock

86. Indecision is like the centipede who was told to be careful and put his best foot forward.

87. Beautiful bubbles, blowing in the cool breeze, bring back half-forgotten, wistful memories of lazy, long-ago summers.

88. Glancing moonlight bursts across the lake to strike a green-blue teal in a moonglow wake.

89. A great thing to do behind a person's back is pat it.

90. A curl of chimney smoke from the flue writes "end of summer" in the autumn sky.

91. Although very swift is our drooped eyelid's flicker, the grapefruit's squirt is even quicker.

92. The pale new moon is a dim but sublime lamp drawing many weary seamen home.

93. Like mischievous imps freshly released from restraining hands, many brightly colored leaves danced about upon our lawn.

94. Yesterday, jets scribbled white chalk marks across the sky's blue bulletin board, then erased them.

95. Nothing makes smoking more hazardous to your health than being surrounded by belligerent nonsmokers.

96. With daredevil abandon, topnotch pilots maneuver vintage open-cockpit biplanes during air show.

97. Maybe money does grow on some trees. Otherwise, why do most big banks carry branches?

98. Stork: The big bird too often held accountable for circumstances that might better be attributed to a lark.

99. Don't be deceived by popular applause; it veers with the wind.

100. If we could just get all those joggers on a treadmill, they'd grind an awful lot of corn.

101. Raging storms battered regions along our eastern coastline causing untold misery.

102. Criticism cannot hurt me unless it should.

103. Party question: Can you name a five letter word whose pronunciation isn't changed by removal of four letters? Answer: Queue.

104. Old-time prospectors maintained no bread can ever beat sourdough; prolonged fermentation produces this flavor.

105. A man must serve his time to learn almost every trade but censure—critics come ready-made.

106. Forgiveness is the subtle fragrance the violet sheds upon the brutal heel that crushes it.

107. I think people could indeed call their automobile insurance "wreck-compense."

108. Long ago I did not heed prevailing rules concerning speed; now I stand and stare aghast when careless people drive so fast.

109. Proper public relations can be aptly described as being adept in the art of treating the public as if they are not your relations.

110. Hardly anybody feels enthusiasm over scientific gadgets after he has been caught in a radar speed trap.

111. Bright, lucid similes in each dull line like glowworms in the dark will shine.

112. "Alleluia," chorused nine loud altos; "amen," countered eight tenors.

113. At a barbecue, the hamburger you get is apt to be a carbon copy of many others.

114. The bird takes a bath; then I see him flying straight to the clothesline to dry himself.

115. Some authors say the going's rough; they can''t find time to write their stuff, but others cannot be prolific unless the pressure is terrific.

116. What a pleasant sound is the merry laughter of many children as they chase the bright flashes of lightning bugs.

117. With hospital costs what they are, no one can possibly be ill at ease.

118. Adopted orphan turns childless farm couple into happy family.

119. Lush green hills form magnificent natural amphitheater for pastoral collegiate chorale.

120. Nature's rich bounty: Beautiful wild flowers grow in abundance alongside country roads.

ANACROSTICS

1. *Author:* Myra Waldo
Work: BEER AND GOOD FOOD*

"Babylonian taverns were maintained exclusively by women (apparently the world's first barmaids), with charges and payments recorded on wet clay tablets. Guests drank on credit, accounts being settled after each harvest, an early form of Diner's Club."

* From BEER AND GOOD FOOD by Myra Waldo. Copyright © 1958 by Myra Waldo Schwartz. Used with permission of the publisher, Doubleday & Co., Inc.

2. *Author:* (Sue) Spencer
Work: AFRICAN CREEKS
I HAVE BEEN UP*

"Up . . . in the African bush . . . there are no new . . . greeting cards . . . to be had, so every one cuts off the old signature and uses them over. They get smaller and smaller. The thoughtful person . . . thinks twice and devotes great care to putting his signature on an expendable part."

* Copyright © 1963 by Sue Spencer. From the book AFRICAN CREEKS I HAVE BEEN UP, published by David McKay Company, Inc. Reprinted by permission of the publisher.

3. *Authors:* (Poppy) Cannon (and)
(Patricia) Brooks
Title: (THE) PRESIDENT'S
COOKBOOK*

"As the Congressmen ate their fruit, buckwheat pancakes, and maple syrup . . . silent Cal . . . consumed his homemade hot cereal. Sometimes not a . . . word was spoken at these official breakfasts . . . Coolidge maintained he did not have to talk to Congressmen . . . Looking them over . . . was sufficient."

* By permission of the publishers, Funk & Wagnalls Publishing Company, Inc. © 1968 by Poppy Cannon and Patricia Brooks.

4. *Authors:* Myron Wood and
Nancy Wood
Work: COLORADO: (Big Mountain
Country)*

"Colorado names were born of frustration, hope, irony, and a sense of humor. Creeks with such names as Starvation, Troublesome, O' Be Joyful, Weary Man, and Stinking Water. Gulches called Poverty and Hog John. Calamity and Sewemup Mesas. No Good Park and Skinny Fish Lake."

* From COLORADO: (Big Mountain Country), by Myron Wood and Nancy Wood. Copyright © 1969 by Myron Wood and Nancy Wood. Used by permission of the publisher, Doubleday & Co., Inc.

5. *Author:* (Bergen) Evans
Work: (THE) NATURAL
HISTORY OF NONSENSE*

" 'Soft living' is difficult to define. If it means lolling on cushions and eating a great deal of custard, it probably would produce a degree of flabbiness, but there is no great need to worry. There are not enough cushions to go around."

* From THE NATURAL HISTORY OF NONSENSE by Bergen Evans. Copyright © 1946 by Bergen Evans. Published by Alfred A. Knopf.

6. *Author:* B. C(ory) Kilvert, (Jr.)
Work: INFORMAL GARDENING*

"To deter starlings . . . fill feeders with . . . sunflower seeds. Starlings have not yet learned to crack the hulls . . . and . . . will not touch them. I don't know how much longer this will hold true . . . because they are highly intelligent birds and enjoy my . . . respect as formidable foes."

* From INFORMAL GARDENING by B. Cory Kilvert, Jr. Copyright © 1969 by B. Cory Kilvert, Jr. Used with permission of the publisher, The Macmillan Company.

7. *Author:* Roger Hilsman
Work: TO MOVE A NATION*

"In spite of the great power they wield, Presidents can rarely command . . . the Executive Branch itself. President Truman, as he contemplated turning the presidency over to Eisenhower, used to say, 'He'll sit here and he'll say, "Do this! Do that!" And nothing will happen. Poor Ike—it won't be a bit like the Army.' "

* From TO MOVE A NATION, by Roger Hilsman. Copyright © 1964, 1967 by Roger Hilsman. Used by the permission of the publisher, Doubleday and Company, Inc.

8. *Author:* R(ussell) B. Nye
Work: THE UNEMBARRASSED
MUSE*

"During the twenties the motion picture brought the mass audience to a level of sophistication in manners, speech, dress . . . and social and ethical attitudes utterly unknown—and . . . undreamed of—by the preceding generation. . . . People copied what they saw on the screen."

* By permission of the publisher, The Dial Press.

9. *Authors:* (Irma S.) Rombauer and
(Marion Rombauer) Becker
Work: (THE) JOY OF COOKING*

"We have always liked the snug phrase 'baked in their jackets' to describe . . . vegetables baked unpeeled . . . but . . . at least one young cook, after encountering it, called a home economist of the local utility company and complained that her grocer was unable to supply her with potato jackets."

* From THE JOY OF COOKING by Irma S. Rombauer and Marion Rombauer Becker. Copyright 1931, 1936, 1941, 1942, 1943, 1946, 1951, 1952, 1953, 1962, 1963, 1964, reprinted by permission of the publisher, The Bobbs-Merrill Company, Inc.

10. *Author:* R(ichard) Jefferies
(1848-1887)
Work: (THE) STORY OF MY
HEART

"I hope succeeding generations will be able to be idle . . . that nine-tenths of their time will be leisure time; that they may enjoy their days, and the earth, and the beauty of this beautiful world; that they may rest by the sea and dream; that they may dance and sing, and eat and drink."

11. *Author:* V(eronica) Geng
Work: IN A FIT OF
LAUGHTER*

"A frightened woman actually phoned the Los Angeles Police . . . and in a distracted whisper said, 'There's a prowler in my back yard.' The officer on switchboard duty asked . . . her address. There was a moment's pause . . . then the woman said, 'I'd better not give it . . . I don't want to get involved.' "

* Used by permission of the publisher, Platt and Munk, Inc.

12. *Author:* E(arl) S(chenck) Miers
Work: THE AMERICAN STORY*

"Nicknames applied to Sherman during . . . his military career tell . . . of his evolution. . . . He was plain 'Cump' Sherman . . . when . . . he entered West Point. After First Bull Run, troops . . . called him 'Old Pills': but experience soon demonstrated that he was a soft touch . . . and they renamed him 'Old Sugar-Coated.'

* Used with permission of Broadcast Music, Inc.

13. *Author:* Evelyn Wells
Work: NEFERTITI*

"During the Eighteenth Dynasty . . . in Egypt . . . the toilette of any great lady was an elaborate ceremony. Nefertiti's** required . . . a supervisor of the bath, a first lady of the eye pencil . . . a keeper of the myrrh, a guardian of jewel boxes, a tender of oil jars."

* From NEFERTITI by Evelyn Wells. Copyright © 1964 by Evelyn Wells. Used by permission of the publisher, Doubleday & Company, Inc.
** Nefertiti was the hauntingly beautiful queen who, with her husband, ruled Egypt in the 14th century B.C.

14. *Author:* Florence Thomas
Work: VOTE, OR ELSE!*

"Belgium has universal suffrage like the United States. Unfortunately, not all U.S. citizens avail themselves of this privilege. Belgians, on the other hand, probably attach the utmost importance to exercising this right . . . especially as they must vote or get fined."

* Used by permission of the author.

15. *Author:* W(ilma) Dykeman
Work: LOOK TO THIS DAY*

"The simple life breaks a fresh crust of bread, and gratefully finds nourishment for the spirit . . . The simple life discovers a clump of fragile . . . ferns flourishing in a winter woods, and happily acknowledges the wonder of all living things."

* Used by permission of Holt, Rinehart and Winston, Inc. Copyright © 1968 by Wilma Dykeman Stokely.

16. *Author:* E(leanor) B. Heady
    Work: COAT OF THE EARTH*

"Grass has been called the 'forgiveness of nature.' It covers our parks, the yards and gardens around our houses and the parking strips nevt to our streets. It heals the scars of our roadsides, growing quickly to soften the sharp outlines of cuts into the earth's surface."

Used by permission of W. W. Norton & Company, Inc., © 1968 by Eleanor B. Heady.

17. *Author:* Alistair Cooke
    Work: ONE MAN'S AMERICA*

"The geography of Long Island is easy to describe. It is a flat fish lying northeast of New York City parallel with the Connecticut shore. Its nose burrows into Manhattan . . . its tail, a hundred miles out to sea, divided into two forks . . . as distinct as those on a tarpon."

Copyright 1951, 1952 by Alistair Cooke. Used by permission of the publisher, Alfred Knopf.

18. *Author:* Vance Packard
    Work: (THE) NAKED SOCIETY*

"A picturesque example of Soviet advances in miniaturization was discovered accidentally by a U.S. military attache at a Moscow bar when he picked up a martini not intended for him. The "olive" in it contained a transmitter, and the tiny toothpick stuck in it was an antenna."

Copyright © 1964 by Vance Packard. From the book THE NAKED SOCIETY, published by David McKay Company, Inc. Reprinted by permission of the publisher.

BOWL-A-SCORE CHALLENGER 4

STRIKES: 1. important; 2. alienated; 3. outspoken; 4. implicate; 5. obedience; 6. buckwheat; 7. scavenger; 8. venerable; 9. anarchist; 10. judiciary.

SPARES: (*Other combinations are possible. Score full credit for them as long as they are correct.*) 1. print, moat; 2. dial, eaten; 3. spook, tune; 4. limit, pace; 5. bode, niece; 6. whack, tube; 7. crag, seven; 8. rebel, vane; 9. chain, star; 10. arid, juicy.

CODE-A-GRAPH SENTENCE

You'll find that it's a wise man who will save something for a rainy day, and here's one thing that some people are very glad to have put up.

KEY-LETTER SCORE 1

The key letter is "e." 1. create; 2. bleach; 3. omelet; 4. please; 5. poetic; 6. overdo; 7. energy; 8. crease; 9. wreath; 10. pierce.
(*Other words are possible.*)

KEY POINTS 1

1. forest (11); 2. slant (10); 3. neutral (12); 4. anthem (11); 5. penalty (12); 6. allow (10); 7. racket (11). TOTAL: 77 points.

MYSTERY DUO

1. THE CASE OF THE SANTA BARBARA TREASURE
The map was dated 1556, but Prufrock knew that the fabled *Santa Barbara* sank in the mid-17th century. Since 1556 was in the 16th century, Prufrock saw that the map would have had to have been drawn nearly 100 years before the *Santa Barbara* sank. Also, Prufrock knew that the ship sank southwest of the Bahamas while the map had the site to the southeast of the islands.

2. THE CASE OF THE CRYPTIC CLUES: The burglar is Michael Smith. Clues: victims were Smith, Meister, Icabod, Thibadeau, Harrison, spelling SMITH. Items taken, map, ice cream, cash, hat, aspirin, emeralds, ladle, spelling Michael; items in the bag anagram into michael, and the message, CLAIM HE THIS, M. anagrams into Michael Smith.

SYLLABLE SAYING

1. taxi; 2. organic; 3. embark; 4. Newton; 5. judo; 6. oversight; 7. yogurt; 8. telegraph; 9. harmonize; 10. elf; 11. final; 12. Romeo; 13. undertow; 14. icicle; 15. tailor; 16. pajamas. "To enjoy the fruit, pick not the flowers."

KEY-LETTER SCORE 2

Our key letter is U. 1. around; 2. return; 3. salute; 4. engulf; 5. reduce; 6. allude; 7. insult; 8. ritual; 9. thrust; 10. deputy. TOTAL: 150 points.
(*Other solutions may be possible.*)

CODED CLICHES

1. d; 2. a; 3. g; 4. e; 5. b; 6. h; 7. f; 8. c.

ANAGRAM QUOTE

1. atom; 2. laid; 3. itch; 4. ache; 5. ring; 6. nave; 7. earl; 8. ever; 9. dire; 10. sail; 11. avid; 12. gear; 13. ogle; 14. once; 15. dive; 16. mare; 17. earn; 18. muse; 19. ours; 20. room; 21. yarn. "A liar needs a good memory."

MENU MATCH-UP

1. e; 2. j; 3. o; 4. g; 5. i; 6. t; 7. r; 8. a; 9. c; 10. q; 11. p; 12. f; 13. s; 14. b; 15. n; 16. d; 17. h; 18. l; 19. m; 20. k.

NUMBER WORD STAR

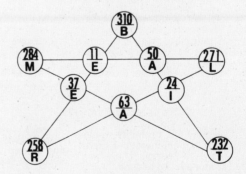

CRYPTOQUIZZES 4

1. stamps, postal cards, aerograms, registered letters, money orders, "wanted" posters, postage meters, windows. 2. piers, ships, anchors, seamen, fishermen, shipyards, gangplanks, longshoremen, dry docks, cargo. 3. salmon, salami, spinach, spaghetti, spareribs, sausage, scallops, strawberries, squash, steak. 4. Dangerous, Jezebel, Dark Victory, Juarez, Now, Voyager, Watch on the Rhine, A Stolen Life, The Petrified Forest. 5. tents, sand, cactus, oasis, camels, rattlesnakes, pack mules, campsite, caravan, vegetation. 6. gem, marquise cut, hardest mineral, pure carbon, April's birthstone, found in South Africa, facets, sparkle.

KEY POINTS 2

1. carrot (11); 2. alias (10); 3. freedom (12); 4. trance (11); 5. lighten (12); 6. place (10); 7. settle (11). Total: 77.

NUMBERAMA

B. 28 (× 2 −10 × 2 −12 × 2 −14 × 2 −16)
C. 18 (÷ 3 ÷ 3 + 6 + 6 ÷ 3 ÷ 3 + 6 + 6)
D. 22 (−18 × 2 −16 ×11 −14 × 2 −12 ×11)
E. 40 (× 6 −24 −16 × 5 −14 −16 × 4 − 4 −16)
F. 5 (+26 ÷ 9 +28 ÷ 7 +30 ÷ 5 +32 ÷ 3)
G. 2 (× 3 + 7 −11 −15 ×19 +23 −27 −31)
H. 19 (+ 5 +13 ÷ 5 + 4 +13 ÷ 4 + 3 +13 ÷ 3)
I. 46 (−21 − 7 +24 + 8 −27 − 9 +30 +10)
J. 3 (÷ 8 × 7 +13 ÷ 9 × 6 +12 ÷10 × 5 +11)
K. 9 (×29 −22 −16 −11 × 7 − 4 − 2 − 1)

FIND-A-WORD

1. Rustle (6); 2. veils (5); 3. nuclear (7); 4. gavels (6); 5. tilting (7); 6. blouse (6); 7. prelate (7); 8. armored (7); 9. deprive (7); 10. platinum (8). TOTAL: 66

WORD ASSOCIATION

1. Wave, 2. animals, 3. blade, 4. crest, 5. title, 6. string, 7. corn, 8. stem, 9. shell, 10. key, 11. roots, 12. spots.

CREATIVE GREATS QUIZ

1. Horatio Alger, Jr.; 2. John Keats; 3. Henry James (whose brother was William James); 4. Truman Capote ("Breakfast at Tiffany's" and "In Cold Blood"); 5. Lewis Carroll ("Alice's Adventures in Wonderland"); 6. Emily Dickinson; 7. Johann Sebastian Bach; 8. Pablo Picasso; 9. Sigmund Freud; 10. Joseph Conrad; 11. Isadora Duncan; 12. Gertrude Stein; 13. Dashiell Hammett; 14. Eugene O'Neill; 15. Sarah Bernhardt.

SEVEN CLUES QUIZ

A. Sahara Desert; B. Venice; C. Nobel Prize Awards; D. Pablo Picasso; E. Mt. Kilimanjaro; F. Golden Gate.

VOCABULADDER

1. AESTHETIC: Sensitive to art and beauty; showing good taste.
2. BLASPHEMY: Profane or contemptuous speech or writing.
3. CALUMNY: A false and malicious statement about a person; slander.
4. DELINEATE: Trace the outline of; sketch.
5. HIERARCHY: A group of persons or things arranged in order of rank.
6. RANCOROUS: Full of bitter hate or malice.
7. MAELSTROM: Any large or violent whirlpool.
8. INCESSANT: Continuing without stopping; constant.
9. POTPOURRI: A mixture of dried flower petals and spices; any medley.

BAKER'S DOZEN

1. wood; 2. ten; 3. Eddie Murphy; 4. beautiful mahogany furniture; 5. mandrill: it is a primate; 6. this sentence doesn't contain the letter "e," the most frequently used letter in English; 7. fresh water; slab ice and ice fields are frozen sea water, but a true iceberg is broken off from a glacier; 8. yes: it comes from *"dent de lion,"* Old French for "lion's tooth", so called because of the outline of its leaves; 9. Spain; the U.S.S.R.; Belgium; 10. No: it is only 21% oxygen; 78% is nitrogen; 11. according to the U.S. Department of Agriculture, about 62 pounds; 12. the Bank of England, which stands on London's Threadneedle Street; 13. Maryland.

SCRAMBLED SENTENCES

Last year, more Americans went to symphony concerts than to baseball games. This may be viewed by some people as an alarming statistic, but it's likely that both baseball and the country will survive.

SHORT SCORE

Our words: quilt, buy, beret.
Scoring:
$Q_2 + U_2 + I_1^* + L_3 + T_1 = 18$ (rule 3)
$B_2 + U_5 + Y_1 = 25$ (rule 3)
$B_2 + E_1 + R_1 + E_3 + T_4 = 11$
Total: 54 points

TIME FOR THE ASKING

1. 7:12 p.m. Let T be the time when Jane met the Professor. The time from midnight until then is T (the time since noon) + 12 (because it is evening). The time until midnight is 12 − T. The time of their meeting can be written as T = ¼ (T + 12) + ½ (12 − T). T works out to be 7 1/5, or 7:12 in the evening. 2. 9:36 a.m. Let T be the time Jane arrived in class in the morning. Now the number of hours since midnight is T. The time until midnight is the number of hours until noon plus another 12 hours, or 24 − T. The time Jane arrived at class can be written as T = ¼ (T) + ½ (24 − T). T works out to be 9 3/5, or 9:36 in the morning.

CROSS PATHS

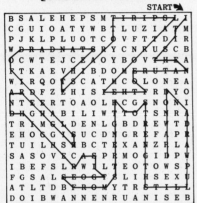

A-LINE-MENT

	W	I	S	C	O	N	S	I	N
		I	D	A	H	O			
	M	A	R	Y	L	A	N	D	
	W	A	S	H	I	N	G	T	O	N
				F	L	O	R	I	D	A
	V	E	R	M	O	N	T		
			A	R	I	Z	O	N	A
W	Y	O	M	I	N	G			
			M	A	I	N	E		
	I	O	W	A					

SKILL-O-GRAM 3

QUOTATION MAZE

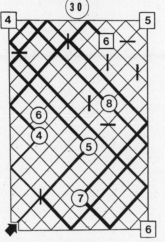

It is the nature of the immortal spirit to raise the standard of ideals higher and higher, as it goes from strength to strength, still upward and onward.

SCOREWAYS

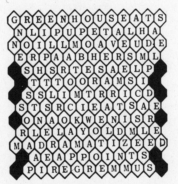

CODE-A-GRAPH

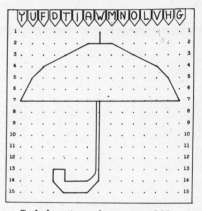

Coded sentence is on page 309.

WORD STAIRCASE

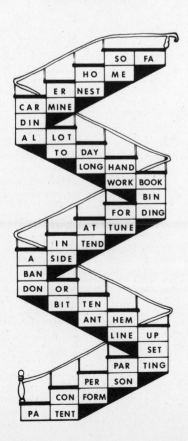

ZIG ZAG

```
G R E E N H O U S E A T S
N L I P U P E T A L H A
N O I L L M O A V E U D E
E R P A A B H E R S M L
S H S R T E S A E L P
S T T O O R A M S I
S S L I M T R R I C D
S T S R C I E A T S A E
O N A O K W E N I S R
R L E L A Y O L D M L E
M A D R A M A T I Z E D
A E A P P O I N T S
P I R E G R E M M U S
```

SEQUENTIAL MAZE

The sequence is +7 −2 +7 −2.

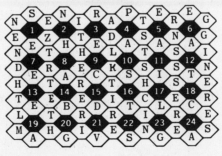

PINWHEEL 2

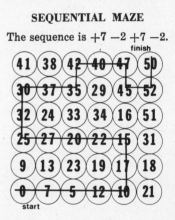

LOCKED-IN LETTERS

1.

S	H	I	N
T	I	R	E
E	D	I	T
M	E	S	S

2.

S	A	S	H
O	L	E	O
D	E	E	P
A	S	K	S

311

ANACROSTIC 1
A. Mannerly
B. Yorktown
C. Refuses
D. Accidental
E. Waterways
F. Advertises
G. Lobby
H. Derisive
I. Outwardly
J. Brain trust
K. Eccentric
L. Emancipate
M. Rashest
N. Annex
O. Nearsighted
P. Dumbbells
Q. Grand O.d Party
R. Ownership
S. On the ball
T. Decency
U. Flagman
V. Overcast
W. Off the beam
X. Distant

ANACROSTIC 2
A. Shrewd
B. Phantom
C. Extent
D. Nest egg
E. Crones
F. Evened off
G. Regatta
H. Audible
I. Feather
J. Rattler
K. Insight
L. Changed
M. Arduous
N. Neutral
O. Courtesy
P. Rotund
Q. Eulogy
R. Emboss
S. Kittens
T. Shipshape
U. Important
V. High-hat
W. Artful
X. Violet
Y. Etching
Z. Bachelor
AA. Earnest
BB. Eased
CC. Never
DD. Undone
EE. Pawns

ANACROSTIC 3
A. Cheddar
B. Academic
C. Newsman
D. Nightfall
E. Octave
F. Nostalgia
G. Beforehand
H. Remiss
I. Overtake
J. Orison
K. Keepsake
L. Seethed
M. Plymouth
N. Rummage
O. Economical
P. Shafts
Q. Impasse
R. Dawes
S. Ecstatic
T. Natural
U. Taciturn
V. Showdown
W. Cleats
X. Outshines
Y. Offset
Z. Knee-high
AA. Benefit
BB. Onlooker
CC. Optimism
DD. Knotted

ANACROSTIC 4
A. Mawkish
B. Youthful
C. Roadster
D. Overhead
E. Nickname
F. Wrings
G. Ominous
H. Observe
I. Dampens
J. Affable
K. Northern
L. Diplomacy
M. Nosegay
N. Adamant
O. Nip and tuck
P. Cherish
Q. Yankees
R. Womanly
S. Outworn
T. Objects
U. Delaying
V. Conjure
W. Oarsman
X. Lawless
Y. Outrage
Z. Rankles
AA. Another
BB. Dispose
CC. Offshoot

ANACROSTIC 5
A. Ethic
B. Visible
C. Agelong
D. Nectar
E. Sober
F. Noted
G. Afghan
H. Toast
I. Ululate
J. Rodeo
K. Absence
L. Lariat
M. Hideous
N. Igneous
O. Staff
P. Torrid
Q. Old maid
R. Record
S. Youthful
T. Officer
U. Fruited
V. Newborn
W. Outpoint
X. Niggard
Y. Stifle
Z. Euphony
AA. Nobles
BB. Swan song
CC. Editing

ANACROSTIC 6
A. Bywords
B. Clench
C. Keyholes
D. Ice-cold
E. Limelight
F. Volatile
G. Esther
H. Rundown
I. The jumps
J. Italian hand
K. Noteworthy
L. Fish or cut bait
M. On the watch
N. Rubs in
O. Mendelssohn
P. All-fired
Q. Life style
R. Groton
S. Affords
T. Rhymester
U. Dead weight
V. Eludes
W. Networks
X. Illegal
Y. Nesters
Z. Gauntlet

ANACROSTIC 7
A. Royalties
B. Off with you
C. Ghoulishly
D. Ensheathed
E. Rabbit ears
F. Hesperides
G. Inch by inch
H. Linkletter
I. Sophistry
J. Meditation
K. Apprehend
L. Newcastle
M. Timed
N. Order arms
O. Mastered
P. On a par with
Q. Vested interest
R. Expediency
S. An even keel
T. Noontime
U. Adolph Rupp
V. Tattletale
W. In the wrong
X. Occidental
Y. New Thought

ANACROSTIC 8
A. Red wine
B. Based
C. Nictitate
D. Yesterday
E. Engage
F. Tiddleywinks
G. High school
H. Erupted
I. Up to snuff
J. New Deal
K. Enthusiast
L. Mecca
M. Brotherhood
N. Appetite
O. Recount
P. Repellent
Q. Apennines
R. Stanchion
S. Shenanigan
T. Epicenter
U. Dichotomous
V. Mildew
W. Uttermost
X. Shorthand
Y. Evacuation

ANACROSTIC 9
A. Romberg
B. Out-and-out
C. Mounding
D. Belittle
E. Attaché
F. Union Jack
G. Ethical
H. Revolved
I. Askance
J. Neatest
K. Dust bowl
L. Bell-bottom
M. Estuary
N. Cheapskate
O. Know-how
P. Eclectic
Q. Refined
R. Jewelry
S. Olympics
T. Yankees
U. Open-hearth
V. Footage
W. Calabash
X. Oligarchy
Y. Oppressed
Z. Keep at it
AA. In-depth
BB. Nautilus
CC. Get ahead

ANACROSTIC 10
A. Ranch hand
B. Jaunty
C. Eat your heart out
D. Fit to be tied
E. Fiddle with
F. Ebb tide
G. Rabble
H. In stitches
I. Embellishes
J. See eye to eye
K. Stand
L. The millennium
M. On the skids
N. Repent
O. Yataghan
P. On the wane
Q. Family tree
R. Mayday
S. Yawl
T. High and mighty
U. Endurable
V. Antedate
W. Read the riot act
X. This and that

ANACROSTIC 11
A. Vichyssoise
B. Gadded about
C. Ends in smoke
D. Northwest
E. Gnomic poets
F. Irascibility
G. Nowadays
H. At the moment
I. Fiddlers three
J. In the winter
K. Taradiddle
L. On the way
M. French prison
N. Lawmaker
O. Aptitude tests
P. Upper hand
Q. Grace of God
R. Howled down
S. Tea ball
T. Earth and heaven
U. Reactivate

ANACROSTIC 12
A. Expletive
B. Simmer down
C. Mouthpiece
D. Incessant
E. Edward Elgar
F. Run of the mine
G. Spoilsport
H. Thickheaded
I. Hold forth
J. Elemental
K. Aunt Chloe
L. Masterful
M. Empyrean
N. Radiale
O. In the dumps
P. Calisthenics
Q. Allhallows
R. Nip in the bud
S. Shortcoming
T. Trespass
U. "Outward Bound"
V. Rosinante
W. Year of the Rat

ANACROSTIC 13
A. Erythrophobia
B. Violation
C. Expeditionary
D. Lee Majors
E. Year-around
F. Namesake
G. Whiffletree
H. Edgeways
I. Language
J. Leprechaun
K. Shortsighted
L. Nabobery
M. Effortless
N. Forty-fifth
O. Edifying
P. Repented
Q. The theater
R. Intestate
S. Trajectory
T. Inadequately

ANACROSTIC 14
A. Father Time
B. Litterbugs
C. Open-hearth
D. Roved
E. Evaluated
F. Nazareth
G. Castanets
H. Eleventh hour
I. Tunnels
J. Higher-ups
K. Otis
L. Monuments
M. Aghast
N. Shish kebab
O. Vitality
P. Off-limits
Q. Tattletale
R. Efficiency expert
S. Oblivious
T. Rightness
U. Ecumenical
V. Logrolls
W. Stupidity
X. Easygoing

ANACROSTIC 15
A. Wrapper
B. Deflect
C. Yellowstone
D. Knightliness
E. Effusive
F. Mephistopheles
G. Assumes
H. Narcissus
I. Landlord
J. Opportunities
K. Order
L. Kindergarten
M. Traffic
N. Overnight
O. Thorough
P. Half-and-half
Q. Intelligible
R. Swordfish
S. Difficile
T. Affirmable
U. Yawning

ANACROSTIC 16
A. Erroneous
B. Bunch grass
C. Hopalong Cassidy
D. Effortless
E. Autosuggestion
F. Distrust
G. Yearling
H. Crow's-nest
I. One-sided
J. Authoritarian
K. Threshold
L. Overturns
M. Frankfurter
N. Take to task
O. Hotchpotch
P. Equivocated
Q. Expertness
R. Assessorship
S. Range finder
T. Trousseau
U. Halfhearted

ANACROSTIC 17
A. Addled
B. Last word
C. In this neck
D. Suspects
E. Toothwort
F. At least
G. Inchoate
H. Rabbit
I. Chin
J. Of the woods
K. Out of sight
L. Kitty Foyle
M. Eared
N. "Of Thee I Sing"
O. Nation
P. Elfin
Q. Morning
R. Adversity
S. Natation
T. Shallow
U. Assassin
V. Mountains
W. Easy does it
X. Roughly
Y. In error
Z. Chipper
AA. Attic salt

ANACROSTIC 18
A. Victimized
B. Appian Way
C. Naiad
D. Cuddlesome
E. Eternal City
F. Point-blank
G. Authentic
H. Castanet
I. Know-how
J. Admitted
K. Rara avis
L. Draw the line
M. Nonharmonic
N. Attachment
O. Katahdin
P. Efficacious
Q. Discontinue
R. Samson
S. On tiptoe
T. Coquettish
U. Iniative
V. Expatriate
W. Timesavers
X. Yul Brynner

LOGIC PROBLEM 5

The obstetrician lives in Montreal (clue 1). Sally is married to the internist, who is Dr. Jones (clues 2, 8). Jane's husband is the G.P. (clue 6) Joe (clue 10). The obstetrician's wife is not Kay (clue 1) or Mary (clue 7); she is Anne. Tom is neither the obstetrician nor internist (clues 2, 7), and he is not the psychiatrist (clue 4), so he is the surgeon. Bob is neither the obstetrician nor internist (clues 1, 2); he is the psychiatrist. Anne's obstetrician husband is not G.P. Joe, surgeon Tom, psychiatrist Bob, or Jerry (clue 9), so he is Bill. By elimination, then, Jerry is the internist whose wife is Sally Jones. Tom's wife is not Mary (clue 7); she is Kay, and Mary is Bob's wife. Anne and obstetrician Bill are not the Bennetts (clue 1), the Browns (clue 3), or the Jacksons (clue 9); they are the Greens. The Bennetts are not Bob and Mary or Tom and Kay (clue 1), so they are Joe and Jane. The surgeon (we already know he is Tom) is not Dr. Brown (clue 5); he is Dr. Jackson, and Dr. Brown is psychiatrist Bob. Tom Jackson, surgeon, is not from San Francisco (clue 4), New York (clue 6), or Chicago (clue 10),—we already know Bill Green lives in Montreal—so he is from St. Louis. The man from New York is not Jerry or G.P. Joe (clue 6), so he is Bob. Joe is not from Chicago (clue 10); he is from San Francisco, and Jerry is from Chicago. In sum:

Jane & G.P. Joe Bennett, San Francisco

Mary & psychiatrist Bob Brown, New York

Anne and obstetrician Bill Green, Montreal

Kay and surgeon Tom Jackson, St. Louis

Sally and internist Jerry Jones, Chicago

SPELL TO SCORE

1. N O V E L T Y   7
2. M A R C H   5
3. Q U I Z   4
4. P R O B L E M   7
5. S H A V I N G   7
6. J O C K E Y   6
7. F L I N T   5
8. E M B A R G O   7
9. T H I N L Y   6
10. W A X E D   5
11. C O N F I R M   7
       ──
       66
      +11
       ──
       77

LETTER COUNT

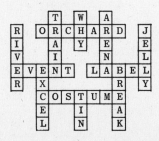

TWENTY QUESTIONS

1. George Bernard Shaw, Irish-born playwright, author of *Man and Superman* and many other plays.
2. Oahu, the most populous island in Hawaii, though third largest in size.
3. Pompeii, southeast of Naples. Most of the city has now been excavated by archaeologists.
4. "in for a pound"; "is a penny earned"; "pound foolish."
5. Hardwood.
6. Two, the Tropic of Cancer in the Northern Hemisphere, and the Tropic of Capricorn in the Southern Hemisphere.
7. They are named for Juan de Bermúdez, the Spanish explorer who discovered them in the early sixteenth century. They were first colonized by English settlers in the early 17th century.
8. No, it is an alloy consisting of 925 parts of pure silver to 75 parts of copper.
9. December 21 or 22, it's considered the shortest day of the year.
10. Graham flour, out of which Graham crackers are made.
11. No, he was the first Republican presidential candidate *elected*. Their first candidate was John C. Fremont in 1856.
12. Cloture.
13. John Brown's, who captured the U.S. arsenal located there in 1859. An ardent abolitionist, he was attempting to provoke a slave uprising, and he was later hanged for treason. The poem *John Brown's Body*, by Stephen Vincent Benèt, is about his exploits.
14. Lake Mead, located between Arizona and Nevada. Its area is 227 square miles.
15. Egbert, from 829 to 839 A.D.
16. Mercury.
17. It would pass 11—every train that left New York for Boston from 7 P.M. to 5 A.M. inclusive. The train that left New York at 6 P.M. would arrive in Boston at the instant the Boston-New York train left, and therefore is not passed en route. And the train leaving New York at 6 A.M. pulls out at the instant the Boston-New York train arrives.
18. It refers to extreme nationalism. The term, suggested by the phrase "by jingo" in a British music-hall song, became popular during the Russo-Turkish War.
19. The U.S.S.R. on the north and northeast, Bulgaria on the south, Yugoslavia on the southwest, and Hungary on the north and northwest.
20. It is a type of mountain railway in which the weight of an ascending car is partly or wholly balanced by that of a descending car.

WORD GRAPH
1. spread; 2. liable; 3. beyond; 4. typist; 5. intend; 6. quaint; 7. melody; 8. prefer.

By clues 1, 6, and 10, four cars—Nan's, Ms. Stuck's, the one having brake repairs, and Ms. Noble's—were ready at one-hour intervals, in that order. Clues 2, 4, and 13 list another such sequence of four cars ready at one-hour intervals: the Chevrolet, the one having radiator repairs, the Plymouth, and Ms. McKay's. Since neither Ms. Hobbs' car nor Ms. Innes's was the first one ready (clues 3, 5), Ms. Cole's was. And since the last one ready was not Jan's (clue 3), Ali's (clue 5), Betty's (clue 11), or Marie's (clue 15), it was Sue's. Returning to the two sets of sequential clues: since there were six cars altogether, these two consecutive sequences must "overlap" to some degree. Ms. Noble's car was not the last one ready (clue 12), so, as you will see if you line up the two lists, there are only two possibilities. One is that the six cars were ready in this order, from 1:00 to 6:00: Ms. Cole's Chevrolet, Nan's radiator repair, Ms. Stuck's Plymouth, Ms. McKay's brake repair, Ms. Noble's car, and Sue's. Ms. Innes would then have to be either Nancy or Sue. But since we have placed the brake repair at 4:00, either would contradict clue 14. Therefore, the second possibility for "overlap" is the correct one: Nan Cole's car was ready at 1:00, Ms. Stuck's at 2:00, the Chevrolet with its brakes repaired at 3:00, Ms. Noble's radiator repair job at 4:00, the Plymouth at 5:00, and Sue McKay's car at 6:00. By clue 14, then, the Chevrolet belongs to Ms. Innes and the Plymouth had the carburetor repair; the latter by elimination, belongs to Ms. Hobbs. Ms. Stuck is Ali (clue 5), and Ms. Noble's car is the Dodge (clue 7). Jan is Ms. Innes (clue 3). Betty is Ms. Noble and Marie is Ms. Hobbs (clue 11). The Ford is Sue McKay's (clue 15). Ali Stuck owns the Olds, while Nan Cole's car—by elimination, the Buick—had the tune-up (clue 9). The tire repair was done on the Olds, and the Ford had the headlight adjustment (clue 8). In sum:

- 1:00—Nan Cole's Buick, tune up
- 2:00—Ali Stuck's Olds, tire repair
- 3:00—Jan Innes's Chevrolet, brake repair
- 4:00—Betty Noble's Dodge, radiator repair
- 5:00—Marie Hobbs' Plymouth carburetor repair
- 6:00—Sue McKay's Ford, headlight adjustment

ARROW MAZE 2

LADDERGRAMS 3

1.

T	TACKS	SACK	ASK	C
O	ORANGE	ANGER	RANG	E
M	MELTS	LETS	SET	L
A	BEAST	BETS	TBS.	E
T	OTHERS	SHORE	HOSE	R
O	MAYOR	ARMY	RAM	Y

2.

H	PEACH	CAPE	PEA	C
E	PRAISE	PAIRS	RIPS	A
A	BEATS	BEST	SET	B
D	BREAD	BEAR	ARE	B
S	SHADES	HEADS	SHED	A
O	GOALS	LAGS	ALS	G
F	FEAST	EATS	SAT	E

3.

Y	YODEL	DOLE	LEO	D
A	ROAST	SORT	RTS.	O
N	LOANS	ALSO	SAL	O
K	DRANK	DARN	RAN	D
E	FEEL	ELF	FE	L
E	AGREES	GEARS	RAGS	E

4.

M	TAMED	DATE	ADE	T
Y	ITALY	TAIL	ALT.	I
C	CASTLE	STALE	LATE	S
O	HOOTS	SHOT	H.S.T.	O
U	FAULTS	FLATS	SALT	F
N	FRONT	FORT	FRO	T
T	THREAD	HEARD	READ	H
R	YEARS	EASY	SAY	E
Y	SAWYER	SWEAR	WARS	E

HI-SCORE 2

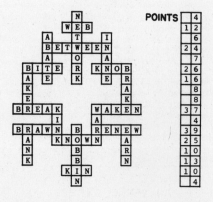

POINTS

| 4 |
| 12 |
| 6 |
| 24 |
| 7 |
| 26 |
| 16 |
| 8 |
| 8 |
| 37 |
| 4 |
| 39 |
| 25 |
| 10 |
| 13 |
| 10 |
| 4 |

TOTAL 253

FORM-A-WORD

1. trend (5); 2. alley (5); 3. wage (4); 4. miracle (7); 5. erase (5); 6. brave (5); 7. camera (6); 8. skiing (6); 9. amaze (5); 10. link (4); 11. detain (6). TOTAL: 58 points.

SOLICROSS™ 1

Our score: 387. Order of words — Note: The word or words given in parentheses were formed in the same DRAW as the word immediately preceding the parentheses —

aim; ice; name (nice, am); art (nicer); lose (names); zinc (close); pen (an); ape (part); lace (can); open; lamp (place); closely; cub (clamp); item; box (by).

SOLICROSS™ 2

Our score: 427. Order of words — Note: The word or words given in parentheses were formed in the same DRAW as the word immediately preceding the parentheses —

earth; reach (hearth); sector; erect; tale; crease; peas (preach); rate (ear, ate); dime; drone (do, in, me); ward; peasant; toward (to); preacher; trial.

SOLICROSS™ 3

Our score: 424. Note: The word or words given in parentheses were formed in the same DRAW as the word immediately preceding the parentheses. Order of words: hat; ban; owl (what); kit (bank); by (bowl); kitten; give; avid (at, in); ray; bids (kittens); trim (tray); dip; soda (stray, or, am); forbids; big (if, go).

SOLICROSS™ 4

Our score 452. Note: The word or words given in parentheses were formed in the same DRAW as the word immediately preceding the parentheses. Order of words: fort; part; odor (of, do, or); comfort; tick; fee (off, doe, ore); office; shelf (stick); paw; fame (fore, am, we); wealth; crown (officer); stay (wealthy); eat (sew, tan, at); sticker.

SOLICROSS™ 5

Our score: 362. Note: The word or words given in parentheses were formed in the same DRAW as the word immediately preceding the parentheses. Order of words: toy; in (it, no); act (tin); party (tint); row; alias (so); ignore (grow); win (grown); winner; arc; earns (winners); let (learns); lot; of (fact); cup (plot).

SOLICROSS™ 6

Our score: 398. Note: The word or words given in parentheses were formed in the same DRAW as the word immediately preceding the parentheses. Order of words: fan; to (at, no); out (too); due (nod); past (nods); glee (tool, paste); pastel; polo (go); tap; as (so); rig (it, gas); row (or, wit); arrow; new (narrow); gem (am).

WHAT'S WRONG AT THE BEACH?

1. Christmas tree; 2. moon out over water; 3. lighthouse has traffic light; 4. water-skier pulling boat; 5. rain coming from sun; 6. TV antenna on beach umbrella; 7. giraffe near palms; 8. Eskimo; 9. man in vest; 10. carrying briefcase; 11. girl with roller skate; 12. igloo on beach; 13. mermaid; 14. snake in picnic basket; 15. stop sign in water; 16. boat flags in opposite directions; 17. swimmer wearing boots; 18. octopus with ice-cream cone; 19. boy wearing earmuffs; 20. fish on leash; 21. umbrella upside down; 22. boy wears mitten; 23. man wears black tie; 24. floating glass; 25. Cold Drinks wagon has hot drinks; 26. vendor wears winter cap; 27. football used in vollyball game; 28. man wearing ice skate; 29. girl using pancake turner in game; 30. fish reading newspaper; 31. man using telephone; 32. woman wearing winter boots; 33. picnic hamper is tool box; 34. boy wearing football helmet; 35. eating ice-cream cone with straw; 36. girl's ice-cream bar says 14 karat gold; 37. she wears winter coat; 38. man has golf clubs; 39. girl carries ice skates; 40. Ice Cream misspelled on vendor's cart.

AROUND THE BLOCK

MAZE 1

LETTER CHASE

1. road (9); 2. arena (10); 3. value (10); 4. balcony (12); 5. hire (9); 6. climb (10); 7. talent (11); 8. level (10); 9. door (9); 10. stack (10). TOTAL: 100 points.

THE DOT GAME

20	25	30	35	15	15

25	5		5	
		20		
	30			
	30			

Our scoring:

2 units of 1 pair .... $2 \times 5 = 10$

2 units of 2 pairs .... $2 \times 15 = 30$

2 units of 1 quartet ..... $2 \times 20 = 40$

2 units of 4 consecutive
numbers ...... $2 \times 25 = 50$

3 units of 1 trio plus
1 pair .... $3 \times 30 = 90$

1 unit of 5 consecutive
numbers .... $1 \times 35 = 35$

(All squares used; no handicap)

Grand Total   255

MAZE 2

WORD ARITHMETIC 3

```
   0 1 2 3 4 5 6 7 8 9
1. B O Y F R I E N D S
2. H A R L E Q U I N S
3. M A N I F E S T L Y
4. L I O N/T A M E R S
5. F I R S T/P L A C E
6. T A X/R E F U N D S
7. P A R K I N G/L O T
8. G R A C I O U S L Y
9. R E D U C T I O N S
```

WHAT IS TIME?

1. Certainly; say you left New York at 1 A.M. Sunday and the plane took one hour to make the trip: because of the three-hour time difference, you'd reach Los Angeles at 11 P.M. Saturday. 2. The change from standard to daylight-saving time and vice versa. 3. Estimated time of arrival. 4. "As Time Goes By." 5. The theory of relativity; Albert Einstein. 6. (a) tide, (b) Procrastination, (c) wounds. 7. 3:30 P.M. Bells are rung every half hour to mark the periods of the watch: The afternoon series begins with one bell at 12:30 and ends at eight bells at 4:00. 8. Father Time. 9. (b) Chapter 3, Verse 1. 10. "Now is the time for all good men to come to the aid of the party." 11. sundials and hourglasses: 12. False; it began during World War I for the same reason. 13. Eastern: c, e, j; Central: a, f, l; Mountain: d, h, i; Pacific: b, g. k. 14. 1c; 2e; 3g; 4d; 5i, during World War II; 6b (opening sentence of "A Tale of Two Cities"); 7h (from "Julius Caesar"); 8a (from "Common Sense"); 9j (to an aide-de-camp); 10f.

UNIGRAMS

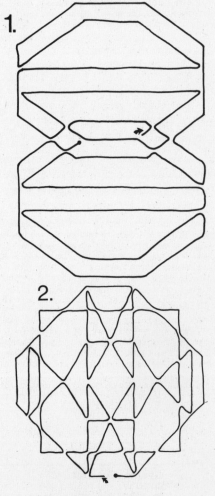

1.

2.

MISSING ALPHABET

1. plastic; 2. expense; 3. amazing; 4. adjourn; 5. squired; 6. flighty; 7. weaving; 8. blanket; 9. thought; 10. balloon.

LOGIC PROBLEM 7

Let us look first at the cost of the calls. The senior's call cost twice as much as Mike's (clue 3), the Ohio State student's twice as much as the one from Stanford, which was the longest of the four (clue 6). Mike is not the Ohio State student (clue 10); nor did he make the longest call (clue 3). Since all the calls were of different lengths, the senior does not attend Ohio State, nor is the senior at Stanford (clue 8). Thus, clues 3 and 6 refer to four separate calls, and either Mike's call or the longest one, from Stanford, cost least. By clue 5, the one costing least was Mike's, which was also the shortest. Mike is thus not at Georgia Tech (clue 4); he must attend Columbia, and the senior attends Georgia Tech. The Stanford student who made the longest call is not the junior (clue 1) or the freshman (clue 4) and must be the sophomore. That student is not John (clue 2). Karen's call cost $3.00 (clue 7). If she were at Stanford, the call from Ohio State would have cost $6.00 (clue 6), a total of $9.00 for those two calls. But by clue 9, that would leave $1.50 for the other two calls, which cost at least $1.00 each—clearly impossible. The Stanford sophomore is therefore Linda. Since she made the longest call, the junior's call was longer than the freshman's (clues 1, 4) and Mike, who made the shortest call, is the freshman, and the Ohio State student is the junior. Karen is either the latter or the Georgia Tech senior. If she were the Ohio State junior, Linda's call would have cost $1.50 (clues 6, 7), with $6.00 remaining for the other two calls (clue 9)—$4.00 for the senior's and $2.00 for Mike's (clue 3). But we know Mike's call cost least—so Karen is the Georgia Tech senior, and the Ohio State junior is John. Karen's call cost $3.00 (clue 7), Mike's $1.50 (clue 3), John's $4.00 and Linda's $2.00 (clues 6, 9). The lowest rate for any call was 10¢ a minute (clue 12). If either Karen or Mike called at that rate, Karen's call would have lasted 30 minutes and Mike's 15 minutes (clue 4), a total of 45 minutes —leaving nine minutes for the other two calls (clue 11). We know Linda made the longest call, so that is impossible. If John's had been a 10¢-per-minute call, he would have talked for 40 minutes—again impossible, for the same reason. So Linda made the call at the 10¢ rate and talked for 20 minutes, and junior John's call lasted 10 minutes (clue 1). The remaining time was 24 minutes (clue 11), meaning Karen's call took 16 minutes and Mike's eight (clue 4). In sum:

John, Ohio State junior, $4.00 for 10 min.

Karen, Georgia Tech senior, $3.00 for 16 min.

Linda, Stanford sophomore, $2.00 for 20 min.

Mike, Columbia, freshman, $1.50 for 8 min.

RECTANGLE LOGIC

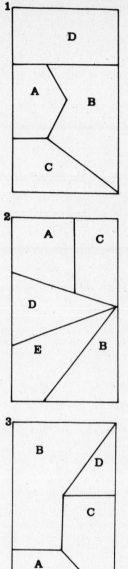

THE CENTER SPELLS IT

1. shut, shout; 2. moth, month; 3. died, diced; 4. find, fiend; 5. host, hoist; 6. door, donor; 7. cost, coast; 8. root, robot; 9. save, salve; 10. pond, pound; 11. spar, spear; 12. coma, comma; 13. lose, loose; 14. stop, stoop; 15. rage, range. Familiar expression: once in a blue moon.

SHOPPER'S SPECIAL

1. b; 2. a; 3. c; 4. c; 5. a; 6. c; 7. b; 8. a; 9. c; 10. b.

CIRCUS ENIGMAS

1. trapeze; 2. elephant.

LETTER CHOICE

1. charter (7); 2. beauty (6); 3. church (6); 4. chamber (7); 5. truant (6); 6. current (7); 7. mental (6). TOTAL: 45 points

LOGIC PROBLEM 8

Baker's is in 204 (clue 5), the toy store in 106 (clue 11). Ogden Cosmetics is on the first floor, with the shoe store directly above it (clue 3); it is not one of those on the north side (clue 1), and it is not one of those mentioned in clue 7, which refers to all the stores situated at the ends of the four rows. Since Baker's is not the shoe store (clue 13), Ogden Cosmetics must be in 102, the shoe store in 202. Stores farthest apart are those diagonally opposite and on different floors —e.g., 200 and 109 comprise one such pair—and there are four pairs altogether. Clue 7 lists them all. Gray's is on the first floor on the north side (clue 1), just under Alden's (clue 16), so from clue 7, the ice-cream parlor is on the first floor on the south side. The music store is on the first floor on the north side (clues 1, 4) so from clue 7, Holden's is on the second floor on the south side. Jackson's is on the second floor (clue 12), so from clue 7, the florist is on the first floor. The art store is directly opposite the florist (clue 14), so it is also on the first floor and is at the end of one of the rows; it must, therefore, be one of the stores mentioned in clue 7. Since we know Jackson's, Alden's and Holden's are all on the second floor, the art store must be Troop's and the pet store is on the second floor. Troop's Art Store is not on the north side (clue 1), and it is not in 108 (clue 10), so it is in 100 and the pet store is in 209. Alden's is then in 201, the ice-cream parlor in 108. The florist (opposite the art store by clue 14) is then in 101 and must be one of the stores named in clue 1; it is Gray's (clue 17), and by clue 7, Jackson's is in 208. We can now place the remaining pair mentioned in clue 7: the music store is in 109, Holden's in 200. Dailey's is in 107 (clue 4), so the music store is Niven's (clue 1). The ice-cream parlor in 108 is Smith's (clue 9). Kelly's is between Palmer's and Mitchell's Gift Shop, and in one order or the other, they are all in a row (clue 8), on the second floor with Queen's directly below Mitchell's (clue 6). Since we already know the names of three second-floor stores on the south side, Palmer's, Kelly's, and Mitchell's are on the north side, and Queen's is either the bake shop or the leather-goods shop (clue 1); it is not the latter (clue 6), so it is the bake shop. Queen's is in either 105 or 103; therefore, Palmer's, Kelly's and Mitchell's Gift Shop are respectively in 209, 207, and 205 (with Queen's in 105) or in 207, 205, and 203 (with Queen's in 103). The jeweler is between Cramer's and the cheese shop (clue 19), and since there is no space for such a sequence remaining on the north side, it is on the south side. There is only one place it could be: the jeweler is Baker's in 204, Cramer's is the shoe store in 202, and the cheese shop is in 206. Egan's and Long's are side by side, and Egan's is not the toy store (clue 20); since we know the names of four stores on each floor on the north side and on the second floor on the south side, Egan's must be in 104 and Long's is the toy store in 106. We now know the names of all the first-floor stores on the south side, so Forrest's, with the sporting-goods store directly above it (clue 2), is on the north side and must be the leather-goods shop (clue 1). It isn't in 105

(clue 18), so it is in 103 and the sporting-goods store is in 203. Queen's Bake Shop is then in 105, with—as previously determined—Mitchell's Gift Shop in 205, Kelly's in 207, and Palmer's Pet Store in 209. Inman's isn't the cheese shop (clue 22), so the cheese shop in 206 is Rose's, and the sporting-goods store in 203 is Inman's. The children's clothing store directly above the women's clothing store (clue 15) must be, respectively, Kelly's in 207 and Dailey's in 107. There is only one remaining pair of opposite stores for which the type of store is unknown, Alden's in 201 and Holden's in 200— so they are, respectively, the furniture store and the restaurant (clue 21). The stationery store is Egan's, and Jackson's sells men's clothing (clue 23). In sum:

North side, first floor:
101. Gray's Florist
103. Forrest's Leather Goods
105. Queen's Bake Shop
107. Dailey's Women's Clothing
109. Niven's Music Store
North side, second floor:
201. Alden's Furniture
203. Inman's Sporting Goods
205. Mitchell's Gift Shop
207. Kelly's Children's Clothing
209. Palmer's Pet Store
South side, first floor:
100. Troop's Art Store
102. Ogden's Cosmetics
104. Egan's Stationery
106. Long's Toy Store
108. Smith's Ice Cream Parlor
South side, second floor:
200. Holden's Restaurant
202. Cramer's Shoe Store
204. Baker's Jewelry
206. Rose's Cheese Shop
208. Jackson's Men's Clothing

3-D DRAWINGS

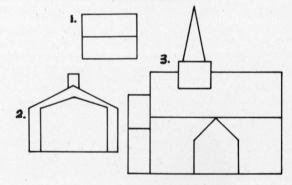

WORD LINK

	C		S								S				
C	O	N	S	E	N	T		N	O	N	S	E	N	S	E
	N		C	E					N		S	E			
B	F	O	N	T	A	R	I	O	S		T	O	N	I	C
O	B	E	R	O	N		O		O		I	O			
N	R		D		N	O	O	N		B	O	N	N	E	T
B					R			N			N			O	N	E
O	N	L	Y			I		M		A	N				B
N		O			O	N	L	O	O	K	E	R		G	O
	N	O	T	I	O	N		N			S	U		U	N
	G		D		N			S		L	O	N	E	L	Y
B	O	N	E		S	O	N	N	E	T		N		O	
N		R		C	E	O		E		E				N	
E			C	O	T	T	O	N		R	A	Y	M	O	N	D
I	R	O	N			E		O			N	O		R	N
C			G					N			R			N	
O		A	R	G	O	N		T	O	N	T	O			
N								O			O		N	O	O	N	E

NUMBER PLACE

1

3	6	5	9	7	2	4	1	8
7	2	8	4	3	1	5	6	9
4	9	1	8	6	5	7	3	2
5	3	9	6	8	4	1	2	7
8	1	4	5	2	7	6	9	3
2	7	6	1	9	3	8	4	5
9	4	3	7	1	8	2	5	6
6	5	7	2	4	9	3	8	1
1	8	2	3	5	6	9	7	4

2

5	4	8	3	7	6	2	9	1
2	7	6	1	5	9	8	4	3
1	9	3	2	4	8	5	6	7
6	8	7	9	2	3	4	1	5
9	3	2	4	1	5	7	8	6
4	5	1	6	8	7	9	3	2
8	6	9	7	3	2	1	5	4
3	2	4	5	9	1	6	7	8
7	1	5	8	6	4	3	2	9

STRIKES: 1. asserting; 2. barometer; 3. antitrust; 4. peaceable; 5. melodrama; 6. arbitrary; 7. clientele; 8. ultimatum; 9. armadillo; 10. demitasse.
SPARES: (*Other combinations are possible. Score full credit for them as long as they are correct.*) 1. rains, gets; 2. amber, tore; 3. trait, stun; 4. palace, bee; 5. alarm, dome; 6. briar, tray; 7. tell, niece; 8. tumult, aim; 9. moral, dial; 10. steam, side.

LETTER PATHS

1. marry
   motto
   musty
   mural
   minor

2. virus
   vague
   value
   vault
   vowel

3. baton
   bulky
   bonus
   bench
   berry

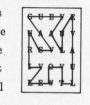

LETTER LINK 2

		F	
H	T	O	N
L	E	S	I
R	A	W	

TANGLEWORDS

(*finished diagram with letters filled in*) (*diagram with circles showing words*)

NUMBER FILL-INS

1.

1	6	11	16	21	26	31	36	41	46	51
3		15			36					61
5		19			46	55	64	73		71
7	15	23			56			79	80	81
9		27	40	53	66			85		91
11			43					91		101
13	24	35	46	57	68	79				111
15					87	90	93			121
17	30	43	56	69	82	95		103	117	131
19								113		141
21	25	29	33	37	41	45		123		151
23		47		71						161
25	37	49	61	73	85	97	109	121		

2.

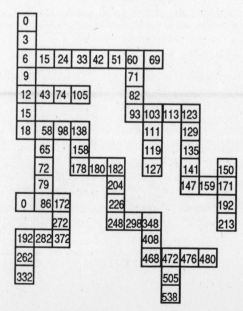

PICTURE MAZE

DIAGRAMLESS STARTING BOXES

Diagramless 3 begins in the 1st box across.
Diagramless 4 begins in the 8th box across.
Diagramless 5 begins in the 4th box across.
Diagramless 6 begins in the 7th box across.
Diagramless 7 begins in the 3rd box across.
Diagramless 8 begins in the 6th box across.
Diagramless 9 begins in the 5th box across.
Diagramless 10 begins in the 3rd box across.
Diagramless 11 begins in the 3rd box across.
Diagramless 12 begins in the 9th box across.
Diagramless 13 begins in the 3rd box across.

CRYPTIC PLACES HELP

Mineral Point, Wisconsin

CROSS SUMS HELPS

2: 978	3: 31752	4: 7216
5: 4938	6: 2538	7: 8975
8: 761	9: 9768	10: 895
11: 8345		

KRISS KROSS HELPS

3: Bennett	5: hockey
6: banyans	7: 346986
8: ermine	12: match
13: incognita	15: sissies

ANAGRAM WORD SQUARES

1.

S	L	O	P
L	I	N	E
O	N	E	S
P	E	S	T

2.

F	L	I	T
L	O	R	E
I	R	K	S
T	E	S	T

WHOSE SHOES?

1. I (fisherman); 2. H (Dutchman); 3. G (Japanese); 4. K (Arabian); 5. C (Indian); 6. B (football player); 7. A (cowboy); 8. Trapper, whose shoes the shoemaker does not have; 9. D (child); 10. E (cavalry officer); 11. J (scuba diver); 12. F (golfer).

LETTER, PLEASE

Sometimes discretion should be thrown aside and, with foolish people, we should play the fool.

CROSS SUMS 10   CROSS SUMS 11

QUOTEGRAM

It is not the revolution that destroys the machinery, but the friction.

"DEAR HATTIE . . ."

1. go, toy, our, Deal, er, sand, as, K, T, hep, rice, soft, hen, E, won, es.
Go to your dealer's and ask the prices of the new ones.

2. hiss, on, select, R.I., C, gui, tar, W, as, re, cent, lyre, posse, SS, Ed.
His son's electric guitar was recently repossessed.

3. way, new, as, G, et, ting, I tin, N.I. net, e'en, Fort, Y, S, even.
Wayne was getting it in nineteen forty-seven.

WORD MATCH

time out, hors d'oeuvres, Ethel Waters, rear admiral, equal rights, navel orange, end run, Veterans Administration, early bird, Roy Acuff, window dressing, apple polisher, steam engine, Academy Award, Glen Campbell, Oxford, England.
"There never was a good war or a bad peace." (Benjamin Franklin)

WORD MINE

4-letter words: able, area, aria, bail, bale, ball, bane, bare, barn, bean, bear, bell, bier, bile, bill, bran, earl, earn, elan, lain, lair, lane, lean, liar, lien, line, lira, nail, near, rail, rain, real, rein, rile.

Less frequently used 4-letter words: abir, abri, aera, aire, alan, alar, alba, albe, alen, alin, anba, anil, arba, aril, arni, bani, bara, bari, bela, bena, beni, bina, bine, birl, birn, brea, brin, eria, lari, lina, rabi, rale, rana, rani, reba, rial, rill, rine.

5-letter words: abler, alien, aline, arena, baler, banal, blare, brain, brine, iller, label, learn, libel, liner, renal.

Less frequently used 5-letter words: anile, areal, ariel, binal, blain, blear, elain, ileal, laine, liana, libra, reban, rille.

ALPHABET TILES

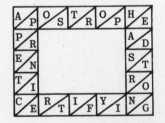

Your solution may be reversed, with APPRENTICE reading across the top of the diagram.

THE TRUTH REMAINS

Crossed off pairs of pictures: anvil, hammer; ashtray, cigarette; chair, sofa; music and bow, violin; cook, kitchen; mailman, letters; ring, hand; apple, tree; logs, fireplace. Remaining pictures: RUler, STatue of Liberty, DOor, ESkimos, WAllet, STar, EMbroidery, ORegon, ETna, HAnger, NUrse, SEven.
Rust does waste more than use.

320